EVENTS MANAGEMENT

SAGE has been part of the global academic community since 1965, supporting high quality research and learning that transforms society and our understanding of individuals, groups and cultures. SAGE is the independent, innovative, natural home for authors, editors and societies who share our commitment and passion for the social sciences.

Find out more at: **www.sagepublications.com**

2nd edition

Razaq Raj, Paul Walters & Tahir Rashid

EVENTS MANAGEMENT

principles & practice

Los Angeles | London | New Delhi
Singapore | Washington DC

Los Angeles | London | New Delhi
Singapore | Washington DC

SAGE Publications Ltd
1 Oliver's Yard
55 City Road
London EC1Y 1SP

SAGE Publications Inc.
2455 Teller Road
Thousand Oaks, California 91320

SAGE Publications India Pvt Ltd
B 1/I 1 Mohan Cooperative Industrial Area
Mathura Road
New Delhi 110 044

SAGE Publications Asia-Pacific Pte Ltd
3 Church Street
#10-04 Samsung Hub
Singapore 049483

Editor: Matthew Waters
Editorial assistant: Nina Smith
Copyeditor: H A Fairlie
Proofreader: Derek Markham
Indexer: Elizabeth Ball
Marketing manager: Alison Borg
Cover design: Francis Kenney
Typeset by: C&M Digitals (P) Ltd, Chennai, India
Printed by MPG Books Group, Bodmin, Cornwall

Library of Congress Control Number: 2012941030

British Library Cataloguing in Publication data

A catalogue record for this book is available from the British Library

ISBN 978-1-4462-0072-8
ISBN 978-1-4462-0073-5 (pbk)

Contents

About the Authors

Dr Razaq Raj is Senior Lecturer in the School of Events, Tourism and Hospitality at Leeds Metropolitan University. He has published work on special events, financial management in events, information technology, cultural festivals and events, sustainable tourism and religious tourism. Razaq is the author of the textbooks *Religious Tourism and Pilgrimage Management: An International Perspective*, *Advanced Event Management: An integrated and practical approach* and *Event Management and Sustainability*. He is a board member of international journals and academic associations, and was formerly Editor in Chief for the *World Journal of Tourism, Leisure and Sport*.

Paul Walters has an employment history that spans over 20 years within the area of music management, exhibition design, festivals, project management, touring theatre management, film production, sponsorship/marketing and public relations. This wealth of knowledge and experience enabled him to undertake a Senior Lecturer position within the area of Events Management at Manchester Metropolitan University. His area of research and current professional activities include festivals and cultural events as well as planning and operational management of large-scale outdoor international events. Paul currently lectures at ANGELL Business School in Germany.

Dr Tahir Rashid is an experienced entrepreneur with a background in retail management, marketing and corporate strategy. As a management consultant Tahir has led government and European sponsored projects to assist SMEs to improve their management and IT capabilities. Tahir has extensive higher education teaching experience and his areas of expertise include relationship marketing, marketing management, internet marketing and corporate strategy. He has published several peer-reviewed journal articles and a book chapter as well as presenting conference papers in the areas of relationship marketing, internet marketing, and e-learning in higher education and SMEs.

Companion Website

Be sure to visit the companion website (www.sagepub.co.uk/raj) to find additional teaching and learning material for lecturers and students

For lecturers:

Full Chapter PowerPoint Slides

Lecturer Teaching Notes

For students:

Student Questions

Video Links

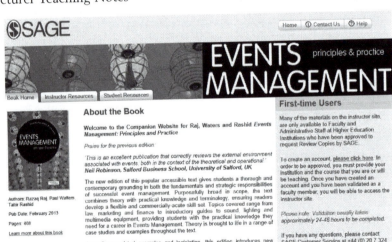

Section A

Concept and Management

Introduction to Events Management

1

In this chapter you will cover:

- the historical development of events;
- technical definitions of events management;
- size of events within the sector;
- an events industry;
- value of areas of the events industry;
- different types of events;
- local authorities' events strategies;
- corporate events strategies;
- community festivals;
- charity events;
- summary;
- discussion questions;
- case studies;
- further reading.

This chapter provides an historical overview of the events and festivals industry, and how it has developed over time. The core theme for this chapter is to establish a dialogue between event managers and event specialists who need to have a consistent working relationship. Each strand of the chapter will be linked to industry best practice where appropriate. In addition, this chapter discusses the different types of events that exist within the events management industry. Specifically, the chapter will analyse and discuss a range of events and their implications for the events industry, including the creation of opportunities for community orientated events and festivals.

The historical development of events

Events, in the form of organised acts and performances, have their origins in ancient history. Events and festivals are well documented in the historical period before the fall of the Western Roman Empire (AD 476). They have an important function within society, providing participants with the opportunity to assert their identities and to share rituals and celebrations with other people. Traditionally, special religious holy days have been celebrated, for example, Christmas and Easter. Sovereign rulers and other leaders have often organised events as a way of controlling the public, as was especially the case in the seventeenth and eighteenth centuries.

In modern society, it may be argued that traditional religious and national festivals are no longer viewed as the key focus for community celebrations. Modern western society instead tends to create events which celebrate *individual* milestones, anniversaries and achievements. Birthday parties, wedding celebrations and house warming parties are all ways in which we get together.

These days, events are considered to make a key contribution to the cultural and economic development of the countries that hold them. Events can have a major impact on the development of cultural tourism to the host communities.

A festival can be defined as a gathering of community or an event which is centred on some theme and held annually or less frequently for a limited period of time. Historical and cultural themes are now often used to develop annual events to attract visitors and create cultural images in the host cities by holding festivals in community settings. Increasingly, larger events and festivals are not specifically designed to address the social and cultural needs of any one particular group but instead are often developed because of the economic benefits they will hopefully bring, primarily through tourism. Such festivals attract increasing numbers of local, regional and international visitors and thus may help to develop links with the global community.

Festivals and celebrations in local communities have generally been accepted and recognised as making an important contribution to society. These local festivals create entertainment for residents and visitors, but also contribute to a sense of community, building bridges between diverse community groups and giving them an opportunity to come together and celebrate their history and the place they live in.

Technical definitions of events management

In order to understand more fully the large array of events that take place today it is important to begin by examining their objectives. Any dictionary definition of an 'event' will include a broad statement, such as 'something happens'.

The word 'event' also has specific meanings in medicine, philosophy or physics. In such sciences we are concerned with happenings or incidents beyond the will of man or woman. When we couple this term with the concept of 'management', the definition of which includes words such as 'organisation', 'administration' and 'control', we begin to see an 'event' as a purposeful human creation. For events to be managed, they must therefore involve other people, and have a predetermined purpose and a location.

Event management can therefore be defined like this:

Event management is the capability and control of the process of purpose, people and place.

It follows, then, that events themselves can be defined as 'happenings with objectives'.

The prime objective for an event can be strictly defined. An objective may be quantitative and financial, for instance to sell tickets and produce a profit. There may also be less tangible, qualitative objectives relating to the thoughts, feelings and emotions, during and after the event, of those attending it. These would be key objectives for a wedding or a private party.

In the next chapter we will look more closely at event objectives and in particular their role within the event planning process. In this section, however, we will explore the way in which 'event objective components' can help us to analyse the full range of international events currently being staged.

Event objective components are the building blocks of event objectives. They are divided into the three categories derived from our earlier definition of event management: purpose, people and place (see Figure 1.1).

So, in order to understand the range of events, we can attempt to classify them by their objective components. But, the process produces so many permutations and overlaps that in the end we must conclude that events cannot be precisely classified. One positive conclusion, though, is that all events involve a community. This community can be local or international; it may be a certain business community or a cultural community.

If we look at events on a scale ranging from the individual to the global, a private and personal event, such as a wedding anniversary or birthday, involves the community of family and friends at a particular calendar date in the individual's life for the purposes of celebration. Culture and community are both expressed and enhanced through the social interaction of the event. At the global end of the scale, an event such as the Olympic Games in London in 2012, or the FIFA World Cup in Brazil in 2014, will probably involve every possible component somewhere in its tiered objectives and stakeholders. This is due to the complexity of such major events, which actually consist of a whole series of events in one. Looking back to our diagram of event object components (see Figure 1.1), we can identify the culture, carnival and celebration of

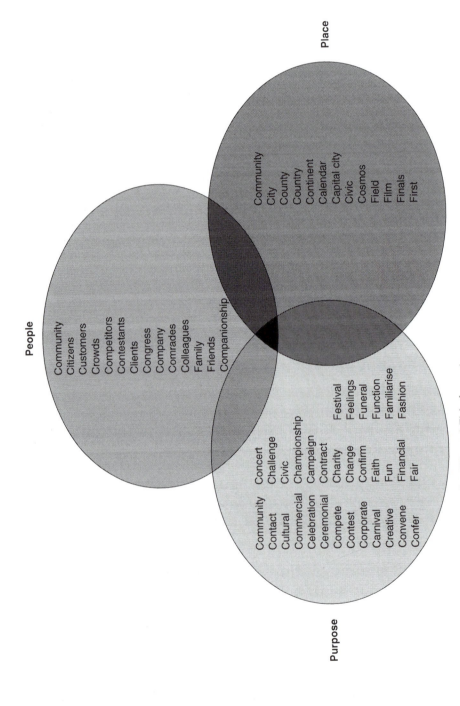

People

Community
Citizens
Customers
Crowds
Competitors
Contestants
Clients
Congress
Company
Comrades
Colleagues
Family
Friends
Companionship

Place

Community
City
County
Country
Continent
Calendar
Capital city
Civic
Cosmos
Field
Film
Finals
First

Purpose

Community   Concert   Festival
Contact   Challenge   Feelings
Cultural   Civic   Funeral
Commercial   Championship Function
Celebration   Campaign   Familiarise
Ceremonial   Contract   Fashion
Compete   Charity
Contest   Change
Corporate   Confirm
Carnival   Faith
Creative   Fun
Convene   Financial
Confer   Fair

Figure 1.1   Event objective components – the 'C's and F's' of events

the Opening and Closing Ceremonies; the many competitors; the corporate elements; and the positive changes these events bring to citizens, communities, city and country.

Community, or communities, is thus the most important of the event objective components. Communities include the international track athletics or football community; the expatriate and descendent communities such as a city's Irish or Caribbean communities who come together to celebrate St Patrick's Day or Carnival; or any field of commerce, such as the UK utilities industry business community. Events are all about the vast and varied communities of people of the world. Events are where people commune!

Size of events within the sector

Modern events vary enormously in terms of their scale and complexity and the number of stakeholders involved, ranging from community festivals to major sporting events.

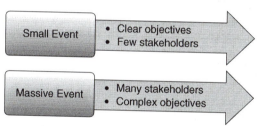

Figure 1.2   How the size of an event links to its complexity

The larger the event, the more objective components it will have, due to the numerous sub-events and stakeholder events which make the whole. This is particularly true, for example, of events such as the Olympic Games. The typology of events in Figure 1.3 shows the different types of events that have been developed around the world by organisers ranging from individuals to multinational organisations.

There have been considerable changes in the nature of festivals over the last decade. Where they previously tended to be associated with key calendar dates, particular seasons and heritage sites, there is now a much broader and more diverse range of festivals and events taking place all over the world. The revolution in festivals has been stimulated by commerce. The changing demand of local community groups has increased business opportunities for event organisers and local businesses.

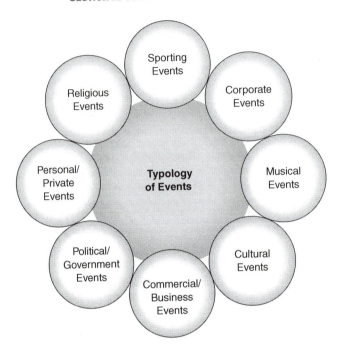

Figure 1.3 Typology of events

Festivals play a major part in the economy of a city and local community. Such events are attractive to host communities, since they can promote a sense of pride and identity amongst local people. In addition, festivals can play an important part in promoting the host community as both a tourist and commercial destination. Events can help to develop the image and profile of a destination and may attract visitors outside of the holiday season. They can also generate significant economic impacts, contributing to the development of local communities and businesses, providing support to those who pursue economic opportunity, and supporting key industrial sectors.

Festivals provide an opportunity for local people to develop and share their culture. If we understand 'culture' to mean the personal expression of community heritage, we can see how festivals may create a sense of shared values, beliefs and perspectives within a local community. The peoples and communities that host festivals also offer their visitors a vibrant and valuable cultural experience. Events enable tourists to see how local communities celebrate their culture, and also give them an opportunity to interact with their hosts. This not only meets their leisure needs but can increase their understanding and appreciation of the local culture and heritage.

An events industry

There is some debate as to whether an events industry actually exists. Those who work exclusively in exhibitions view themselves as part of the exhibition industry; those who work in live music might define themselves as part of the music business. Others, such as wedding organisers, may see themselves as part of a standalone industry.

The common link that binds all of these diverse event organisers together is the multitude of suppliers who rely on events for all or part of their business. A ticket printer's trade exclusively depends upon orders from events, be they sporting, cultural, musical or corporate. In order to prosper, a professional sound company needs contracts with event venues and event organisers, ranging from sound systems installed permanently in churches or nightclubs, to those set up temporarily for a concert or conference. A printer may have a wide range of other customers, but events businesses that need posters, flyers and brochures may account for a significant part of their work. Events can also be a component of an hotelier's business, if the hotel is available for use as a venue for meetings or conferences. Yet business tourism is a vital part of the UK tourism industry and it is one of the largest industries in the UK economy, generating around £19 billion per annum from 180,000 businesses and employing over 1.4 million people across the whole tourism and events sector. Over the last 10 years it has provided growth and employment for the UK and European economies. In addition, tourism is a vital source for the events and hospitality industry, especially where delegates are attending large MICE (meetings, incentives, conferences and exhibitions) events. For example, 22,000 jobs in the West Midlands are sustained by the NEC Group of venues alone (this group includes the National Exhibition Centre, the International Convention Centre, the Symphony Hall, and the National Indoor Arena (British Tourist Authority, 2010)).

Value of areas of the events industry

Estimating the financial value of such a diverse UK events industry is a very difficult task. The typology of events shown in Figure 1.3 breaks the events industry down into different sectors and sub-sectors, some of which have information more readily available than others. These facts and figures, however, do take full account of the importance of events in economic and employment terms.

The British Conference Market Trends Survey 2010 estimates that conferences and meetings are worth £18.8 billion annually. Exhibitions and trade fairs are calculated to be worth £2.04 billion annually, excluding the value of business transacted at them. This means that exhibitions are the fifth largest marketing medium, attracting 11 per cent of media expenditure in the UK (British Tourist Authority, 2010 [online]). The value of the corporate events sector is estimated to be between £700 million to £1 billion annually. Figure 1.4 highlights the overall income generated by the business visits and events sector.

The UK Events Market Trend Survey shows a contrasting view of the conference industry within the UK, attributing the downward trend directly to the global market recession in 2008 (UKEMTS, 2011 [online]). As documented in the report, there was a slight downturn between 2006–8 in terms of direct revenue to venues: the report shows 375 events in 2006–8, compared with 396 in 2005–7. There were an estimated 67 million attendances at venues in 2008, at 1.31 million events. Interestingly, the report also shows some changes relating to time, including a further shortening of lead times for events, a longer wait for confirmations and increased cancellations. The location of the venue has a significant impact: city venues hosted on average 447 events a year; whereas in comparison events hosted in rural areas averaged 250 events per year (Eventia, 2010 [online]).

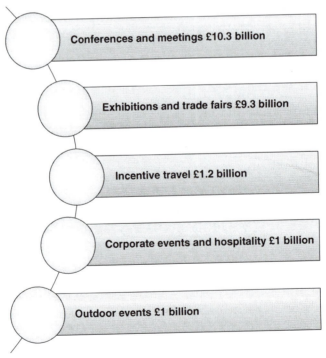

Conferences and meetings £10.3 billion

Exhibitions and trade fairs £9.3 billion

Incentive travel £1.2 billion

Corporate events and hospitality £1 billion

Outdoor events £1 billion

Figure 1.4   Income from the business visits and events sector

Source: www.businesstourismpartnership.com/pubs/BVE_Leaflet_low_pages.pdf

Outdoor festivals have seen a steady increase over the past five years, which can be assessed in terms of customer attendance, the amount of money they spend and the amount of festivals that proliferate in the urban and rural environment. In 2009 a comprehensive document was published by UK Music, a snapshot view of customer spend at UK music festivals which was pulled together with the assistance of Bournemouth University International Centre for Tourism and Hospitality Research. The data gives an indication of the positive contribution of music festivals to the UK economy. The team analysed data from 2.5 million ticket purchases to concerts and music festivals, to show that 7.7 million visitors from the UK and overseas attended the events. This group of people has a spending power of £1.4 billion, and represented a boost to the UK economy of £864 million. Alongside this growth in music festivals, the overall revenue for recorded music sales for the UK rose 4.7 per cent to £3.9 billion in 2009, and the value of the recorded music industry, including physical and digital sales was £1.36 billion in 2009, the same as in 2008. The Performing Rights Society (PRS), which represents and collects revenue for UK songwriters, composers and music publishers, reported income of £511million in 2009, up 4.1 per cent Advertising and sponsorship revenue rose 4.2 per cent from 2009–10, and the licensing of music services such as Spotify, advertising and sponsorship were up 4.4 per cent to £967 million (PRS for Music, 2010 [online]). There is a marginal decline in recorded sales for the music industry, but even taking into account the economic instability that existed in the period from 2008 to 2011, and the cancellation of 34 festivals in 2010 (*Guardian*, 7 August 2011 [online]), UK music festivals have outperformed consumer trends and create a strong economic profile for the UK economy.

Sports events would merit an in-depth study in their own right, such is the range of both events and stakeholders. Given that many sporting events are part of international competitions, it can be difficult to define the boundaries of the market within the UK alone. The clearest example is perhaps Premier League Football – the UK's most popular sport in terms of spectator admissions and television viewing. The Football Association Premier League, in its last published accounts (for the 2006–7 financial year), had a turnover of nearly £598.5 million.

The most revealing figure is the increase in the value of the broadcasting rights contract between the League and Sky broadcasting. An initial five-year deal for £200 million was signed when the League was formed in 1992. The three-year contract which followed in 2007 was worth £1.782 billion. In addition, the new contract which was negotiated in 2012 for the next three years has been increased to £3.018 billion. (Source – www.premierleague.com).

There is also a core group of companies and organisations that work across these various specialist sectors of the events industry. These organisations, known as 'event support services', constitute the foundation of the industry.

Different types of events

Religious events

The largest event in the world in terms of actual attendance is the Hajj in Makka, Saudi Arabia. This annual event is a pilgrimage, which is sacred to the Muslim faith; it is the fifth and final pillar of Islam and is undertaken by approximately 3.4 million people each year (The Saudi Arabia Information Resource, www.saudinf.com, the Saudi Ministry of Culture and Information website and Official News Agency of Saudi Arabia). This figure not only includes the world's largest number of 'religious tourists' who fly in from all over the world, but also the large numbers who converge upon Makka from within Saudi Arabia and neighbouring countries. Papal visits are another example of large religious events. When Pope John Paul II visited Ireland and the United States, he said mass to a million people in Dublin, New York and Boston.

These enormous gatherings of people share the objective components, drawn from Figure 1.1, of faith and feelings, culture, community, ceremony and contact.

The date of such religious event experiences becomes etched into the memory of the people attending, alongside their feelings and emotions. The same is also true of individual religious events such as Bar Mitzvahs. A Jewish male automatically becomes a Bar Mitzvah after his thirteenth birthday. The popular Bar Mitzvah cerebration is a relatively modern innovation and the elaborate ceremonies and receptions that are commonplace today were unheard of as recently as a century ago. The Bar Mitzvah is a celebration of the Jewish faith by friends and families, and the local Jewish Community.

A Bar Mitzvah takes place on a Saturday shortly after the boy's thirteenth birthday. Saturday is the Jewish Sabbath, a day of rest and spiritual enrichment. The boy is called upon to lead sections of the weekly service at the Synagogue. This may be as simple as saying the blessing but often involves much more and varies from congregation to congregation. The boy then often makes a speech which, tradition dictates, begins with the phrase, 'Today I am a man'. His father responds by reciting a blessing, thanking God for taking the responsibility for the son's sins from him (www.barmitzvahs.org).

The religious service is nowadays invariably followed by a reception and celebration. It is this event which is also a cultural and indeed a personal event; however, this celebration would not take place without the religious ceremony.

Bar Mitzvahs have the function of convening a community to celebrate their faith. They can rival weddings in terms of size and scale and are consequently significant to the events industry.

Cultural events

Some cultural events have a religious aspect and some may be held for commercial reasons. However, the primary purpose of such events is the celebration or confirmation of culture. Cultural events, such as concerts or carnivals, incur costs. They also create important economic opportunities and impacts, though a district, town, or city may not directly benefit on a festival's balance sheet. For example, Liverpool's Matthew Street Festival is held every year at the end of August at a cost to Liverpool City Council; yet the event generates £30 million for the local economy (Liverpool Culture Company [online]).

At one level, cultural events facilitate the integration and inclusion of smaller communities of families and friends within the wider community. On another level, they allow outsiders and tourists from different cultures to join and share in the process. For example, St Patrick's Day's parties are held not only in Dublin and Belfast but also in New York, Boston and around the world. Whilst these events are a celebration of Irishness, they also give anyone that wishes to the opportunity to enjoy Irish food, drink and music.

Musical events

Musical events range from the Glastonbury or Roskilde Music Festivals to the Last Night of the Proms in the Royal Albert Hall and all manner of concerts and performances in between. Musical events are often commercial in purpose but they are also about culture and fashion. They can even be concerned with change or charity and they are a celebration of creativity. A concert is about a shared feeling, fun with friends and new companions. Music festivals in particular promote a sense of belonging to the crowd.

An example is T in the Park, which has become Scotland's leading music festival. The first festival was at Strathclyde Country Park on the outskirts of Glasgow in 1994; however, in 1997 T in the Park moved to a more central location at Balado near Perth. This larger and more easily accessible site certainly enabled T in the Park to grow. The event now features hundreds of musicians from many countries around the world. They perform a wide range of popular music on four different stages to a combined audience of over 85,000. This takes place every year on a weekend in early July. In 2011, 45 per cent of people buying tickets for T in the Park came from outside Scotland, making the event one of Scotland's larger annual tourist attractions.

The event is strongly supported by the local council and surrounding communities, thus it does not experience the licensing problems of some comparable events in England. In 2004, T in the Park became the only festival in the UK to have been awarded a three-year licence for the second time. T in the Park has a large number of stakeholders with different objectives. For the organisers, DF Concerts, and the title sponsor, the Scottish lager brand Tennents, the event's purpose is commercial. Yet to its audience, it is a celebration of music and specifically of the Scots' love of music and partying which they wish to share. This is what gives the event its atmosphere. The event is about country but it is also about fun; it is the date on the calendar for the popular music community of Scotland. The event's objectives now go beyond the commercial ones it began with. Scotland's First Minister, Jack McConnell, when attending T in the Park in 2003, said: 'It is great to see so many young people enjoying themselves. The festival is very valuable to the Scottish economy and it symbolises the modern Scotland we want to portray' (www.tinthepark.com).

Sporting events

These range from the largest of international events to local leagues and competitions for communities and children. Their purpose is contest, challenge and competition but they also involve companionship, camaraderie and colleagues. They can often take the form of a championship, where there are displays of differing skills or prowess depending on the sport. Examples range from the US Open Golf Tournament or the Formula One Grand Prix Drivers' Championship to a city's schools' swimming gala and countless others, both large and small.

As professional sports men and women are often very well paid and as some sports attract large numbers of spectators, including huge global television audiences, there is invariably a strong commercial purpose in any large sports event. The success of teams or individual sports men and women from a community, city, county or nation is often a cause for great celebration, particularly if not expected. A perfect example is Greece's victory in the 2004 European Football Championships in Portugal. This had a very positive impact upon Greek national pride, which continued throughout and after the Athens Olympics. Sports events may therefore have political significance. With so many stakeholders and such high stakes, sports events require a high degree of professional events management.

Manchester City Council successfully bid for the staging of the 2008 UEFA Cup Final. It took place on 14 May, and was part of the Manchester World Sport 08 programme, a long-term strategy to bid for and host many international sporting events in 2008. The Northwest Regional Development Agency calculated that Manchester's 08 programme of sport attracted over 317,000 visitors to the city, and was worth an estimated £23 million in terms of financial impact. Manchester City Council and its partners commissioned Ipsos MORI North, in conjunction with Experian, to research the economic benefits. In that same year Manchester won the accolade of the world's top Sport City at the SportBusiness Sports Event Management Awards, ahead of Melbourne, Berlin, Doha, Moscow and New York.

Personal and private events

Personal events are celebrations of special occasions with friends and family. These could be viewed as a subsection of cultural events because when they are cross-cultural the format of weddings or funerals may vary. But the celebration of the union of two people, or the mourning and respect at the passing of a life are the oldest and most widely practised events. Many other life stage celebrations occur, linked either to age or achievement, including birthdays, anniversaries, graduations and homecomings. These events concern family and/or friends and their purposes are celebration and feelings.

Political and governmental events

From annual party political conferences and trade union conferences to events held by specific government departments, these events may be commercial in that they can be costly to organise; but the profit they seek is not financial currency but political change. As the media play a major part in such events, some, especially the party conferences, have become contests. This can range from subtle internal contests, played virtually behind the scenes, to blatant competition for public opinion and future votes between opposing parties on the stage provided by the attendant media.

In order to drive ticket sales and engage with their audience successfully, most events may require some form of media alliance, and none more so than political conferences. Without a media broadcaster(s) attached to the event, essential political messages may be lost at the point of delivery. As the national broadcaster the BBC has a moral undertaking to present a fair and objective coverage on all media platforms.

Commercial and business events

These often involve a whole section of industry or business. Exhibitions tend to be the most complex type of event within this category since each stand can be regarded as a sub-event, particularly where new products or services are being presented. Every stand has its stakeholders and all are competing for customers or clients. These events are key points on the calendar at which an industry convenes or confers in order to coordinate campaigns, make contacts and agree contracts. The overriding purpose is thus commercial.

Major exhibitions such as motor shows or, the largest of all, air shows are such spectacular events that, alongside bringing together the crucial business buyers and manufacturers, they also attract many thousands of members of the general public who pay for tickets. A good example of this is the British International Motor Show. By 1978, the motor show had outgrown the London exhibition facilities and was moved to the then new Birmingham National Exhibition Centre (NEC). Attracting around 700,000 visitors annually, The British International Motor Show now ranks alongside similar international motor shows in Detroit, Brussels and Turin. Since 2006, it has been back in London, at ExCel (www.britishmotorshow.co.uk; www.excel-london.co.uk/).

Business events also include 'association events' – the annual conferences of a very wide range of professional and business associations. From dentists to banking, ocean technology to e-marketing, all spheres of human industry and endeavour have at least one association conference.

Corporate events

Events of this type involve just one single business, company, corporation or organisation. They may include annual conferences, product launches, staff motivation events, or awards ceremonies. They draw their audience from within the organisation and often include an 'incentive' element in their choice of venue or location. Their purpose may be to give colleagues the space and place to confer in order to create change within the organisation. Key tasks may include considering competitors, clients or customers, reviewing the challenges faced by the organisation, and generating creative solutions to those challenges.

Special events

The term 'special events' is used to describe events that are first class or extraordinary in terms of the widespread public recognition they receive. Special events enrich the quality of life for local people and attract tourists from outside the area on account of their uniqueness.

Special events sometimes become synonymous with and dependent on the place where they are held. For example, the annual Edinburgh International Festival, which is a prime example of a special event, would not hold the same prestige should individual festival organisers ever decide to move any of its components to another city.

The primary goal of special events is to develop recognition for the local community and festival organisers. Examples of such events include Notting Hill Carnival, Bradford Mela, Berlin Love Parade, Toronto Street Festival and the Queen's Jubilee celebrations in the UK. Such events create images for the tourism market and attract visitors to the location. A city wanting to upgrade its infrastructure or its political image may also use a large-scale event as a tool to generate funds from corporations and higher levels of government.

The host community benefits from special events both socially and economically. Yet special events are also typically dependent on the large outlay of public monies, which may arise not only from hosting them but also from bidding to host them in the first place. Despite the enormous costs and benefits for host communities, the full impact of special events, socially and environmentally as well as economically, is rarely calculated.

Special events range in size from small community fairs to large-scale sporting events. Community and local festivals can be classed as special events, since they can create a cultural and social environment for tourists who are attending the event. Major cities use special events to celebrate the city and highlight what it has to offer in terms of sport, music, culture and art.

Leisure events

Large scale leisure events are capable of attracting substantial numbers of visitors, gaining global media coverage and reaping vast economic benefits for the hosts. There is generally a competitive bidding process to determine who will host such large-scale events such as the Olympic Games, the FIFA World Cup and the Commonwealth Games.

Events on this scale are extremely important for the host community, not only because of the number of visitors, but because they create legacies, which may continue to have an impact on the host community long after the event has taken place. The bids for large-scale sporting events often incorporate urban regeneration goals into their strategies in order to justify the high costs of such events to all stakeholders, especially the local community. Large-scale leisure events are linked to government funding programmes, which enable the construction of facilities and infrastructure, and the redevelopment and revitalisation of urban areas. This process creates a physical, economic and social legacy which may have long-term benefits for the local communities. Law suggests that such events

act as a catalyst for change by persuading people to work together around a common objective and as a fast track for obtaining extra finance and getting building projects off the drawing board. (1993: 107)

Leisure events can act as a tool for urban regeneration, since through them host cities are given the opportunity to present new or promote existing images of themselves and thus enhance their profile on a global scale. Improving the image of the location as a destination will attract tourists to the area and hence generate future local employment in the tourist industry.

Crucially, leisure events provide an opportunity to acquire funding to regenerate cities and develop new facilities. The planning for these events should include a legacy plan to ensure that local communities continue to benefit from the event and associated investments in the future. This should consider the urban regeneration and social impacts of the event on host communities, identifying any adverse effects and ensuring that benefits to the surrounding communities are not squandered. How new facilities are utilised once the event has moved out of the host city is of great importance, as improper planning can mean they may not be used to their maximum potential. The facilities for the Commonwealth Games in Manchester in 2002 were fully utilised, since it was agreed at the planning stage that the main stadium would be handed over to Manchester City Football Club and that the athletic village would be passed on to the local authority to provide accommodation. In this century, with competitive bidding for large-scale sporting events by local authorities, countries and cities, it is no longer acceptable to stakeholders for central and local governments to host a large leisure event without developing a comprehensive post-event strategic plan.

There has been much discussion over who benefits most from large-scale leisure events and whether the costs and benefits are shared equally by the different stakeholders. It is clear, for example, that the games can produce tangible benefits for governments and businesses, especially within the tourism industry. The non-tangible benefits for the community are less self-evident, aside from the privilege of participating in the mega-event in one way or another.

Community festivals now play a significant role in generating income for local businesses and attracting tourists to the local area. These economic impacts have increased considerably over the past decade as the festivals have grown in size. The expansion of information technology and media networks has contributed to the development of these events and the industry which promotes and runs them. Festival organisers now utilise these new communication tools to advertise their events to wider audiences. Festivals now attract visitors from all over the country and from other countries, not only for the duration of the festival but also possibly, as a result of the media attention attracted by the event, in the longer term. A festival can, however, bring both positive and negative associations to an area; but if the positive impacts are stronger, it can help to develop a sense of local pride and identity. Examples of this include Glastonbury, Reading Festival and The Edinburgh Festival. These events have all taken the host community's name and have therefore reinforced the relationship between event and host community.

Local authorities' events strategies

Many local authorities are using events to position their destinations in the market, and thus support their cultural, tourism and arts strategies. Over the last decade, local authorities' strategies have begun to state the importance of festivals in promoting tourism and developing the social and economic cohesion, confidence and pride that connect local authorities with the communities they serve. Through events, councils can secure political power and influence among the local residents and businesses. Local authorities undertake the development and direct delivery of festivals to pursue specific economic and community development objectives. Given their responsibility for public spaces, they have some advantages in presenting outdoor public events.

Manchester City Council (and the North West Development Agency) put forward a Major Event Strategy after hosting the 2002 Commonwealth Games. The prime objective was to encourage international events to come to the city, and also to build on the existing events to attract a greater number of visitors. With five bespoke venues built, one upgraded site and a total spend of £160 million it would be inconceivable not to extract the potential long-term economic benefits from those venues. The strategy consisted of a number of objectives to become a destination city, and can be summarised as follows:

- To ensure that the region can take maximum advantage of, and be adequately prepared for, staging and bidding for major events;
- As far as is reasonably practicable, to manage intra-regional competition to avoid wasted effort and resource;
- To develop a regional mechanism for sharing and developing expertise in the staging and bidding for major events;
- To develop evaluation tools to consistently measure the impact of major events and guide investment decisions;
- To provide a strategic framework to support bids to national and international organisations for the funding of major events in the Northwest; and
- To maximise the opportunities to secure engagement and funding from the public and private sectors. (North West Development Agency, 2004)

To acquire the international status as a destination city it was imperative for Manchester to have an International Festival. This event came to market in 2007 as a biennial festival. In 2007 it had £6 million support from Manchester City Council and a number of business-related, Manchester-based stakeholders to supplement the financial shortfall.

Local authorities in the UK are developing event-led strategies in cities and using events to serve as marketing tools to boost the national and international profile and image of their cities, so as to attract hundreds of thousands of visitors every year. There are many public and private companies and agencies in the UK events sector at present, working to deliver successful events and festivals. Local authorities are increasingly promoting awareness of the events industry and the role it can play to provide inspiration and ambition to local communities to deliver large festivals and events on an international stage.

Although not all local authorities have an explicit event-led strategy, many can be seen to use events and festivals as marketing tools to achieve some of their goals and objectives. Events and festivals can promote urban regeneration and enhance the profile of the city. The international hosts of major sporting events have all experienced positive benefits in terms of their economic and social development. For example, the London Olympics in 2012 had a major impact on the local economy and the city as a whole.

Corporate events strategies

The corporate events sector has been the fastest growing industry in the UK over the last decade. Corporate events are used by companies to attract and maintain customer loyalty, to raise their business profile, and to increase the motivation level of their workforce to maintain high standards. Over the last decade, companies have become increasingly strategic in their planning of corporate events so as to maximise their impact on business profile. They may, for example, hold a team-building activity at a unique time of year or link their event to a specific ritual, ceremony or large scale sporting event.

Corporate events can be broken down into two main types:

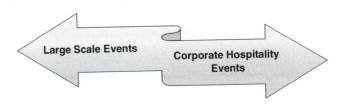

Figure 1.5   Two main types of corporate events

Large-scale events may include sports events such as the Olympic Games, the Commonwealth Games, Royal Ascot, the Grand Prix, and the FA Cup Final. They also could include cultural and lifestyle events such as the Notting Hill Carnival, the Berlin Love Parade, the Chelsea Flower Show, and major music festivals.

Corporate hospitality can be defined as events and activities organised for the benefit of companies who want to entertain clients, prospective clients or employees at the company's expense. A variety of options for entertaining are available, including evening receptions and dinners with a private view of current exhibitions.

Corporate hospitality events are a form of non-financial reward to employees and are increasingly being used by companies in order to motivate employees, to foster team spirit and secure employee loyalty in the long term. Corporate hospitality events may include cultural, team-building and sporting events. The increasing demand for high quality and high profile corporate hospitality events has enabled the expansion of events management companies around the world who specialise in organising them. Corporate events are big business within the UK market. The Events Industry Forum estimated the industry's value at £36.1 billion in 2010, and £42.2 billion in 2015. The corporate hospitality industry has also increased over the years, to £1 billion (Eventia, 2010 [online]).

Community festivals

The concept of 'community' has complex social, psychological and geographical dimensions and there are divergent views as to what constitutes 'a community'. Traditional views of 'community', as defined by the parameters of geographical location, a sense of belonging to that locality, and the mix of social and economic activities within the area, have been supplemented with greater degrees of complexity by analysts. 'Interest communities' rely not on the focus of place, but are anchored in other characteristics, such as ethnicity, occupation, religion, etc. This type of community thrives on social networks and social/psychological attachments. Britain has always been a multicultural society and people with diverse histories, beliefs and cultures have settled here. People from South Asia, Africa and the Caribbean initially arrived in the UK after the Second World War to help meet labour shortages. These multicultural communities now play an important role in enhancing the cultural diversity of Britain. Multicultural communities are spread all over the country, with approximately 30 per cent settled in the sub-region of Yorkshire and Humberside.

Clearly, whilst some communities might have a shared locality and common interests, there are underlying complexities which have ramifications for public policy making, particularly in terms of community development goals. A misconception of what 'community' is, or a lack of precision or understanding regarding some of these elements can lead to imprecise and ultimately unsuccessful and wasteful policy initiatives.

Community festivals now play a significant role in income generation for local businesses and create tourism for the local area. The expenditure in the local economy is more likely to *support* supplier jobs in tourism-related sectors of the economy rather than *create* new jobs; however, many other factors will also have an impact.

Community festivals or cultural events are those produced primarily for the community and only secondarily as a tourist attraction. There are various reasons for organising community events, including a celebration of religious festivals such as Diwali. Community events can be part of regeneration schemes aimed at giving communities a sense of involvement and community spirit. Community events are organised by members of the community, community leaders, and professional event managers or festival producers. These events are often seen by government and community leaders as a way of improving communication between various sections of the community.

In addition to creating community cohesion, such festivals and events have the potential to improve the economic life of the host destination, by developing employment, trade and business, by investing in the infrastructure, and by providing long-term promotional benefits and tax revenues. Events and festivals not only generate significant economic benefits, they also provide host destinations with the opportunity to market themselves nationally and internationally, bringing people from diverse backgrounds to the destination for the duration of the event or festival. As a result, they have the potential to provide host destinations with a high-status tourism profile and may enhance the links between tourism and commerce. Events may do this by improving the image of a place, by generating economic impacts, such as the development of local communities and businesses, by providing a tourist attraction, which may overcome seasonality, and by supporting key industrial sectors.

The economic impacts of events are the most tangible and therefore the most frequently measured impacts. Economic impacts can be positive and negative. The positive effects may include visitor expenditure, investment in infrastructure and increased employment. Examples of negative economic impacts include price inflation on goods and services to cash in on the influx of visitors, or local authority-funded events which run at a loss leading to an increase in local Council Tax. The latter actually occurred following the 1991 World Student Games in Sheffield. The economic impact of the World Student Games was not fully realised due to a lack of foresight from the major stakeholders. Bramwell (1997) made reference to the fact that mega events can be significant assets to a host city if and only if there is a strategic plan. Bramwell (1997) also made reference to a strategic plan not materialising until 1994 – the Friel plan as it was known rolled out in 1995 and looked at events as a means to drive tourism to the city.

Charity events

Charity events have developed as a major provider in employing event professionals and setting out a working model to achieve an objective. The alignment of a celebrity and a media channel orchestrated around a worthwhile activity can bring forward consumer support, revenue and media attention. The organisation of in 8, 10 and 12km runs in cities throughout the UK has become commonplace in raising awareness and finance for a particular cause. The most prominent of these, which is recognised by the International Athletes Association Federation (IAAF) and endorsed by them in 2010, is the Bupa 10K city run televised by the BBC. This event does not carry charity status; however, a large percentage of the runners are doing it to raise funds for a particular charity.

The charity sector has expanded substantially over the last two decades. Currently, there are over 164,000 registered 'general charities' in the UK with a total income of £31 billion in 2005–6 and expenditure of just over £29 billion. These charities employ 611,000 paid staff (2.2 per cent of the overall workforce). By comparison, in 2002 there were around 150,000 registered charities with a total annual expenditure of £20.4 billion.

Data supplied by the Charity Market Monitor (2008) also gives an overview of government support, which shows that there is a disparity in the amount of support depending on the type of charity and its turnover.

Total government funding represents 35.7% of the sector's earnings. Charities with an income of between £100,000 and £1 million rely most on government funding, while charities with an income of less than £10,000 rely the least (9.2%). There has been a shift from grants to contracts since 2002. (Philanthropy UK, 2011 [online])

Summary

In this chapter we have explored the ways in which events and festivals have changed over the years. In the past, festivals were associated with key calendar moments, linked specifically to particular seasons and heritage sites. Events and festivals have been revolutionised to meet the commercial needs of the market in response to the changing demands of local community groups and increased business opportunities for event organisers and local businesses. Local authorities are now using events as a major tool to promote their city and are justifying their bids for large-scale sporting events on the grounds that these form part of their regeneration strategies. Events and festival managers are now using historical and cultural themes to develop annual events to attract visitors and create cultural images in the host cities by holding festivals within community settings. Such events provide an opportunity for local people to develop and share their culture, enhance their own values and beliefs and promote local culture to visitors and tourists.

In addition, the typology of events has been thoroughly examined and many examples of diverse events have been discussed. The focus in this review has been on the objectives of these different events, or to be more precise, the components that make up their objectives, in terms of people, place and purpose. This chapter has identified the most fundamental of these objective components as being that of 'community' in all its many applications. There is no doubt that events and festivals do achieve economic goals and develop community cohesion through their functional role in attracting visitors to the area. We have also noted that the spending by visitors on local goods and services has a direct economic impact on local businesses and that these benefits pass more widely across the economy and the community. On the other hand, cultural tourism does not take into account the loss of local beauty, environmental degradation and the effects it creates on the local people of the host communities through their direct and indirect involvement with tourists. In addition, events and festivals can play an important part in promoting the host community as both a tourist and commercial destination. Events and festivals can help to develop the image and profile of a destination and may attract visitors outside of the holiday season.

The various sectors of the events industry have been introduced. These include both specialists who organise a huge range of different events and the core event support services who are subcontracted to work across these different events.

■ Discussion questions

Question 1

Discuss why event managers target communities to host festivals and events.

Question 2

Critically analyse and discuss the role festivals and events play within tourism industry.

Question 3

How might strategic event management be able to integrate the various components of the people, place and process model to augment value throughout the lifecycle of the event, i.e., prior to, during and after an event or festival?

Question 4

Identify and discuss the benefits of corporate hospitality strategies for events.

Question 5

Investigate the influence music events have on the local community and regional tourism boards.

Question 6

Identify and discuss any problems that are associated with events and festivals which are developed in the local community environment?

CASE STUDY 1 LEEDS WEST INDIAN CARNIVAL

The Caribbean carnival is an annual event which has been celebrated in the city of Leeds since the 1960s. The carnival is one of the oldest Caribbean carnivals in Europe.

The carnival has created a multicultural spirit for people of all races and nationalities to attend the event during the August bank holiday each year since 1967.

Originally, the Leeds West Indian carnival used to go into the city centre, but that tradition changed during the 1980s. The carnival has outgrown the original concept and now it takes place around Chapeltown and Harehills.

Behind the colour and music of the carnival there is a deeper meaning, rooted in the experiences of Caribbean people arriving in England around a time of great change in the late 1950s and early 1960s. So it was a search for identity, for community and belonging that initially led to the carnival being developed.

The carnival has created a platform for the Caribbean people to come together and share their social and cultural traditions with the local community who come from a range of differing backgrounds. It is about people coming together and having fun.

In 2011 over 80,000 people enjoyed the mixture of local and international talent. This magic music was mixed with the wonderful smells of Caribbean cooking. In the afternoon over 100,000 people watched the carnival procession.

(Continued)

(Continued)

The carnival day starts early with the J'ouvert procession at 6.00 am. In the afternoon the procession leaves Potternewton Park for three and half hours of non-stop dancing around the streets of Chapeltown and Harehills. In 2011, 800 revellers joined the procession, which included two sound systems and a colourful mixture of people from all backgrounds and cultures. Figure 1.6 illustrates the site plan for the carnival.

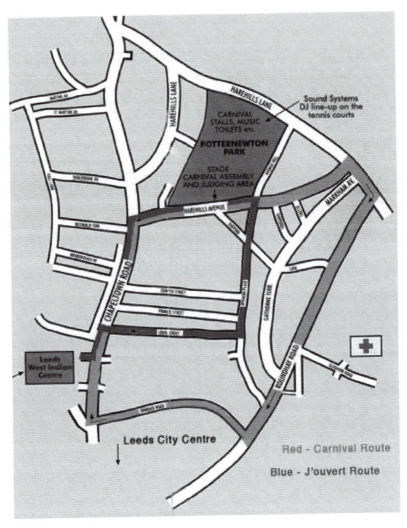

Figure 1.6   The site plan for Leeds carnival

Source: http://www.leedscarnival.co.uk/

The carnival creates cultural variety for the local community and encourages party-goers to enjoy the sights and sounds of the spectacular costumed troupes, the parade, and the traditional Caribbean music. It also brings together people of different ages, races and nationalities to enjoy the great day of fun.

Over the last ten years tourism in the area has also grown, because the event itself attracts those interested in the culture and spectacle created, which highlights an otherwise invisible side of local culture. The carnival has created a very special image for the city of Leeds, because it has brought the local community together and attracted tourists from all over the country and overseas.

CASE STUDY 2   DAILY TELEGRAPH BOARD-X FESTIVAL

Board-X was first set up seven years ago and showcased the best riders in snowboarding, skating and BMX. In 2003 the event was held at Alexandra Palace, London, on 8, 9 and 10 November. Over the three days an estimated 25,000 people passed through the doors. Alexandra Palace provided organisers with a large area to build an indoor full-size street course for skaters and BMX riders but the highlight of the event was the outdoor Big Air kicker for the snowboarders. The kicker was as big as it has ever been, standing at 25 metres tall and 100 metres long. One of the event organisers, George Foster, explains that 'as the number of snowboard enthusiasts in the UK continues to grow, Board-X has matured into an event that caters for all levels of rider and follower while maintaining the support of the industry it seeks to provide for'. With the introduction of a title sponsor in the Daily Telegraph, the event should continue to grow along with the snowboard culture and is now arguably the most comprehensive snowboard festival in Europe.

Having visited the event in 1997 and 2003 the standard of both the event and the riding has increased phenomenally. The event has a totally original vibe, it is the home of the British snowboard scene and it superbly combines, with the aid of top DJs, break dancers, skaters, BMXers and retailers, all aspects of this lifestyle which can be enjoyed by pros and amateurs.

(Source: forums.mxtrax.co.uk/showthread.php)

Further reading

British Tourist Authority (BTA) – www.visitbritain.com

British Visits and Events Partnership (2007) 'Moving business visits and events up the agenda' [online]. Available at: www.businesstourismpartnership.com/pubs/BVE_Leaflet_low_pages.pdf [accessed 19th September 2011].

Getz, D. (2005) *Event Management and Event Tourism*, 2nd edn. New York: Cognizant Communications Corporation.

Glasson, J., Godfrey, K., Goodey, B., Van Der Berg, J. and Absalam, H. (1995) *Towards Visitor Impact Management: Visitor Impacts, Carrying Capacity and Management Responses in Europe's Historic Towns and Cities*. Aldershot: Avebury.

Goldblatt, J. (2002) *Special Events Best Practices in Modern Event Management*, 3rd edn. New York, International Thompson Publishing Company.

Guardian   www.guardian.co.uk/commentisfree/2011/aug/07/are-pop-festivals-over debate?INTCMP=SRCH [accessed 9th September 2011].

Hall, C. (1994) *Tourism and Politics: Policy, Power and Place*. Chichester: John Wiley & Sons.

Philanthropy UK (2011) 'Charitable sector overview' [online]. Available at: www. philanthropyuk.org/publications/guide-giving/how-give/charitable-sector-overview [accessed 9 September 2011].

Raj, R. and Morpeth, N.D. (2007) *Religious Tourism and Pilgrimage Management: An International Perspective*. Oxford: CABI Publishing.

Tomlinson, J. (1992) *Cultural Imperialism: A Critical Introduction*. Baltimore, MD: The Johns Hopkins University Press.

Yeoman, I., Robertson, M., Ali-Knight, J., Drummond, S. and McMahon-Beattie, U. (2004) *Festival and Events Management*. Oxford: Elsevier Butterworth Heinemann.

2 Events Destinations Management

In this chapter you will cover:

- events tourism;
- cultural tourism;
- niche tourism through events;
- developing communities culture through events/festivals;
- managing visitors for events;
- cultural and economic impacts;
- summary;
- discussion questions;
- case studies;
- further reading.

This chapter introduces the concept of events tourism. Events tourism and tourism destination are intrinsically linked. Cities and regions throughout the UK and the European Union have developed strategic policies for encouraging tourism when associated with festivals and events. Festivals attract cultural tourists to local community events and promote enriching exchanges between tourists and residents. Where there are established migratory travel routes, and communities which have emerged through patterns of diaspora and immigration, these are sites which are often able to host particularly distinctive festivals and events. The case studies within this chapter explore the development of cultural tourism and multicultural festivals and events within the UK, and the positive contribution that these events play in solidifying community relations.

Events tourism

Festival organisers are now using historical and cultural themes to develop annual events to attract visitors and create cultural images in the host cities by holding festivals in community settings. The desire for festivals and events is not always specifically linked to the needs of any one particular group. Events are often developed because of the tourism and economic opportunities they present, and also the social and cultural benefits they offer. Many researchers have contested that local communities play a vital role in developing tourism through festivals.

The government now supports and promotes events as part of their strategies for economic development, nation building and cultural tourism. In turn, events are seen as an important tool for attracting visitors and building the image within different communities. According to Stiernstrand (1996), the economic impact of tourism arises principally from the consumption of tourism products in a geographical area. According to McDonnell, Allen and O'Toole (1999), tourism-related services, which include travel, accommodation, restaurants and shopping, are the major beneficiaries of the event.

As far as events and tourism are concerned, the role and responsibilities of the government, private sector and society in general have significantly changed over the last decade. Where previously the state had the key responsibility for tourism development and promotion, we are now in a world where the public sector is obliged to reinvent itself by relinquishing its traditional responsibilities and activities in favour of provincial, state and local authorities. This suggests that festivals impact on the host population and stakeholders in a number of ways, including social, cultural, physical, environmental, political and economic. All of which can be both positive and negative.

The current trend in almost all regions of the world is towards semi-public but autonomous tourism organisations engaged in partnerships with both private sector and regional and/or local authorities. Together they have a role to play in the development, organisation and promotion of destinations. Host organisations, in marketing terms, reach niche as well as mass audiences, not simply through increasing visitor numbers at events but by creating powerful associations of the destination in the mind of visitors. In this respect, multicultural communities have a key role to play in creating narratives and themes which are the basis for diverse festivals and events. To paraphrase the eminent cultural studies academic, Stuart Hall (1995), multicultural events and festivals have the capacity to create linkages between culture, place and identity.

Events and festivals are found in all societies, and are seen as a unique tourist attraction for the organisers and destinations image makers, constituting one of the most exciting and fastest growing areas within the tourism industry.

The phenomenon known as 'event tourism' originated in the 1980s. Events and festival organisers recognised the opportunity to enhance the development of event tourism as a brand to attract consumers and also to reassure the tourist that they will get the promised benefit from the chosen destination. The approach, as Getz (2005) explains, advocates a mixture of science and art:

> Actual mechanisms of image-making are part science and part art. The science is in researching the needs, motives and perceptual processes of potential customers. The art is producing an event or products to meet the needs and in effectively communicating the strengths of the attraction. (Getz, 2005: 369)

Getz (2005) believes that many countries and destinations fail to recognise the advantages of events and are often unable to manage negative images and publicity. Getz (2005) also states that due to rising competition, tourist regions and communities should strategically plan in order to achieve their environmental, social and economic objectives.

Events have the potential to generate a vast amount of tourism when they cater to out-of-region visitors. Although definitive data on the impact of event-tourism is not available due to the complexity and diversity of the industry, Key Leisure Markets (2010) claim that day trips in England are now worth more than domestic and inbound tourism combined. The report commissioned by X-leisure states:

> Family Leisure, a major £90 billion segment of the UK market, is continuing to show resilience and stability despite the current constriction of all aspects of consumers' discretionary spend. (X-leisure, 2010 [online])

Key Note's report for 2010 states that the market for leisure activities outside the home was valued at £60.4 billion in 2009, representing just 7 per cent of total consumer spending.

In addition, festivals have an important role in the national and host community in the context of destination planning, enhancing and linking tourism and commerce. Festivals have become more of a tourist attraction over the last ten years, which has had a great economic impact on the host communities. The event industry has developed due to the expansion of information technology and media networks. Festival organisers now utilise these new communication tools to advertise their event to a wider audience.

Community events are developed to create cross-cultural diversity within the wider community and to enhance economic value for local ethnic minority communities. Events such as African and Caribbean carnivals and Asian melas have given the local communities a sense that they are of long-term cultural benefit to the host city. Such events can promote cross-cultural understanding and social integration amongst local communities and visitors.

Cultural tourism

Cultural tourism is defined by international Cultural Tourism Charter professionals in the following way:

> Domestic and international tourism continues to be among the foremost vehicles for cultural exchange, providing a personal experience, not only of that which has survived from the past, but of the contemporary life and society of others. (ICOMOS, 1999 [online])

Culture can be seen as a sense of identity; it also refers to the importance that individual people place on local and national social organisations, such as local governments, education institutions, religious communities, work and leisure. Cultural tourism describes tourists who take part in cultural activities while away from their home cities. The purpose of cultural tourism is for travellers to discover heritage sites and cultural monuments on their visits. Keillor (1995), in an address to the White House Conference on Travel and Tourism, best described cultural tourism by saying:

> We need to think about cultural tourism because really there is no other kind of tourism. It's what tourism is... People don't come to America for our airports, people don't come to America for our hotels, or the recreation facilities...They come for our culture: high culture, low culture, middle culture, right, left, real or imagined – they come here to see America. (Keillor, 1995 [online])

The theme of culture has grown over the last few decades but no clear definition of culture has been accepted. Culture in modern day terms is generally seen as a product by governments, large organisations and individual people to develop their own standing in a given market. Tomlinson (1991) explains that there are a plethora of definitions, and that culture can encompass aspects from these different definitions. Culture is wide ranging; as Yeoman et al. (2004) state, it ranges from high culture, such as the arts, to popular culture, which embraces diverse subjects such as football, music and television.

Reisenger and Turner argue that:

> Culture is a multivariate concept. There are many definitions of culture. These definitions of culture are complex, unclear and there is no consensus of a definition that can be widely accepted. The majority refer to culture in psychological terms. There is a dominant culture that influences the majority of people, and there are subcultures with regional differences.

For Stuart Hall, the term 'culture' includes:

> the social practices which produce meaning as well as the practices which are regulated by those shared meanings. Sharing the same 'maps of meaning' gives us a sense of belonging to a culture, creates a common bond, a sense of community or identity with others. (1995: 176)

Moreover, cultural tourism relates to those individuals or groups of people who travel around the world, to individual countries, local communities and individual events and who seek to experience heritage, religious and art sites to develop knowledge of different communities' ways of life. This can include a very wide range of cultural tourist experiences, for example, performing arts, visits to historic sites and monuments, educational tours, museums, natural heritage sites and religious festivals. The model in Figure 2.1 shows the process through which cultural tourism attracts visitors to different destinations and famous heritage sites.

The future of event tourism in developing cities or countries relies significantly on event tourism strategies. Therefore, it is important for governments to develop clear and effective event tourism planning strategies. It is also important for destinations and countries to understand the potential needs and expectations of customers/tourists, and to introduce the consumer decision-making process for events. As levels of tourism in the future are difficult to predict, it is essential that governments and other related authorities do not rely on certain events to attract tourists, but have a variety of future event tourism strategies in place to increase cultural tourism. Moreover, it is difficult for some countries or cities to control negative images of their destination and events through the media. So it is important for governments to avoid negative

Figure 2.1 Types of cultural tourism

media publicity for their destination and to encourage event tourism through highlighting the cultural element of the country or city. Festivals and events can play a major role in generating a positive image of the destination, and amending negative images of a country can be important both economically and socially for the host community.

Strategic decisions made by a variety of governments in the past have resulted in poor support from the local community. Therefore, it is important for governments to work with local communities to attract visitors to cultural and heritage sites. Also they need to improve transport, accommodation and food facilities in the tourism areas. Governments should provide tax breaks for those companies which are catering for local and international tourists to the destination.

Event tourism allows locals to become independent. Government laws allow the locals to make and sell handicrafts, to rent rooms from their own housing, as well as to cook for tourists. This is an advantage both to the local community as well as to the country's economy. Government strategies, with support from locals, involve regular improvements on heritage buildings, such as museums, churches and large sports facilities. They provide facilities for visitors, ensuring that the locals are not disturbed during their time in the area. Events can be used to develop community pride and self-sufficiency as well as intercultural communication.

Niche tourism through events

Many researchers, including Raj et al. (2009), Yeoman et al. (2004) and Kim (2002), have contested that local communities play vital roles in developing tourism through cultural festivals, sporting events and hallmark events.

On the other hand, in spite of the tremendous increase in tourism and events, cultural festivals are now assessed by visitor numbers attending the event, and the tourist experience is disregarded and treated as an economic tool to generate income for events managers and organisers. This can disguise the wider significance of festivals in establishing the link between culture, identity and place (Hall, 1995).

Richards (2001) argues that event-led strategies which market the 'cultural capital' of towns and cities have to consider balancing benefits between tourists and residents, warning of the pitfalls of 'social spaces' being utilised for commercial gain and competitive advantage over other urban centres. Event-led strategies, according to Richards (2001: 62), create 'the danger, however, that the city will become trapped on a treadmill of investment, requiring a constant supply of events to ensure visitor flow'. He suggests the possibility that more appropriate and sustainable strategies should focus on improving the 'cultural capital' of a city, which might benefit both residents and tourists. The inference is that the 'hijacking' of contested social spaces creates environments for events and tourism to the exclusion of community needs (Richards, 2001: 14).

Festivals can be big business for a destination. Festivals become part of destination tourism strategies because they can bring in new money to the local economy.

It now seems the importance of cultural events is higher than ever. Festivals can act as a spectacle in attracting tourists' attention and concentrating their focus on a particular city during a short intense period. This can enable the hosts to showcase their destination on a world stage and highlight key attractions and activities they offer. Therefore, local authorities are using events to position their destinations in the market, and thus fulfil their cultural, tourism, festivals and arts strategies – see Raj and Morpeth (2007), Yeoman (2004), Hall (1992).

Developing communities' culture through events/festivals

The revolution in festivals has primarily been driven by the need both to meet the changing demands of local community groups and to address the increasing business opportunities for event organisers and local businesses. Festivals are attractive to host communities because they help to develop local pride and identity for the local people. In addition, festivals have an important role in the national and host community in the context of destination planning, enhancing and linking tourism and commerce. Some aspects of this role include: events as image makers, economic impact generators, and tourist attractions; overcoming seasonality; contributing to the development of local communities and businesses; and supporting key industrial sectors.

Organisers and communities hosting a festival provide the visitors with a vibrant and valuable culture. In addition, culture is the personal expression of community heritage and community perspective. Festivals also provide support to those who pursue economic opportunity related to sharing community culture with the broader world. UNEP (2002) suggest that cultural tourism is boosted through the development of festivals and events. Tourism can add to the vitality of communities in many ways. One example is that events and festivals in which local residents have been the primary participants and spectators are often rejuvenated and developed in response to tourist interest. The local authorities in UK and other countries have provided grants and support for local festivals to add additional activities to cater for the visitors. Priority is given to those events and festivals which include some of the following themes (Figure 2.2) in their events.

The prime objective of local authorities' support for festivals and events in the local area is to create economic wealth for the local economy. Tourism plays a critical role in providing jobs and income for many local communities. In addition, visitors to an area are likely to visit more than one place, and this creates more revenue for the local community and local businesses.

Event tourism over the years has developed into a massive income generator for local communities. Visitors are staying longer in urban areas and spending per head has increased, having a positive effect on the local communities.

Figure 2.2 Essential activities for events visitors

However, getting visitors to stay for an extended period in an urban area is much harder than it first appears. Unless the area is renowned for its history or culture, many cities do not own the credentials to bring in tourists on a regular basis. Large sporting events are one of the key areas for countries and cities to create events tourism. A sporting event generates global exposure and raises interest from local and international visitors. Large sporting events can act as a spectacle in attracting the world's media attention and concentrating their focus on a particular city during a short intense period; enabling the hosts to showcase their destination on a world stage and highlight key attractions and activities they offer. Large sporting events are extremely beneficial for cities to promote themselves as a tourist destination and to enhance the visitors' experience. According to UNWTO, international tourist arrivals grew by nearly 7 per cent in 2010 to 940 million compared in 2008. In particular, as destinations attempt to differentiate their brands and engage visitors at a deeper level, unelected officials, namely destination marketers, may find themselves not only deciding how the events they host will present the destination and how they want the world to relate to their own destination, but also what the destination wishes to say about the world.

CASE STUDY   THE BRADFORD FESTIVAL MELA

The Bradford Festival Mela has been held annually at Peel Park since 1988. An intoxicating festival in its own right, the Bradford Festival Mela is the largest outside Asia and a rare blend of party and pleasure trip. The Bradford Festival Mela has created a unique image in the city, over the last 23 years. The Mela perfectly illustrates its unique role in the communities where it brings people from different cultures together demonstrating various forms of expression. This also brings with it pride and traditional Asian arts to the city of Bradford.

The Bradford Festival Mela attracts 80,000–100,000 people over two days. This has a great economic impact on the city of Bradford when local small businesses in particular gain vital revenue from the festival. Visitors spend great amounts of money during the duration of the festival and this outweighs the social and physical problems that are encountered by the locals.

Moreover, Bradford Festival Mela brings the local community together to celebrate the diverse cultures within it. Over the last decade Bradford Festival Mela has become a major multicultural event for the city of Bradford and has demonstrated the advantages of cultural diversity to the rest of British society. In addition, the festival has created great economic impacts for the local community and enhanced local businesses that benefit from the actual event.

The Bradford Festival Mela over the years has developed into an international event that attracts audiences from the UK and throughout the world. It attracts family and friends from abroad due to the large South Asian Community in Bradford. They often pick festival time to visit close family and friends in the city, which increases

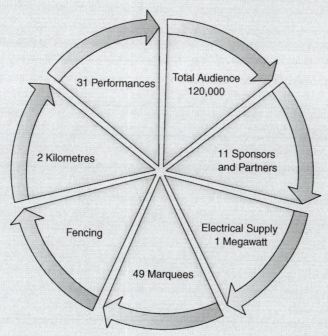

Figure 2.3 Bradford Mela key facts

Source: Bradford Mela (2011)

(Continued)

(Continued)

the tourism in the area. Councillor Adrian Naylor, Bradford Council's executive member for regeneration, stated:

> Bradford Mela, the first in Europe, helped give the city a worldwide recognition. In terms of businesses this is a great showcase, as you walk around you see everything, from the voluntary sector to the private sector.

(*Bradford Telegraph and Argus*, 14 June 2009 [online])

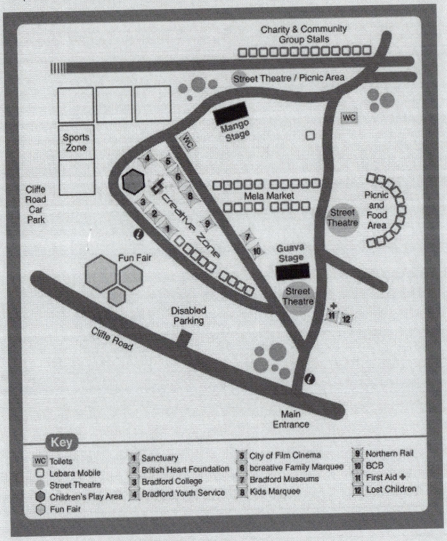

Figure 2.4   Bradford Mela site plan

Source: [accessed 2nd May 2012]

The visitors to the festival provide great financial support for the local economy by overnight stays in the city, which generates direct income from the festival for local businesses. The festival also has a major impact on the host city by creating extra employment for the period leading up to the event and even after the event has taken place. The data in Figure 2.3 highlights the actual benefits the event brings to the city.

The Bradford Festival Mela has developed into one of the centrepieces of the Bradford International Festival programme. The Mela has demonstrated cultural display over the last 20 years to attract tourists and build the image of the city of Bradford. Figure 2.4 illustrates the site plan for Mela 2011. In recent years many local businesses have been inspired by Bradford Mela to hold stalls at the Mela market.

The Bradford Festival Mela now attracts tourists from different community groups and creates cultural experiences for the visitors in a general context. Traditionally, the Bradford Festival Mela depended on local visitors. In its early years the Mela attracted over 95 per cent of local people to the festival. This image has changed over the last decade and now 42 per cent of visitors attending the event come from outside the city of Bradford. Some of the visitors come from as far as countries like Pakistan, India and Bangladesh. Other cities in England have adopted a similar approach to the City of Bradford to develop cultural festivals like the Bradford Festival Mela, to create an enhanced image, reputation and status among South Asian communities to help attract visitors to the area.

Without any deliberate planning, the festival has become a PR event for the Asian community and added an educational focus for other cultures to understand the different aspects of South Asian communities. Finally, Bradford Festival Mela has created an image to enhance tourism for the City of Bradford.

Managing visitors for events

Hosting and staging events as part of tourism strategies to promote destinations has become an increasing focus for tourism agencies and national governments around the globe over the last decade. From staging international events to promoting community festivals within localities, events can shape tourist perceptions of a region and can shape the geography of the imagination.

By analysing event provision within tourism, insights can be gained into not only what the destination wants to present to visitors but also what the destination aspires to be. Events thus serve to provide potential visitors and other nations with an insight into a country's vision of their past, present and their future.

Community festivals provide displays of local cultures deemed appropriate for the eyes of passing audiences. Mega event hosting can raise the status of a country and offer an opportunity for it to showcase its cultures and aspirations on a global stage. Events have become part of an image-making process playing a critical role in positioning destinations against their competitors.

Events can be marketed to reach niche as well as mass audiences, not simply through increasing visitor numbers at events but by creating powerful associations of the destination in the minds of visitors. These associations may be connected to the nature of events, such as religious festivals, but event associations can also result in an overall perception of a country or locality as 'dynamic', 'youthful', 'historic', 'sporting', 'showbiz', etc. The case study below looks at the destination management of Manchester local authority.

CASE STUDY   MANCHESTER AS TOURISM DESTINATION

The North West region of England and in particular Manchester with the City Council as the main driver, set out a strategic model to drive the economy forward and for Manchester to become an international destination by 2010, benchmarking the city alongside New York, Barcelona and Paris, etc. Manchester has a population of approximately 2.5 million inhabitants and is considered to be the second city in the UK after London.

Of the five objectives written in 2003, festivals and events were given prominence as an objective to enhance the city and region. In 2007 Manchester City Council launched The International Festival to the world market, a biennial festival of original and new work. It is an international cultural and arts festival which has become the signature event for Manchester. In January 2004, Manchester City Council approved a £2 million underwriting of the International Festival. This funding was also complemented by money from the Arts Council of England and the North West Development Agency. Early economic impact studies estimated that the festival contributed £34 million to the Manchester economy, also supported by the private sector with a potential audience of 270,000.

Financial backing for this event was published in the Manchester City Council report and resolution in 2007.

> MIF has now obtained committed or contracted sponsorship deals equalling £2.5 million towards its target of £2.8 million, as well as public funding of £1.5 million, consisting of £1.25 million from Arts Council (including £500,000 Urban Cultural programme funds) and £250,000 from Salford City Council. The original target being £3 million for all other public and private income to match the Council's contribution of £2 million.

> The independent evaluation of the first International Festival in June–July 2007, by Morris Hargreaves McIntyre, was titled 'The Ascent of Manchester'. The report presented through quantitative research, that the festival had attracted 200,930 attendees, created 34 jobs, and it was estimated that the festival achieved an economic impact value of £28.8 million.

Cultural and economic impacts

Events have several types of impacts on the host city, ranging from cultural and economic, to social and environmental. Events have both positive and negative impacts on their host cities, but emphasis is often focused on the economic analysis. It is the role of event organisers to focus on impacts other than the purely economic ones that may be created by the event.

The impact of events on host cities is changing in accordance with significant developments in the events market developing during the past ten years. Consequently, the post-event evaluation is extremely important not only to review the situation but also to identify and manage the impacts to assist in maximising future benefits. However, it is quite common for event managers to pay such attention to the financial impacts of the events that they can become myopic concerning other possible impacts occurring during the event. It is important for the event manager to realise this potential situation and identify and manage both positive and negative impacts resulting from the event.

Economic values are often placed on the benefit of publicity obtained for the event, which may occur before, during and after its occurrence. Column inches and advertising costs are used to quantify such impacts.

Undoubtedly, in addition to creating community cohesion, festivals and events potentially give greater economic life to host destinations, by developing employment, additional trade and business development, investment in infrastructure, long-term promotional benefits, and tax revenues. Events and festivals not only generate significant economic benefits, they also provide host destinations with the opportunity to market themselves nationally and internationally bringing people from diverse backgrounds to the destination for the duration of the event or festival. As a result, they have the potential to provide host destinations with a high-status tourism profile. Economic impacts of events are the most tangible and therefore the most often measured impacts. Economic impacts can be positive and negative, but the positive economic impacts of events are visitor expenditure, investment in infrastructure and increased employment.

Summary

Over the last decade local authorities have identified the importance of using festivals to stimulate tourist demand. Many countries have realised the positive effects that event tourism can have. Countries such as the USA, Australia and China have all attracted a wide variety of events, such as the Olympic Games, that have been successful to the development of the country as well as increasing the number of annual tourist arrivals. Examples such as these have shown that events are definitely an effective tool to attract tourists, not only to the events but in the future as well.

This chapter has suggested that events tourism has been increased through the development of local festivals and provided greater economic and cultural benefits to the local area. Visitors are attracted to these festivals from as far away as Europe and Caribbean Islands. It was found that social and economic factors contributed to events tourism growth in these festivals. The Bradford Mela and Leeds West Indian Carnival festivals have become major tourist attractions for local, regional and international visitors.

Festivals have contributed to the development of events and cultural tourism. Festivals attract events tourists to local community events to promote cultural exchanges between tourists and residents. Events tourism brings benefits to cities, but these benefits are not being analysed in any great depth. Tourism festivals have major effects on the local economy directly and indirectly. The spending by visitors on local goods and services has a direct economic impact on local businesses and also these benefits pass more widely across the economy and the community.

■ Discussion questions

Question 1

Critically evaluate and examine the role of cultural events in developing community cohesion.

Question 2

Festivals attract culture tourists to local community events to promote cultural exchanges between tourists and residents.

Critically evaluate the above statement.

Question 3

What are the advantages and disadvantages for destinations in the holding of major community and cultural events?

Question 4

Identify and discuss the economic impact of outdoor events on host cities.

Question 5

Investigate the importance of managing visitors' experience attending cultural events.

Question 6

Critically evaluate the success of the autonomous tourism organisations engaged in partnerships with both private sector and regional and/or local authorities.

CASE STUDY 1 THE TURKS AND CAICOS ISLANDS

The Turks and Caicos Islands is a chain of over 40 islands in the Atlantic Ocean. The island chain lies at the end of the Bahamian archipelago and is situated on what the country's tourism board claims is the 'third largest coral reef system in the world'. The Islands form a self-governing British overseas territory with a population of over 25,000.

The tourism industry brings over 150,000 tourists to the islands per annum, with approximately 70 per cent coming from North America and the remaining tourists visiting from Canada (20 per cent) and Europe (10 per cent). Scuba-diving on the coral reef is a major attraction, although increasingly visitors come to the islands for beaches and essentially to 'do nothing'. In the mid-1990s, the country developed the slogan 'beautiful by nature' to promote the natural beauty of the islands.

The Turks and Caicos Islands had to compete against bigger and more established destinations with larger budgets and market share within the Caribbean. The differentiation of specific products within the region is a challenge as countries promote the same key messages of beaches, sunshine and sea. In addition, a majority of the destinations market scuba-diving as a niche product. At the start of 2000 in such a competitive marketplace, the Turks and Caicos Islands were encountering difficulties in selecting appropriate marketing mediums. Ever increasing numbers of publications were approaching the destination for advertising and the Islands had a limited budget that could not make much impact on its own.

In 2002, the Turks and Caicos Islands Tourism Board decided to host a free diving World Record attempt and sponsor free diver and environmentalist Tanya Streeter. This new strategy was based on the need for the destination to travel beyond the travel pages and hit more worldwide special interest and potentially mass markets in a manner that could not be achieved within limited advertising budgets. The key success of the strategy would rest on the risk/excitement involved in hosting such a niche and special interest sports event. It was believed that the special nature of the sport and the risks would attract news coverage.

Source: Mulligan, J. and Raj, R. (2008) 'Destination marketing', in C. Vignali, T. Vranesevic and D. Vrontis (2008) *Strategic Marketing And Retail Thought*. Zagreb: Accent.

CASE STUDY 2 LONDON 2012 OLYMPIC GAMES – SUSTAINABILITY

Background

London is the first summer host city to embed sustainability in its planning from the start. Sustainability underpins everything we do towards our vision 'to use the power of the Games to inspire lasting change'.

These guidelines have been developed to help ensure that all events and related activities hosted by, or associated with, London 2012 are positive examples of sustainability in practice. The

(Continued)

(Continued)

London Games in 2012 are subject to the full sustainability management system developed by the London 2012 Organising Committee (LOCOG) for compliance with BS 8901 (2009)1 – British Standard for sustainable events – and, therefore, went beyond the provision of these guidelines.

Early planning

Early planning is essential to hosting a more sustainable event. It is important to identify the main sustainability aspects of the event from the very outset. As a starting point, we expect the organisations we work with to have evidence of relevant policies relating to environment and/or sustainability; accessibility; health and safety; and security. In addition, we would seek assurance on compliance with all applicable legal requirements and a commitment from these organisations to at least be working towards implementation of BS 8901.

Stakeholder engagement

Liaison with all parties involved in putting on the event (including the venue, suppliers, sponsors and so on) and those potentially affected by the event (such as local communities) will help identify the most important sustainability impacts and issues. Stakeholders will provide vital local knowledge, understand community sensitivities and help avoid potential timing, location or cultural clashes with other events being planned in the area.

Stakeholders typically include sponsors/partners, venue owners or managers, suppliers, local residents, potential workforce, customers/spectators and/or participants, statutory bodies, the emergency services, security services and relevant non-governmental organisations. It is always worth mapping out a list of relevant stakeholders for any given event to ensure you have identified as far as possible all the key parties that need to be engaged.

Identifying potential impacts and issues

We have selected ten key topic areas which we consider most relevant to the types of events we will be organising in the lead-up to the Games. The following guidance points for each of these topics provide a good starting point for delivering positive change.

Measuring outcomes

Progress recording also extends throughout the event phase, to help the event team ensure that the targets are being delivered or are on track for delivery. For example, how much waste has been recycled, reporting any accidents or near misses, or checking sightlines are suitable for the audience during the event.

Taking accurate measurements is essential to understanding that the actions taken in the pre-event phase have delivered results and identifying what delivered the most significant results. It will also enable you to decide where best to focus resources for your next event and enable continual improvement.

Communicating achievements

Take the opportunity to be proud of what you have achieved through implementing these guidelines. Good ways to spread the word about the lessons you have learned include:

- providing sustainability facts and figures in speeches, presentations, briefings or as rolling text on screens – for example, resources saved, sourcing of materials, what will happen with the set afterwards; encourage others to 'spread the word';
- displaying signage detailing the measures undertaken;
- displaying signage to promote more sustainable ways of working, such as switching off electrical appliances when not in use;
- publishing press releases or case studies about sustainability;
- integrating sustainability messaging into press releases; and
- ensuring printed documents and materials such as tickets and brochures carry information about recycled content and printing processes.

Source: LOCOG (2012) [online]

Further reading

Dwyer, L., Mellor, R., Mistillis, N. and Mules, T. (2000) 'A framework for assessing "tangible" and "intangible" impacts of events and conventions', *Event Management*, 6: 175–89.

English Heritage (2000) *Tourism Facts 2001*. Swindon: English Heritage.

Getz, D. (2005) *Event Management and Event Tourism*, 2nd edn. New York: Cognizant Communications Corporation.

Greater London Authority (2004) *Notting Hill Carnival: A Strategic Review*. London: Greater London Authority, www.london.gov.uk

Key Note (2010) 'Leisure outside the home market review' [online]. Available at: www.keynote.co.uk/market-intelligence/view/product/10374/leisure-outside-thehome?utm_source=kn.reports.browse

Leslie, D. (2001) 'Urban regeneration and Glasgow's galleries with particular reference to the Burrell Collection', in G. Richards (ed.), *Cultural Attractions and European Tourism*. Oxford: CABI Publishing.

Richards, G. (ed.) (2001) *Cultural Attractions and European Tourism*. Oxford: CABI Publishing.

X-leisure (2010) 'Making the case for leisure' [online]. Available at: www. x-leisure. co.uk/case/download.pdf

3 Event Entrepreneurship

In this chapter you will cover:

- what is entrepreneurship?;
- entrepreneurship today;
- characteristics of entrepreneurs;
- types of entrepreneurs;
- the entrepreneurial process;
- starting a new event business;
- buying an existing event business;
- summary;
- discussion questions;
- case studies;
- further reading.

The aim of the chapter is to provide an overview of entrepreneurship in the events industry. Theories of entrepreneurship will be discussed in order to identify the prime methods and techniques which would help events managers to develop the necessary skills and attitudes to deal with the challenges and at the same time take advantage of the new opportunities presented by the evolving events industry.

The events industry is a key player within the key economic sector of creative industries. The events industry mainly includes the designing, promoting, advertising and delivery of an event, but also includes a range of supporting professions and boundary industries.

Most entrepreneurs start their first venture in their own field of interest and expertise. This implies that emerging entrepreneurs with event skills (particularly event graduates) are more likely to identify an opportunity within the event industry. Therefore, it is important that, as a prospective event entrepreneur, you should understand the full extent of the event industry and where you might find potential business opportunities.

Despite the global economic downturn and the challenges and opportunities presented by the emerging economic superpowers like India and China, the event industry in the West is still thriving, with plenty of opportunities for innovative and intuitive event entrepreneurs.

What is entrepreneurship?

The word *entrepreneur* is widely used both in everyday conversation and as a technical term in management and economics. It is a French word dating back to the 1700s, and originally referred to an individual commissioned to carry out a particular commercial project by someone with money to invest. This was often an overseas trading project and carried with it risk for both the investor (who could lose money) and the entrepreneur (who could lose a great deal more). Therefore the chance of risk with entrepreneurial activity is evident from the start.

Since then the term has evolved to mean someone who undertakes a venture, particularly starting a new business. This meaning is central to the understanding of the word 'entrepreneur' in the English language, although the French would prefer to use 'créateur d'entreprise' (creator of an enterprise). From the word entrepreneur, a number of concepts have been derived such as *entrepreneurship, entrepreneurial*, and *entrepreneurial process*. Entrepreneurship is what an entrepreneur does. It is more of a process, a way of doing things that transforms innovation into market opportunities or competitive advantage. The entrepreneurial process is the means through which new value is created as a result of the project – the *entrepreneurial venture*. Entrepreneurial is an adjective describing how the entrepreneur undertakes what they do.

Nevertheless, there are many definitions of entrepreneur found in the management and economic literature and it is certainly a task to provide a concise and unambiguous definition. Attempts to define it have focused on using the skills that characterise the entrepreneur, using those processes and events which are part of entrepreneurship, and using those results that entrepreneurship leads to (Davidsson, 2003). Most of the existing definitions are a mix of these three. For instance:

> An entrepreneur is a person who identifies an opportunity or new idea and develops it into a new venture project. (Burke, 2006)

In this respect, enterprise is an outcome of entrepreneurship, i.e. the organisation created is an enterprise. However, to some people it is basically about using enterprise to create a new business, and in this respect enterprise is a means of entrepreneurship. It is important to note here that it is generally accepted that entrepreneurs are agents of change and they provide innovative and creative ideas for enterprises to grow and make profit. They act to create and build a vision from virtually nothing, thus being enterprising.

Taking into consideration the above ideas, therefore, the event entrepreneur is the key innovative person who is managing the entrepreneurial process. This will usually involve planning, organising, promoting, directing, controlling, managing and delivering an event with the help of team members together with the associated business risks.

Entrepreneurship is acknowledged as the driving force behind innovative change in society and the event industry is no exception. Taking the definition above, an event entrepreneur can therefore be defined as someone who sets up a new event venture. To achieve this, the event entrepreneur needs to spot new commercial opportunities and determine the needs of the customers by co-ordinating the resources to deliver an event.

Entrepreneurship today

Today, with the internet boom, entrepreneurs represent one of the most dynamic forces in the economy. It is they who are driving the technology boom, which in turn is driving much of the world's economic growth. This makes entrepreneurs very important from a macro-economic perspective. Entrepreneurs, therefore, are an economic phenomenon that has a major impact on the global economy and thus as the globalism of business becomes even more widespread, this impact will be felt even more deeply. Entrepreneurs are already becoming a major force in developing nations and in the economy worldwide.

The scope of what entrepreneurship involves will continue to change and evolve, and yet there are some common issues of how to start a business, how to finance the business, how to share our business with the community and how to learn from each other. Something that is common for all entrepreneurs is the challenge of starting their own business, be it through inventing something, looking for a new idea within a business, finding the right opportunity to break into a business or buying into a franchise. This involves planning and organising all the aspects so that the goals can be achieved. All entrepreneurs are also faced with financing their entrepreneurial enterprise. Even intrapreneurs (those who are entrepreneurial within an existing organisation – internal entrepreneurs) usually are faced with financial hurdles within corporate rules. So unless the funding for the venture comes from your own pocket, getting money is a challenge that requires preparing funding proposals or applications to be written and/or presented for loans and venture capital. There is so much information written about these stages of an entrepreneurial venture that sorting the good from the bad is an overwhelming challenge in itself.

Characteristics of entrepreneurs

Integral to the concept of entrepreneurship is the ability to take action. It is this ability which sets them apart from others. In addition, a wide range of competences are seen as entrepreneurial and useful to entrepreneurs. These include knowledge, skills and personal traits such as:

- management skills – the ability to manage time and people (both oneself and others) successfully;
- being a team player;
- being good at planning and organising;
- being self-motivated and able to motivate others;
- being disciplined and adaptable;
- being an innovative and creative thinker;
- being single-minded;
- having the ability to work under pressure and persevere;
- being very competitive;
- being a good networker and able to communicate with others;
- having the ability to market and sell a new product or idea.

Furthermore, many pieces of research over the years have shown that entrepreneurs are risk takers, or more willing to engage in risky activity. That is, people higher in risk-taking propensity are more likely to exploit entrepreneurial opportunity because risk-taking is a fundamental part of entrepreneurship. Aspects of risk-taking among entrepreneurs include investing their own money, leaving secure jobs, and the stress and time associated with starting and managing a business. Kobia and Sikalieh (2010) argue that enterprising individuals seek to realise productive opportunities and consequently function in uncertain environments.

Types of entrepreneurs

Although potentially anyone can become an entrepreneur, it may be of interest to examine some demographics such as age, gender and race in their relative roles in entrepreneurship.

Young entrepreneurs

It is evident from several studies that the entrepreneurs are most likely to be between the ages of 25 and 40 when creating a new venture. In fact, studies have also shown that entrepreneurship can emerge even amongst young people between the ages of 8–24. This is illustrated by the case study below.

CASE STUDY   YOUTH ENTREPRENEURSHIP SURVEY 2010

Despite a difficult economic climate, many young Americans are still interested in entrepreneurial pursuits. A Harris Interactive® online poll, conducted on behalf of the Ewing Marion Kauffman Foundation, released in conjunction with the start of Global Entrepreneurship Week, revealed that 40 per cent of youth aged 8–24 would like to start a business at some future point, or have already done so. Additionally, young people are overwhelmingly optimistic about the possibility of owning their own business. Seventy-five per cent of the 8 to 12-year-olds, 62 per cent of the 13 to17-year-olds, and 62 per cent of the 18 to 24-year-olds agree that they can successfully start their own businesses if they work hard.

Results from the August 2010 survey of 5,077 young people are consistent with a previous study conducted in 2007.

'The economic downturn, it seems, has done nothing to dissuade young people from their dreams of business ownership', said Carl Schramm, president and CEO of the Kauffman Foundation, who launched Global Entrepreneurship Week in front of more than 1,700 entrepreneurs at the Ernst & Young Strategic Growth Forum in Palm Springs, California, the largest gathering of high-growth companies in the country. 'The survey findings are good news, because economic recovery hinges on entrepreneurship. The survey results also attest that connecting with successful entrepreneurs inspires young people to pursue their entrepreneurial aspirations, which is what Global Entrepreneurship Week was founded, in part, to accomplish.'

The survey shows that youth who know an entrepreneur personally have the strongest interest in starting their own businesses. (To access the complete youth poll findings, go to www.kauffman.org/youngentrepreneurs)

Connecting young people to successful business owners is just one aspect of Global Entrepreneurship Week. It also inspires them to get started on their ideas and shows them what it takes to turn them into real-world projects and ventures. Co-founded by the Kauffman Foundation, the world's largest foundation dedicated to entrepreneurship, and Enterprise UK, a business-led, government-backed campaign in the United Kingdom, Global Entrepreneurship Week helps current and would-be entrepreneurs gain knowledge, skills and networks to inspire and enable them to grow sustainable enterprises.

About Global Entrepreneurship Week

With the goal to inspire young people to embrace innovation, imagination and creativity, Global Entrepreneurship Week will encourage youth to think big and turn their ideas into reality. From 15–21 November 2010, millions of young people around the world will join a growing movement to generate new ideas and seek better ways of doing things. Tens of thousands of activities are being planned in dozens of countries. Global Entrepreneurship Week is founded by the Ewing Marion Kauffman Foundation and Enterprise UK.

The Ewing Marion Kauffman Foundation is a private nonpartisan foundation that works to harness the power of entrepreneurship and innovation to grow economies and improve human welfare. Through its research and other initiatives, the Kauffman Foundation aims to open young people's eyes to the possibility of entrepreneurship, promote entrepreneurship education, raise awareness of entrepreneurship-friendly policies, and find alternative pathways for the commercialisation of new knowledge and technologies. In addition, the Foundation focuses on initiatives in the Kansas City region to advance students' maths and science skills, and improve the educational achievement of urban students, including the Ewing Marion Kauffman School, a college preparatory charter school for middle and high school students set to open in 2011. Founded by late entrepreneur and philanthropist Ewing Marion Kauffman, the Foundation is based in Kansas City, Missouri, and has approximately $2 billion in assets.

(Adapted from Kauffman Foundation, 2012 [online])

Women entrepreneurs

Women's entrepreneurship has been on the rise to the point where women are opening their own businesses faster than any other segment of small businesses start-ups. In the United States they account for 29 per cent of all enterprises. Although a very high percentage of women-owned businesses are in the retail sector, women are now branching out into male-dominated industries such as mining, manufacturing, construction and transportation. This rise is further illustrated in the case study below.

CASE STUDY   WOMEN-OWNED BUSINESSES ARE PROLIFERATING IN THE UNITED STATES

Women-owned businesses are proliferating faster than men-owned businesses in the United States, according to The American Express OPEN State of Women-Owned businesses Report.

(Continued)

(Continued)

Between 1997 and 2011, when the number of businesses in the United States increased by 34 per cent, the number of women-owned firms increased by 50 per cent – a rate of 1.5 times the national average. As of 2011, there are over 8.1 million women-owned businesses in the United States, generating nearly $1.3 trillion in revenues and employing nearly 7.7 million people, the report found.

Despite the fact that the number of women-owned firms continues to grow at a rate exceeding the national average, and accounts for 29 per cent of all enterprises, women-owned firms only employ 6 per cent of the country's workforce and contribute just under 4 per cent of business revenues. Further, the employment and sales growth of women-owned enterprises between 1997 and 2011 (8 per cent and 53 per cent, respectively) lags behind the national average (17 per cent and 71 per cent).

'Within the population of women-owned firms, we see steady growth but a lack of progress up the size continuum', American Express said in the report. 'And, when comparing like to like, small and midsize women-owned firms are keeping pace with the national average – and are topping the very sluggish growth seen among men-owned firms in the 1997–2011 period.' However, something is putting women-owned firms off their stride as they grow larger; they fall behind toward the end of the entrepreneurial marathon, when entering the 100-employee and million-dollar 'anchor leg' of the race.

Article adapted from: http://entrepreneurs.about.com (2011)

Minority entrepreneurs

Certain ethnic minorities have shown a greater propensity than others, including the indigenous populations, to engage in self-employment. Minority entrepreneurs such as Asians, Chinese and Eastern Europeans find starting their own businesses as a way out of poverty and a chance to move up the class system. For instance, historically, in the UK it was the Jewish community who led the way of starting their own businesses after the Second World War, followed by Asians from the Indian Sub-continent and China in the 1950s and 1960s. Then it was the turn of Asian-Africans who arrived in the 1970s followed by Eastern Europeans who came to the UK after the opening of the European Union borders. Interestingly, what is common amongst most of these groups is that they possessed some kind of entrepreneurial characteristics from their home countries and took advantage of the opportunities presented by the open UK business systems. Research has shown that there could be many factors for their success including culture, religion, family, network support, determination, commitment and hard work.

Asian people were twice as likely to be involved in autonomous start-ups as compared to their white counterparts. However, these Asian entrepreneurial activities have historically been in low-profit, low-growth industries such as minority ethnic retail and clothing (Rashid, 2006).

Family-owned businesses

A family-owned business can be described as one that is run by two or more members of the same family, and the family has overall financial control of the business. These are an integral part of many economies.

Copreneurs

Copreneurs are couples who start and own their own business. Each one brings a special expertise to the enterprise and both are regarded as equal in terms of ownership and decision making. To some this may be a recipe for divorce. Nevertheless, couples should set rules and clearly define their roles very early on at the start of the business in order to reduce friction and conflict. One key area to address is to keep family matters separate from business matters and keeping family time set aside from the business.

Corporate entrepreneurs

Three types of corporate entrepreneurs can exist within organisations: the intrapreneur, the venturer and the transformer (Bolton and Thompson, 2003). The intrapreneur is the enterprising person in the organisation. They are the innovators who develop new products, new services, new processes, new market opportunities and new distribution channels. They are already to change and are often the instigators and champions of change in large organisations.

The venturer is the next level up in the entrepreneur hierarchy. They have the talent to spin off a new business from an existing one. They either leave an established business to start up a new one; or they seize an opportunity when companies develop new ideas but which do not fit into their existing setup but still have growth potential; or they come to a decision that some businesses within their portfolio would be better off by divesting.

The transformer is the growth entrepreneur in the corporate world. They are the leaders at the top of the entrepreneur ladder and have the expertise and skills to lead transformation in large corporations. The relationship between these three types of corporate entrepreneur is shown by the triangle below (Figure 3.1).

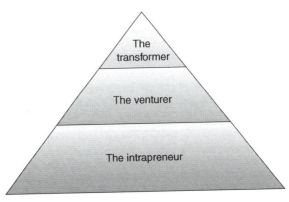

Figure 3.1 The relationship between the intrapreneur, the venture and the transformer

The entrepreneurial process

The entrepreneurship process gives us a framework to understand how entrepreneurs create wealth and helps us to make sense of the detail in specific ventures. According to Wickham (2006) the process is based on four interacting contingencies: the entrepreneur, market opportunity, a business organisation and resources (see Figure 3.2).

The entrepreneur is the person, or team of entrepreneurs, who is at the centre of the process and drives it. Entrepreneurs may be individual or they

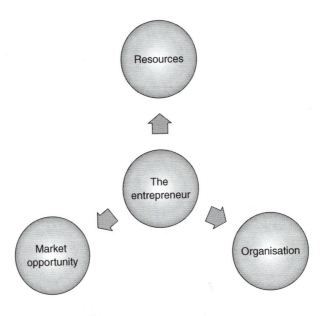

Figure 3.2 The entrepreneurship process

Source: Adapted from Wickham (2006)

may act as a team and have different roles and responsibilities. They may be from the same family, copreneurs, or an existing management who have started their own venture after a management buyout.

Opportunity in the marketplace is the gap which has been left by existing players and is recognised by the entrepreneur either to serve customers better than they are being served at present or to do something differently. The role of the event entrepreneur involves researching the market for those opportunities and possibilities which have not been exploited. However, in all situations, it is important that the customer recognises that the new offering by the entrepreneur is something of enough value to them that they are willing to pay for it.

The organisation is the new business created by the entrepreneur, in which the activities of different people need to be coordinated to supply the innovation to the marketplace. The entrepreneurs within these organisations often show strong and charismatic leadership.

Resources can be thought of as tangible assets and intangible assets. Tangible assets include: money; people who contribute their efforts; machinery and production equipment; buildings; and vehicles. Intangible assets include: brand names; knowledge and skills of people; company reputation; and customer and supplier goodwill. All these resources can be subject to investment. The entrepreneur plays a key role in attracting the investment to the venture and using it to build up these assets effectively to supply the innovation to the marketplace competitively and profitably. Figure 3.2 illustrates the entrepreneurial process.

Starting a new event business

As part of the entrepreneurial process the question is often asked by an entrepreneur: should I start a new event business or buy an existing one? In this section we examine the pros and cons of both.

Starting a new venture is not easy and accepting that at the outset will avoid any disappointments and regrets. It is to be expected that working patterns will change substantially, the hours may be irregular and the business may take precedence over everything else including family and friends. This is when the support from family and friends will be really crucial, especially at the beginning, when the going is tough and the road is hard.

One of the challenging questions a budding event entrepreneur may have is: 'what kind of event business can I start easily and will it be successful?' This is a very difficult question to answer, as it depends on the entrepreneur, trends at the time, the global national and regional economic situation and the needs of the market. However, most successful ideas for starting a business come from identifying gaps in the market or problems that people face. Potential event entrepreneurs could begin asking and answering the following questions:

- What skills and capabilities do I possess?
- What business experience and expertise do I have?
- What is my rationale and motivation for starting a new business?

It is so important to seek answers to these questions and evaluate thoroughly your talents, skills, experiences, and contacts to see if these could be translated into a successful business.

Further points to consider when starting a new events business include:

1 Research that there is a market for your new event idea before embarking on the venture.

2 Who are your customers and where are they?

3 Carry out a feasibility study to find out whether to pursue your event business idea or not.

4 Identify who are your potential competitors. Improve upon their weaknesses and avoid trying to compete against their strengths.

5 Seek out trends in events that are just beginning and take advantage of them quickly.

6 Develop a business plan and design a long, medium and short-term business strategy.

7 Consider starting the venture from your home but be professional at all times.

8 Always try to negotiate the terms and conditions of any contract.

Another possibility is to consider starting a venture in an event management area that you are familiar with, and that you have given clear thought to in terms of its uniqueness. You could use existing contacts and networks for advice and help while searching around for a variety of sources for financial backing. It is important to cover the financial bases really well as it's no longer the employer's money which is on the line but yours and/or your investors'.

Buying an existing event business

The trend of buying an existing business and making it more profitable is growing amongst entrepreneurs. This is particularly popular amongst displaced workers who are ambitious to become entrepreneurs, and amongst large corporations which are seeking out specialist small businesses to provide them with innovative products in new markets.

Many entrepreneurs are not the creative types in starting a new venture but are more successful in buying existing businesses and turning them around by growing them and making them more profitable. They have the flair to recognise

Table 3.1   The advantages and disadvantages of buying an existing event business

Advantages of buying an existing business	Disadvantages of buying an existing business
• Risks associated are lower	• Market is saturated and there is intense competition
• Lower asset costs	
• Seller may finance whole or part of the business	• Hidden costs associated with the business
	• Seller is dishonest and may back out
• Buyer has clearer idea of the operations	• Inadequate market potential
• The business may have established markets	• The business is not worth much
• There is a history of the business	
• Established suppliers	
• Established customer base	
• Seller may provide management training to run the business	

good business opportunities when they see them and revitalise and revolutionise them rather than creating new businesses from scratch. Buying an existing business is a good idea when the business opportunity is thoroughly analysed, thought through and matches the existing expertise and experience of the purchaser.

Although the advantages of buying a new event business outweigh one starting from scratch, the disadvantages should not be ignored.

Summary

This chapter has presented an overview of entrepreneurship in the event industry. An event entrepreneur is the key innovative person managing the entrepreneurial process, particularly starting a new business such as a wedding planning or conference organising enterprise. Today, with the internet boom, entrepreneurs are a dynamic force in the economy, helping to drive the technology boom, which in turn is driving much of the world's economic growth. This makes entrepreneurs very important from a macro-economic perspective. Entrepreneurs, therefore, are an economic phenomenon that has a major impact on the global economy and thus as the globalism of business becomes even more widespread, this impact will be felt even more deeply.

Entrepreneurship is an activity which leads to the creation and management of a new organisation designed to pursue a unique and innovative opportunity in the marketplace. Although there are many characteristic traits of an entrepreneur, the most important is the ability to take action and risk. Moreover, entrepreneurs are people who have a strong need for self-realisation and independence.

Research has indicated that most entrepreneurs are between the ages of 25 and 40; women represent the fastest growth segment in the start of new businesses; and ethnic minorities such as Chinese, Asians and Eastern European have shown a greater propensity than others to engage in self-employment.

Although there are advantages and disadvantages in deciding whether to start a new event business or to buy an existing one, as an entrepreneur you should consider your existing skills, capabilities, experience, and your motivation. Careful consideration and planning given to these points would reduce the failure risk of the new event enterprise.

■ Discussion questions

Question 1

Discuss why the events industry is still growing despite the economic downturn.

Question 2

Describe the difference between entrepreneur and intrapreneur.

Question 3

Explain the entrepreneurship process as applied to the events industry.

Question 4

Analyse the character traits of an entrepreneur.

Question 5

Discuss the arguments as to why young people, women and people from Asian and Chinese ethnic minorities are more successful as entrepreneurs.

Question 6

Evaluate the advantages and disadvantages of buying an existing event business or starting a new venture.

CASE STUDY 1   STARTING AN EVENT MANAGEMENT BUSINESS

Event management is a broad industry, with many companies choosing to specialise in one area. Over the last 10 to 15 years, the events industry has seen huge growth. According to the International Special Events Society (http://www.ises.com), global spending on events is US$500 billion (£300 billion) annually.

What do event planners do?

Events are held for a variety of reasons in many forms. Some of the main types of event include:

- Corporate events (conferences, meetings, team building days, seminars, workshops, networking)
- Educational events (training seminars, workshops, conferences)
- Private events (weddings, birthday parties, other celebrations)
- Public events (festivals, gigs, carnivals, fairs, protests, rallies)

Although the list is by no means exhaustive, you can probably see why so many event managers choose to specialise in one area.

When an event manager is asked to organise an event, they may be required to cover one or all of the following areas:

Research – especially for events for which tickets are sold. Will people want to attend the event? Who are the competitors? Is anything else occurring on the same date in a nearby location?

Event design – how will the event look? Will there be a theme? For some events this may include lighting and sound – these may be best left to a professional.

Sourcing a location – how many guests will you need to accommodate? Does the location fit with the event? If a bar is required at the event, does the location have the right kind of licence? Will your client require a specialist bar, e.g. cocktails, for which you would need to find the right kind of bartenders?

Catering – for most events any menu will be pre-agreed. You will need to ensure that enough food is provided and that it is made to a good standard, within all health and safety laws. For some events waiting staff may also be required.

Entertainment or speakers – the majority of celebratory events will require some form of entertainment, usually a band or DJ. Always check your client's requirements – they may have something very specific in mind. In other cases, some venues may have in-house DJs – although it may be worth attending an event they are performing at before deciding to book them. For educational events and conferences, you may have to arrange speakers – although in some cases the client may already know exactly who they want there.

Decoration – again, this is most commonly required at celebratory events.Confirm everything with the client, and ensure you're very organised – you wouldn't want to end up putting 'Happy Birthday' banners up at someone's wedding!

Transport and accommodation – in the UK, this is most likely to be required at corporate events. Some companies will pay for their staff to attend training events in other towns and cities and sometimes these have a very early start. Often, hotel conference suites are used for such events, so if this is the case see if the hotel hosting the event would organise a group accommodation discount. Alternatively, try the same with a nearby hotel – ensure that employees are able to get to the event from their hotel, though.

(Continued)

(Continued)

Invitations and guest list – although you will probably only have to send out invitations to private events such as weddings and birthday parties, it is likely that the majority of events will have a guest list so you can ensure that the correct people are attending.

Supervising – you, or a member of your team, will probably have to attend the majority of events you organise to ensure that they run smoothly. You will also need to co-ordinate the running of the event, e.g. ensuring that everything runs to schedule – although for some events, such as conferences, the venue may have a team that will ensure everything runs according to plan.

Source: Adapted from www.inspiresme.co.uk

CASE STUDY 2 TEN REASONS WHY EVENT BUSINESS OWNERS FAIL

If you are just starting an event company, there are 10 ways not to grow your business.

Here are some of the reasons why so many people in the live event business work long, crazy hours and have little to show for it (and that includes: caterers, event planners, wedding planners, photographers, designers, decorators, entertainment, event services …).

Not thinking right

The number one reason why event people fail at business is that they think of themselves as 'wedding planners', 'event planners', 'party planners' or 'caterers' but not business people. Thinking this way limits their ability to grow the company. Your business will struggle if marketing, sales and money management are not your first priority. You'll lose business to more business-minded competition.

Your top priority must be building a business. If you lack the skills needed to promote and manage a growing company – you can either develop these skills or collaborate with someone who has them.

Stuck in a rut

How do you find exciting new ideas that will thrill your clients and build your reputation? The very best in the event and catering business are active members of trade associations and attend trade shows and conferences.

ISES (International Special Events Society) and ICA (International Caterers Association) are two outstanding groups to consider joining. However, don't just join – be an active participant and leader.

Attend trade shows like those sponsored by BizBash, Catersource/Event Solutions. Subscribe to outstanding publications like BizBash, Special Events, Events Online, Catersource and Event Solutions.

No systems

Building a steady stream of new leads and creating a client base is more important than ordering new linens for that party next week – but marketing tasks don't seem as urgent.

Realise that your primary mission as business owner is to create new clients. To do that efficiently you need systems. Systems to attract new clients, systems to make existing clients happy and systems to make sure all the nitty-gritty details get done.

Marketing

Marketing and selling event services is neither easy nor time-sensitive. Many event people hate selling and are clueless about marketing. Therefore, they put it off, although its not that they're lazy. Event planners tackle impossible challenges every day (and nights and weekends). It's just so easy to get caught up in the day-to-day stuff.

Poorly-defined goals

By accomplishing a shallow and ill-defined goal, a caterer who works twelve hours a day, seven days a week achieved her goal of 'making more money', but she's miserable for it. She's overweight, grouchy and heading for a divorce. She got what she wanted – but a whole bunch more which she didn't want.

An intelligent goal is essential to the success of your marketing plan, and more importantly, your life.

No strategy

What is your marketing strategy? When asked this question, event planners list the things they do: advertise, Yellow Page ad, ad in the local paper, postcard mailers and so on. These are tactics, not a strategy. What's the difference?

The right strategy makes any tactic work better. The right strategy puts less pressure on executing your tactics perfectly.

It's important for you to identify your worthy and meaningful short-term and long-term goals. Figure out the 'why'. Why you are in the (event, hospitality, wedding, event, catering) business. Then build a plan that fulfils that bigger vision.

Selling skills

Is the telephone the best way to try to talk a stranger into booking an event? No, but sadly so many new event organisers think it's the way to do it. Discovering how to help people buy is important. Plus when you market correctly, you don't waste any time talking to people who aren't already 'sold' on you. Learn how to sell and market the right way.

(Continued)

(Continued)

Financial controls

The event industry attracts many 'non-financial' and 'non-analytical' types of people. The industry tends to draw in creative and social personalities – but only those who have or develop analytical and executive skills survive as business owners.

Partner, outsource and delegate – but never abdicate your financial controls.

Employee management

You probably know one or two business owners who pay and treat their employees poorly. They don't like or trust their own employees and the feeling is mutual. The workers only do what they're told to do and only if their activity is closely monitored. Remember, your employees are more important to your long-term success than any client is. Hire the best, take care of them and they'll treat your clients like gold.

Burnout

Burnout is a very big cause for failure in any business – and very easy to do in the event business.

Set realistic goals that include all aspects of your life. Working yourself to an early grave is no way to live. Make sure your business plan includes your vision of a good life.

Source: Adapted from www.brianmcgovern.com

Further reading

Davidsson, P. (2003) 'The domain of entrepreneurship research: some suggestions', in J. Katz and D. Shepherd (eds), *Cognitive Approaches to Entrepreneurship*, Vol. 6. Cambridge, MA: Elsevier Science, pp. 315–72.

Kobia, M. and Sikalieh, D. (2010) 'Towards a search for the meaning of entrepreneurship', *Journal of European Industrial Training*, 34(2): 110–27.

Rashid, T. (2006) 'Relationship marketing and entrepreneurship: South Asian Business in the UK', *International Journal of Entrepreneurship and Small Business*, 3(3/4): 417–26.

Wickham, P. (2006) *Strategic Entrepreneurship*, Harlow: Financial TimesPrentice Hall.

4 Human Resource Management

In this chapter you will cover:

- Human resource management;
- types of organisations;
- the human resource planning process;
- legal rights of employer and employees;
- training and professional development;
- supervision and appraisals;
- retaining personnel in event organisations;
- termination of employment;
- evaluation of the process;
- HRM theories;
- summary;
- discussion questions;
- case studies;
- further reading.

This chapter aims to provide an overview of Human Resource Management (HRM) for festivals and events. Theories of HRM will be discussed in order to identify the prime methods and techniques which can help events managers to develop the necessary skills and attitudes to deal with employees in the workplace. In Japan, the recognition that people should be seen as a key resource within strategic plans changed attitudes to employment and resulted in increased quality for Japanese products and business practices. This allowed Japan to challenge for industrial dominance. This example suggests that people are indeed the key asset of any organisation and that the management of people has to be at the heart of any strategic issue, rather than a necessary inconvenience.

Human resource management

Over the last hundred years or so human resource management (HRM) has become a distinct feature in organisations. HRM has its origins in studies of Japanese firms undertaken by American academics interested in the development of the Japanese manufacturing industry. They discovered that Japanese personnel policies revolved around performance, motivation, flexibility and mobility (Blyton and Turnbull, 1992).

HRM is the process of organising and effectively employing people in pursuit of organisational goals. Dessler has stated that HRM refers to:

> the policies and practices one needs to carry out the people or human resources aspects of a management position, including recruiting, screening, training, rewarding and appraising. (2000: 2)

According to Krulis-Randa, HRM involves the following characteristics:

- A focus on horizontal authority and reduced hierarchy; a blurring of the rigid distinction between management and non-management.

- Whenever possible, responsibility for people management is devolved to line managers – the role of the personnel professional is to support and facilitate in this task and not to control it.

- Human resource planning is proactive and compound with corporate planning; human resource issues are treated strategically in an integrated manner.

- Employees are viewed as subjects with a potential for growth and development; the purpose of HRM is to identify this potential and develop it in line with the adaptive needs of the organisation.

- HRM suggests that management and non-management have a common interest in the success of the organisation. Its purpose is to insure that all employees are aware of this and committed to common goals. (Krulis-Randa, 1990: 136)

Whatever the characteristics of HRM in event organisations, the planning process for human resources needs to be carried out carefully in order to fulfil the needs of the different types of event organisations.

Types of organisations

Flexible Organisations

A pulsating organisation is one whose workforce increases and decreases with demand. This means that the organisation must be flexible, with a core of permanent workers and a periphery of other staff. Due to the peripheral nature of temporary workers they will raise their own management issues.

In a corporate hospitality organisation, for example, the number of temporary staff used means that the organisation will be pulsating and so therefore flexible. Flexibility can be placed into two distinct areas: functional, and numerically flexible labour (Goss, 1994).

Functional flexibility

Functional flexibility allows employees who are multi-skilled to perform various jobs and roles.

A corporate hospitality organisation will operate both functional and numerical flexibility due to the fluctuations in its labour demands. Functional flexibility could refer to an employee who, in the time leading up to the event, was responsible for the logistical operations, but during the event is required to perform as a section manager due to their prior role being completed.

Numerical flexibility

Numerical flexibility in terms of corporate hospitality will refer to the many agency staff employed solely for the event's duration. This is numerical flexibility because they are not required before and after the event.

The fact that numerically flexible staff are employed for short periods raises issues of how to achieve maximum output from them, how to build effective relationships, and how to have high service levels.

The human resource planning process

Human resource strategy

In this stage of events many activities are involved including job analysis and job descriptions.

Job analysis

Job analysis is a very important part of this stage of the HR planning process. It includes defining a job in terms of specific tasks and responsibilities and identifying the abilities, skills and qualifications needed to perform it successfully.

The level of the job analysis process will be different from event to event; however, some small-scale events that depend on volunteers may simply attempt to match people to the tasks in which they have expressed an interest. Under these conditions, it is still nevertheless important to consider factors such as skills, experience and the physical abilities of the volunteers.

Job description

This is another result of the job analysis process that you need to be familiar with if you are to effectively match people (both employees and volunteers) to jobs. A job description is a statement identifying why a job has come into existence, what the holder of the job will do, and under what conditions the job is to be conducted.

Policies and procedures

Policies and procedures are required to provide the framework in which the remaining tasks in the HR planning process take place, including: recruitment and selection; training and professional development; supervision and evaluation; termination; outplacement; re-employment; and evaluation. Stone (2002) states that policies and practices serve to:

- reassure all staff that they will be treated fairly (e.g. seniority will be the determining factor in requests by volunteers to fill job vacancies);

- help managers make quick and consistent decisions (e.g. rather than a manager having to think about the process of terminating the employment of a staff member or volunteer they can simply follow the process already prescribed);

- give managers the confidence to resolve problems and defend their positions (e.g. an event manager who declines to consider an application from a brother of an existing employee may point to a policy regarding employing relatives of existing personnel if there is a dispute).

The event manager needs to make sure that policies and procedures are communicated to staff and that they are applied. Furthermore, resources will need to be allocated so that the policy and procedure documents can be stored, accessed and updated/modified when needed.

Recruitment

Recruitment is about making sure that the right staff are taken on to do the right job. For large events, it is more than likely that there will be a budget for this purpose in order to cover costs such as recruitment agency fees, advertising, travel expenses of non-local applicants and search fees for executive placement firms. For smaller events in reality, however, event managers will have few resources to allocate to the recruitment process.

Once the right staff are recruited, event organisations need to provide the appropriate training and development.

Legal rights of employer and employees

The Health and Safety at work Act 1974 has direct links with UK and European regulations. It states that if you have five or more employees, a health and safety policy must be in operation, with a clear health and safety certificate displayed at a location visible to all employees. The employer, apart from developing a health and safety policy, is also required to undertake a full risk assessment of the working environment for all employees. Consideration should also be given to employees where working conditions may endanger their health. Therefore, an occupational risk assessment could be part of the health and safety policy. The organisation can seek insurance once a full health and safety policy has been developed and introduced to all employees and a risk assessment has been carried out.

Employers' liability insurance is compulsory for all businesses with employees under the Employers' Liability Compulsory Insurance Act, 1969. If your organisation has employees based abroad they must also be covered by your company insurance. In general, the minimum level of insurance cover for any UK business is £5–10 million. However, insurance liability may fluctuate on the type of business, and the type of event planned, managed and delivered. Organisations have a legal responsibility to inform employees and to display a copy of the employers' liability insurance certificate. This certificate must be displayed where all employees have access to it. There are some exemptions to employers' liability and one area is where family members are employed.

The Information Commission must be notified if an event company stores personal data on employees, and in particular where a Criminal Records Bureau (CRB) clearance is required. A vast majority of event companies actively partake in direct marketing, but personal information, such as contact details, held by a company can only be used once authorisation has been obtained from each individual. Websites that have an option to collect personal data must protect the individual's rights. You can find more information about health and safety, and public liability, in Chapter 8.

Another piece of legislation concerning employing security at events is the Security Industry Act (SIA) which arrived on the statute book in 2001, and was implemented in 2006–7. The main purpose of this legislation was to remove/clean up rogue security companies that permeate the leisure and entertainment industry. It also has a further remit linked to seven other licensed activities.

It is vital to ascertain the legality of security personnel employed at the venue when your organisation approaches a venue for the purpose of securing it for an event. Once you have undertaken these operational and legal requirements, it is then the responsibility of the company to issue employment contracts that meet UK and European legislation on employment rights. Any employer must be fully aware of the minimum wage, human rights, disability discrimination, equality and race discrimination legislation when selecting employees and during staff development/training and awareness.

Training and professional development

The prime motive for event managers should be to treat individuals as a vital asset and enable them to make maximum contribution to the organisation. This can only be done if the individual is educated and fully trained on the job. Training is the most vital tool which can motivate and enhance the knowledge of the workforce.

Therefore, it is important to help new and current staff to develop new skills that will help them to contribute to the overall goals of the event organisation. Training courses and workshops for staff can be set up which address different skills and areas of development and enhance the knowledge of staff for the future. Figure 4.1 shows what the training programmes should include.

If your organisation addresses training and staff development issues you are much more likely to have satisfied employees, and also to avoid high rates of staff turnover, which is a notorious problem within the events industry.

Boella and Goss-Turner (2005) have stated that an employee needs to develop and effectively achieve their role by developing the following:

- knowledge required for the job;
- skills developed over the years;
- attitude towards the job.

The authors describe how these can only be improved upon by effective training and clear mentoring to achieve the required task. By providing clear and effective training to the workforce it helps the organisation to achieve the set tasks quicker and more effectively.

Mullins (2007) describes how training is a key element in the ability, morale, job satisfaction and commitment of staff, which will lead to improved levels of service and customer satisfaction.

The events and festival industry is very complex and changes in line with the nature of the event. For this reason, it is important for events organisations to offer on-the-job training and appoint individuals according to their skills

Figure 4.1   Training programme for event managers

and knowledge. To support this, the US Department of Labor has outlined the role of human resource professionals as follows:

> In an effort to enhance morale and productivity, limit job turnover, and help organizations to increase performance and improve business results, they also help their firms effectively use employee skills, provide training and development opportunities to improve those skills, and increase employees' satisfaction with their jobs and working conditions. Although some jobs in the human resources field require only limited contact with people outside the office, dealing with people is an important part of the job.
>
> (US Department of Labor, Bureau of Statistics, 2011 [online])

The importance of training is unquestionable but it is not always sustainable within events due to the short period of time staff are required and the flexible nature of the organisation. Due to the strong customer focus of both the events and the hospitality industry, much of an employee's time will be spent at the customer interface. This means that much training may be considered 'on the job' (Boella and Goss-Turner, 2005). In the context of corporate hospitality at large-scale events, this may place extra pressures on a manager who themselves may be unfamiliar with the event.

The need for orientation at events is evident, due to the large amount of staff on site and their temporary nature. Within a permanent sustained corporate culture, orientation takes the form of socialisation and can be described as acquiring a firm's cultural perspective and an understanding of others' expectations and their personal role boundaries (Foote, 2004). If this understanding is not reached then it may lead to misconception and a dysfunctional organisation.

This poses the question: how can you best help orientate a temporary employee who is arriving at an event on the morning it goes live?

Supervision and appraisals

This function may be carried out through a variety of means, including having potential supervisors shadowing an existing supervisor, developing a mentoring system, or encouraging staff to study professional courses.

One of the main tasks of supervisors and managers is that of performance appraisal. This task normally involves evaluating performance, communicating that evaluation and establishing a plan for improvement. The main outcomes of this process are a better event and more competent staff and volunteers.

Once an appraisal has been conducted there should be a follow-up review. This will allow a review of job responsibilities, how these responsibilities have been carried out and also find out how performance could be improved. Training should be provided for managers/ supervisors involved in this process.

Part of the appraisal system also involves rewards which, in the case of paid staff, come in the form of salaries, bonuses, profit sharing, promotion to other jobs or other events, and benefits such as cars and equipment usage (e.g. laptop computers). A range of options also exists to reward volunteers for their efforts. These include:

- training in new skills;
- free merchandise (e.g. clothing, badges, event posters);
- hospitality in the form of opening and closing parties, free meals/drinks;
- certificates of appreciation;
- opportunities to meet celebrities, sporting stars and other VIPs;
- promotion to more interesting volunteer positions;
- public acknowledgement through the media and at the event;
- free tickets to the event.

Discipline also needs to be considered by managers. Thus it is useful to have in place specific policies and practices that reflect the seriousness of different behaviour/actions, and these should be communicated to all staff (paid and voluntary). A disciplinary policy is likely to begin with some form of caution and end with dismissal. It also needs to be noted that many of the approaches to disciplining paid employees (e.g. removing access to overtime) are not applicable to volunteers. Approaches that may be applied to this group include reassignment, withholding rewards/benefits, and simple admonition by a supervisor.

Retaining personnel in event organisations

Retention of staff is a fundamental issue in generic organisations. But this is a specific problem for event organisations because they are different from other organisations in the way they pulsate. Event organisations often transform their structure overnight, expand personnel by significant numbers for an event, and then reduce to their original size in a matter of weeks. This pulsating feature places unique and specific demands on event managers in relation to retaining personnel. For example, for major sports event organisations, there are three quite distinct stages in the operating cycle and there are different elements that need to be taken into consideration by managers in each stage. The three stages are: lead-up to the event, during the event, and post-event (Hanlon and Jago, 2004).

In the lead-up to the event stage, an event can be put at risk if key personnel depart. Since in many events most personnel are seasonal, minimal notice is required before such staff can leave, which has the potential to pose problems. During the event itself, loss of staff can be unfortunate. Many part-time personnel involved in events generally begin to look elsewhere for employment in the concluding stages of the event. Some personnel may even leave during the final days of the event. The nature of the three stages means that major sports event organisations require more complex and tailored retention strategies than might be necessary at generic organisations. Hanlon and Jago (2004) recommend that in order to overcome these problems organisations should have a guide illustrating their retention practices, which recognises that different strategies are required for various personnel categories at different stages of the event cycle. This would assist event managers to optimise performance. In addition, they suggest that the proposed strategies are made available to all personnel.

Termination of employment

Occasionally, event managers will be faced with the need to terminate the services of an individual. This may be necessary in circumstances where an employee violates the employment contract (e.g. repeatedly arriving late at the workplace) or under-performing.

This need may also arise when economic or commercial circumstances of the organisation conducting the event are such that it needs to let staff go (e.g. insufficient revenue due to poor ticket sales).

Evaluation of the process

A regular review is necessary to see how well the process is working. To carry out such a review it is necessary to obtain feedback from relevant supervisory/management staff and from organising committee members in the case of a voluntary event. A specific time should be set aside to analyse the extent to which the process and its individual parts achieved the objectives. Once the review has been done, revisions can then be made to the process for subsequent events.

HRM theories

What motivates staff and how can they be encouraged to pursue excellence? Some staff may be motivated by empowerment, others may be motivated by promotion, while others may be motivated by a pay rise. These questions can be answered by understanding the various theories of human resource management.

Empowerment

Knowing your job roles leads to another management issue, this being empowerment. This can be described as permitting staff to undertake duties and accept responsibilities which were previously practised by management (Mullins, 2007).

This description is consistent with the HRM idea that empowerment will increase efficiency by removing unnecessary layers of management. In the live event context, empowerment is associated with the art of delegation.

Delegation involves the passing on of authority and responsibility throughout the structure of an organisation (Mullins, 2007). It can be conducted at an organisational level or at an individual level.

Empowerment may concern management as it could lead to various control failures due to a more remote management style (Boella and Goss-Turner, 2005), but it is also possible that it will lead to a more positive and committed workforce due to them having more control over the way in which their roles are performed.

Commitment

The next HRM issue to consider when managing temporary workers is the theory of organisational commitment. This is a contentious issue as its main purpose is to develop an employee to be committed to the organisation and their work.

The basic assumption underlying this theory is that if you are committed to the organisation and believe in its objectives and goals, it is likely you will perform for them. However, in order for you to be committed to the organisation, what must the organisation first deliver to you? In relation to events an employee may not be committed to the organisation, but might be committed to the event or the work they are responsible for. It is therefore the organisation's responsibility to enhance and maintain this commitment.

To develop commitment an organisation must fulfil the needs of its employees. This will be a hard task to achieve as each employee will be different and have different needs, and they will also have different expectations referring to the psychological contract.

Diversity

This leads to the issue of workplace diversity. Diversity can be defined as follows:

> Valuing everyone as individuals – as employees, customers and clients.
>
> (CIPD, 2011 [online])

The Chartered Institute for Personal Development places diversity into three separate types as shown in Figure 4.2.

1   The first type is social diversity, which relates to demographic differences such as age and race.
2   The second type is informational diversity. This acknowledges the differences in people's backgrounds, such as knowledge, education and experience.
3   The third type is value diversity. This refers to the difference in people's personality and attitudes and is also known as psychological diversity.

Diversity is an issue that runs parallel with the other HRM theories and practices. It is an element that needs managing simply because it is the make-up of an events workforce. An employee's background, age, experience and race may impact on their motivation, commitment and how to achieve the maximum output from them.

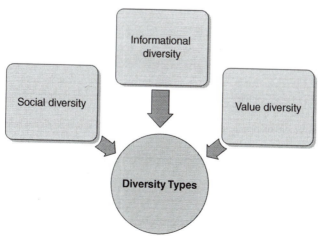

Figure 4.2   Three diversity types

As a manager, you can help with the issue of diversity by taking the following actions:

1   Examine your own styles of behaviour, beliefs and attitudes.

2   Consider your own feelings and reactions to people.

3   Be a role model.

4   See things from other people's perspective.

5   Be honest with staff.

6   Make sure that everybody feels part of a team.

7   Look at how flexibly you treat your staff.

Motivation

Motivation is one of the key factors in every individual's daily life. It is important to understand that motivation underpins an individual's ability to perform their duties. For this reason an employee's level of work performance is determined by their ability and through their motivation, which has been developed through job satisfaction and individual needs. Theories to help understand motivation have been developed through carrying out studies in the workplace.

Motivation is a very complex concept and there is no universal answer for ascertaining which motivation theory applies to any given individual. Carrell et al. define motivation as:

> the force that energizes behaviour, gives direction to behaviour, and underlies tendency to persist, even in the face of one or more obstacles. (Carrell et al., 2000: 127)

Maslow (1943) provides a theory of individual development and motivation. The idea behind this is that people want better living standards and job satisfaction, and they will always desire more. This desire is dependent upon what they already have. Maslow suggests that this desire can be arranged into a hierarchy, which he named *the hierarchy of needs*. This is shown in Table 4.1.

In this model, each need or level has to be satisfied for the person to be motivated in order to progress to the next level. The first three levels are seen as deficiencies. They must be satisfied in order to compensate for a lack of something. In contrast, satisfaction of the two higher needs is necessary for an individual to grow emotionally and psychologically.

However, the problem with this model is that, when it is applied to a work situation, many of the needs could be considered personal and are

Table 4.1   Maslow's hierarchy of needs

Type of need	Examples
1 Physiological needs	Develop self-satisfaction of hunger, food, shelter and sex
2 Safety and protection	Look for security and stability, feel secure and safe for the future
3 Social (support)	To care for others, love and be loved by others, developing social activities and friendship
4 Self-esteem (respect)	Admiration, self-respect, good opinion
5 Self-actualisation	Developing self-confidence and fulfilling individual potential capabilities

not necessary for motivation at work. It should be noted that Maslow's theory relates to individual life and not just to work behaviour (Mullins, 2007). Furthermore, it has been argued that the Maslow model is now outdated, and does not sit so well alongside modern thinking in managing organisations.

Nevertheless, it is important to understand that an employee in any organisation will attend work in return for a salary or wage that has been agreed in advance. The level of effort from each employee will be different, because it will depend on the individual's motivation. In addition, Maslow's model has implications for human resources managers in that if the organisation can give the individuals a reasonable pay and competitive wages or salaries according to national requirements, and also provide the workers with a safe and clean working environment, this will satisfy the basic needs of individuals.

Expectancy theory

Expectancy theory focuses on the need to link performance outcomes to rewards that are valued by employees. Expectancy theory is really a framework for performance management (Mabey, Salaman and Storey, 1998).

Its main premise is that the motivation of an employee is determined by the perceived strength of the link between:

- effort expended;
- performance achieved;
- rewards obtained.

Expectancy theory linked with Maslow's hierarchy of needs provides a strong theoretical base for motivating factors when discussing temporary staff.

The social aspect to work

Supportive working relationships and social interactions with work colleagues can be strong motivating factors. These tie in with both Maslow's hierarchy of needs and the expectancy theory of motivation.

The social elements at corporate hospitality events will have a bearing on motivation, whether it is workforce-to-workforce interaction or workforce-to-customer interaction. Figure 4.3 shows the links with the hierarchy of needs, and how needs expectations at work link to social relationships, intrinsic satisfaction and economic rewards.

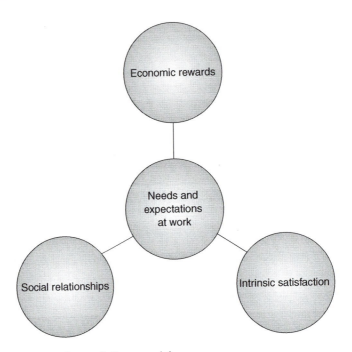

Figure 4.3   Needs and expectations model

Source: Adapted from Mullins, 2007: p. 252

Summary

Human resource management is a process of staffing and organising the right kind of people that will benefit the organisation and the event. As a manager, you need to understand that this is a process of integrated activities including: human resources strategy, policies and procedures; recruitment; training and professional development; supervision and evaluation; termination, outplacement and reenlistment; and evaluation. Why are these activities and techniques so important? Perhaps it is easier to list the personnel mistakes that managers need to avoid. For example, hiring the wrong people for the job – both paid and volunteer; experiencing high turnover; finding that staff are not performing to their best; wasting time with useless recruitment and allowing a lack of training to undermine the organisation's effectiveness.

The final part of the chapter discussed the issues of empowerment, commitment, diversity and motivation, examining Maslow's hierarchy of needs for understanding what may motivate an individual, and expectancy theory for understanding motivation at work.

■ Discussion questions

Question 1

Explain what HR management is and how it relates to the management process.

Question 2

Why is it important for an event company to make its human resources into a competitive advantage? How can HR contribute to doing so?

Question 3

How can HR contribute to integrating various functional processes into an integrated 'bundle of event/festival celebration'?

Question 4

What items are normally included in the job description and what items are not normally shown?

Question 5

Explain the techniques that can be employed by an organisation to motivate their employees?

Question 6

How can Investors In People help events organisations to enhance the CPD of their employees?

CASE STUDY 1   YOUTH SPORT TRUST EVENT VOLUNTEERING

Launched in September 2008, the event volunteering programme, funded by the HSBC Education Trust and *V* (the implementation body of the Russell Commission), seeks to create a new generation of young people as sports event volunteers.

Working in partnership with six of England's major host cities for international sports events from 2008–2011 and beyond, this project aims to create a structure and everlasting legacy of young people as volunteers. The aspiration for this programme is to reach across community divides, inspire young people to 'get involved' and tackle negative perceptions of young people by providing high profile examples of the positive contribution that young people can and do make.

Over 367 Young Event Volunteers have been deployed to support circa 65 events across six host cities, totalling over 1,000 volunteer opportunities. Roles have included marshalling, media support, admin roles, and event manager support.

Young Event Volunteer crews have supported a range of sporting events including:

- Paralympic World Cup
- Bath half marathon
- Basketball BBL League Cup Final
- Athletics AVIVA Indoor grand prix
- National Badminton Championships
- National Squash Championships
- British University Championships
- Flora London marathon
- 5K your way, Regents Park
- IMG moonwalk
- ASA Water Polo National Champs
- Great Manchester run
- FINA Diving World Series

'It has been a privilege to be a part of making a major event a success. Hearing the athletes comment on the fact that it's the volunteers who make such events a fantastic place to compete in, motivates me to volunteer and help others to reach their potential.' Young Event Volunteer.

Six young people have been recruited as Young Event Volunteer development officers who play a crucial role in identifying, recruiting and training the 'event crews'. The 'event crews' are led and managed by young people from higher education institutes who take on the role of Team Manager, supported by circa 8–10 Young Event Volunteers. Each young person, recruited from local school sport partnerships, will be deployed at a minimum of three major events over a 12 month period. The project is aiming to recruit 350 young people per year and offer more than 1,050 volunteering opportunities.

Source: Adapted from www.youthsporttrust.org

CASE STUDY 2   EDINBURGH INTERNATIONAL CONFERENCE CENTRE

Opened in 1995, the Edinburgh International Conference Centre (EICC) was set up by the local authorities to generate additional economic impact for Edinburgh and the surrounding area by drawing in 'business tourists'. The intention was that these tourists would not only generate new income for hotels but also for other related businesses such as pubs, shops and taxis among others.

The centre operates in a highly competitive arena, and finds itself up against other state-owned, private, government-run or commercially-run conference venues both in the UK and overseas. However, in order to fulfil its goal of economic output, the centre has to strike a balance between targeting high economic impact events and high revenue events.

The centre's unique selling point is its service including event management, technical production, themed catering, event planning and accommodation finding.

The challenge

'The conference and events industry is all about people – they determine whether we are successful or not,' remarks Geoff Fenlon, Business Excellence Director of the EICC. 'It made sense for us, therefore, to look for a framework such as Investors in People in order to develop our human resource policies to ensure our business is successful,' he says.

'We also needed to develop a culture that would encourage individuals to move from being just another member of the team to ones who would strive to become business-focused and ultimately business leaders.'

The strategy

'We dedicate time and funds to developing an individual and we see 360 degree appraisals as key to this process and have continued to fine tune them year on year. The most recent change has been to reduce paperwork and conduct appraisals as a team around a table as well as provide workshops on the subject for team leaders. We have also introduced a psychometric tool to make the appraisals more objective.'

'Getting our people involved and making them feel empowered is also essential – we want them to "own" the event, the issue, the success, the business,' says Geoff. 'All staff are encouraged to find creative ways to make life easier without compromising quality. We are firm believers that no one has a monopoly on good ideas and we have processes in place that support this while ensuring any output is sensitive to all stakeholder needs.'

'We have adopted a unique approach for the industry,' says Geoff. 'We use the Human Resources/Total Quality Management staff as internal consultants and facilitators so that team members are given help to meet any challenges without actually being provided with the

(Continued)

(Continued)

answers. So, by people working with other teams to find solutions, not only do we get a solution but also ownership, learning and commitment.'

EICC also has other mechanisms to hand ranging from proactive, such as brainstorming, to reactive and preventative.

The result

Edinburgh was the first congress venue to become an Investor in People back in 1997.

However, Geoff is quick to point out that achieving Investors in People is not a rigid procedure: 'Processes rather than detailed procedures have been important,' he stresses. 'These would have to change for just about every event – maybe even during an event.'

'Investors in People is highly valued within the organisation,' he adds. 'Such qualitative assessments are of vital importance and we pay close attention to what they say. We have reviewed whether to adopt a more quantitative approach but have decided that our current approach suits our culture of open communications and allows people to fully express themselves.'

The EICC has achieved dramatic results for the regional economy since it was created and has undoubtedly achieved world-class status. It has also increased its operating profit by over 400 per cent.

'Occupancy is increasing and, in line with our target, we have generated over £149.5 million for the local economy,' confirms Geoff. 'We also compare well with other venues around the world where the EICC is the fifth highest occupied venue and the fifth top venue at turning over its space.'

'But as we develop we will not lose our focus on people. Within the centre management team, including sub-contractors for catering and cleaning, there is a constant focus on quality systems and meeting the Standard,' concludes Geoff. 'Investors in People has been key in our success and will remain one of our main tools in taking the business forward.'

Source: www.investorsinpeople.co.uk

Further reading

Blyton, P. and Turnbull, P. (1992) *Reassessing Human Resource Management*. London: Sage.

Boella, M. and Goss-Turner, S. (2005) *Human Resource Management in the Hospitality Industry*, 8th edn. Oxford: Elsevier Butterworth Heinemann.

Carrell, M.R., Elbert, N.F. and Hatfield, R.D. (2000) *Human Resource Management: Global Strategies for Managing a Diverse and Gobal Workforce*, 6th edn. Dallas, TX: The Dryden Press.

Chartered Institute of Personnel and Development (2011) 'Reflections on the 2005 Training and Development Survey', CIPD, London [online]. Available at: www.cipd.co.uk/guides [accessed 3 October 2011].

Dessler, G. (2000) *Human Resources Management*, 8th edn. London: Prentice Hall International, London.

Foote, D.A. (2004) 'Temporary workers and managing the problem of unscheduled turno-ver', *Management Decisions*, 42: 863–74.

Goss, D. (1994) Principles of Human Resource Management. London: Routledge.

Hanlon, C. and Jago, L. (2004) 'The challenge of retaining personnel in major sport event organizations', *Event Management*, 9(1–2): 39–49.

Kandola, R. and Fullerton, J. (1998) *Diversity in Action: Managing the Mosaic*. London: Chartered Institute of Personnel and Development.

Krulis-Randa, J. (1990) 'Strategic human resource management in Europe after 1992', *International Journal of Human Resource Management*, 1(2): 131–9.

Mabey, C., Salaman, G. and Storey, J. (1998) *Human Resource Management: A Strategic Introduction*. Malden, MA: Blackwell Publishers.

Mullins, L.J. (2007) *Management and Organisational Behaviour*, 5th edn. London: Financial Times/Pitman Publishing.

Stone, R. (2002) *Human Resource Management*, 3rd edn. Brisbane: John Wiley & Sons.

US Department of Labor, Bureau of Labor Statistics. Available at: www.bls.gov/home [accessed 3 March, 2006].

Section B

Finance and Law

5 Financial Management in the Events Industry

In this chapter you will cover:

- the principles of financial management;
- the regulatory framework of accounting;
- understanding financial statements;
- the financial crisis and the events management industry;
- summary;
- discussion questions;
- case studies;
- further reading.

The aim of this chapter is to provide clear-cut explanations of accounting terms for event managers/businesses, enabling you to familiarise yourself with the financial management process. Financial management effectively controls growth and should be carried out by event organisations for the protection of creditors and shareholders and to keep the company in business. Finance is at the centre of every business and at the heart of management; it is concerned with everything to do with obtaining money for an organisation and recording and controlling how that money is being spent. The most important point to remember for events managers, even if you have no direct responsibility for managing financial resources, is to be aware of the financial procedures that are used in your organisation, particularly for those items which cost money or which generate cash for the business.

The principles of financial management

Financial accounts are concerned with classifying, measuring and recording the transactions of a business. At the end of a period (typically a year), financial

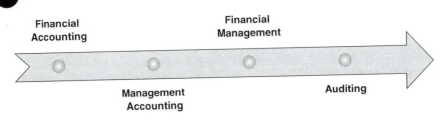

Figure 5.1   Traditional accounting disciplines

statements are prepared to show the performance and position of the business, through the systematic recording, reporting, and analysis of its financial transactions.

Traditionally, finance is split into four major accounting disciplines, as highlighted in Figure 5.1.

Financial accounting is a technique which involves recording the results and financial position of a business. Financial accounting reports on how the organisation has performed in the previous accounting period or year. The information is based on what has already happened. It is only concerned with summarising the historical data that has been collected over the year. Financial accounting is mainly concerned with financial reports which are produced at the end of each period for external users and shareholders.

Management accounting provides information to managers for day-to-day decision making, as well as for short- and long-term planning. Management accounting produces detailed information for each department; it is also responsible for preparing budgets and helping the managers and board to set prices for the products.

Financial management is a method used to analyse the future for management and to help managers to make better long-term decisions for the organisation. In addition, it helps the management decide where to obtain money and to choose the best options for the use of the monies available to an organisation.

Auditing is an evaluation process for organisations to maintain quality control and also provide an assessment of an organisation's internal control. The generic definition of an audit is an assessing of a system, process, product and business. The role of the auditor is to carry out the financial audit as a part of the investigation. The purpose of the audit is designed by the law-making bodies to determine whether financial statements which are produced by the companies are fairly presented in accordance with International Financial Reporting Standards (IFRS), Generally Accepted Accounting Principles (GAAP) or by the individual countries' own legal requirements.

In UK the audit is carried out under the Companies Acts 1985, 1989 and 2006. The annual accounts of a limited company must be audited by a person independent of the company. In theory, the company should appoint Chartered or Certified accountants to carry out an annual investigation of accounts prepared by the company.

Each year the auditor will investigate the accounts prepared by the company. He or she will then complete a report explaining the work that has been done and noting whether or not the accounts show a 'true and fair view' of the company's performance. If the auditor agrees with annual accounts, he or she will state that the work has been carried out according to the auditing standards as laid out in the Companies Acts. If in the auditor's opinion the accounts show a true and fair view, this is called an **unqualified audit report** (in other words it is a clean report). If the auditor disagrees with the company's board of directors in the preparation of the company's account, it is the responsibility of the auditor to ask the company's board of directors to make changes and report to shareholders at the annual general meeting, setting out the concerns on which he or she has disagreed with the board of the directors. In accounting terms this is called a qualified report.

Under the Companies Acts, the auditor must investigate and compile his or her report on four key financial statements, as shown in Figure 5.2.

In addition, the auditor's report needs to be included as a part of the final annual accounts for the company. Therefore, it is also important that the auditor addresses the reports to the shareholders, not to the directors of the company or anybody else within the company.

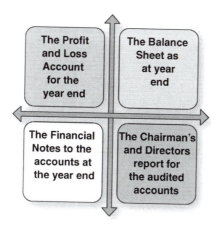

Figure 5.2   Fundamental statements for an auditor's report

The regulatory framework of accounting

In UK the preparation of financial accounts is governed by the Companies Acts 1985 and 1989, particularly for limited companies. The UK is a member of the European Union and companies need to comply with legal requirements which are set by the EU. The regulatory framework is based on three main accounting laws.

Company law

Company law provides the legal framework within which businesses operate in the UK. The Companies Act 1985 brought together all the previous Acts. This Act was amended on the enactment of the Companies Act 1989. The Companies Act 2006 repeated certain parts of the 1985 and 1989 Act and inserted new sections.

Limited companies are required by law to prepare financial accounts for each financial year for shareholders and other groups who are interested in accounts. Under the Companies Acts, financial accounts need to be registered with the registrar of companies and available for inspection by any member of the general public. The published accounts need to be lodged with the registrar of companies within four weeks of the end of the financial year.

Limited companies are required to keep all accounting records and accounting files for each accounting period with Companies' House. Under the Companies Act 2006, company directors are responsible for preparation of the accounts and ensuring that accounts are delivered to Companies' House within the given time period. If accounts are not delivered on time, directors can be penalised for late submission.

The annual return which is submitted by the company is a snapshot of company information giving details of its annual financial activities and providing details of its chairman, directors, company secretary, registered office address, shareholders and share capital. Each year Companies House sends an annual return form to the company's registered address asking for any changes during the year to be noted, and that all details should be checked. The form needs to be signed off by the company's secretary and returned within 28 days with a fee.

The legislation also requires directors to produce accounts which show a true and fair view of the company's accounts for the accounting period and which highlight the financial position at end of the period. The board of directors needs to sign off the annual accounts, and the independent auditors then attach their report. The accounts are presented to the shareholders of the company at the annual general meeting. Once the accounts have been adopted by the members they are sent to Companies' House for the registrar to file.

Accounting standards

In the UK, apart from company law the key principles or regulations which affect accounting procedures are derived from guidelines issued by the professional accounting bodies. The accounting standards were devised in the UK and around the world due to the need to standardise the ways in which companies' accounts are measured. The accounting standards had the effect of narrowing the areas of difference between each company, and standardising the preparation and presentation of accounts. This helped to eliminate deliberate manipulation in accounts and also served to enhance comparability between companies. The Accounting Standards Board (ASB) was set up in 1970 to crack down on the manipulation of published accounts that were being presented to shareholders. This was the first step taken by the UK government and professional accounting bodies to protect investors in the wake of accounting scandals. The Accounting Standards Board (ASB) introduced Statements of Standard Accounting Practice (SSAPs) for companies to follow in 1973.

Following the recommendations of the Dearing Report in 1990, accounting standards are now governed by four accounting bodies (see Figure 5.3).

Over the last 15 years, the ASB has revised the Statements of Standard Accounting Practice (SSAPs), replacing them with Financial Reporting Standards (FRS). While some of the SSAPs have been superseded by FRSs, some remain in force. Before 1990, SSAPs were the major accounting standards being used by companies. As these contained a number of loopholes, they have now been replaced by FRSs. Below are the main FRSs and SSAPs used by sole traders, partnerships and limited companies in the UK.

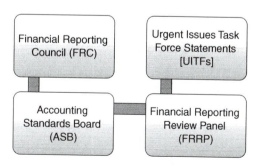

Figure 5.3 Accounting bodies

FINANCIAL REPORTING STANDARDS (FRS)

FRS 1 (Revised 1996) – Cash flow statements
FRS 2 – Accounting for subsidiary undertakings
FRS 3 – Reporting financial performance
FRS 4 – Capital instruments
FRS 5 – Reporting the substance of transactions
FRS 6 – Acquisitions and mergers
FRS 7 – Fair values in acquisition accounting
FRS 8 – Related party disclosures
FRS 9 – Associates and joint ventures
FRS 10 – Goodwill and intangible assets
FRS 11 – Impairment of fixed assets and goodwill
FRS 12 – Provisions, contingent liabilities and contingent assets
FRS 13 – Derivatives and other financial instruments: disclosures
FRS 14 – Earnings per share
FRS 15 – Tangible fixed assets
FRS 16 – Current tax
FRS 17 – Retirement benefits
FRS 18 – Accounting policies
FRS 19 – Deferred tax
FRSSE (effective June 2002) – Financial reporting standard for smaller entities
FRS 20 (IFRS2) – Share-based payment
FRS 21 (IAS 10) – Events after the balance sheet date
FRS 22 (IAS 33) – Earnings per share
FRS 23 (IAS 21) – The Effects of changes in foreign exchange rates
FRS 24 (IAS 29) – Financial reporting in hyperinflationary economies
FRS 25 (IAS 32) – Financial instruments: disclosure and presentation
FRS 26 (IAS 39) – Financial instruments: measurement
FRS 27 – Life assurance
FRSSE (effective January 2005) – Financial reporting standard for smaller entities
FRS 28 – Corresponding amounts
FRS 29 – (IFRS 7) Financial instruments: disclosures

STATEMENTS OF STANDARD ACCOUNTING PRACTICE (SSAPS)

SSAP 4 – Accounting for government grants
SSAP 5 – Accounting for value added tax
SSAP 9 – Stocks and long-term contracts
SSAP 13 – Accounting for research and development
SSAP 15 – Status of SSAP 15
SSAP 17 – Accounting for post-balance sheet events

SSAP 19 – Accounting for investment properties
SSAP 20 – Foreign currency translation
SSAP 21 – Accounting for leases and hire purchase contracts
SSAP 24 – Accounting for pension costs
SSAP 25 – Segmental reporting

International accounting standards

In 2003 the UK government announced that from January 2005, all UK companies will be able to use the International Financial Reporting Standards (IFRS) as an alternative to UK accounting standards. In addition, European Union law now requires all listed UK companies to use International Accounting standards (IAS) following the 2006 act, when preparing their financial consolidated accounts.

Understanding financial statements

Trial balance

The trial balance is a schedule which lists all the ledger accounts in the form of debit and credit balances to confirm that total debits equal total credits.

The balance sheet and trading and profit and loss account are prepared from a list of the various balances, which then produces a trial balance. Traditionally, the trial balance is derived from the ledger accounts at the end of the financial year or accounting period. These accounts are drawn up by the owner or the accountant for the business. The business accountant records every single transaction that takes place in the business during the year.

In reality, the accountant or book-keeper for the business will use a technique called double entry book-keeping with which to write up individual transactions in the ledger of accounts. The accountant needs to enter every transaction over the year twice in the books of annual accounts. This double entry process results in the forming of a trial balance for the business. In return, this equation balances both sides of the trial balance.

Total debit £ amount + Total credit £ amount

Traditionally, businesses use the following principles in preparing a trial balance:

- Find the balance of each account on the ledger account.
- Businesses should record the ledger account balances in the right column of the trial balance.

- Once the ledger account balances have been recorded on the trial balance, then each column can be totalled up.

- Then both totals of the two columns of the trial balance are compared, to see if they match with each other or not.

- If the totals do not match, then the book-keeper or financial record keeper may have made a mistake in the ledger accounts.

This proof that debits and credits match the ledger accounts offers the business the opportunity to verify that the individual accounts are correct and accurate. It helps the accountant to prepare the final account with clear and effective proof that the accounting information is correct and efficient for the year. It is vital for businesses that the correct debit balances have been entered into the debit column and the credit balances are entered in the credit column of the trial balance.

The trial balance is used by the accountant to put together the final accounts and at the same time uses the legal framework to ensure that the accounts meet requirements of the Companies Acts 1985, 1989 and 2006. Businesses need to

Table 5.1   Example layout for a working trial balance

Trial balance for a logistic event as at 31 December 2011		
	DR	CR
Event income		
Sales		£223,400
Capital		£112,600
Event expenditure		
Purchase	£71,800	
Motor expenses	£7,450	
Office expenses	£13,900	
Premises	£77,300	
Motor vehicles	£22,155	
Fixtures and fittings	£14,790	
Light and heat	£1,200	
Debtors	£25,900	
General expenses	£3,000	
Creditors		£35,650
Bank	£27,800	
Cash	£4,565	
Drawings	£6,000	
Stock at 1st Jan 2011	£34,500	
Salaries and wages	£39,790	
Rent and rates	£21,500	
	£371,650	**£371,650**
Stock at 1st Jan 2012	£16,800	

produce a working trial balance at the end of the year, usually using a layout such as the one shown in Table 5.1.

The balance sheet

The balance sheet is one of the main financial documents used by any company, and provides information about its financial state. A balance sheet is a financial snapshot of the company's financial situation at any given moment in time. It is one of the financial statements that limited companies and PLCs produce every year for their shareholders.

Essentially, a balance sheet is a list of the assets, liabilities and capital of a business. In addition, the purpose is to show the financial position of the organisation on a certain date during the year. Under the Companies Act 1985, 1989 and 2006 the balance sheet needs to be produced at the end of company's financial year. An example layout of a balance sheet for a sole trader is shown in Table 5.2.

Table 5.2   Example layout of a balance sheet for a sole trader

Balance Sheet as at 31 December 2011			
Fixed assets			
Land and building			xxx
Fixtures and fittings			xxx
			xxxx
Current assets			
Stocks	xxx		
Debtors		xxx	
Cash in hand	xxx		
		xxxx	
Current liabilities			
Creditors		xxx	
Bank overdraft		xxx	
Net current assets			**xxxx**
			xxxx
Long-term liabilities			
Long-term loan			xxx
			xxxx
Capital			
Capital as at 1 January			xxx
Profit for the year to 31 December 2011			xxx
			Xxxx

Traditionally, a balance sheet is divided into two halves, the top half of the balance sheet shows where the money is currently being used in the business, and the bottom half of the balance sheet shows how the money has been raised by the business.

Fixed assets

Long-term assets are known as fixed assets. A fixed asset is an asset purchased for use within the organisation and which helps the business to earn income from its use on a regular basis. Examples would be machinery, equipment, computers and so on, none of which actually get used up in the production process.

Fixed assets = Property + Machinery + Equipment

Current assets

Short-term assets are known as current assets – assets which are used on a day-to-day basis by the firm. In the balance sheet layout shown in Table 5.2, the fixed assets are followed by current assets. The current assets are items which are owned by the business. The purpose of current assets is to turn them into cash within one year. In addition, current assets are continually flowing through the business at regular intervals, so these are assets which can be quickly changed to liquid cash. The current assets may include cash in hand and in the bank, anything owed to the business by debtors, any advance payment of bills, stock and so on.

Current assets: Stock + Debtors + Cash / Bank + Prepayments

The current assets are shown on the top half of the balance sheet, and the current liabilities are subtracted from them to show net current assets.

Long-term liabilities

In a balance sheet, just like the fixed and current assets, long-term liabilities and current liabilities are shown separately. The long-term liabilities are debts which are not payable within the one-year period. Under the terms of the Companies Acts 1985 and 1989, limited companies must show any long-term liabilities by using the term 'creditors' (amounts falling due after more than one year). The amounts can be owed to suppliers, creditors, employees or the government. In addition, if the business receives money in advance of an event taking place, they have a liability to carry out the event or service.

Long-term liabilities = Bank loan + Long-term creditors

Current liabilities

Current liabilities are the short-term debts of the business, which are due to be paid within one year, and usually refer to amounts owed to creditors or suppliers. Under the terms of the Companies Acts 1985, 1989 and 2006 limited companies must show their current liabilities by using the term '**creditors**' (amounts falling due within one year).

Current liabilities = Creditors + Accruals

Capital employed

The other half of the balance sheet includes capital employed. Capital employed is debt owed to the business owners. The three main areas which are shown on the balance sheet under this heading are: the amount invested by the owner(s) in the business; the profit earned by the business during the year; and the amount of money of which has been drawn from the business by owner(s) for personal use (also known as drawings).

Moreover, capital employed is considered as a liability by company accountants, because this is money owed by the business to the owner(s). Finally, on the balance sheet, the owner(s) equity is shown as a liability, as illustrated in Figure 5.4.

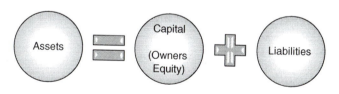

Figure 5.4   The owner's equity is shown as a liability on the balance sheet

Profit and loss account

The profit and loss account differs significantly from the balance sheet. The profit and loss account is a record of the firm's trading activities over a period of time, whereas the balance sheet is the financial position at a given moment in time.

The purpose of the trading account is to measure the actual gross profit on trading of the business over the last twelve months. This is done by taking the total sales for the year minus the cost of sales (cost of goods sold). An example of a trading account is shown in Table 5.3.

The purpose of a profit and loss account is to define the gross profit of the business by deducting from it all the genuine expenses incurred in running the business over the last twelve months and arriving at a net profit for the given period. There are a number of different types of expenses that are incurred during the year in a business cycle, which are deductible from gross profit.

The profit and loss account looks at how well the firm has traded over the time period concerned (usually the last 6 months, or the last year). It shows

Table 5.3   The trading account

Sales			61409
Less Cost of Sales			
Opening Stock		8500	
add Purchases	37302		
less Discounts received	1222	36080	
		44580	
less Closing Stock		8800	35780
Gross profit			25629

Table 5.4   Example of a profit and loss account for a sole trader

Gross profit			**25629**
Less expenses			
Lighting and heating	2557		
add accrued electricity	82	2639	
Wages		7565	
Rent and rates	5788		
add rent owing	559		
less rates prepaid	121	6226	
Telephone	223		
add accrued	45	268	
Insurance	483		
less prepaid	56	427	17125
Net profit			8504

Gross profit – Expenses = Net profit

Figure 5.5   Formula for net profit

how much the firm has earned from selling its product or service, and how much it has paid out in costs (production costs, salaries and so on). The net of these two is the amount of profit the business has earned. An example of a profit and loss account for a sole trader is shown in Table 5.4.

The basic principle of a profit and loss account is to show the net profit of the business for the financial year, that is, any money which is left after all relevant business expenses have been deducted from the gross profit.

Put simply, in order to understand the concept of a profit and loss account, you can use the following formula to calculate the net profit.

As indicated in the profit and loss account, the expenses are those which have been incurred in the business over the last 12 months. These are expenses which are not included in the trading account. The expenses for a sole trader are not classified into any category, however, for a limited company expenses are classified into three main categories:

Table 5.5   Example layout of a trading, profit and loss account for a sole trader for the end of a financial year

Trading, Profit and Loss Account for the year ended 31 January 2012			
Sales			xxx
Less cost of sales			
Opening stock	xxx		
Add purchases	xxx		
Less closing stock		xxx	xxx
Gross profit			xxx
Less expenses			
Lighting and heating	xxx		
Wages	xxx		
Rent and rates	xxx		
Telephone		xxx	
Telephone		xxx	
Insurance		xxx	
Total expenditure			xxx
Net profit			**xxx**

- Selling
- Administrative
- Distribution

Table 5.6 shows an actual example of a trading, profit and loss account and balance sheet, for the Logistics Events Company, for the year 2011.

Accounting ratio analysis

The ratio analysis is the most essential information contained within financial statements, besides the trading, profit and loss account, and the balance sheet. The financial position of the business needs to be measured in order that the key stakeholders within the company are able to appreciate how the business has performed during the financial year. The only way you can enhance the understanding of the key stakeholders how the company is performing is through ratio analysis.

Ratio analysis is a technique which compares crucial relationships between numbers in a readily understood form (usually a percentage). It is essential for the event organisation to carry out evaluation of the performance of the business or event, to examine the profitability, growth, return on fixed and current assets, return on equity capital and general expenses of the business. This will provide an indication for the company to compare the financial performance of the business with other companies in the industry. It is important to understand that ratios on their own are not particularly useful. You need to be able to compare ratios over time or against other ratios to be able to build up a useful picture of the performance of the company.

Ratio analysis compares company financial accounts to generate vital figures by using the following techniques.

- **Performance ratios**: these include profit, capital employed and turnover.
- **Liquidity ratios**: these are concerned with the short-term financial position of the company.
- **Gearing ratios**: these are focused on the long-term financial position of the company.
- **Investments ratios**: these are concerned with the return for the shareholder.

Profitability ratios

These ratios help the business and key stakeholders to judge how well the firm's profit has performed over the last 12 months. Profitability ratios are expressed

Table 5.6   Example trading, profit and loss account and balance sheet for Logistics
Events, 2011

Logistics Events

Trading, profit and loss account, for the year ending 31 December 2011

	£	£	£
Sales			£223,400
Less cost of sales			
Opening stock		£34,500	
add purchases		£71,800	
		£106,300	
less closing stock		£16,800	£89,500
Gross profit			£133,900
Less expenses			
Lighting and heating	£1,200		
Salaries and wages	£39,790		
Rent and rates	£21,500		
i. Office expenses	£13,900		
ii. Motor expenses	£7,450		
General expenses	£3,000		
iii. Drawings	£6,000		
			£92,840
Net profit			£41,060

Logistics Events

Balance sheet as at 31 December 2011

Fixed assets			
Premises			£77,300
Fixtures and fittings			£14,790
Motor vehicles			£22,155
			£114,245
Current assets			
Stock	£16,800		
Debtors	£25,900		
Cash at bank	£27,800		
Cash in hand	£4,565	£75,065	
Current liabilities			
Creditors	£35,650		
		£35,650	
Working capital (or net current assets)			£39,415
			£153,660
Financed by:			
Capital			£112,600
add net profit			£41,060
			£153,660

Table 5.7   Ratio analysis techniques

Type of ratio	Ratio
Performance	Profit margin
	Days sales in stock
	Asset turnover
Liquidity and gearing	Current ratio
	Gearing ratio
	Interest cover
Investments	Earnings per share
	Return on equity
	Dividend yield
	Dividend per share
	Price/earnings ratio

either in terms of the profit earned on sales, or the profit earned on the capital employed in the business. In addition, profitability ratios relate to a company's ability to earn a satisfactory income. A company's profitability is closely linked to its liquidity because earnings ultimately produce cash flow. The key profitability ratios are explained below.

Profit margin ratio

The profit margin ratio measures the level of profit compared to the sales of the firm for the financial year. It therefore shows the percentage profit on the sales. It can be measured as either a gross or net profit margin.

Gross profit as a percentage of sales $\quad\dfrac{\text{Gross profit} * 100}{\text{Sales}}$

Net profit as a percentage of sales $\quad\dfrac{\text{Net profit} * 100}{\text{Sales}}$

Return on capital employed ratio

The return on capital employed ratio measures the level of profit of the firm compared to the amount of capital that has been invested.

Return on capital employed $\quad\dfrac{\text{Net profit (before tax)} * 100}{\text{Capital employed}}$

Liquidity ratio

The liquidity ratio measures the liquidity of the firm. The business needs to ensure that it has enough liquidity in place to meet all it commitments. The liquidity ratio shows if the firm has sufficient assets to convert into liquid cash to meet the business commitments for 12 months, and it is important for the business to not have all their assets tied up as capital.

Current ratio

The current ratio is calculated by dividing the current assets by the current liabilities.

$$\text{Current ratio} \quad \frac{\text{Current assets}}{\text{Current liabilities}}$$

Acid test ratio

The acid test ratio excludes stock from the current assets, but is otherwise the same as the current ratio.

$$\text{Acid test} \quad \frac{\text{Current assets} - \text{stock}}{\text{Current liabilities}}$$

Gearing ratios

Traditionally, all businesses have to borrow money regardless the size of the business. If the company wants to expand, they need to borrow money from banks or other financial institutions. In addition, most businesses fund their investment from profits they have made from business over the years. The other means of investment is met by the issue of shares. In reality, most of the investment is met by borrowing money from banks. The only disadvantage of borrowing money for business is that the business has to pay interest on the sum which has been borrowed, regardless of whether the investment is a success or not.

The key stakeholders and potential investors look at a set of accounts to assess how big that risk is and they use gearing ratios to analyse business stability in the industry.

Shareholders' equity ratio

This ratio measures and determines how much shareholders would receive in the case of a company going out of business (liquidation).

$$\text{Shareholders' equity ratio} = \frac{\text{Shareholders' equity}}{\text{Total assets}} \times 100$$

Interest coverage ratio

This measures how easily the company can pay its interest out of its profit.

$$\text{Interest coverage ratio} = \frac{\text{Profit before interest and tax}}{\text{Periodic interest charges payable}}$$

Investment ratio

The investment ratio is key for current and potential investors, and measures a standard return on investor's equity.

Price/earnings ratio

This ratio measures the market price per share to earnings per share and is useful for comparing the value placed on a company's shares in relation to the overall market.

$$\text{Price/earnings ratio} = \frac{\text{Market price per share}}{\text{Earnings per share}}$$

Dividend yield ratio

The dividend yield ratio measures the rate of return an investor gets by comparing the cost of his shares with the dividend receivable.

$$\text{Dividend yield ratio} = \frac{\text{Dividend per share}}{\text{Market price per share}} \times 100$$

The financial crisis and the events management industry

Over the past 5 years companies have witnessed the most catastrophic banking and financial crisis in history. The financial crisis has hit the events industry very hard, particularly the corporate events market, which hit rock bottom due to the collapse of large financial institutions. The corporate events industry has seen a number of evictions and foreclosures of events companies who were organising major corporate events for the large financial institutions and government departments, due to their plummeting budgets and revenues, and shrinking employment opportunities. Recent statistical reports may insinuate that economies around the globe are on the road to recovery from the recession, but fuel prices and unemployment are still intensifying, small and medium enterprises are still feeling the burden during the revival process, banks are yet to replenish their reserves and countries are still dependent on financial rescue packages and excessive borrowing from organisations like the International Monetary Fund (IMF) as a source of relief. These crises, issues and controversies in global financial markets have highlighted several glitches in the world's banking policies, financial regulations, and government enforcements, making it clearly evident that global economies are a part of a deeply unified system and any impact on the financial position of a particular country can have a snowball effect on all the nations worldwide (Nanto, 2009).

Such global crisis brought the world's financial system to its knees; economically, politically, and socially (Milne, 2009). The downturn in the events and tourism industry has impacted on local businesses and caused a slowdown in the tourism market.

According to Papatheodorou, Rossello and Xiao (2010), the global credit crunch and subsequent recession has had unavoidable impacts on the events and tourism industry around the world. According to figures provided by the United Nations World Tourism Organization (UNWTO), international tourism had dropped considerably in the second half of 2008 and the first half of 2009. Even the Office of National Statistics (ONS) (2011) in the UK suggests that the number of foreign tourists travelling to the UK, and their spending, have dropped by 2 per cent respectively.

Even domestic tourism has been hampered, as UK residents travelling within the country and their spending have dropped by 9 per cent and 7 per cent respectively. The £9.3 billion budget for London Olympics 2012 had to go through severe negotiation due to the credit crunch. The same is true for the development of the athletes' village – the biggest section of the 500-acre Olympic park in East London. This makes it clearly evident that tourism, events, venues, and all the subsequent sectors are profoundly affected by the credit crunch.

Summary

In this chapter it has been suggested that understanding finance is vital for events managers. Traditionally, there are three main forms of business organisations that exist in the UK: sole trader, partnership and limited company. For events managers, it is important to understand the principle of financial statements of a business, and also the legal financial accounting concepts which are governed by the Companies Acts 1985 and 1989. In order to understand financial accounting, it is important to look at finance as a whole, and to see where it fits in the organisation. Under UK law, limited companies need to produce annual accounts, which must be audited by a person independent of the company. This will provide a clear and effective process for companies to report their annual return within the given framework. In theory, the company should appoint independent Chartered or Certified accountants to carry out an annual investigation of accounts prepared by the company.

The financial reporting standards (FRS) issued by the Accounting Standards Board have been changed over the last 15 years to close the loopholes that were left open by the Statements of Standard Accounting Practice (SSAPs). Over the years, financial reporting requirements have been getting more detailed and so updating is necessary to enhance the structure for large companies to report accurate information.

Ratio analysis provides a means of comparison for events managers and organisers. The financial position of the business needs to be measured in order that the key stakeholders within the company are able to appreciate how the business has performed during the financial year, in line with other competitors in the industry. Ratio analysis provides investors with a clear and effective comparison of financial data for the company's financial activities for the year. In addition, ratio analysis is a prime technique to help managers and event organisers to assess and evaluate how well the event has performed in terms of profitability. Ratio analysis compares crucial relationships between numbers in a readily understood form (usually a percentage). Finally, the chapter has discussed the increasing importance of the financial crisis that has hit the events and tourism industry over the last five years, which may continue for another five years to come. The corporate event industry has suffered due to lack of sponsorship and corporate deals collapsing.

 ■ **Discussion questions** ■■■■■■■■■■■■■■■■■■■■

Question 1

The information in Table 5.8 was extracted from the books of V2000, as at 31 December 2011.

Prepare a trading and profit and loss account for the company, for the year ending 31 December 2011.

Table 5.8   Accounts information for V200, 31 December 2011

Sales	2,000,000
Purchases	750,000
Vehicles hiring cost	40,000
Trade debtors	23,500
Trade creditors	45,000
Capital	500,000
Security charges	65,000
Salaries	215,000
Lighting and heating	19,500
Stationery	559
Sundry expenses	89,000
Vehicle expenses	9,955
Postage	455
Telephone	5,690
Insurance	6,000
Rent	49,000
Equipment hire	104,500

Question 2

The information in Table 5.9 was extracted from the books of Global Events Management Limited, as at 31 October 2011.

Prepare a trading and profit and loss account and balance sheet for the company, as at 31 October 2011.

Table 5.9 Trial balance for Global Events Management Ltd, as at 31 October 2011

Event income	DR	CR
Cash sales (usually tickets)		£76,450
Credit card sales (usually tickets)		£23,900
Sponsorship		£6,700
Fees from clients		£3,570
Donations		£650
Capital		£53,400
Expenses		
Director's salary	£29,750	
Event assistant's salary	£16,600	
Employer's National Insurance and tax	£6,550	
Office rent	£12,340	
Office rates	£1,300	
Office telephone	£1,050	
Water rates	£1,460	
Mobile phones	£860	
Electricity	£1,690	
Gas	£1,985	
Company ad and promo	£1,130	
Motor expenses	£4,800	
Public liability insurance	£2,000	
Bank charges at 1% pa	£835	
Creditors		£12,670
Stock at 1st Nov 2010	£18,400	
Depreciation on car	£5,600	
Depreciation on computer	£990	
Premises	£32,000	
Motor vehicles	£8,000	
Fixtures and fittings	£7,600	
Debtors	£5,700	
Bank	£16,700	
	£177,340	**£177,340**
Stock at 31 November 2011	£13,475	

Question 3

a Discuss the difference between 'capital' and 'revenue' expenditure.

b Discuss the role of ratio analysis and describe different types of ratios.

Question 4

a Explain the difference between financial accounting and management accounting.

b Critically outline the role of the balance sheet within private and public limited companies.

Question 5

The information in Table 5.10 was extracted from the books of World Events Ltd, as at 31 March 2012.

Prepare a profit and loss account for the company for the year to 31 March 2012.

Table 5.10   The trial balance of World Events Ltd as at 31 March 2012

The trial balance of World Events Ltd as at 31 March 2012

220,000 Ordinary shares of £1		220,000
10,000 6% Preference shares of £3 each		60,000
Dividends: Ordinary	11,000	
Preference	3,600	
Taxation	35,000	
Interest paid	6,500	
Bank loan	50,000	
Admin cost	35,000	
Turnover	200,300	
Cost of sales	182,500	

Question 6

Calculate the profit margin ratio for Logistics Management Ltd, using the trading and profit and loss account and balance sheet 31 December 2011, as shown in Table 5.11.

Question 7

Calculate the liquidity and gearing ratios for Logistics Management Ltd, using the information in Table 5.11.

Table 5.11   Trading and profit and loss account and balance sheet for Logistics Management Ltd, as at 31 December 2011

Logistics Events
Trading profit and loss account, for the year ending 31 December 2010

	£	£	£
Sales			34949
Less cost of sales		4569	
Opening stock			
add purchases	18422		
less discounts received	1248	17174	
		21743	
less closing stock		5721	16022
Gross profit			18927
Less expenses			
Lighting and heating	4146		

Logistics Events

Trading profit and loss account, for the year ending 31 December 2010

	£	£	£
add accrued electricity	76	4222	
Wages		6947	
Rent and rates	2659		
add rent owing	403		
less rates prepaid	133	2929	
Telephone	176		
add accrued	43	219	
Insurance	956		
less prepaid	65	891	15208
Net profit			3719

Logistics Events

Balance sheet as at 31 December 2010

Fixed assets			
Van			3571
Fixtures and fittings			8503
			12074
Current assets			
Stock	5721		
Debtors	5150		
Cash at bank	6725		
Cash in hand	30		
Prepaid	198	17824	
Current liabilities			
Creditors	3048		
Accrued	522	3570	
Working capital (or net current assets)			14254
			26328
Financed by:			
Capital		29194	
add net profit		3719	32913
less drawings			6585
			26328

CASE STUDY 1   BROADSTAIRS BIG TOP

Broadstairs Folk Week has recently considered an option to replace the annually-hired marquee with a more innovative temporary structure. This has a 500 flat floor seating capacity and they

(Continued)

(Continued)

have rented it for the last 6 years from Dover Marquees for around £4,000 per week, including transport and labour for putting it up and taking it down.

They have an ambition to purchase a new structure for their own festival and then rent it out to other festivals and events when not in use. Their business model relied on an application for funding from the Foundation for Sports and the Arts which unfortunately has just been turned down. They are unsurprisingly keen to find another public sector supporter although the model could, in theory, work without public investment.

Broadstairs have approached Roustabout Ltd to purchase a Big Top structure suitable for their site in Pierremont Park. Broadstairs recognise that they don't have the skills or experience to operate the structure and have asked Roustabout to consider storing, maintaining, hiring and installing it for Folk Week, and for other events at a hire charge.

The cost of the structure would be £43,500 and Roustabout estimate that it could be rented out at £2,000 for a typical 7–10 day period, giving a payback time on the capital cost of 22 weeks. They further estimate that there might be a market for 4–5 weeks' hire a year in addition to the Folk Weeks, resulting in a 5–6 year payback period. In addition, installation costs a further £2,000, depending on location, which is born by the hirer. However, Roustabout would be required to store and maintain the structure and make a profit for operating it. This might leave Broadstairs with £1,000 profit per hire.

The problem with this approach is that the Broadstairs site is unusual and the structure they want will need to be purpose built. Although it can be used for other hirers, the potential to achieve 22 weeks' hire over its lifetime might be limited. Broadstairs are not able or willing to raise the investment commercially, and providing public funds would save them £2,000 a year, and potentially give them a further income stream of £4–5,000 a year if the project achieved its targets.

The risk:return ratio for this type of project is not sufficient for it to be of interest outside a publicly-funded model.

Source: SEEDA, the Regional Development Agency for the South East of England, 2009 [online].

CASE STUDY 2 LONDON 2012 OLYMPIC AND PARALYMPIC GAMES

Financial position

Cash flow

The outcome of the spend analysis up to the end of December 2010 is as follows:
    November 2007 Forecast spend to end December 2010 = £5,466 million
    Actual spend to end December 2010 = £4,730 million

Savings

A total of over £780 million in savings has been achieved by the Olympic Delivery Authority (ODA) since the November 2007 baseline was agreed, including £33 million in the last quarter.

The majority of these savings have been achieved on Structures, Bridges and Highways, Logistics, Security, Transport, Enabling Works, IBC/MPC and savings from inflation. Most have been used to offset increases across the programme which has meant lower levels of contingency have been utilised.

Park operations

As reported since the February 2010 Annual Report, the ODA will take on additional responsibilities for the operation of the Olympic Park and its venues and facilities between 2011 and the handover to legacy owners by 2014. This includes facilities management, logistics and access arrangements and security, which protects the assets and supports their use through the test events period and the Games until handover to a successor body.

In February 2010 the ODA estimated that the additional cost of this work would be up to £160 million depending on the finalisation of scope, delivery approach, procurement and other factors. A business case has now been agreed and the additional budget for this work has been finalised at £158 million.

It has now been agreed that LOCOG are best placed to carry out some elements of this work as they scale-up and move onto the Olympic Park during 2011–12. Therefore £67 million of the funding for this additional scope will be transferred to LOCOG. The remaining £91 million is allocated to the ODA, of which £57 million is allocated to this quarter and £34 million has already been allocated in previous quarters.

As anticipated since February 2010, the ODA has also reallocated £105 million from its Programme Contingency to Park-wide Operations – a move which does not affect the ODA's overall AFC.

Contingency under current arrangements

During the last quarter, a total of £304 million of contingency was released, the majority of which reflects the finalisation of the budget for Park Operations, including the funding transferred to LOCOG.

Also included in that figure is: £47 million of contingency to cover the increase in the VAT rate from January 2011; £11 million of contingency funding that had previously been provided for Park Operations from savings achieved by the ODA, which has now been reallocated; and £17 million for anticipated additional costs at the shooting venue at the Royal Artillery Barracks in Woolwich and for Games-time training venues.

As at the end of December 2010, the gross allocation of contingency was £1.133 billion (£1,066 million to the ODA and £67 million to LOCOG), leaving a total balance of £839 million before the revised contingency arrangements apply from April 2011.

Contingency arrangements from April 2011

As announced in November 2010, from April 2011 as part of the Spending Review settlement, the total funding package for the Games will be reconfigured as set out in Table 1, with £587 million of the £9.298 billion funding package being held as an Olympic contingency for cross-programme

(Continued)

(Continued)

issues, including any material change in security circumstances. This cross-programme contingency will be separate from the Programme Contingency that forms part of the ODA's budget.

All contingency will continue to be strictly controlled and will only be released to meet costs that are essential and for the delivery of the Games, where they cannot be reasonably met from existing budgets.

Source: Government Olympic Executive, 2010 [online]

Further reading

Brearley, R. and Myers, S. (1999) *Principles of Corporate Finance*, 6th edn. Maidenhead: McGraw-Hill.

CAROL website for European, UK and Asian financial reports. Available at: www.carol.co.uk

Dyson, J.R. (2010) *Accounting for Non-Accounting Students*, 8th edn. London, Pitman.

Fowler, F.J. (2002) *Survey Research Methods*. London: Sage.

Glautier, M. and Underdown, B. (2001) *Accounting Theory and Practice*, 7th edn. Harlow: Financial Times Press/Prentice Hall.

Journal of the British Accounting Review

Kotas, R. (1999) *Management Accounting for Hospitality and Tourism*, 3rd edn. London: International Thomson Business Press.

Weetman, P. (2010) *Financial and Management Accounting: An Introduction*, 5th edn. Harlow: Financial Times Press/Prentice Hall.

Wood, F. (2005) *Business Accounting 1*, 8th edn. London: Pitman.

Costing, Pricing and Capital in the Events Industry

In this chapter you will cover:

- classification of costs;
- traditional cost accounting concepts;
- marginal costing;
- absorption costing;
- contract costing;
- the structure of a contract;
- break-even analysis;
- the role of capital investment decisions;
- investment appraisal methods used in businesses;
- summary;
- discussion questions;
- case studies;
- further reading.

This chapter will examine the accounting methods a company uses for its internal reporting and decision-making, in order to give events managers sufficient financial knowledge to manage the company. One of the most important aspects of management accounting is to provide the managers and board of directors of companies with information related to its costing. The reason why costing information is important is that it helps managers to understand and know what selling price would lead to a profit. The chapter will also explore the relationship between profit and investment expressed through a measure referred to as capital investment appraisal. Capital investment appraisal methods consider the rate of return, and they therefore overcome the main weakness of cost-oriented methods by focusing on profit and taking account of the investment necessary to generate that profit.

Classification of costs

Management accounting is a management information system for analysing past, present and future data for decision making. Cost accounting is defined by the Chartered Institute of Management Accountants (CIMA) as

> that part of management accounting which establishes budgets and standard costs and actual costs of operations, processes, departments or products and the analysis of variances profitability or dual use of funds. (Association of Accounting Technicians, 1990: 3)

Traditionally, the elements of costing for events organisations are classified as shown in Figure 6.1.

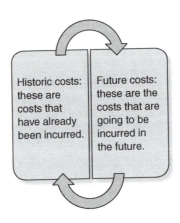

| Historic costs: these are costs that have already been incurred. | Future costs: these are the costs that are going to be incurred in the future. |

Figure 6.1   Traditional costing concept for events

The organisation incurs a number of different costs when it produces products or in carrying out a service. Under the cost accounting system these costs need to be split in various ways. One way is to split them into fixed costs and variable costs as highlighted in Figure 6.2.

Fixed costs

Fixed costs are not related to products or services. These costs are totally independent of company's output. Fixed costs have to be paid out by the company regardless of whether the company has produced any activity or not. Fixed costs remain fixed for a period and are unaffected by the increases or decreases

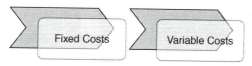

Figure 6.2   Fixed and variable costs

in the level of activity produced by the company. Fixed costs only change with the time span; as the span increases, the fixed costs increase too. By keeping fixed costs under control, the business can enjoy a very healthy profit and achieve successful development in the future. Figure 6.3 below demonstrates the fixed cost classification.

The most common fixed costs include the following:

- business rates paid to local authority;
- interest paid on bank loans;
- rent paid for the use of buildings or venues;
- staff costs for a permanent member of staff;
- company liability insurance.

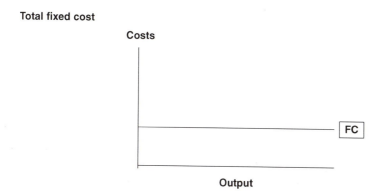

Figure 6.3   Fixed cost classification

Variable costs

Variable costs depend on the level of production or service being provided. Variable costs change with the level of activity being carried out by the organisation, and so they will change with the size and type of event. Variable costs are hard to control and are determined by the level of activity being produced or sold. By controlling the variable costs the organisation can create more effective and efficient products or services. It is important for event organisations to bear in mind the larger the event or festival, the larger will be the variable costs to control. Figure 6.4 below demonstrates the variable cost classification.

The most common variable costs include the following:

- hiring of venue;
- printing of marketing material;
- advertising;
- guest speakers;
- weekly wages paid to the staff working on the event;
- gas and electricity bills.

Total variable cost

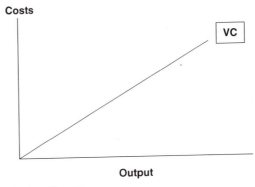

Figure 6.4   Variable cost classification

Managers need to bear one important element in mind regarding fixed and variable costs. The clear difference between fixed and variable costs lies in whether the amount of costs incurred will rise as the level of activity increases during the period of the event, or whether the costs remain the same during the event, regardless of the level of activity.

Traditional cost accounting concepts

It is important for managers to analyse and classify costs according to the purpose for which each cost is being used. The following are the most common cost concepts the management accountant and costing managers are concerned with:

1   Total cost: the sum of all items of expense which have been incurred in the process of the event or festival or in providing services to customers.

2   Standard cost: the target or budgeted cost predetermined by the management or business prior to starting the event. The standard cost is estimated by management in advance and then it is compared to the actual results incurred during the event or activity.

3   Marginal cost: determined by the level of activity, the fixed cost under this concept is considered separately.

4   Direct cost: the cost which is directly related to the specific event or service. The direct cost is easily traceable within the event cost. For example, direct costs would include staff working on the event, security, equipment hiring and advertising for the event.

5   Indirect cost: the opposite of direct costs, indirect expenses cannot be traced to the finished product or event. These are costs which are incurred in the business or on the event from its start to its finish. This may include office expenses which are not related to the event. For example, salaries of company directors, rent, rates, and insurance for the whole year cannot be directly related to one particular event.

6   Functional cost: the cost which relates to a specific event or festival. It is the cost that is attached to an area of operations in a business. This could be security, administrative, marketing, personnel and development costs.

7   Controllable and uncontrollable costs: this accounting method provides management with clear guidelines in advance as to which costs can be controllable and which uncontrollable costs are unachievable by management action.

8   Incremental cost: this is incurred only when the individual event or project is undertaken. The incremental costs include both additional fixed costs and variable costs arising from the individual event or festival, besides standard costs that are already being incurred by the business.

Marginal costing

In the marginal costing concept, only variable costs are charged as the cost of sales and contribution is being calculated by accountants. They ignore fixed costs and overheads. Under marginal costing, fixed costs are treated as period cost and fully charged to the period in which they are incurred. CIMA defines marginal costing as:

> [a] principle whereby variable costs are charged to cost units and fixed cost attributable to the relevant periods is written off in full against the contribution for that period. (Association of Accounting Technicians,1990: 221)

It is impossible to calculate marginal costing without working out contribution. The contribution is the difference between the revenue achieved during the event and the marginal cost of the event.

Contribution per event ticket can be defined as: Selling price less Variable costs. Total contribution can be calculated by businesses as shown in Figure 6.5.

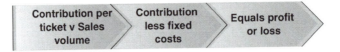

Figure 6.5   Contribution formula

Tables 6.1 and 6.2 below look at operating statements set out in a marginal costing format. Notting Hill Carnival and Leeds Film Festival host

Table 6.1   Notting Hill Carnival operating statement, marginal costing format

					Volume	Per ticket	Total
Sales					10000	£50	£500,000
Variable costs					10000	£30	£300,000
Contribution per ticket					**10000**	**£20**	**£200,000**
Fixed costs							£75,000
Profit and loss							**£125,000**
Notting Hill Carnival's break-even point						£75,000	
						£20	3750

Table 6.2   Leeds Film Festival operating statement, marginal costing format

					Volume	Per ticket	Total
Sales					100	£30	£3,000
Variable costs					100	£20	£2,000
Contribution per ticket					100	**£10**	£1,000
Fixed costs							£600
Profit and loss							**£400**
Leeds Film Festival's break-even point						£600	
						£10	60

annual events in London and Leeds, which each have variable costs and fixed costs.

Marginal costing is a management accounting system for business managers to analyse the company's individual costs. It distinguishes between fixed costs and variable costs and can be compared to the absorption costing method.

The advantages of using a marginal costing by accountants and business managers for pricing the product or service are as follows:

- Marginal costing is simple to understand compared to absorption costing.

- It provides information for managers and boards of directors for short-term decision making.

- It helps the businesses to focus on achieving break-even point.

- It calculates the difference between sales volume and variable costs.

- It helps managers to avoid having to make different allocations for fixed and variable costs.

- Fixed costs are charged fully to the accounting period in which they have been incurred.

- Under marginal costing, by not charging fixed overheads to the cost of the production or event, varying of charges per ticket is avoided.

- Marginal costing also eliminates large balances overdue in the overhead control account and provides greater flexibility for management to control the overheads.

However, there are disadvantages of using marginal costing methods:

- Under the marginal costing method it is difficult for management to raise prices for event ticketing, if the contribution per ticket is set too low at the start of the event.

- Marginal costing can cause a high risk for management when setting the ticket prices, because it may not recover the company's fixed costs set at the beginning.

- If contribution is set very low at the start, it can cause businesses to make major losses at the end of the event.

- The division of costs into fixed and variable is difficult to understand and sometimes does provide misleading impressions of results to management.

- The marginal costing concept does take into account that stock and works in progress are understated. By not including the fixed costs in the actual event or service it can affect the organisation's profit.

Absorption costing

Absorption costing is the opposite of marginal costing. Under absorption costing full cost is passed on to the event or service. It does not disregard the fixed cost from an individual event or service. In absorption costing, the fixed cost is included in the pricing of the event or service; under marginal costing the event or service is valued at the variable cost only.

The prime difference between marginal costing and absorption costing is that under absorption costing all costs incurred during the event are allocated to particular costing areas, for example, direct costs, indirect costs, semi-variable costs and semi-fixed costs, etc. In addition, absorption costing allocates all indirect costs more accurately to the specific cost area where the cost was incurred during the event or service.

For example, let's look at the operating statements again, this time set out in an absorption costing format (see Tables 6.3 and 6.4).

The advantages of using an absorption costing for pricing the event or service are as follows:

- Under absorption costing the fixed production costs for events are incurred in order to make an output, therefore it is fair to charge all output with a share of costs that have been incurred during the event production process.

- Absorption costing is the technique which helps management to take into consideration all the costs that have been incurred during the production of an event or service, regardless of its nature. Particularly, it takes into account fixed costs, where marginal costing techniques ignore the fixed costs involved for each event or product.

Table 6.3   Notting Hill Carnival operating statement, absorption costing format

Notting Hill Carnival produced 10700 tickets for the event.							
Direct production cost £18 per ticket							
Direct labour £12 per ticket							
Fixed costs are £75000 a month £7 per ticket							
Sales are 10000 tickets at £50 per ticket							
						Per Ticket	Total
Sales						£50	£500,000
Cost of Sales:							
Direct production cost						£18	£180,000
Direct labour						£12	£120,000
Overheads						£7	£70,000
Total cost of sales						£37	£370,000
Profit and loss						£13	£130,000

Table 6.4   Leeds Film Festival operating statement, absorption costing format

Leeds Film Festival produced 120 tickets for the event.								Per Ticket	Total
Direct production cost £10 per ticket									
Direct labour £10 per ticket									
Fixed costs are £600 a month £5 per ticket									
Sales are 100 tickets at £30 per ticket									
Sales								£30	£3,000
Cost of Sales:									
Direct production cost								£10	£1,000
Direct labour								£10	£1,000
Overheads								£5	£600
Total cost of sales								£25	£2,600
Profit and loss								£5	£400

Disadvantages of using the absorption costing method:

- The fixed cost is carried over to the subsequent accounting period under the absorption costing technique.

- The absorption costing is dependent on the levels of output of the business, which vary from one accounting period to another.

- This practice does not provide clear and effective cost per unit prices, because it depends on the existence of fixed-cost overheads, which could not be related to the same period.

Contract costing

Contract costing is the name given to job costing where contracts are to be carried out at a sophisticated level between the supplier and the customer. The company draws up a formal contract for each large piece of work that is undertaken.

Contract costing provides the company with an up-to-date picture of expenditure and revenue associated with specific and large-scale contracts or projects. The majority of contracts are carried out away from the company's head office, therefore it is important for organisations to keep separate records for each individual contract which has been agreed. From the accounting point of view, each contract or project is regarded as a separate unit or product. Large contracts may take a long time to complete, and the time period for large-scale contracts is hard to predict at the initial stage. The contracts may even be spread over two or more accounting periods. However, problems may arise within contract costing in the following areas:

1 Adding overheads.

2 Identifying direct costs.

3 Dividing the profit between different accounting periods.

4 Difficulties of cost control.

5 Identifying indirect costs.

Therefore, it is important to have some clear guidelines in place, and to make sure that standard documents are used by the management to record the costs of each contract. In addition, very specific rules are laid out by the Companies Act 1985 for disclosing long-term contracts in a company's financial accounts. These rules need to be followed for internal management accounting purposes by the management.

The structure of a contract

A standard contract should cover the following areas:

- the period of the contract;
- the specification of the contract;
- the location of the work of contract;
- the agreed price for the contract;
- the end product of the contract;
- the agreed date for the contract to finish.

Once the structure of the contract has been agreed by both the parties, it is important to work out the total cost for the contract. This can be done in three different ways:

1 Total cost for the project.

2 Pricing based on stages of the contract.

3 Time scales for the contract.

The central focus for the costing is to bridge the gap between customer and supplier by providing an up-to-date financial picture of the contract at each stage to both parties. In addition, the contract costing brings together both the financial accounting functions and the operational activities of the business, by anticipating any potential problems and taking action to rectify the situation.

Contract costing is the main accounting method used by events and festivals organisers to bid for large-scale events or to subcontract the work out to individual clients. This method was used, for example, for bids for the Commonwealth Games, the FIFA World Cup, the Olympic Games, and also for large music festivals.

Break-even analysis

Break-even analysis is one of the most common techniques used by management accountants. Under this technique the costs are categorised into fixed and variable costs. The break-even analysis technique does not compare the total fixed and variable costs with sales values or revenue. Instead, it looks at points at which neither profit nor loss occurs, that is, it analyses the point at which sales revenue covers all expenses. At this stage no profit is being made by the festival organisers, but loss will begin to show as soon as the sales revenue begins to fall below the break-even point. Break-even analysis provides clear and very effective information to management about expected future costs and sales revenue for decision-making processes. This technique is used by management accountants to help managers to plan the budgets for future activities.

The break-even point can be calculated arithmetically by managers or budget planners by using the formula which takes the number of tickets that need to be sold in order to break-even compared to total costs, then divides it by the contribution per unit (see Figure 6.6).

However, break-even points can also be calculated by representing figures as a graph. Let's look at a worked example (see Table 6.5 and Figure 6.7).

The various cost levels of activity are shown on the same chart as the sales revenue, variable costs and fixed costs. The festival fixed costs and variable costs make up the total costs (the straight line parallel with the X axis). The sales revenue appears on the straight line through the origin of the graph. The graph below indicates the break-even point at the intersection of the revenue and total costs lines.

The role of capital investment decisions

Capital investment appraisals relate to the future and look at the ways in which organisations can make a strategic financial decision on whether to

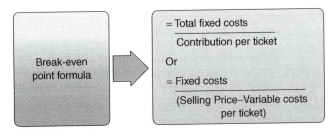

Figure 6.6 Break-even analysis point

Table 6.5 A graphical approach to break-even

Graphical approach to break-even

Real Festivals Limited sell events tickets at £100 each. They pay the festival organisers' company £60 for each ticket.

Office and admin costs are £4000 however many are sold.

With only a little thought we can produce a table like this:

	Quantity sold	
	0	200
Sales (£)	0	20000
Variable costs	0	12000
Fixed costs	4000	4000
Total costs	4000	16000

The next step is to produce a chart from the figures in this table (see Figure 6.5)

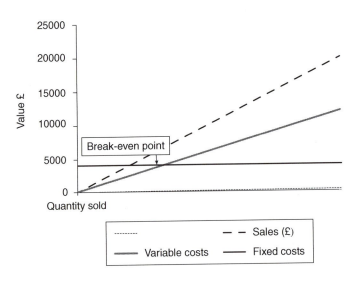

Figure 6.7 Break-even festival ticket sales

invest in or decline to take part in the project. It also provides an organisation with the opportunity to choose between a number of different projects which are available to invest in. Capital investment appraisal techniques are used by accountants to analyse and collect the information for senior managers to make better decisions.

Event organisations operate in a dynamic environment and must gain competitive advantage over their competitors through continual improvement. The development of large-scale events will require investments of capital expenditure to meet the demand. The amount of money can vary between businesses, for example it may be thousands of pounds for a small event organisation or millions of pounds for a large-scale event organisation, but the amount is usually substantial relative to the size of the organisation. This factor dictates that decisions on capital investment should be thoroughly explored and all options and consequences clarified.

Drury (2007) states that once the organisation has committed to the investment, the decision is often irreversible, increasing the risk for the organisation and putting a greater emphasis on the need for extensive analysis prior to the decision being made.

Investments usually involve the allocation or reallocation of resources to a project or product which will benefit the organisation. This could involve replacing or updating equipment to improve efficiency, expanding the existing organisation through office space or resources, or establishing a new area of business to gain market share. If capital resources are restricted, this results in strategic business units (SBUs) within the company bidding against one another to have their proposal accepted. A successful proposal will gain not only investment and development of that SBU, but will lengthen its product life within the organisation. In addition, capital investment decisions cover a wide range of projects to produce cash flow for years. For example, the main type of projects may include:

- research and development projects;
- replacement of existing assets;
- expansion of existing services and products;
- new services and products;
- property;
- large advertising campaigns;
- social and welfare programmes.

Figure 6.8 shows the four methods which are used by senior management in the events industry. Each method will be discussed and simple examples provided of how to work out the calculations and apply them to your own organisation.

Payback period

This is a simple method of calculating how long it will take before the cash inflows from an investment are equal to the sum of any costs incurred, including the initial capital investment. This is the most tried and trusted method among managers and financial accountants. The payback method refers to initial investment in the project and provides analysis to the management team as to what date the investment will start to make a profit. Projects which meet the payback within the target period are accepted.

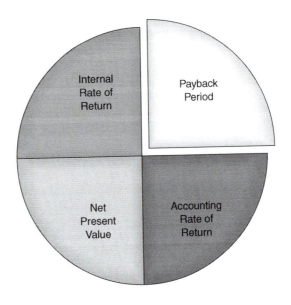

Figure 6.8   Capital investment techniques

The payback period is calculated by dividing the total initial investment by the expected annual inflow. For example, if a company invested £100,000 and expected to have an annual income of £25,000, then £100,000 divided by £25,000 would give a payback period of four years.

However, if the cash inflow varies per year, as is likely due to demand, then the payback period is calculated using a cumulative total of cash inflows (as shown in Table 6.6). The initial investment is shown as a negative and when the cumulative total turns positive the payback period is reached. This

Table 6.6   Payback period calculation

Year		Project A		Project B	
Cumulative Year		Annual	Cumulative	Annual	Cumulative
0	Cost	(100,000)	−100,000	(100,000)	−100,000
1	Cash inflow	24,000	−76,000	18,000	−82,000
2	Cash inflow	18,000	−58,000	26,000	−56,000
3	Cash inflow	21,000	−37,000	40,000	−16,000
4	Cash inflow	16,000	−21,000	14,000	−2,000
5	Cash inflow	16,000	−5,000	16,000	14,000
6	Cash inflow	25,000	20,000	11,000	25,000
		20,000		25,000	

Project A: 5 + $\frac{5,000}{25,000}$ years = 5.2 years*

Project B: 3 + $\frac{22,000}{24,000}$ years = 4.1 years*

often occurs part way through a year but the rounded estimations shown in Table 6.6 are acceptable, due to the uncertainty attached to the prediction of future income.

Table 6.6 indicates calculated payback period, describing how many years it will take to recover the original investment outlay from the cash flows which result from an investment project.

The application of payback period method in Table 6.6 favours the acceptance of project B, as the initial cost would be paid back in less time. However, this method also reflects that the total profit gained by project A is lower than project B.

Advantages and disadvantages of payback period

Advantages

- It is a popular method compared to others, due to its simplicity.
- Managers favour this method, it is easy to understand and calculate.
- This method is more objectively based; it uses projected cash flows rather than projected accounting profit.
- It favours fast-return projects and reduces time-related risks for the organisation.
- It saves management time otherwise spent in calculating forecasted cash flows for the whole of a project or event.

Disadvantages

- The payback period does not take into account the time value of money.

- Under the payback period rule, if the two projects or events are similar, the project or event which has the shorter time period will be considered.

- It ignores the end values of the project and wealth maximisation.

- It presents the problem of ambiguity: at what point do you start counting the cash flows?

Accounting rate of return

The accounting rate of return (ARR) can be defined as the ratio of average profits of the initial capital invested. The average rate of return also expresses the profit which has been generated from a project as a percentage, after taking away depreciation. There is no clear definition for ARR and different authors provide different definitions of profits and capital cost.

ARR is also known as 'return on capital employed' (ROCE), or 'return on investment'. These terms can be defined differently, causing confusion.

Pike and Neale (2006) define ROCE as indicating an organisation's efficiency in generating profits from an 'asset base'. ROCE is concerned with the comparison of profitability and capital employed within a single year. This is likely to fluctuate, increasing in profitability as the project becomes established. On the other hand, ARR finds the 'average rate of return', or annual percentage of profit, over the entire life of the project.

In Table 6.7, Proposal B has better ARR value than proposal A, so would be the preferred investment. However, proposal B has a higher cash flow in the first three years so would benefit the investor if they have high liabilities as they could be paid back more rapidly.

The ARR technique has no concept of the lifespan of the project or its size. If project B was extended into year seven, yielding a profit of £1,000, this would make the profit seem more attractive. However, the ARR would then decline from 8.33 per cent to 7.42 per cent as it is the average over seven years as opposed to six years. ARR also ignores the timing of cash flows as it works out the average profit per year even though the large returns may only occur in the latter stages of the project's life.

The previous examples use the average investment for the proposal but an alternative ARR technique is:

$$\text{ARR (total investment)} = \frac{\text{Average annual profit}}{\text{Initial capital invested}} \times 100$$

Table 6.7   Accounting rate of return

	Project A	Project B
Accounting profit = ($\sum$ inflows) – initial investment	= £120,000 – £100,000 = £20,000	= £125,000 – £100,000 = £25,000
Average annual profit = accounting profit ÷ n years	= £20,000 ÷ 6 = £3,333	= £25,000 ÷ 6 = £4,167
Average investment = (initial asset value + closing asset value) ÷ 2	= (£100,000 + £0) ÷ 2 = £50,000	= (£100,000 + £0) ÷ 2 = £50,000
ARR (average investment) = Average annual profit × 100 Average investment	= £3,333 × 100 £50,000 = 6.67%	= £4,167 × 100 £50,000 = 8.33%

Both are acceptable methods and give appropriate results when applied correctly. Confusion can be caused, however, if the same equation is not applied routinely and to all proposals, as the result from each produces wide variations and could lead to a wrong investment decision.

Drury (2004) states that the ARR method is inappropriate as it is based on profits instead of cash flows; profits are not equal to cash flows because financial accounting profit measurement is based on the 'accrual concept'.

Advantages and disadvantages of accounting rate of return

Advantages

- It is easy to understand and calculate.
- It is a popular method due to its simplicity.
- Accounting rate of return is simple for managers and business planners to understand, because it is expressed in percentage terms.

Disadvantages

- It ignores the time value of the money.
- It ignores the timings of inflows and outflows of cash generated from the project.
- There is no standard concept of calculating accounting rate of return.
- It uses the concept of accounting profit; profit can be very subjective and is not appropriate for capital investment decision making, because cash is generated by the project.
- It does not help managers to make investment decisions, because it does not give very clear and definitive answers.

Discounted cash flow methods

Discounted cash flow (DCF) can be worked out by the following equation:

$$PV = \frac{FV}{(1+r)^n}$$

PV: Present Value of a cash flow

FV: Future Value of a cash flow

r: The required rate of return/ interest rate

n: The number of years until the cash flow takes place

For example, Project A receives £21,000 in year 4 of the investment, if this had a required rate of return of 5% then actual value would be:

$$\frac{25,000}{(1 + 0.10)^4} = £20,575$$

These manual calculations can become lengthy if the investment lasts for a number of years, so discount tables containing annuity factors are produced by HM Treasury in *The Green Book* to simplify the method.

For the previous example, using this table and cross-referencing three years with a discount rate of 10% gives the following equation:

$$£25,000 \times 0.823^* = £20,575$$

(*The Green Book* shows the discount rate for 4 years at 5% is 0.823)

This published discount rate contains a small margin of error due to rounding but makes the DCF method of appraisal a lot more accessible to non-accountants. However, it is advised that a declining long-term discount rate should be used for investments over thirty years due to uncertainty about the future. These long-term discount rates are shown in *The Green Book*. A higher percentage can also be used when calculating high-risk investments to give a more cautious present value.

The two main techniques within the discounted cash flow group are: net present value and internal rate of return.

Net present value

The net present value (NPV) appraisal method utilises discounted cash flow to estimate the current total value of future inflows compared with the initial investment. If, when the total cash inflow at present value is subtracted from the total cash outflow at present value, the grand total is negative, then the investment should not be made; but if it is positive, the organisation should accept the proposal.

NPV explains whether the capital would be worth more if invested for several years, or whether it would be worth more lent into the capital market. Theoretically, this means if the NPV was zero then the investor should be indifferent.

This concept of present value clearly helps the company to assess the wealth of a project at the initial stage, by using NPV technique to look at cash flows expected in future years. The value of money varies over time and between different nations. This happens due to changes in interest rates and inflation. It is important to understand the concept that the current value of £1 will not be the same in future years. It is important to work out how much present capital will be worth in the future. NPV ignores any depreciation as the full cost of the asset is treated as the initial investment, so it would mean 'double-counting' the cost.

The formula for calculating NPV is:

$$NPV = \frac{FV1}{1+r} + \frac{FV2}{(1+r)^2} + \frac{FV3}{(1+r)^3} + \ldots\ldots + \frac{FVn}{(1+r)^n} - I$$

NPV: Net present value

FV: Future value of cash flow

r: The required rate of return/interest rate

n: The number of years until the cash flow takes place

I: Initial investment

By applying the discount factor of 4 per cent to project A and B, both have positive NPVs so should be accepted. When compared with a higher discount rate of 10 per cent, as shown in Table 6.8, project A remains acceptable yet

Table 6.8   Net present value with a 4 per cent discount rate factor

Year		Amount	Discount Factor 4%	Present Value	Amount	Discount Factor 3.5%	Present Value
0	Cost	−80,000	1	−80,000	−80,000	1	−80,000
1	Cash inflow	20,000	0.962	19,240	19,000	0.962	18,278
2	Cash inflow	19,000	0.925	17,575	15,000	0.925	13,875
3	Cash inflow	20,500	0.889	18,225	36,000	0.889	32,004
4	Cash inflow	14,000	0.855	11,970	16,000	0.855	13,680
5	Cash inflow	12,000	0.822	9,864	12,000	0.822	9,864
6	Cash inflow	27,000	0.79	21,330	8,000	0.79	6,320
				NPV = 18,204			NPV = 14,021

Table 6.9   Net present value with a 10 per cent discount rate factor

Year		Project A			Project B		
		Amount	Discount Factor 10%	Present Value	Amount	Discount Factor 10%	Present Value
0	Cost	(100,000)	1	(100,000)	(100,000)	1	(100,000)
1	Cash inflow	28,000	0.9091	25,455	21,000	0.9091	19,091
2	Cash inflow	23,000	0.8264	19,007	28,000	0.8264	23,139
3	Cash inflow	20,000	0.7513	15,026	38,000	0.7513	28,549
4	Cash inflow	18,000	0.683	12,294	15,000	0.683	10,245
5	Cash inflow	18,000	0.6209	11,176	9,000	0.6209	5,588
6	Cash inflow	35,000	0.5645	19,758	9,000	0.5645	5,081
				NPV = 2,716			NPV = −8,307

project B makes a loss. The NPV for project A, using a discount rate of 10 per cent from *The Green Book* is shown in Table 6.9. The ARR method suggested that project A would have a profit of £12,000 but the NPV approach shows that in reality the investment would only make a profit of £2,716.

Advantages and disadvantages of net present value

Advantages

- NPV allows management to compare and analyse a number of different projects with the same discounting factor.
- NPV considers all the cash flows which have been generated from the projects.
- NPV takes into account the time value of money.
- NPV takes into account the risk of future cash flows.
- NPV ensures that the organisation gains maximum wealth from the investment.

Disadvantages

- NPV is very complicated to calculate and understand.
- It is difficult to apply the appropriate discounting rates.
- NPV is time consuming.

NPV allows a decision-maker to compare a number of projects with the same risk factor. A negative aspect is the assumption that the cash flows occur at the end of the year, which is often false. In addition, it is difficult to say that any investment appraisal method can give a definitive decision to a decision-maker as to whether to invest in the project or not. NPV merely acts as a guide for managers to analyse the future cash flow.

Internal rate of return

The internal rate of return (IRR) is one of the most important methods in investment appraisal techniques to analyse the future cash flow of the project. In other words, it is a capital budgeting method used by companies to make financial decisions as to whether to invest in the project in the long term. IRR is used by managers to access a positive return from the investment.

IRR calculates the capital investment return on each individual project. If the project produces a positive IRR that is higher than the rate of the interest, it helps the organisation to make better decisions and to compare alternative options.

Moreover, IRR can be defined as the discount rate which gives the net present value of zero to different sets of cash flows. IRR is a method of working out the discount rate of a project. This can be used when there is a predefined discount rate and the decision-maker wishes to know if the project meets or exceeds this target.

'If the project's IRR exceeds the comparison rate (cost of capital) accept the investment; if IRR is less than the comparison rate, reject the investment.' (Brayshaw, R. et al., 1999: 63)

IRR is calculated by calculating the value of 'r' when the NPV is zero.

$$\frac{FV1}{1+r} + \frac{FV2}{(1+r)^2} + \frac{FV3}{(1+r)^3} + \ldots\ldots + \frac{FVn}{(1+r)^n} - I = 0$$

This equation can be rearranged if the project only lasts for a year, and is simple to work out:

$$\frac{FV_1 - I = 0}{1+r}$$

$$\frac{FV_1}{1+r} = I$$

$$FV_1 = I\,(1+r) = I + Ir$$

$$FV_1 - I = Ir$$

$$\frac{FV_1 - I}{I} = r$$

FV: Future value of cash flow

r: The required rate of return/interest rate

n: The number of years until the cash flow takes place

I: Initial investment

If the investment is for a period of two years, the equation can be solved using a quadratic equation. However, when an investment is for several years the equation is a lot more complicated.

$$\frac{FV1}{1+r} + \frac{FV2}{(1+r)^2} + \frac{FV3}{(1+r)^3} + \ldots\ldots + \frac{FVn}{(1+r)^n} - I = 0$$

This complex polynomial equation can be solved using computer programmes. For example Table 6.8 shows project B with a positive NPV with a discount factor of 4 per cent and Table 6.9 shows project B with a negative NPV with a discount factor of 10 per cent.

Therefore the IRR discount factor must lie between 4 per cent and 10 per cent.

$$IRR = 4\% + \left(\text{difference between the two discount rates} \times \frac{\text{positive NPV}}{\text{NPV range}}\right)$$

$$= 4\% + \left(6\% \times \frac{14{,}021}{22{,}328}\right)$$

$$= 4\% + 7.8$$

$$= 7.7\%$$

This shows that for project B to be accepted the discount rate, or rate of interest, must be below 7.7 per cent. In a stable economy this is possible, but risk factors such as reliance on demand can be used in conjunction with discount factors. IRR enables decision-makers to calculate the level of interest a project can withstand, and competing projects with the highest resilience will have greater appeal. In addition, IRR is a very difficult technique to use in the industry, due to the nature of the method and practical difficulties which are attached to this technique of investment appraisal. NPV and IRR will usually show the same result when carried out on an investment proposal, and will indicate whether it should be accepted or rejected. Unlike NPV, however, IRR calculates the average discount per year, and does not allow for different discount rates to be used in different years.

Advantages and disadvantages of internal rate of return

Advantages

- IRR uses the time value of the money.
- IRR is a break-even discount rate used by the management accountant to analyse future cash flow.
- The IRR method is more popular than the NPV method among managers.
- Compared to NPV the IRR method is easier to use and more understandable to the managers in the industry.
- IRR is a method used by firms to minimise errors in the calculations obtained by using NPV.

Disadvantages

- IRR often provides unrealistic rates of return compared to NPV.
- IRR expresses the return in percentage rather than in forms of currency.
- IRR is time consuming compared to the payback method and ARR.
- IRR ignores the scale of investment, it only takes into consideration the percentage derived from the project.

Investment appraisal methods used in businesses

Over the past two decades research has shown an increase in the use of the more sophisticated methods of investment appraisal involving discounted cash flow, NPV and IRR. However, these techniques are still less popular in smaller companies. This may be due to the companies' lack of understanding, or that smaller companies concentrate on short-term investments so do not take account of the difference in value of money.

Although the payback method ignores profits, it is still widely used in UK industry as it can be a comprehensive, simple argument used by a manager to convince others, who do not have a financial background, that a certain proposal should be accepted. This is emphasised by companies' focus on profits; projects with larger profits seem more attractive despite the decreasing value of money.

The proposed projects for investment can be independent (unrelated to the acceptance or rejection of other projects) or mutually exclusive (which precludes the acceptance of one or more alternative projects). As resources are limited, however, projects may have to be adapted as capital is shared, and this can endanger the effectiveness of that investment.

Decision-making process in investment appraisals

When any decision is made, be it large or small, it will go through a type of decision-making process. The formality and time taken to carry out this process will vary according to the implications of the decision and the investment required. For a non-biased capital investment decision a formal procedure should be adhered to and applied to each proposal to ensure the correct proposal is accepted.

Time can be a major factor in how the decision process is carried out. If a company is reactive, then they will want to reach a decision quickly to maintain competitive advantage in the dynamic environment. However, if the organisation is proactive the time period will be extended as they are predicting changes and planning for them rather than making decisions after the change has taken place. This is beneficial as they can apply a more extensive decision-making process and ensure that all proposals are considered equally and any elements of risk are considered.

Capital investment appraisal methods provide a quantitative analysis giving a firm logical basis from which a decision can be made. However, it is important to note that capital investment appraisal methods are only part of the final decision and other factors must be taken into account.

Strategic decisions are subject to external and internal influences. This makes it difficult to come to a non-biased decision but by following a routine process it is more likely that the project that holds the greatest benefits for the organisation is accepted.

The application of capital investment appraisal methods enables a company to set benchmarks and have a standard of comparison; it also helps the management to make better strategic decisions. This is due to an extensive proportion of businesses using the same investment appraisal techniques to enhance business growth and develop benchmarking tools; all of this helps businesses to compare their performance with other competitors and internal managers.

Accounting managers and experts within financial investment extensively consider this decision process; however, strategy texts put heavy emphasis on past financial analysis instead of ways to direct capital expenditure. Prior to carrying out an investment appraisal there must be a strategic need for the project, therefore strategy is interlinked with the investment at all stages of the decision-making process.

Therefore, strategic management involves making investment decisions by identifying, evaluating and selecting the projects that are likely to help the business to have greater impact and have a competitive edge. Capital investment appraisal helps the senior management to make the right decisions and these techniques have been proven successful over the years. As Idowu states:

> The question to address is whether or not the future returns will be sufficient to justify the sacrifices the investing entity would have to make. (2000, p. 1)

For this reason, strategic investment decision-making helps managers in all elements of cost benefit analysis and ensures that future capital can be raised through future returns, to invest in the business for future growth.

The time factor can be a major element for any decision-making process. In modern events management, decision-making needs to be quick in order to prevent competitors from securing market share, which results in little benefit for a business. However, if the organisation is being proactive the time period is extended and techniques like capital investment appraisal can be applied. A successful event company should have processes for both types of decision to ensure resources are allocated correctly, competitive advantage is maintained and future development projects are feasible. Capital investment appraisal can be initiated due to an environmental change or it can be used for an idea at development stage; it can therefore be either reactive or proactive. However, due to the nature of capital investments, in which a large amount of resources may be utilised and in which the cost may be recouped over several years, the organisation must go through a methodical process to ensure the correct decision is made.

The identification of an investment need by the organisation is the primary step. This is achieved through a thorough internal and external strategic analysis of the company. A company analysis is an imperative preliminary to the evaluation of investment projects as this will determine the financial and other resources available.

It is important to note that capital investment appraisal is only part of the decision-making process and other factors must be considered. These are often intangible and so are more difficult to measure.

Summary

This chapter has critically evaluated the analysis of cost accounting. Costing is a vital tool for any company, regardless of its size or business activities. The main aspects of cost accounting are to provide information which will be useful for the board of directors, managers and employees of the organisation. In reality, the majority of them are not economists or accountants. The other reason that cost accounting information is important is that it helps managers to understand and know what selling price would lead to a profit. When looking at the individual costs, it is important for the costing manager or director to analyse and classify the costs according to the purpose for which the cost will be or has been used.

Traditionally, costs are broken into direct or indirect, but there are several other ways of presenting the costs. The types of costing classification used by managers will depend on the purpose of the exercise. In addition, organisations will also use the marginal and absorption costing methods to calculate final costs. The marginal costing method only takes into account variable costing, whereas absorption costing takes into account total cost.

Another technique which has been explored in this is chapter break-even analysis. This is the most common technique used by management accountants. In this technique the costs are categorised into fixed and variable costs. Break-even analysis technique compares the total fixed and variable costs with sales values or revenue achieved, and focuses on the point at which neither profit nor loss occurs.

The developments of large-scale events will require investments of capital expenditure to meet the demand. The amount of money can vary between businesses, but because the amount can be substantial relative to the size of the organisation, all decisions on capital investment should be thoroughly explored and all options and consequences clarified.

In this chapter four traditional methods of capital investment methods have been explored. There are similarities between all four models. NPV and IRR are more sophisticated methods of investment appraisal involving detailed calculations and taking into account the time value of the money. However, these techniques are less popular in smaller companies, which may be due to the companies' lack of understanding, or that smaller companies concentrate on short-term investments so do not take into account the difference in value of money.

 ■ **Discussion questions**

Question 1

Discuss and evaluate the essential differences between marginal and absorption costing concepts.

Question 2

Explain and critically discuss why contract costing is important for events and festival organisations.

Question 3

Explain and critically evaluate the role of the following appraisal methods used in capital expenditure decision-making:

a Payback period

b Internal rate of return

c Net present value

Question 4

A company is considering two capital expenditure proposals. Both proposals are for similar products and both are expected to operate for four years. Only one proposal can be accepted.

The following information is available.

	Proposal A	Proposal B
Initial Investment	46,000	46,000
Year 1	17,000	15,000
Year 2	14,000	13,000
Year 3	24,000	15,000
Year 4	9,000	25,000
Estimated scrap value at the end of year 4	4,000	4,000

Depreciation is charged on the straight line basis.

The company estimates its cost of capital at 20 per cent per annum.

	Discount factor
Year 1	0.833
Year 2	0.694
Year 3	0.579
Year 4	0.482

i   Calculate the following for both proposals.

   a The payback period.

   b The average rate of return on initial investment.

   c Net present value.

ii Give two advantages for each of the methods of appraisal in (i) above, and state which, if any, proposal you would recommend and why.

Question 5

Define and critically evaluate the role of developing costing strategies for a new event.

Question 6

What are the advantages and disadvantages of the accounting rate of return method of investment appraisal?

CASE STUDY 1   EVENTS GLOBAL LIMITED

Events Global Limited is an events production company with many large departments that each make separate musical lighting for events. One department makes marquees. Events Global Limited is planning to invest in new machinery which will develop marquees for clients.

The following information relates to three possible capital expenditure projects.

Because of capital rationing only one project can be accepted.

		A	B	C
Initial cost		£305,000	£279,000	£195,000
Expected life		5 years	5 years	4 years
Scrap value expected		£15,000	£13,000	£11,000
Expected cash inflows		£	£	£
End year	1	120,000	123,000	50,000
	2	102,000	113,000	60,000
	3	93,500	78,000	100,000
	4	83,000	43,000	120,000
	5	89,000	62,500	0

The company estimates its cost of capital is 20 per cent and the discount factors are as follows:

Year	0	1.00
Year	1	0.83
Year	2	0.69
Year	3	0.58
Year	4	0.48
Year	5	0.40

CASE STUDY 2   CHEVIN HOUSE EVENTS

Chevin House Events, which was set up by two former Event Managers in 1990, is a well-known events management company, with a high reputation for quality. The company is based in a seventeenth-century country mansion on the outskirts of Leeds within easy reach of Leeds Bradford airport. Although Chevin House Events focuses its core business on organising conferences and corporate training courses, the directors recently decided to expand by using their exclusive historical and geographical situation. This was done by organising events that would capitalise on their unique situation (events such as music concerts, family days, historical re-enactments, trade fairs, etc). Leeds City Council has given the go-ahead for a huge expansion of the airport. With this in mind Chevin House Events has exhibited at German business fairs resulting in winning contracts with 5 German companies to hold their international conferences at Chevin House Events. This is a sound business with a good reputation and, according to its current business plan, is set to expand.

The company employs 50 full-time members of staff at its Leeds headquarters, and generally relies on casuals, agencies, and outsourcing to supply relatively low-skilled labour for its events. Some specialist functions are bought in for events. Its conference business tends to use volunteers recruited from those associations for which it regularly organises conferences. A permanent core of 100 volunteers has been recruited to staff the newer site-based activities. Permanent members of staff at HQ are: older males in their 50s in senior managerial positions; women in their 30s head up Conferences, Human Resources, and Marketing departments; men in their 30s head up the other 3 Departments; a relatively even gender mix, mostly in their 20s and 30s, of Event Managers and Event Co-ordinators; women aged 22–55 predominate in secretarial and administrative posts. Black and ethnic minority (BME) workers are employed mostly in secretarial posts although there is one long-standing male BME worker employed as an Event Co-ordinator. The volunteers are overwhelmingly white British.

Annual labour turnover: non-existent at senior management level; relatively low (5 per cent) at Head of Department level with slightly more males than females leaving; higher at about

(Continued)

(Continued)

10 per cent amongst Event Managers and Co-ordinators; highest at about 15 per cent annually amongst secretarial and administrative workers.

The company at headquarters is divided into 6 departments which operate separately from each other:

- 3 business support departments – Finance, Marketing, Human Resources; and
- 3 event specialisms – Conferences, Corporate Training, Chevin House Events.

Further reading

Alkaraan, F. and Northcott, D. (2006) 'Strategic capital investment decision making: a role for emergent analysis tool?', *The British Accounting Review*, 38(2): 149–73. London: Elsevier Ltd.

Brayshaw, R., Samuels, J. and Wilkes, M. (1999) *Financial Management and Decision Making.* London: International Thomson Business Press.

Burns, P. (2005) *Corporate Entrepreneurship.* New York: Palgrave Macmillan.

Butler, R., Davies, L., Pike, R. and Shaap, J. (1993) *Strategic Investment Decisions.* London: Routledge.

Drury, C. (2007) *Management and Cost Accounting,* 7th edn. London: Thomson Learning.

Journal of Business Finance and Accounting

Lumby, S. and Jones, C. (2000) *Investment Appraisal and Financing Decisions,* 6th edn. London: Chapman & Hall.

7 Project Management and Financing

In this chapter you will cover:

- project management within the events industry;
- the project life cycle;
- the events life cycle;
- project management tools and events;
- identifying sources of finance for events and festivals projects;
- fundraising strategies for events organisations;
- summary;
- discussion questions;
- case studies;
- further reading.

This chapter will investigate and explore the theories and practices that are associated with project management, as appropriate to the events management industry, and will also evaluate a range of techniques that are available for event managers in the context of organisational transformation and density. In addition, the chapter will look at the different sources of finance and the wide range of fundraising strategies available to events managers. This should enable events managers to understand, negotiate and make decisions regarding the financial opportunities that may be presented to them.

Project management within the events industry

Project management has been a cornerstone of all projects that have been implemented since the early days of major projects such as the construction of the Hoover Reservoir Dam and the Manhattan Project (Luecke, 2004). Today, project management is applied to all kinds of activities and even the events industry is discovering the benefits and realising the significance of project management. Over the last two decades expectations about the quality and efficiency of events have increased (GCB, 2009 [online]), and some discussion is needed as to which project management tools are most suitable to ensure the successful planning and control of events. It is questionable whether the importance of project management only grows with the complexity of an event, or whether project management offers planning and control tools which benefit the success of any kind of event, no matter what size or scale. Undoubtedly, the more complicated and long-lasting the planning of an event is, the more essential it is to introduce methods guaranteeing its progress and success.

As several leading authors such as Getz (2005) emphasise, every event has to be completed by a specific date, and its budget is limited and closely linked to its quality and performance. Organising an event can thus definitely be characterised as a project. So, we now need to investigate to what extent the application of project management can contribute to more successful events.

The project life cycle

Project management approaches generally divide the project life cycle (PLC) into a number of phases, in order to support a project's progress and success. Figure 7.1 summarises the six fundamental framework phases of the product life cycle for an event.

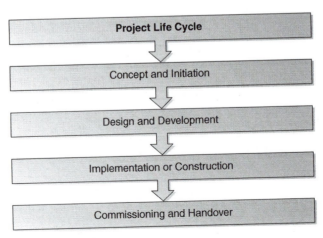

Figure 7.1   Fundamental framework of project management

To correctly apply these phases to the events industry it is necessary to define them briefly.

Concept and initiation

The two most important things to be covered in the first phase are to establish 'a need or opportunity for the product, facility or service' and to conduct a feasibility study, to assess whether or not the project is realisable.

Design and development

If it is decided that the project is to go ahead, the second phase is concerned with very important tasks. Undoubtedly, failures in this phase will have very damaging impacts on a project as discrepancies within the planning process will affect a project's quality and time management.

Implementation or construction

Afterwards, the third phase uses the outcome of the second phase to implement the project. Effective management is very important here as monitoring and controlling will be undertaken throughout this phase. The reason for this is the interdependence between the parameters time, budget and quality – any shortfall in one of these parameters will very likely endanger the whole project.

Commissioning and handover

The fourth and last phase 'confirms that the project has been implemented or built to the design' and in the end terminates the project (Burke, 2006: 28). Luecke (2004) even stresses that learning from experience is also a very important activity of this phase. For the events industry, this phase offers a great opportunity to improve on the ways things have been done for future projects, as a lot of events take place annually or might at least repeat within a few years. This short definition of the PLC reveals how dependent all these phases are on each other. Every end result of one phase determines the success and progress of the following. As events, just like any other project, are in most cases organised over a long period of time, it is best to divide the planning of an event into several phases.

The events life cycle

The PLC of events is called the events life cycle (ELC), and is considered to have five phases (as shown in Figure 7.2).

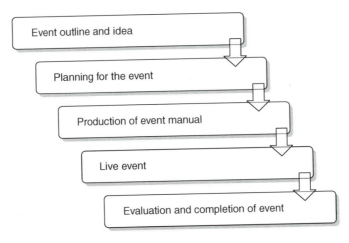

Figure 7.2   The events life cycle

The aim of the different phases is to provide clarity to the confusing tasks involved in events management. The most important action of the last phase is learning for the future. Understanding how the different phases overlap and determine each other, in the opinion of authors like Goldblatt (2002), can only be improved by experience, since the basic framework of, for example, planning, leading, designing, marketing, controlling, budgeting, staging and evaluating an event does not necessarily depend on the type of event. Remember, every event is unique and therefore sets new standards.

Event outline and idea

The outset phase of the ELC is concerned with the presentation of the project's idea, for which objectives have to be set. This phase can also include a feasibility study to determine whether the event is realisable or if the idea has to be rejected. According to this, the outset phase clearly offers decision-makers the opportunity to evaluate if any investment in a potential event should be undertaken or not.

Planning for the event

The planning phase supports event organisers with clearly structured plans and schedules if developed and implemented in the right way. Better coordination means that any risks and dangers can be identified before they cause serious damage to the successful completion of an event.

Well-conceived and detailed plans and schedules facilitate an event's planning and as there is only one opportunity to get it right, the planning phase should provide events industry professionals with security and clarity to successfully plan, control and implement an event. Thus, it is at this stage where project management tools can be deployed to contribute to an event's success.

Production of event manual

The implementation phase deals with the monitoring and controlling of all actions undertaken and furthermore offers the opportunity to compare the initially set objectives with reality. It is this phase that offers events industry professionals the opportunity to intervene and adapt plans to the objectives if they might sheer away and endanger an event's success.

Live event

In this phase the event takes place. Any last-minute difficulties have to be solved on site. If serious problems and risks have not been worked out in the planning or implementation phase there is hardly anything that can be done to bring the event to a successful termination.

This stage of the ELC clearly reveals how important it is to have a well-structured plan for an event. Dividing the organisation of an event into different phases reduces pressure, provides an overview and the opportunity to react early enough if potential threats and risks might arise.

Evaluation and completion of event

It is important for event managers to take the completion of an event very seriously, because to do so always helps the preparation for future events. Therefore, event evaluation becomes an important part of this phase, in helping to improve future performance.

The evaluation and completion of an event means more than just paying the bills and closing the venue. It is an opportunity to evaluate an event's success and to improve the way an event is planned, monitored, controlled, and brought forward. As revealed above, using the ELC to divide the organisation of an event into different phases provides clear structures and support to successfully organise an event.

Project management tools and events

What tools does project management have to offer to guarantee an event's success? Which phases can be supported and what limitations might exist which could weaken or endanger an event? Project management is built upon a diverse number of project management tools. However, some project management tools might be more efficient and beneficial for most projects than others. The choice of appropriate tools depends on the kind of project, the most common project management tools used in the events industry include:

- breakdown structures;
- the critical path method;
- the Gantt chart;
- risk management.

These are usually initiated and applied in the planning phase of an event or project, which again emphasises the fact that the planning phase is the most important one within the ELC. The following sections will look at each of these tools in more detail.

Breakdown structures

There are five tools within this category: work breakdown structure (WBS), resource breakdown structure (RBS), contract breakdown structure (CoBS), location breakdown structure (LBS), and breakdown by sub-projects. Let's look at each of these in turn.

Work breakdown structure

The WBS is a suitable tool for events to be handled and structured successfully. The graphical subdivision of an event into manageable work packages is an important feature of the WBS, which leads to benefits such as the improvement of communication or the early identification of risks and uncertainty factors. The WBS also provides clear structures which support all team members with explicit ideas about their responsibilities.

Resource breakdown structure

RBS subdivides the event in terms of the total resources available. Resources like money or manpower are issues which have to be considered and treated with greatest attention, as for example, failing to budget properly will surely endanger the successful completion of any event.

Contract breakdown structure

Contract breakdown structure (CoBS) simply helps to understand the relationships between large numbers of contractors that might exist in an event. It also facilitates the setting of priorities in favour of an event's success as some stakeholders are more or less important, and able to express their expectations on an event.

Location breakdown structure

Large-scale events often include a wide spread of work over different locations. To stay on the top of things the LBS supports a listing of the physical locations of the work.

Breakdown by sub-projects

The subdivision of a big event into several smaller sub-projects is a measure to keep lines clear and to identify risks as early as possible. The process and structure of the event is demonstrated graphically, so that every team member is able to reconstruct the project's progress.

Application to events

The various breakdown structures show that there are many ways of subdividing an event. Therefore, the choice of the right breakdown structures certainly depends on the kind of event. Events certainly feature characteristics which demand continuous monitoring and control, so breakdown structures can help to improve the way an event is handled and planned. WBS can help managers to address the fact that events are characteristically non-routine, as potential risks can be identified, eliminated or minimised before they harm an event substantially. However, breakdown structures do not provide a time flow, which in the case of events is very important as deadlines have to be met.

Critical path method

CPM helps to determine the total time needed to accomplish a project and to identify critical tasks which might endanger a project's completion on time. To make use of the CPM, the WBS has to be first transformed into a networking diagram.

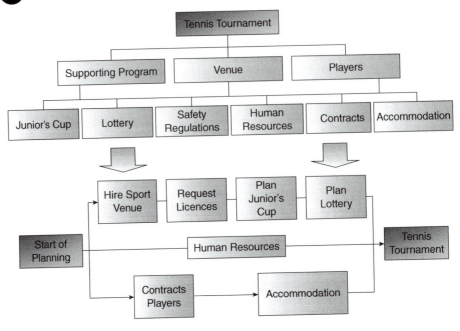

Figure 7.3   WBS into a networking diagram

In this context the networking diagram (Figure 7.3) diagram can be seen as an extension to the WBS. Although both are a graphical presentation of an event, the networking diagram is more suitable to demonstrate dependencies and to provide certain activities with time needed to accomplish them (Lock, 2001).

Activities are marked with the latest starting time (LST) and the earliest finish time (EFT) to determine whether a specific task can be delayed without delaying the project as a whole. Any delay on the critical path will delay the whole event. These are valuable features as most events are characterised by fixed end-dates, and events industry professionals are expected to meet the deadlines. Any delays might evoke costly miscalculations which in return will weaken stakeholders' satisfaction and future business.

Therefore, effective communication among all parties concerned when staging an event is important. Applying the CPM supports the early identification of critical tasks and any misunderstandings can be eliminated before any damaging consequences occur. All in all, the CPM is an indispensable tool for events planning, and in fact it becomes even more important as the complexity of an event increases. Nevertheless, WBS and CPM might also provoke some issues. Shone and Parry (2010) stress that the application of these tools might hinder team members from free thinking, collaboration and the use of their own creativity as both WBS and CPM provide 'ultimate' plans which permit no variances. Therefore, the right balance between fixed plans and room for manoeuvre has to be found to prevent the planning of an event from becoming self-driven.

The Gantt Chart

Another widely used project management tool is the Gantt chart (GC), which is named after its inventor, Henry Gantt, an American engineer and social scientist.

A definite advantage of the GC is that it puts all activities in a time-sequenced order. This helps to identify the different tasks and to decide on how long they should take, that is, when they should be completed. It assists events industry professionals in developing scenarios that might occur if critical tasks are delayed. Another very valuable characteristic of the GC is the simple act of thinking through an event which increases the awareness of all work that has to be done.

Identifying sources of finance for events and festivals projects

Events managers rarely have the pleasure and luxury of sufficient funds to sustain their current and planned business expenditure. However, they need to obtain sufficient funds in order to compete within the industry, and must therefore look to external sources of finance to meet their business obligations. Generally speaking, there are two methods of raising money for business development. Firstly, there is business equity, which covers funds invested by the owner of the business, shareholders and any other interested parties. Secondly, there is debt, which is generated by borrowing the money through banks, trade credit or leasing. The business needs to pay this money back to the lender at some point in the future.

The most common sources of business funding are outlined below.

Internal sources of finance

Personal savings

Personal savings are most commonly used to raise funds for businesses. The savings invested are normally those of the business owner, partner or shareholder and this type of financing is frequently found in small businesses or businesses which are at the early stages of their development. Investing substantial personal savings in a business can help to demonstrate commitment to external finance providers.

Sales of assets

Businesses may decide to sell some of their surplus fixed assets in order to raise funds for current or future projects; to expand the business; or to pay off debts. By selling fixed assets, the organisation can avoid borrowing, which would mean incurring interest charges and increasing the overall liability of the business.

Retained profit

Using retained profit is the simplest method by which a business can finance its own activities. The retained profit is the money which has been generated by the business in the past through net profit and which has not been spent on any other project or activity. Retained profit is typically used by businesses to help them to buy new assets or to expand in other ways. Sometimes business owners save profits to provide security during any difficult periods in the future.

External sources of finance

Bank loans

Borrowing money from the bank is the traditional method used by businesses to raise funds for their current and future projects. Interest must normally be paid on any money borrowed from the bank. There are different forms of bank loan which are available to businesses. It is generally more difficult for new businesses to secure cheaper rates of interest; these are usually only offered to reputable businesses with good track records. The business will need to repay the bank loan in regular instalments, with interest rates being set according to the Bank of England rate. Typically, banks charge businesses interest rates of at least 4 per cent above the Bank of England rate.

There is an endless range of loans on offer, to suit all types of businesses. These vary according to:

- the amount required by the business;
- the length of time over which the business will repay the loan;
- the type of interest rate being charged by the bank (e.g. fixed or variable).

Choosing the right type of interest rate is very important for the business in the long run. This can be difficult, since both fixed and variable rates have advantages and disadvantages. For example, taking out a fixed rate loan means that the company can accurately predict the size of the monthly repayments. On the other hand, repayments on a variable rate loan can fluctuate if the base rate changes in line with the Bank of England rate. In addition, the banks charge individual customers different rates, usually ranging between 3 per cent and 4.5 per cent on top of the Bank of England rate.

Overdrafts

An overdraft is the most common form of debt available to businesses in the short term. An overdraft is easy to arrange and does not have a minimum borrowing term. It is a flexible method to use in order to finance a business shortfall over a short period. The money can be drawn down by the business fairly quickly and repaid over the period agreed with the bank manager; though interest rates and ease of borrowing will depend on the state of the business and on the history of the company. If a company has no previous track record, banks will require some form of security, perhaps involving the assets of the business or the personal property of the owner. Where a business uses its assets to secure an overdraft, this clearly limits its ability to sell these assets or to use them to secure any other sources of finance. However, if the business has a good track record, an unsecured overdraft facility is easy to arrange.

One of the main advantages of this type of borrowing is that the debt can be paid off at any time without incurring a penalty. On the other hand, an overdraft is repayable on demand from the bank. Since overdrafts are given and the interest rate set according to the status of the individual account, new customers are normally charged more than long-standing customers. Overdrafts are one of the most expensive forms of finance since the interest rate is usually higher than that set for medium- and long-term borrowing and a business arrangement fee of between 1 per cent and 2.5 per cent of the agreed overdraft facility is commonly charged. It is therefore important only to use the overdraft facility for a short period of time.

Leasing

Leasing is the most common method of obtaining assets, such as backstage equipment, vehicles or computer equipment, without immediate large-scale capital expenditure by the company. Traditionally, the leasing company buys and owns the assets and claims any capital allowances due against them. A number of different types of leasing agreement exist within the market. The two most commonly used by businesses are:

- finance leases
- operating leases.

The finance lease is a form of loan repaid by the company in monthly instalments throughout and up to the end of the economic life of the product. An operating lease is an arrangement whereby the product is used by the company for less than its full economic life and the leasing company therefore takes the risk of the equipment becoming obsolete during this period. Normally, the leasing company will pay for the maintenance and insurance of the product.

The main benefit of leasing an asset is that the business does not have to pay a deposit or a large amount of money up front. This allows the finance to be spread over time in monthly or quarterly instalments that are generally fixed and means that costs can be shared with other parts of the business. This can make it much easier for small and medium-sized companies to manage their cash flow and plan their use of capital over the year.

Business angels

Business angels are individual investors who provide finance to support either the start up or further growth of businesses which can demonstrate the opportunity for good future returns. Private investors are usually individuals who are prepared to make a long-term investment of £50,000 or more in promising businesses which are at a very early stage in their development. Business angels usually select local companies or those which are of personal interest to them in which to invest. Some business angels also have specific knowledge of the business and can bring a great deal of added value.

Generally, investments by business angels take the form of share capital (as defined on page 153) in exchange for a share of the business and its future profits. It is their intention to help the business develop and they may join the board of directors in order to safeguard their investment and provide support, knowledge and guidance.

Corporate sponsorship

Corporate sponsorship is another method of finance used by events and festivals. It may take the form of cash donations, goods or services from a large corporation in return for specific opportunities to promote their business. These may include using a corporate logo on promotional materials; displaying a special corporate banner at the event or calling the event by the corporate name.

Formal stock markets

The formal stock markets method is the most efficient and proven technique used by large corporations to raise finance. Large organisations have a clear advantage over smaller ones since, once their listing has been established on the stock market, shares in the company can be bought and sold readily and thus become more stable and liquid assets. At the same time, being listed on the stock exchange provides the individual shareholders and company with better rating on the stock market.

Moreover, once the company's shares are registered and held publicly on the stock market, the stock exchange imposes conditions and rules upon the business, which the company's board of directors have a duty to follow by law.

In the UK, various types of stock market listings are available. The type of listing normally depends on the market valuation of the company being floated on the stock exchange. Figure 7.4 describes four traditional world stock markets.

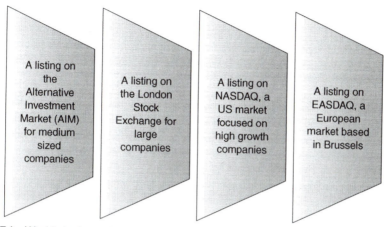

A listing on the Alternative Investment Market (AIM) for medium sized companies

A listing on the London Stock Exchange for large companies

A listing on NASDAQ, a US market focused on high growth companies

A listing on EASDAQ, a European market based in Brussels

Figure 7.4   World stock markets

Debentures

A debenture is a loan which is given to an organisation for a long period of time, by a wealthy investor. Money is lent on a secured basis and with interest rates that may be either fixed or floating. Debentures usually have a number of different conditions attached with regard to interest rates, security and, most importantly, the preferential treatment that debenture holders are given over external shareholders. The debentures are normally rolled over to future periods if the company fails to make a profit; however, even if a company makes a loss, they will still need to pay interest charges to the debenture holder.

Moreover, debenture holders have the right to receive their interest payments before any dividends or interest are paid out to external shareholders. Secured debentures are usually tied to one specific asset like a building or a particular activity, such as a special event.

Share capital

This is the simplest method by which a company can raise finance. However, this option is only open to those companies which are listed on the stock market.

This method normally involves a permanent interest-free loan, given in exchange for a part share in the ownership and profits of the business. The share capital scheme is used by investors to buy shares in individual companies through the stock market without stipulating fixed interest rates for their investment. The only payment they will get is their share of the profit, in the form of dividends, at end of the financial year.

There are a number of types of share capital in each company. The voting rights of shareholders at the end of the financial year are determined by the grade of shares that they own. The ordinary shareholders are the least powerful; whereas the preference shareholders have stronger voting rights and also receive their fixed dividend before any other dividends are paid out.

Government grants

Governments are normally very keen to provide support to businesses, both in the form of grants and through the provision of expert advice and information. It is in the public interest that new businesses are started and existing ones developed, since successful businesses provide employment and create wealth for the country by helping the economy to grow. To this end, the UK government has provided finance to companies over the last 30 years, through cash grants and other forms of direct assistance.

Government grants have been made available through a number of different initiatives. Over the last decade, the government has created Business Link to help small and medium-sized enterprises with business planning, marketing and legal advice. Government grants are always attached to a specific purpose or project and it can sometimes be difficult for small and medium-sized enterprises to meet the government's criteria. The government applies very strict terms and conditions to all its grants and if a company does not follow these they may be required to repay immediately. However, the government normally provides clear guidelines and assistance, so companies rarely break the terms and conditions.

Most government grants require businesses to match the public funds they are being awarded. It is important for a business to show that it can provide its share of the total amount before applying to the government for a grant. Businesses normally generate match funds through retained profits, owner's own funds, bank loans, or through partnership.

Fundraising strategies for events organisations

Financing can take many different forms and a mix of several approaches will increase the campaign's chances of success. There are various sources from which an organisation can seek funds to put on an event, including individual donations, grants, corporate and business donations, partnerships or sponsorship.

The majority of contributions come from individuals who believe in a project or cause. Sometimes a company may ask the relevant private, community and government foundations for a grant. Grants are donations or interest-free loans that are given to groups or projects in accordance with strict standards and procedures. In order to apply for such funds, the organisation must usually submit a formal proposal.

Corporate and business giving is the other form of fundraising. Creating a partnership with a business to receive cash, in-kind support, product donations or even employee involvement can be a smart move. Businesses of all sizes have resources to offer, if asked in a proper and timely manner. There are two main methods by which a business may donate funds: corporate underwriting is where a business provides cash to cover a specific item in the budget and corporate sponsorship involves the donation of cash, goods, or services by a corporation in exchange for specific marketing opportunities.

Direct-request campaigns are excellent strategies that can be used both to increase contributions and get the word out about the project. Recently, the trend in fundraising has changed from individual involvement to mass communication and public participation.

Successful financing requires a regular programme of communication to keep the company visible to the target audience and the potential funders. A range of media can be developed, including: news releases; television or radio advertising; e-mail newsletters; and websites. Such a marketing strategy can have long-term benefits by building a relationship with the public ('friendraising') and saving time later by educating people now about the firm and forthcoming events. A good communication strategy will help the company to focus its energy on raising money (Freedman and Feldman, 1998).

Nowadays, fundraising for events can be a worldwide process, since international mass media enables people of all ages and a wide range of groups and organisations to access both the fundraising programme and the marketing of the event. As a result of this trend, many organisations in both the profit and not-for-profit sectors are turning their attention to the fundraising event business.

Financing through sponsorship and ticketing

Sponsorship is a central source of fundraising for many large-scale events. In the last decade, sponsorship has become essential to the events industry providing the means to finance many events. In today's market sponsorship has also become an integral and recognised part of event operations, with many savvy sponsors fully exploiting the marketing opportunity, often through promotional activity, to enhance the consumer's event experience. Sponsorship managers have recognised that they need to adopt a much more hands-on approach.

Lee, Sandler and Shani, define sponsorship as:

> The provision of resources (e.g., money, people, equipment) by an organization directly to an event, cause or activity in exchange for a direct association (link) to the event, cause or activity. The providing organization can then engage in sponsorship-linked marketing to achieve either their corporate, marketing or media objectives. (1997: 161)

It is very clear that large-scale events, such as music festivals and sporting tournaments like the Olympic Games, cannot take place without the commercial support that comes from sponsorship.

Generating revenue through ticket sales

Ticket sales are one of the major revenue-generating strategies for the events organiser to adopt in the modern events market, and are the main source for income generation at events. Ticketing helps the business to overcome cash flow problems which are encountered by events. Selling tickets in advance can provide an organisation with the opportunity to raise revenue early on and potentially ease the cash flow problem in the short term. Selling tickets or charging conference fees in advance increases the opportunities for event organisations to take advantage of this method of raising funds.

Over the years, many large- and small-scale events have generated revenue by ticketing. Figure 7.5 shows the revenue generated by the corporate meetings and events market in the UK.

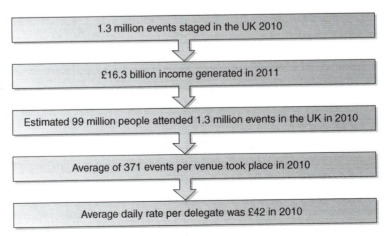

Figure 7.5   Revenue generated by the corporate meetings and events market

Source: UK Events Market Trends Survey (UKEMTS), 2011

There are a number of difficulties with the ticketing concept, particularly in setting ticket prices. The events attendees are attracted to the events for several reasons, but one of the main reasons will be the price being charged at the event. Therefore, this can cause major problems especially for the pricing strategies which are set by the events organisers to cover all costs or to break-even from the event. The dilemma for organisers is to attract the customer to the events and at the same time cover the cost. For this reason it is important for businesses to raise funds from other sources as well. Some of the common sources which can be used to raise funds are explored in the following sections.

Sales of merchandise

Brassington and Petit describe merchandise as

> [a] physical good, service, idea, person or place that is capable of offering tangible and intangible attributes that individuals or organisations regard as so necessary, worthwhile or satisfying that they are willing to exchange money, patronage or some other unit of value in order to acquire it. (cited in Doyle, 2004: 262)

Events can provide many opportunities for merchandise sales and this is yet another source of income. The most obvious use of merchandise is to generate direct income for the event through sales of programmes, for example such as at the Edinburgh Festival. Merchandise sales are particularly popular at events as it is a way of combatting their intangible nature. Another benefit of selling merchandise such as programmes is that advertising space in the programme can be sold or offered to sponsors, generating additional funds for the event organisation.

Donations

Donations are sums of money that are given to an organisation, and which do not require any privilege or service in return. In this way they must not be confused with sponsorship. Obtaining donations can also take a substantial amount of time, effort and resources. Donations often need to be requested, either from existing donors (a database of previous donors would ease the process slightly), identified targets or the general public. Charities are the normal recipients of donations (Getz, 2005), which means this method of fundraising may not be particularly useful to other types of event organisations. Edinburgh Festival, however, does list donations in the same category as sponsorship in their accounts suggesting that they do benefit from this area.

Summary

This chapter has explored the key fundamentals of project management. It has analysed the issues which events managers needs to consider in order to achieve success during events. The key tools of project management and finance can support event organisers with clearly structured plans and schedules if developed and implemented in the right way, no matter what size or scale the event happens to be.

Finance is vital to the existence of any business in the industry. In addition to bringing in money, fundraising also helps an organisation to develop relationships with the people who can support it. The basic sources of finance for any business include: personal savings; debt; grants; and earnings from business activities. Few business managers have the luxury of sufficient funds to sustain current and future planned expenditure. The approach to raising funds is not the same for each organisation, and this will vary according to the size and ownership of the business. Generally, the longer the business has been running, the easier it will be to acquire finance for it.

Businesses are funded from two main sources of finance: internal funding streams, including retained profit and the owner's own funds; and banks and other financial institutions, which are the principal source of borrowed money for businesses. These institutions apply very strict conditions before they agree to lend money to any organisation. Other approaches to borrowing include leasing, business angels, debentures and government grants.

■ Discussion questions

Question 1

Investigate and discuss the role of project management in events management.

Question 2

Describe and investigate how project management fits best into events and festivals.

Question 3

Critically evaluate how events and festivals managers develop project management into practise.

Question 4

Discuss and critically evaluate how an event organisation can implement fundraising strategies for their current and future growth and development.

Question 5

'Where (and how) will we make money in the future?'

Discuss this statement by critically evaluating the strategies that have been implemented in the hosting of major events.

Question 6

Describe and discuss how fundraising helps an organisation to develop relationships with the people who support the business.

CASE STUDY 1   CO-OPERATIVE VILLAGE EXPERIENCE 2012

Increasingly, many sponsors are aware of the benefits of supporting an event via financial assistance as a means to drive their brand to the target audience. However, many corporate organisations have taken it upon themselves to create their own experiential brand experience.

The Co-operative Bank with its history and head office in Manchester for the second year created the 'village experience' a sponsor of the Manchester Day Parade on June 8 - 10th 2012, hosted in Albert Square in front of Manchester City Town Hall. The event has a schedule to tour throughout the country attaching itself to major events. It toured between June and September, going to the Royal Highland Show after Manchester, The Royal Welsh Show with over 200,000 visitors in 2011, Bristol Balloon Fiesta which has a history dating back to 1979 and the Thames Festival London. It is obvious why the Co-operative made a strategic decision to align themselves to the type of events on offer. Three strategic reasons will be highlighted to demonstrate the method of brand alignment and positioning. First each of the events listed have a significant history in terms of event delivery over many years and therefore already has a committed target audience. Secondly, the target audience for all shows have a strong family appeal, which is at the corner stone of the cooperative brand. Lastly, the Co-operative society can drop into an existing event without undertaking a significant budget to market their concept. In following this method of dual alignment it can bring some issues that relate to the professional delivery of the existing event and thus have a negative impact on all brands attached to the various shows. In 2009 a hot air Balloon crashed into a wall in Bristol.

The Royal Highland Show is the only event with a headline sponsor in place, where there is more than one sponsor at an event and if those sponsors have a similar business profile it could

(Continued)

(Continued)

be difficult for the audience to distinguish who has exclusivity and dominance. Therefore it is essential for brands to create an experience beyond the standard branding one can see at most events.

This type of experience is not uncommon for major brands, for example Smirnoff Vodka, Adidas and many more have taken to creating the event experience and therefore have a significant amount of control over the means by which customers experience the brand. The Co-operative Bank has many facets to its business and thus requires an experience that can display and communicate to the target audience. Currently the Co-operative has six facets to their business profile which featured at all locations in 2012. The Co-operative Bank, travel, pharmacy, electrical, food and legal service. In the village branding was significant throughout with enough staff to direct participants to various activities; the purpose of the activities to create a long lasting experiential experience for customers and with that research shows a significant return on investment for the brand. Many of the activities were targeted towards children allowing the family atmosphere to take precedence. The activity that had significant coverage at the event was the kitchen demonstrations which involved members from the audience to participate and walk away with a memorable experience.

Another record charity haul by London Marathon runners. (Table 7.1)

Table 7.1   Five record years of charity fundraising

2007	£46.5 million
2008	£46.7 million
2009	£47.2 million
2010	£50.6 million
2011	£51.8 million

Source: My Next Race's marathon, www.mynextrace.com/2011/09/london-marathon-announces-impressive-charity-fund-raising-figures/

CASE STUDY 2   LONDON 2012 OLYMPIC AND PARALYMPIC GAMES

From April 2011 Government funding for the programme, excluding security which sits with the Home Office and other Government Departments, will be held by DCMS. The Greater London Authority (GLA) and the Olympic Lottery Distributor (OLD) will continue to contribute, as per the

2007 Spending Review agreement. Security funding will be provided primarily by the Home Office, based on the principle that costs lie where they fall.

The maximum contribution of the Lottery remains unchanged. However, the London Development Agency's (LDA) contribution to the Public Sector Funding Package has fallen by £300 million, as reported in July 2010, from £550 million to £250 million. Net of £27 million reduction in the overall Public Sector Funding Package the Exchequer contribution therefore increased to £6,248 million as reported in July 2010.

Under the confirmed arrangements, the interests of the Lottery under the 2007 Memorandum of Understanding between the Government and the Mayor are still protected. Meanwhile, the Memorandum is being updated as necessary to reflect the latest position as a result of the Spending Review and the transfer of land ownership from the LDA to the Olympic Park Legacy Company, which has now been completed.

The overall National Lottery contribution to the 2012 Games remains at up to £2.175 billion, including contributions of £750 million from dedicated Olympic lottery games; £340 million spending by sports lottery distributors out of their existing funds (including £290 million of support for elite and community sport); and £1.085 billion to be transferred from general lottery proceeds held in the National Lottery Distribution Fund.

Source: GOE London 2012 Olympic and Paralympic Games Annual Report 2011 www.culture. gov.uk/images/publications/DCMS_GOE_annual_report

Further reading

Berridge, G. (2006) *Event Design and Experience.* Oxford: Butterworth Heinemann.

Brearley, R. and Myers, S. (1999) *Principles of Corporate Finance*, 6th edn. Maidenhead: McGraw-Hill.

Brown, S., Blackmon, K., Cousins, P. and Maylor, H. (2001) *Operations Management: Policy, Practice and Performance Improvement.* Oxford: Butterworth Heinemann.

Burke, R. (2006) *Project Management: Planning and Control Techniques.* China: Everbest.

Getz, D. (2005) *Event Management and Event Tourism*, 2nd edn. New York: Cognizant Communication Corporation.

Glautier, M. and Underdown, B. (2001) *Accounting Theory and Practice*, 7th edn. Harlow: Financial Times Press/Prentice Hall.

German Convention Bureau (GCB) (2009) Frankfurt: GCB. www.gcb.de/pdf/Meeting_und_EventBarometer_Studie.pdf

Government Olympic Executive (2011) 'London 2012 Olympic and Paralympic Games Annual Report 2011' [online]. Available at: www.culture.gov.uk/images/publications/DCMS_GOE_annual_report

Johnston, R. and Clark, G. (2008) *Service Operations Management.* London: Prentice Hall.

Lock, D. (2001) *The Essentials of Project Management*, 2nd edn. Farnham: Gower Publishing Limited.

Luecke, R. (2004) *Managing Projects – Large and Small*. Boston, MA: Harvard Business Press.

Meredith, J.R. and Mantel, S. J. (2009) *Project Management: A Managerial Approach*, 7th edn. Chichester: John Wiley and Sons.

My Next Race's marathon (2011) www.mynextrace.com/2011/09/london-marathon-announces-impressive-charity-fund-raising-figures/

Shone, A. and Parry, B. (2010) *Successful Event Management: A Practical Handbook*. 3rd edn. Andover: Cengage Learning.

UK Events Market Trends Survey (UKEMTS) (2011) www.meetingsreview.com/news/view/64560

8 Legal, Security, Safety and Risk Management

In this chapter you will cover:

- legal structure for limited companies;
- public liability and health and safety requirements for events organisers;
- the Licensing Act and permits for events/festivals;
- the Consumer Protection Act 1987;
- the Private Security Industry Act;
- contracts and their legal complexity;
- risk management;
- level of risk management changes;
- summary;
- discussion questions;
- case studies;
- further reading.

The purpose of this chapter is to give an overview of the standard legal requirements for event organisers. The chapter will present in the first instance a number of pieces of statutory legislation under UK jurisdiction. While the context of the chapter is the UK legal framework, the European market and the wider international business environment will be introduced in order to alleviate any confusion on operating procedures and legal jurisdiction. The chapter will also show that the legal structure for limited companies and the Licensing Act have significant financial impact on international revenue.

Legal structure for limited companies

To operate as an event organiser within the UK, no formal registration or licence is required at present. Each individual business should look at registering the business through Companies House, under the Companies Act 2006. This particular legislation has direct lineage from the 1989 Company Act. The 2006 Act covers limited and unlimited companies, private and public companies, companies limited by guarantee and having share capital, and community interest companies. The most popular type of company registered by event organisers in the UK is a company limited by guarantee.

Formal registration of a limited company can be done by an individual but a chartered accountant is required in submitting year-end business accounts to Companies House under company law. A company with share capital may require the assistance of a solicitor who specialises in company law in drafting articles for shareholders.

Registering a company not only gives direct access to particular operating company procedures but also allows your organisation to have credible prominence in its particular market. From a consumer perspective, it demonstrates legitimacy and accountability for consumers. Investors will be given protection under company law along with shareholders. Outside contractual relationships with suppliers, agencies, partners and other companies also operate according to a legal framework to establish sustainable working relationships; and, when operating outside of the UK, organisations have legal protection for employees and contractual disputes. Company annual accounts can be accessed via the gate keeper (Companies House) for a nominal fee by any interested individual or organisation. This information could help in determining the type of business relationship that could be entered into by any outside organisation.

Once your company is registered with Companies House there are a number of legal requirements to undertake before the business can become operational. It is not a legal requirement to register your business with the Health and Safety Executive (HSE) or the local authority. However, various types of organisations may require permits or certificates from the local authority, including the Health and Safety Executive, before commencing business operation. From an event perspective, it is advisable to register with the local authority through the HSE website. Where your event has a construction build as part of the event planning process it is necessary to complete a HSE 'Notification of Construction Project Form' which is available from the HSE website. As many outdoor event organisers work with suppliers that have health and safety regulations attached to their particular type of activities, it is advisable to access the HSE website and make sure that you have the necessary information that will enable you to interpret, manage and sign off, where required to do so, work carried out by outsourced companies.

Public liability and health and safety requirements for events organisers

The Health and Safety at Work Act 1974

The Health and Safety at Work Act 1974 states that if you have five or more employees, a health and safety policy must be in operation, with a clear health and safety certificate displayed at a location visible to all employees. The employer, apart from developing a health and safety policy, is also required to undertake a full risk assessment of the working environment for all employees. Consideration should also be given to employees where working conditions may endanger their health. Therefore, an occupational risk assessment could be part of the health and safety policy. The Health and Safety at Work Act 1974 has direct links with UK and European regulations (and this area will be highlighted later in the chapter). Once a full health and safety policy has been developed and introduced to all employees and a risk assessment has been carried out the organisation can seek insurance.

Employers' liability insurance

Under the Employers' Liability Compulsory Insurance Act 1969 employers' liability insurance is compulsory for all businesses with employees. If your organisation has employees based abroad they must also be covered by your company insurance. Company insurance should be obtained from authorised insurers. The Financial Services Authority (FSA) maintains a register of authorised insurers in the UK. Your insurance company may undertake their own risk assessment or ask for a copy of yours. This will determine the level of insurance liability required for any particular type of business. In general, the minimum level of insurance cover for any UK business is £5–10 million. However, insurance liability may fluctuate on the type of business, the type of event planned, and how it is managed and delivered. If your organisation has witnessed previous insurance claims, this may affect the overall premium. Therefore, it is the requirement of each organisation to seek further advice and guidance from their insurer on each event if not identified in the organisation's insurance policy.

As a company, you have a legal responsibility to inform employees and to display a copy of the employee's liability insurance certificate. This certificate must be displayed where all employees have access to it. There are some exemptions to employer's liability and one area is where family members are employed.

For further advice on employee insurance, contact a registered insurance company regulated by the FSA. Further advice can be obtained from the HSE and the Department for Work and Pensions. Self-employed people, regardless of the contractual status between the organisation and the person(s) can also be covered by your employees' liability insurance. This would depend upon the nature and relationship of control that you have with that individual whilst they are working for your organisation. Within the event industry there are a number of activities by outside individuals or an employee of your organisation that may require an individual insurance cover to support their type of work. 'Riggers' by definition undertake very high risk intensive operational procedures, therefore it is essential to ensure that any rigger has full insurance cover that allows them to carry out their type of work. In some local authorities within the UK it is a requirement to obtain a permit before a rigger can undertake their activities.

Public liability insurance

Public liability insurance is different and voluntary; it covers against claims made by the general public. As an event company that may manage, produce and deliver events of many types to the general public, it will be essential for you to obtain public liability insurance. This particular cover is mandatory by many local authorities when applying for a temporary entertainment licence for outdoor events open to paying or non-paying members of the general public.

Data protection

Many organisations today have a legal remit to register their company with the Information Commission under The Data Protection Act 1998. The Data Protection Act was brought into existence to address a number of issues; one of the principles was to protect individual personal data held by organisations. It also has a remit to allow individuals to have access to their personal data. The Information Commission can provide training courses to staff and assist organisations in developing data protection handbooks and policy.

Where an event company stores personal data on employees and in particular where a Criminal Records Bureau (CRB) clearance is required the Information Commission must be notified. A vast majority of event companies actively partake in direct marketing, but personal information held by a company can only be used once authorisation has been obtained from each individual. Websites that have an option to collect personal data must protect the individual rights.

Employment contracts

Once an organisation has undertaken these operational and legal requirements, it is then the responsibility of the company to issue employment contracts that reflect and meet UK and European legislation on employment rights. Minimum wage, human rights, disability discrimination, equality and race discrimination should be given full representation when selecting employees and staff development/training and awareness. The Disability Discrimination Act, as written and made law in 1995, has had a far-reaching impact on event organisers and venue operators. Local authorities, educational establishments and their facilities had specific inclusion and amendments were made to the 1995 Act for the 2006 edition. Therefore, we now operate within a climate whereby all individuals within society should be given equal chance without prejudice or discrimination.

The 2006 Act states that an organisation must show 'reasonable' effort to meet the needs of everyone in society. Entertainment venues, exhibition halls, conference venues and outdoor spaces have a legal remit to demonstrate that they are working to meet the requirements within the amended Act.

Legal requirements for UK venues

Apart from the initial start up and legal requirements to that process, the business may need ongoing legislative adherence. This, however, will be reflected in the type of events developed and delivered by the organisation and while the organisation expands. To illustrate this, let's have a look in detail at the legal requirements event organisers need to be aware of when negotiating with a venue.

When an event company negotiates with a venue for the purpose of delivering an event, there are a number of regulations and statutory requirements to meet before final contractual negotiation. It is the responsibility of a representative from the event company to ascertain if the venue has all the legal requirements and documentation necessary. A fire certificate will be granted by the local fire service which allows the venue to be used as directed under the fire certificate. This document may have representations as to the use of materials within the venue such as curtains or drapes, and the requirement of those materials to meet British Standards on fire retardant capability. A separate fire certificate will also be required for any material that is brought into the venue that does not meet British Standards on fire retardant materials. Under new legislation it is also the requirement for a venue to undertake an independent fire risk assessment. The venue must present a recent and full risk assessment, including a health and safety policy indicating a full emergency and evacuation procedure. An entertainment licence denoting the type of entertainment granted by the local authority with any restrictions associated to the said licence should also be presented along with a full alcohol licence and associated certificate which should be displayed at the venue. The event company has a legal responsibility to relay the health and safety and evacuation procedures presented by the venue to all employees of the event company, suppliers or outside contractual staff working within the venue. This information must be presented and understood prior to any outside employee commencing work within the venue.

To accompany any health and safety policy an event organiser must have an understanding of the different type of regulations that will have an impact on the event, staff and venue. The most common group of regulations are known as the 'six pack' and were developed by the EU and represented into UK law. The 'six pack' includes: management of health and safety at work regulations; manual handling operations regulations; display screen equipment (DSE) regulations; workplace (health, safety and welfare) regulations; provision and use of work equipment regulations; and personal protective equipment (PPE) regulations. (For more information on these, go to the Unite union website, at www.unitetheunion.org/member_services/health_and_safety/health_and_safety_resources/the_six_pack.aspx)

Food hygiene

Food hygiene falls under local authority control; the Environmental Health Department within the local authority will take full responsibility for the issuing of a Food Hygiene Certificate along with the procedures for checking that each establishment or temporary catering unit(s) continually meets the legal requirements. The Environmental Health Department is also responsible for issuing closure notices and legal proceedings for contravention of food hygiene. Further advice and guidance can also be obtained from the HSE or your local authority.

The Licensing Act and permits for events/festivals

The 2003 Licensing Act was introduced to modernise licensing arrangements, to meet European standards and to improve control over places of entertainment. It also extends to temporary entertainment licences along with the sale of alcohol. The 2003 Act only has jurisdiction for England and Wales. In Scotland, entertainment is governed by the Civic Government (Scotland) Act 1982. All applications for entertainment, renewals, and alcohol licences in Scotland must be sent to the local authority. For entertainment in Scotland where no fee is charged for admittance an entertainment licence is not required.

In England and Wales the entertainment requirements were previously regulated by the 1982 Miscellaneous Provision Act. The changes brought in by the 2003 Act were broad and far reaching. Administratively, the 2003 Licensing Act gave control of licensing and its administration to the Licensing Department within each local authority. The Licensing Act requires the issuing of two licences, one for the event or building, and a separate and national licence for the individual. A personal licence is valid for ten years and can be obtained from the local authority where the person resides and may only be renewed at the end of the ten-year period by the same local authority. This enables a person to sell or authorise the sale of alcohol. A premise licence under the new Act is valid indefinitely unless it is revoked, or the business decides not to continue in its current form issued under licence. If the building requires a change then a change of use can be applied for via the local authority.

Figure 8.1 shows the four clear objectives within the Act that must be translated into practical operational duties for licensed purveyors of alcohol.

If the local authority or appointed agencies charged with upholding these four objectives obtain evidence that a breach of these objectives has occurred, they have the power to enforce a closure of an establishment or use the full legal due process available.

Alongside that, each holder of an entertainment licence must produce what is known as an 'operational document'. This document should set out the full operational duties related to the event or venue, including substantial

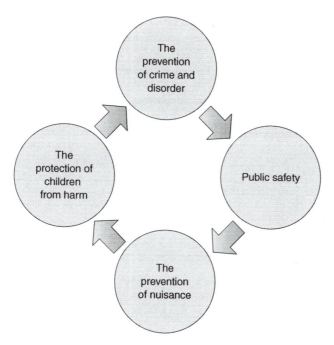

Figure 8.1 Licensing Act objectives

information about all regulatory documents that support any particular activity. The document should act as a footprint for any agency, authority or contracted service and above-line management charged with the responsibility for a particular aspect of the event or building. The document should also clearly specify the roles and responsibilities for all parties involved.

Apart from the legislative requirements, each local authority has the opportunity to produce supporting conditions for obtaining and operating a temporary licence within that local authority's jurisdiction. The condition to the licence, as it is usually known within the industry, carries enormous influence on a successful application and continued use of the licence for the agreed length of time. The cost incurred by an organisation for obtaining an entertainment licence will be an internal matter for each organisation. However, each local authority will charge an administration fee for processing an application and each licence will relate to a sliding scale in relation to costs and customer capacity. Another aspect to the application process is the requirement for the organisation applying for the licence to place an advertisement in the classified section in the local newspaper for a period of one month.

The full legislation as passed by Parliament can be accessed at the Department of Culture Media and Sport's website (see www.culture.gov.uk). Not only is it possible to read the full document but a copy of the guidance document associated to the Act is also available.

As part of the event planning experience an organisation may wish to obtain a road closure around a building or site which may be in a residential, commercial or non-residential location. For this to take place an organisation or representative must make an enquiry to the local police in the area where the event is taking place. The permit for a temporary road closure order is regulated under the Town Police Clauses Act 1847, section 21. This type of arrangement is generally enforced at outdoor music festivals and the application should be completed early within the event planning process. Where disruption to daily traffic flow is considered to be outside of the norm for that location, consideration to public safety and emergency vehicle access must take precedence.

Entertainment licences

When there is a need to obtain an entertainment licence or temporary entertainment licence with singing and dancing attached to that licence, further legal consideration must be given if live or pre-recorded music is part of the event or played within the facility.

Under the Copyright, Designs and Patent Act 1988, events or venues that provide live music performances to the public, will be subject to the requirements of the Act to safeguard writers and music publishers, therefore an application to the Performing Rights Society (PRS) must be made for a music licence. PRS has over forty different tariffs for premises and types of performance. Where your venue or event would like to play original sound recorded music it is essential that a PPL Licence is obtained. Phonographic Performance Ltd represents the record companies who own the copyright in the recording.

Alongside PRS and PPL there is also the Mechanical Copyright Protection Society (MCPS). The main remit of MCPS is to collect and distribute royalties. These charges will be levied against anyone who wishes to record music for TV, radio, websites, feature films and so on.

The guiding principle for the use of live or prerecorded music at events and venues, where the music will be played to the public, is that there is a cost/tariff and a licence will be required.

As previously mentioned in relation to other legislation presented thus far there are also exemptions regarding the obtaining of the music licence. For further clarification and guidance it is essential to access the MCPS-PRS alliance website for a more conclusive discussion (see www.prsformusic.com).

A Video Performance Ltd (VPL) licence is needed for the public playing of music videos. VPL represent the companies who own the 'film' copyright in the music videos themselves. Contact VPL through PRS and MCPS.

UK trade mark registration

This next section is not considered to be a legal requirement under UK law. However, to protect the individual identity and integrity of your company, product or event and securing the merchandising rights, this particular process would be a necessary requirement. The UK Patent Office is where all UK Trade Mark registrations can be applied for and held. This process protects the intellectual design/logo given to a company or event. Registering that design, name, logo or sound gives your organisation immediate protection once the application has been successful. Upon receiving notification from the Trade Mark Office it is a simple process of filling in a form supplied by the Patent Office at no cost for the merchandising rights.

Obtaining the merchandising rights and the permission to produce items under the licence could potentially be a huge income generator for many events as they increase in size, frequency and become successful. This also allows the company to sell the merchandising licence to an agency for the production of official merchandise. With that licence an organisation can also franchise the event/product to any interested party. Further Trade Mark registration must be taken out in each separate country if you consider that your event has an international reach, audience profile and locations.

Registering with the Patent Office is not a straightforward process and can take up to a year to receive a final application notification. Therefore, a considerable amount of pre-planning in the formulation of a business idea to the intended market is essential.

Not all applications sent to the Patent Office will be approved. There are some names and designs that will never be approved, such as the five rings for the Olympic Games. It is necessary to contact the office with any queries concerning trade mark registration. Trade mark registration is held within the UK office and has a renewal date every ten years. (Glastonbury Festival was first registered in 1999 at the UK Patent Office, although the festival has been in existence since 1970. It was first licensed as an entertainment event in 1983.) Upon receiving full trade mark registration there is no legal requirement to place the official trade mark logo on company letter-headed paper or on any communication materials, products or associated items that fall under trade mark law.

The Consumer Protection Act 1987

Consumer protection is essentially a piece of government legislation that protects the rights of consumers. Trading Standards are the authority that will act on behalf of consumers when rights have been infringed. Alongside Trading Standards the Financial Services Authority also has powers where unfair terms are represented in consumer contracts.

Within the event management selection process for contractors and sub-contractors who supply goods and services at events, it is imperative that all contractors have all the legal requirements associated with their particular task or activity before commencing work or supplying a service. If products that are supplied, sold or used at events are found to be defective when in contact with the consumer, product liability under the Consumer Protection Act will enable a person to request a refund or exchange of goods and in some cases sue for damages. The latter will only come into play when that consumer's rights cannot be resolved via the normal channels of negotiation.

Where an event organiser imports goods into the UK, including from the EU, the liability will rest with the first importer. By placing a company name on a product that gives the impression to the consumer that they are the producer, liability will rest with the company.

Within this type of business arrangement it is vital that the event organiser takes great care in selecting products and service providers who meet all the regulatory requirements under health and safety law including all regulations which support their particular activity. This will ensure that consumer rights are protected at events, thus avoiding refunds, defective products/services or possible litigation.

The Private Security Industry Act

The Private Security Industry Act arrived on the statute book in 2001. The implementation of this legislation came in 2006–7. The main purpose of this legislation was to remove/clean up rogue security companies that permeate the leisure and entertainment industry. It also has a further remit linked to seven other licensed activities.

When an organisation approaches a venue for the purpose of securing it for an event, it is vital to ascertain the legality of security personnel employed at the venue. A full list of all licensed security operatives should be logged with the local authority. The local police may also have a copy of the same information. If security checks on operatives are required by event organisers, the local police can assist with that process. It is an offence to employ security staff who have not been trained, security checked by the police or who do not have the appropriate licence to carry out a task. Stewards at events, as titled, have a different operational remit and do not require a licence to undertake their designated operational task. Working within a football stadium, stewards will fall under different licensing requirements and certificates and must be regulated accordingly. The sports industry made a representation for exclusion from the Private Security Industry Act. This was presented on the basis that sporting facilities are governed by the Safety of Sports Grounds Act 1975 and the Fire Safety of Places of Sport Act 1987. The representation was not successful and sporting events remained bound by the requirements of the Act. Adequate training must be given to stewards before permitting them to work.

Contracts and their legal complexity

Another area within the event management remit is to construct contracts which are fair in their content and expected outcomes. Contracts by definition are legally binding agreements. Event managers will ultimately encounter many types of contracts while producing events. Apart from the terms and conditions attached to a contract a service agreement could also be an addition. It is necessary to have an understanding of the different levels of contracts available.

Contracts are formulated to ensure that all parties' rights and obligations are not infringed, and if breached they can be enforced in the civil courts usually with an outcome of an award of compensation to the aggrieved party. Contracts can be divided into two main areas: contract by deed, or simple contracts. The majority of event managers will work under simple contracts. These can be written, delivered orally or they may be implied by general conduct.

Another way of classifying contracts is according to whether they are 'bilateral' or 'unilateral'. Bilateral contracts generally relate to the sale of goods. Unilateral contracts are those where an offer is made not to a specific party but to anybody. A unilateral contract can be best explained using the example of a competition online, which is promoted to anyone via a website. When producing an event and working with suppliers a simple contract under a bilateral agreement will be the standard approach. An event provider promises to make available access and an area on the site for the safe erection of a temporary structure. The company supplying the temporary structure promises to deliver and erect the structure within an agreed time frame that meets all the regulatory requirements, and that it will be handed over upon completion of all safety checks.

It has become standard practice for many event providers and suppliers to include a service agreement alongside the contract. The two may have similarities but are different in the general style and approach. As stated earlier, the contract is written from the point of view upholding rights and obligations. A service agreement is written from the point of view of the delivery of the service or product and all its associated complexities. The service agreement gives a greater understanding as to the level of service or product that could be supplied and its intended use throughout its lifetime at the event. Therefore, any disagreements as to service delivery or product defects have a direct point of reference.

In the early negotiation stage there are a number of elements to consider before signing a contract. A legally binding contract must possess an offer, an acceptance of that offer and due consideration to promise to give or do something for the other. The parties must be legally capable of entering into the contract, and knowingly have the capability to carry out the given task or provide the product/service. Consent to deliver on the contractual promise must be without duress or undue influence. On the whole, contracts should be drafted by a legal representative with sufficient knowledge of this particular area of the law. Mistakes in contracts, even down to the name of the individual, can render a contract void.

A breach of contract can occur if one party does not uphold their side of the bargain as set out in the original contract. A claim for unfair contract terms may come about at a later stage if one party believes that the original draft had expectations far beyond the scope that was required.

Risk management

Risk management, when aligned to health and safety, can be viewed as a mechanism to apply further control and disseminate responsibility beyond the scope of the event. The wider ramifications regarding risk can be seen when assessing an organisation and the risk associated to the stability of the enterprise. Enterprise risk management addresses risks born out of everyday operational activities. Risk management shouldn't be confused with risk assessment as the two have specific theoretical principles and protocols; risk management has a broader remit. Event agencies have consistently requested the services of companies to undertake a risk assessment; however, risk management is something which many companies overlook. PricewaterhouseCoopers have written extensively on this subject and published a number of guidance documents that cover financial and operational risk, in response to the recent meltdown of the global financial banking sector in 2008, and its subsequent impact on many commercial organisations. This guidance allows an organisation to apply a 10-point plan as taken from the paper titled, 'Facilitating sound practice in risk management'.

The nature of a commercial business ultimately places an entity in a risk averse environment. The potential survival of that entity is to strike a balance between risk and return for the entire organisation. The Enterprise Risk Management Framework appoints a person to manage risk within the organisation; this is done by applying some basic rules.

It is necessary to establish what a health and safety policy is, why it is required and in what ways it may achieve organisational security. A health and safety policy is a document that sets out a clear working standard for all employees while working on behalf of the company. This document should be written with direct reference to the Health and Safety at Work Act 1974. The policy will set out the company's duty to ensure that individuals can carry out their tasks in a safe environment. It will also specify what is acceptable for employees while undertaking their particular tasks. Acceptable measures may also state that training is to be provided before undertaking a particular activity or using equipment. The document may also be supported with guidance notes that will give an employee further information before commencing a task. The policy can also make reference to regulations to which an employee must adhere to 'when completing a task' or 'before commencing a task'. If protective clothing is essential to a particular activity, it should be indicated in the document as a necessity. An event manager should request a copy of the Health and Safety Policy from any organisation that has a contractual agreement with the event company, and where employees are working under the direction of a contractor or subcontractor. By neglecting the health and safety policy an organisation can jeopardise the employee's safety, human rights plus the organisation's ability to remain operational and within the law.

The term 'risk assessment' in today's business climate has more than one function when aligned to an organisation. It can protect the employees from harm; it can also ensure customers can use a product/service with a minimum level of risk to themselves and others. The risk assessment concerns the long-term stability of the organisation to carry out its daily business and remain competitive. For all events it is essential that the principles of risk assessment are applied. Figure 8.2 highlights the key Health and Safety Executive (HSE) guiding principles.

The five steps to risk assessment as presented by the HSE should become the cornerstone of any organisation/event internally and externally. Due to an increase in the litigation culture within the UK over recent years, due diligence on behalf of the organisation to protect employees is considered paramount for many organisations. Where risk assessment is not given sufficient attention, it could have a negative effect on the organisation's insurance liability for employees and customers.

Risk assessment is a legal requirement in the UK in order to execute the 'duty of care' under the Health and Safety at Work Act 1974. It is essential that a risk assessment is fully presented as part of the production process. The risk assessment should be formulated in line with the five key steps set out above. Upon identifying the activity or task, it is necessary to look at ways of limiting exposure, removing, controlling or transferring risk. In some documents you may also find a risk rating, which gives further information about the likelihood of the risk accruing and the impact of the risks to person(s) in the immediate vicinity.

By using a matrix, as shown in Figure 8.3, a priority can be established. If likelihood is high, and impact is low, it is a medium risk. On the other hand if impact is high, and likelihood is low, it is high priority. A remote chance of a catastrophe warrants more attention than a high chance of a hiccup.

The risk matrix is a more scientific method of developing risk control measures. The document should also highlight who has responsibility for

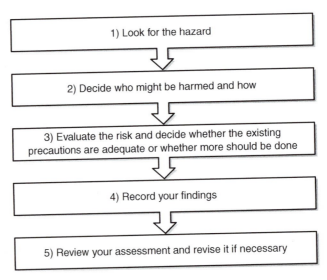

Figure 8.2 Health and Safety Executive principles

monitoring and controlling the identified risks. For more complicated or hazardous production processes, further guidance will be required by the production company and associated agencies.

Risk assessment is not to be confused with risk management, which should be regarded as any other management function. It should involve the identification, analysis and control of risk which has the potential to threaten assets or enterprise. The risk assessment document, when presented to the venue, local authority and event manager allows all parties to engage in reasonable discourse to manage production safely. Within the production process it is also essential to document injuries that have occurred as a direct result of any of the risks identified in the risk assessment or the management thereof. The documentation should be in a separate incident log book. With regard to regulation, registration and inspection, event companies with ten or more employees must register their business with the Social Security Claims Payment Regulation 1987. When a business falls under leisure and entertainment, inspection for health and safety/risk assessment will be with the local authority. However, the HSE have the authority to inspect fair grounds. On the other hand, local authority events can be inspected by the HSE if they are on local authority land. If the event business has fewer than five employees there is no requirement under health and safety to produce a health and safety policy for employees.

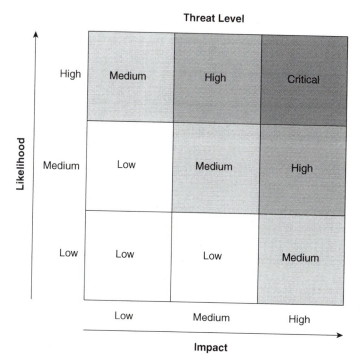

Figure 8.3   Risk matrix

To improve operational and production procedures, many production companies also include a method statement in the information they give to event managers. This document aims to ensure the duty of care for employees, as do the risk documents. A method statement is given to production personnel before they undertake a specific task to ensure they are fully aware of what to do and how to do it. It sets out a step-by-step approach to completing a task, especially where equipment is required to complete a task or is the finished article. If technical illustrations are required, they must also accompany the method statement. A method statement should either be prepared by the production manager or should accompany equipment. It should also identify all of the tools and supplementary equipment to be used in order to create a safe working environment in which to carry out work. There should be a method statement for each task or operation and copies should be held at the production office on site. This document can also create a safe working environment and safeguard against insurance claims from employees.

Where an organiser has arranged for an event to be held, whether inside a venue or outdoors, it is essential to obtain electrical test certificates for electrical equipment powered by fuel or mains supply. This process of testing electrical equipment is called a PAT test (portable appliance testing) and it must be signed off by a qualified electrical engineer. It will give a degree of assurance to organisers, venue managers, licensing authorities and production personnel that electrical equipment has been tested and is ready for use. It is not possible to provide complete assurance of the electrical stability of the tested equipment but this process will go some way to ensuring that equipment is safe for its intended use.

From the information presented so far, we can see the fundamental relationship between the production company and the event organiser. Each has a direct responsibility to ensure that individual employees are given sufficient training, information, certification, method statement, insurance, permits, protective clothing and well-maintained equipment to carry out each specific task. All this information should be written down and given to the event organiser and associated agencies (which may include fire, local authority and police) in the pre-planning stage of the event.

When the production company is satisfied with the information they have in turn obtained from the site/venue, an official undertaking to commence work will be ordered. Any sub-contracted companies must also adhere to all the agreed documentation and regulations, in accordance with the requirements set out for the main contractor for whom they are working. If sub-contracted production companies have any special requirements, all new details must be forwarded to the relevant organisation.

Level of risk management changes

With the best planning, risks get identified as early as possible. The level of risk and opportunity to minimise a risk is very high at the start of an event (outset and planning phase), whereas the amount at stake is very low. This relation changes dramatically while the event proceeds, as decisions are made and plans get implemented. Therefore, the opportunity to minimise a risk declines, whereas the amount at stake continuously increases as resources are invested to accomplish the event.

The case study below, of the Bupa Great Manchester Run, further provides example of how risk management can be assessed at large-scale events.

CASE STUDY   THE BUPA GREAT MANCHESTER RUN

The case study provides an overview of the application and results of the risk and vulnerability analysis for a 10km mass participation run in Manchester.

Event format

The Bupa Great Manchester Run is a 10km mass participation road race, and takes place within Manchester City Centre in the month of May on Sunday each year. The event is a joint promotion by Nova Limited and Manchester City Council, and includes:

- an elite wheelchair race;
- an elite women's race;
- a mass race for an anticipated field of up to 29,600 male and female runners aged over 15.

Each of the events listed above fall directly under the Nova organisation but has in place their own management team, planning meetings and own event safety plans, plus risk assessment.

On site, the event liaison team (ELT) will coordinate all necessary contractors during the crucial stage of the event set up. The official start of the race will see operational control fall under the Event Director and Course Director; their task is multifaceted but they have overarching operational decision-making powers for the event. Further delegated responsibility is given to competent individuals who manage the start and finish of the race. To assist with the management and control, the ELT is located in a building to record and respond to all communication

(Continued)

(Continued)

traffic and decisions made throughout the event with the assistance of the police, senior medical and senior security operatives. This dual approach to operational management and control, as seen from the on-site Event Director and ELT, has immediacy due to the fast nature of the event and response time that is required to assist and deal with any given situation. This approach to managing the event helps to reduce and respond to known and unknown risk. This particular race has five waves of runners, designed to help reduce congestion on the course, and to allow more space for the competitors during assembly. Each wave also leaves at different times, with the elite runners given first position. Runners are placed into waves by a colour-coded system from information submitted in their online application, based on the time that each individual considered appropriate to finish the race. Before each wave arrives at the start line they have the opportunity to participate in an orchestrated warm-up session. This ultimately helps to reduce the risk for runners who may require medical attention due to muscle spasms during the race and after. To assist in the recording of times for runners, they each have an individual electronic chip which records when they start and complete the race.

For a run of this magnitude, there are many risks for the organisation to contend with. The one which has the highest priority while the run is under way, is the risk that a runner that may collapse due to over exertion, a pre-existing medical condition, or due to warm or cold weather conditions. Therefore, it is paramount that the course is set up to mitigate those potential risks.

The 10km race is designed with clear markers for all runners. Showers and water stations are strategically located along the race route, as are medical professionals with full resuscitation equipment (water is positioned and available at the start, finish and at 5km). When runners approach the last two kilometres a fast response medical team are on alert, as past experience has shown that runners tend to require medical assistance during the latter stage of the race.

The risk assessment with the event manual identifies 126 individual risks associated with the event, of which only twenty are marked as medium risk, with the further 106 ranked as low risk. The fact that the event has a significant amount of risk ranked as low is testament to the planning, organisational management and competence of the individuals in the above-line management associated with the event. An event of this nature is susceptible to extreme weather conditions which ultimately increases the risk in a number of specific categories. In particular, there is a risk of dehydration through prolonged and intense heat or humid weather. Extreme rain and cold can decrease the core body temperature dramatically. Where cold weather is a problem, aluminium space blankets are given out before and after the race to keep the core body temperature at a stable level. There is also an area for 7,000 people to have shelter if required.

In situations where the weather can have a dramatic influence on the event, spectators and more importantly the participants, the event will bring forward a wet weather or hot weather plan. If this has been activated, medium-level risk may be ranked as high if not dealt with immediately, thus having a dramatic effect on a person's chance of survival. It is not a common situation within events of this nature; however, participants have died when participating in road races due to a number of issues such as pre-existing complication, insufficient medical service/equipment available to assist at any given time. As noted above, through the process of delivering events of this nature, event organisers know that participants have a higher propensity to require medical attention in the last few miles before the finish line. In their online application, participants are asked to inform the event company of any pre-existing medical condition; this is an optional request but may be essential if medical assistance is required. If that medical information is forthcoming the event company can identify that person by a colour code given to them with their official number. If that person requires any medical attention their information is available via a database shared with the medical operatives and above-line management team (ELT). Individual official race numbers given to each participant are directly linked to all data supplied by that person. Therefore, to pass on an official number to another participant not only increases the potential confusion and risk if a person requires medical attention.

In order to reduce the risk in those areas, there are a number of protocols and secondary checks made to ensure that a person is correctly linked to a given number. Correct information connected to next of kin becomes absolutely essential in the event of a serious incident or a fatality. Figure 8.4 illustrates the start position

Figure 8.4   The start position for each colour wave

(Continued)

(Continued)

for each colour wave; they are released in a controlled manner to reduce the risk of injury to runners and to ensure spectators and TV broadcasters can locate runners by their colour code.

Figure 8.5   The Bupa Great Manchester Run route map

Figure 8.5 gives an overview of the route with a key that indicates crucial aspects of the race design for runners and spectators in the first instance. The distance markers act as sector timers for runners and give the ELT a degree of control for monitoring the times of the last runner in each wave. This route map is also available online.

Summary

This chapter has outlined many of the regulatory requirements to which event organisers must adhere. In order to keep up-to-date with changes in legislation and regulations, you should register your organisation with the HSE, via their website, which will provide you with regular updates on new legislation and regulations associated to particular activities and organisations. Apart from this there is a requirement for operational deployed staff at events to have undertaken training courses in key areas such as health and safety, demountable structures, crowd management and licensing law.

This type of approach will help to ensure that events are planned, organised and delivered within the confines of the law and operational procedures. Apart from UK legislation, there are regulations, policies, procedures and benchmark standards which you must also take into account in the international market place. Many companies within the event sector have a long history of delivering events across international boundaries. Operating outside of the UK brings with it many new challenges and obstacles. Exporting goods to another destination could render the entire operation redundant if the paperwork is inaccurate. If you have opted for a handler to collect goods on arrival and store them at a secure location, if appropriate use a reputable company that has been fully investigated.

For employees who travel, work and reside within a different international jurisdiction for a month or a year and beyond, it is essential to ensure that insurance covers their entire stay and also the activities they do while they carry out their job. If further insurance is required due to the nature of the location, political situation or potential instability, environmental or otherwise, then seek further advice from your insurance company. Most insurance companies allow for cover outside of the UK but this must be negotiated and continually risk assessed.

Operating an event business requires not only business acumen in setting up the business in the first place. It also involves knowledge of the vast number of operating policies and procedures that are necessary while delivering an event. This is even more the case when the business is supported by contractors and business partners/stakeholders. Setting the appropriate business 'tone' is essential for future growth and long-term partnership development. To develop this area of partnership in business, the Department of Trade and Industry (DTI) has been working in the business community over a number of years to pioneer this business formula.

 ■ **Discussion questions**

Question 1

Under the 2006 Company Act name three different types of companies available for registration through Companies House, and indicate which company requires the assistance of a solicitor for the administration and formal registration process.

Question 2

State which particular Licensing Act was in use in England by local authorities and event providers, prior to the 2003 Licensing Act for England.

Question 3

Outline your understanding of the two types of business cover from an insurance company, and why event companies should consider them before trading commences.

Question 4

In what way can extreme weather conditions have an effect on the operational delivery of a road race?

Question 5

In an attempt to reduce the risk to runners at a 10 kilometre run, why is it necessary to increase medical facilities and operatives in the last few miles?

Question 6

What agencies are required to reduce the risk when closing down the roads over a Saturday night/morning for a 10 kilometre run?

CASE STUDY 1   KOREAN FOOD FAIR

Anticipated crowd size: up to 20,000

Event activities

Food stalls and eating areas, information stalls, speeches and entertainment at main stage, Korean dance troupes, music groups and martial arts demonstrations, amusement rides (see program), children's stage, Hyundai car auction.

Venue description

Beamish St is the main street of Campsie. The fair was held in the area north of the station and the Anzac Mall. Anzac Mall is a paved pedestrian mall, closed to traffic. There is a variety of Korean shops which line the mall and were open during the festival. The event attracts families, with a majority of Korean visitors (over 80 per cent) and the remainder a combination of Chinese and other ethnic mixes. There is public parking in nearby streets. The venue is also readily accessible from Campsie railway station.

Existing facilities

The street litter bins (approx. 55 litre bin inside a metal frame) along Beamish Street and Anzac Mall were supplemented with 60 240 litre wheelie bins for the event.

Other relevant information

Canterbury City Council has in the past offered free cleaning and waste disposal at the Korean Food fair as the event is a council-run event. The value of labour and tipping fees is approx. £5,000. For the past 2 years, the Southern Sydney Waste Board has sponsored the festival by supplying the envirotrays and biodegradable cutlery for use by all of the food vendors via the packaging supplier D&JC Trading. A standard size envirotray was used as a unit of measurement, as all stalls were charging £5 for a selection of foods in the same tray. The food vendors are discouraged from bringing their own packaging and were not charged to use the envirotrays and corn starch sporks (combination of spoon and fork).

Source: www.environment.nsw.gov.au/resources/warr/cs_koreanfoodfair2001.pdf

CASE STUDY 2   OUTDOOR MUSIC FESTIVAL

Staff at a major music festival were exposed to very high noise levels without adequate care for their safety. This was a large music festival with more than 50,000 people present and with two major outdoor stages.
   The following problems were found:

- Security staff were less than one metre from the front of the bass speakers for the main stage.
- Food vans for the main stage were facing the stage and positioned close to the PA delays.
- There was no refuge from the noise. Sound levels in staff rest areas reached or exceeded 79 dB, and there were no quiet areas or refuges where staff were working.
- There was little or no evidence of control of the noise levels that the staff were exposed to, or limiting of the time spent in the noisy locations, or warning of the risks due to the noise.
- Hearing protection had been provided without training on its use. In some cases security staff receiving the highest exposures were choosing not to use any hearing protection.
- Hearing protection had not been considered for staff at the food outlets.

(Continued)

(Continued)

Table 8.1 below gives the daily noise exposure for workers at the festival.

Table 8.1   Daily noise exposure for workers at the festival

Job	Location	Hearing protection	LEP, d dB
Paramedic	Side of main stage	Muffs	100
First aider	Tent at side of main stage	Muffs when outside tent	97
Food service	By PA delays of main stage	None	100
Gate security	Side of main stage	None	101
Gate security	Wheelchair area for main stage	None	95
Door security	Secondary venue tent - 1	None	99
Stage security	Secondary venue tent - 1	Earplugs	108
Door security	Secondary venue tent - 2	None	103
Drummer	On stage	None	104
Bass guitarist	On stage	None	101
FoH sound engineer	Tower approx. 30 m from stage	Earplugs	99
Monitor engineer	Side of stage, behind PA	None	96

Commentary

The use of noise control and hearing protection was inadequate. Both the event organiser and the individual employers were in clear breach of the law.

Under the law employers have a duty to protect their own employees from the risks associated with high noise exposures. In addition, there is a duty to other workers who are also put at risk by their noisy activities. These duties had clearly been neglected.

Exposure needs to be reduced by means other than hearing protection as outlined in this chapter. Where a risk still remains the correct fitting and use of hearing protection needs to be enforced.

Employees have a duty to use hearing protection provided for them if their exposure is likely to exceed 85 dB.

Source: www.soundadvice.info/amplifiedlivemusic/casestudies.htm

Further reading

McKendrick, E. (2007) *Contract Law*, 7th edn. Basingstoke: Palgrave Macmillan.
Murphy, J. (2007) *Street on Torts*, 12th edn. Oxford: Oxford University Press.
Richards, P. (2007) *Law of Contract*, 8th edn. Harlow: Longman.
Silvers, J. (2008) *Risk Management for Meetings and Events*. Oxford: Butterworth Heinemann.
Tarlow, P. (2002) *Event Risk Management and Safety*. New York: Wiley.
Turner, S. (2007) *Unlocking Contract Law* (Unlocking the Law), 2nd edn. London: Hodder Arnold.
Webster, I., Leib, J. and Button, J. (2007) *The Concise Guide to Licensing*. Leicester: Matador.

Section C

Marketing and Media

9 Event Sponsorship

In this chapter you will cover:

- the role of sponsorship in the events industry;
- securing support, partnership and strategic alliance;
- major sponsorship deals;
- external influences effecting sponsorship deals;
- naming rights;
- exclusivity deals through sponsorship and ambush marketing;
- summary;
- discussion questions;
- case studies;
- further reading.

This chapter will look in detail at the process of events sponsorship, investigating the relationship between sponsors and the events industry on local, national and international levels. What are event sponsors seeking to achieve? The chapter will examine tendering and pitching ideas, and also look at the concepts of support, involvement and funding. It will outline the guiding principles for developing and presenting a sponsorship package in line with particular types of events, making clear distinctions between the various types of sponsorship levels within a sponsorship deal. The chapter will also look at the new and emerging trends in sponsorship allocation across the events sector.

The role of sponsorship in the events industry

The concept of sponsorship has been developed over the years and is now considered as a specialist area within the marketing framework. Many organisations today employ what is known as a 'sponsorship manager'. This position can either be taken up by an individual (who may also have a team of people working in support) who looks at supporting events as part of the company's strategic vision. Alternatively, organisations may employ an individual to acquire sponsorship as part of the event's financial and operational requirements.

Sponsorship comes in many forms and guises. Not all sponsorship deals look to increase market share or competitive edge for the company product or service directly. Indirectly, some companies use sponsorship to maintain a public image. An organisation may find it necessary to maintain their public image by associating their product/service with a particular event.

However, sponsorship is also applied when an organisation is faced with unacceptable/negative publicity and therefore adopts a strategy to maintain an acceptable level of public image.

Cadbury, the chocolate confectionery company, saw its milk chocolate sales slip 2.5 per cent in 2006, on the back of a salmonella scare. The recall of 1 million chocolate bars brought an estimated £30 million loss to the company. Cadbury's ten-year relationship with *Coronation Street*, a British TV series, came to an end in 2007. That relationship had achieved marked success for both organisations, as the biggest in financial contribution and the longest TV sponsorship deal in British history. We are not attempting to imply a direct cause and effect scenario here, of negative impact on a business and its decision to relinquish its sponsorship relationship with a TV series – we do not have the necessary data to make that claim. However, there is room to see a cause and effect situation between Cadbury relinquishing their deal with *Coronation Street* and a drop in sales due to bad publicity via a food scare in chocolate production. With Cadbury no longer part of the sponsorship market, the big food chains in the UK went into a bidding war for the sponsorship rights to that TV series.

Securing support, partnership and strategic alliance

Sponsorship acquisition in its true form within the event industry looks at seeking out an appropriate sponsor, or sponsors, to meet the combined strategic vision of the event and sponsoring company, and in particular where financial assistance is a necessary business requirement for the short- to long-term sustainability of the event. There are also ethical and political issues that should be taken into consideration when researching potential companies.

The combined strategic vision is the level of knowledge and work required in developing a business partnership. This will be looked at in more detail throughout the chapter. Within this model the chapter will demonstrate how to match appropriate sponsorship companies to particular types of event.

When undertaking any type of sponsorship research it is a good idea to obtain historical data on the type of events sponsored by the company you are looking at. You may not be able to see the exact level of financial assistance that the company has given to events overall. However, there are some routes you can use to find detailed financial information. Company accounts, if published via Companies House, could give you some statistical data to begin with. Internal/external newsletters may also carry this information. Articles on the company website, along with local or regional newspapers, where the event has a public image, civic pride or has newsworthy appeal, could contain useful information. Industry-related trade magazines may also give a specific viewpoint. These are just some of the areas where information can be obtained and may help to build a picture of the type of events and financial assistance given as part of the sponsorship deal. This invaluable information when analysed could demonstrate a profile of events sponsored, frequency of sponsorship deals, and long-term sponsorship deals including financial assistance. Where the event is attached to local authority resources or a local authority event, information on that type of event should be in the public domain. The Freedom of Information Act 2000 places requirements on public authorities relating to the disclosure of information in order to promote greater openness and transparency. Therefore, information should be accessible through the local authority or stored at the local public funded library. The Manchester Commonwealth Games in 2002 were supported by the local authority and commercial sponsorship. Information on this event is held at the Manchester public library and available via the web.

CASE STUDY   SPORT INDUSTRY INTERVIEWS

This sponsorship case study will investigate the different type of sponsorship arrangement, and the trend towards sponsoring an award ceremony within a business context.

On the back of London winning the 2012 Olympics in 2005, the Mayor of London's office set up an event titled 'Sport Industry Interviews'. This event ran for the first time in 2006. The purpose of the event was to address the UK sport industry business leaders and stakeholders on the key milestones, challenges and opportunities ahead in the preparations for the London 2012 Olympic Games.

In the pre-publicity information posted on the web from the Mayor of London's office, a sponsorship package was made available, outlining the sponsorship opportunities for supporting the 2006 Sport Industry Interviews.

The package clearly stated the different types of sponsorship levels and benefits attributed to each option.

The event was by invitation only, for approximately 260 attendees; it was aimed at CEO/Director level key decision makers in sport. As part of the event there was also the sports industry awards, which have been described by the media as the 'Oscars of the sports world'. The award ceremony received coverage from BBC, ITV, Sky and

(Continued)

(Continued)

national newspapers – extensive media coverage which helped to enhance the sponsorship package on offer.

There are a number of reasons as to why any organisation would deem this event worthy of sponsorship. From the point of view of the potential sponsor, the main constituent parts that made up this event were that it was:

- linked directly to the 2012 London Olympics;
- organised and represented by Ken Livingstone, then Mayor of London;
- covered by three national broadcasters and national newspapers;
- offering networking opportunities with major decision makers in the sports industry;
- attended by 260 hand-picked delegates by invitation only;
- an established event with a recognised award ceremony;
- the largest sport business event in Europe.

The seven points above are considered to be the sponsorship pitch. This information would be translated via printed media or verbal communication to potential sponsors. Alongside this information the event will have a sponsorship package that outlines the different levels of sponsorship deals. These deals are closely linked to financial commitments from a potential sponsor. The different deals within the package will give an indication of the level of exposure prior to, at the event and post-event. The level of sponsorship is calculated on the cost of hosting the event and the economic value of media coverage in all areas. Levels of sponsorship deals generally fall within three categories. For this particular event we have one headline sponsorship deal and other multi-layer deals for the award ceremony. As a headline sponsor an organisation has complete confidence that no other company can compete within the same arena. Exclusivity is given to the headline sponsor. This would be demonstrated by areas within the venue where branding opportunities are given. Press and media coverage would also carry the headline sponsor on all communication associated to the event for a given period of time.

It is essential to remember that each sponsorship document must be constructed around the specific and general opportunities that can entice a potential sponsor. Marketing and advertising, along with credible presentation, are what makes the sponsorship package a saleable item. In constructing the package you might want to consider a particular business sector, with a strategic vision that can drive their product/service to a wider audience through association with the event.

Major sponsorship deals

Major sporting events today such as the Commonwealth Games and the Olympic Games can only function effectively with a substantial level of financial funding. Financial support for the Olympic Games dates back to Ancient Greece, when prominent citizens gave financial support. Historically, the Olympic Games also received funding from the state, as does the Games today in most cases.

In 1924 in Paris, advertising hoarding made its first and last appearance. Four years later the Olympic rights were extended to other sectors. It is now possible for companies involved in brewing to open bars/restaurants within areas where the customers are. Advertising did return to the Olympic Games but not inside the competition areas. In 1936 at the Berlin Olympics television made its first appearance. In 1947 at the London Olympics, television rights were assigned for the first time. In 1994 the Los Angeles Olympics were marketed as the beginning of organised contribution to sponsoring the games by groups of companies. The International Olympic Committee (IOC) set out a marketing plan and divided it into three categories. The three categories are: Major Sponsor, Official Sponsor and Official Supplier; with 34 companies acquiring contracts with the IOC as official sponsors, 64 companies acquiring the right to supply and another 65 being granted authority to use the Olympic symbols. The Los Angeles Olympics television rights were brought by 156 countries. At the Seoul Olympics it was decided to reduce the number of sponsors to increase the value of the rights. In 1992 Barcelona Games continued the reduction of companies acquiring rights. In 1996 the Atlanta Games turned the whole organisational structure upside down. All expenses were covered by private funding, through TV rights, sponsors and ticket sales. TV viewers from 214 nations watched the Games, and 11 million tickets were sold, more than for the Barcelona and Los Angeles games combined. The Sydney Olympic Games in 2000 only covered 63 per cent of expenses; the rest was covered by the Australian Government. It is evidently clear that major sporting events around the globe rely heavily on corporate sponsorship. It also demonstrates that over time sponsorship has developed and become an enormously complicated mechanism in driving a product/service to potential consumers on a global scale, or maintaining the continual presence of a major sporting event. The concepts highlighted earlier for major sporting events have also been grafted onto many of our national and regional events in many business sectors, e.g. the demarcation of categories within sponsorship profiles, the selling of TV rights to acquire substantial revenue, and funding from regional and central government along with associated agencies. Exclusivity deals and service deals are now entrenched within many of the sponsorship proposals/packages in the marketplace today.

External influences effecting sponsorship deals

The marketplace for acquiring sponsorship does not operate in isolation and sometimes can be very fragile. It is prone to fluctuation with the influence of geopolitical events. The downturn in the global economy through political or economic market forces has a direct effect on the stock market.

With economic fluctuations emanating from various parts of the globe, there can be both short- and long-term impacts on available financial revenue from corporate organisations listed on the stock market. Within any business, the departments most likely to be affected by these situations are marketing and advertising, where revenue spend is curtailed. A geopolitical event, such as the 9/11 attack on the twin towers in the USA in 2001, can have a major negative economic and ripple effect across the globe. The robustness of the global market and in particular the US stock exchange at that time meant that the world did not experience a recession. There was, however, a downturn in stocks for some businesses and in particular the airline industry. Companies laid off staff at home and abroad, and also reduced their spending in many territories.

Event companies seeking sponsorship must be fully aware of the economic and political landscape before attempting to approach a business for sponsorship. Research is essential and will save time and resources, a valuable commodity for most small-to medium-sized event companies.

Within this sophisticated sponsorship market, we have what are called 'brand agencies'. Many companies today relinquish the responsibility to place their product/service in a suitable marketing environment. This function is instead passed on to brand agencies, where the strategy is delivered by 'brand managers'. They work on behalf of the client, in essence becoming the gate keepers for managing the product/service. Therefore, these clearly defined processes show that, in order to be successful, sponsorship proposals need to have natural synergy with their intended audience. This must not merely be implied but well documented throughout. Brand agencies, as with the client, on the whole are looking for maximum exposure and return on investment. Therefore, sponsorship proposals must demonstrate a strategy that communicates across all communication channels, enabling the sponsor to maximise investment.

Within the event management tool kit for delivering a sponsor's message via a partnership, we now have what is called 'new media'. This is not just a simple matter of branding on a web page, rather it should be seen as moving towards a fully integrated and interactive procedure, whereby data can be collected and analysed with a view to establishing a method for customer relationship marketing. This will assist the event company and the sponsor in building future marketing campaigns, and where long-term sponsorship deals are in place this method can help to solidify a working relationship.

With this audited data event, companies can back up their proposal with facts and figures to attract future sponsors. Sponsorship has its original heritage in marketing, advertising and public relations; this area of business management works well when marketing campaigns fully recognise the target audience. The proliferation of new media has fragmented the consumer market. Therefore, targeting a consumer or potential audience now needs to be a sophisticated scientific approach. Audience profiles have become expansive with the digital media network through the web, digital satellite and cable TV, and digital radio. These communication platforms have become further delivery portals with the introduction of integrated mobile phones. It is essential for event providers to recognise the changing and developing technological landscape and use new media where appropriate to enhance the event experience and acquire synergy with the customers.

Naming rights – part of the marketing mix

Within the sponsorship portfolio there are a number of income-generating strategies. Naming rights is a concept that has its historical and commercial development firmly rooted in the USA and dates back over 50 years.

In defining naming rights we need to look at the process in the first instance from the sponsor's perspective. It is a tool to acquire intangible and tangible benefits by purchasing the space and length of time to apply a name to a facility.

'The global market for sponsorship naming rights on venue/stadia is estimated to be approaching $4 billion worldwide, with 75% of the market in the USA' (Sports Business Group, 2001: 48 [online]).

Naming rights within the UK is a relatively new business concept; with naming rights on sport stadiums within the UK football Premier League introduced for clubs such as Bolton Wanderers with the Reebok stadium, completed in 1997. In 1994, BT Cellnet signed a 10-year deal for £3.5 million with Middlesbrough football club for sponsorship at the Riverside Stadium. In 2006, Arsenal football club opened their new stadium with a £100 million naming rights deal with Emirates Airways; this is the largest naming rights deal in the UK at present. With exclusive worldwide rights the new stadium is officially called 'Emirates Stadium'. This deal will conclude in 2020–1. This deal also includes an eight-year shirt sponsorship deal which began in 2006.

Naming rights sponsorship deals have seen a steady increase over the past ten years in the UK. However, the large financial spend is predominantly located within the sports industry.

The live music industry within the UK has also seen an injection of commercial sponsorship on live music facilities. Academy Music Group (AMG) is the UK's largest owner and operator of nationwide live music venues. This organisation was formally known as McKenzie Group Ltd. The management buyout of the McKenzie Music Group in 2004 included the promoters SJM Concerts, Metropolis Music and MCD Productions. This strategy also included bringing online new academy venues in Birmingham, Bristol, Glasgow, Liverpool and Islington.

Within the AMG business portfolio there are now a number of live music venues which carry the naming rights of the Carling beer company: Carling Academy Brixton, Carling Academy Birmingham, Carling Academy Bristol,

Carling Academy Glasgow, Carling Academy Liverpool and Carling Academy Islington. Carling Academy Islington opened in 2003, and it is clear that AMG has a strategic direction to acquire and develop venues as part of their business strategy, with the inclusion of sponsors purchasing the naming rights for a period of time. It signifies a new direction for facilities owners and managers to support their financial business model with sponsorship revenue.

The Department of Culture Media and Sport (DCMS) estimates the music industry as a whole contributes £5 billion to the UK economy annually. The music industry within the UK is relatively buoyant according to a report compiled by Burns Owens Partnership, published by DCMS, titled 'Music business growth and access to finance 2006'. Three hundred and thirty-nine small-to medium-sized business contributed to the report.

There are many factors that have contributed to the fall in profits for some areas within the music sector. The biggest factor can be seen in the digital revolution and in particular across the internet, with downloadable music from legal and illegal websites. As is indicated from the report, the live music sector, and in particular management and promoting, is still a profitable business. This can be seen in the case of AMG from the strength given to the business model from the three main partners and the offset of financial liability through sponsorship naming rights with Carling Lager.

Naming rights have also filtered into outdoor live music events over the years. From 1997 to the present, the Virgin brand has been working alongside the dual-sited V Festival. V Festival, Carling Festival, O2 Wireless Festival and T in the Park are some of the very few events that have effective naming rights sponsorship deals in the UK.

Of the 100-plus outdoor festivals that pop up in the UK landscape on a yearly basis, less than 5 per cent carry any corporate naming rights sponsorship deals. Evidently there is room for commercial growth in this area along with entertainment facilities.

It is argued that within the UK, as opposed to the rest of Europe, there is a resistance to change. Naming rights are not considered a tangible part of the sponsorship/marketing mix. (See Chapter 10 for more detail on the concept of the marketing mix.)

> According to John Knight, an independent sponsorship consultant involved in a handful of UK deals and an advisor to the *Manchester Evening News* (that acquired the naming rights to the MEN Arena in Manchester), it has taken a lot longer for naming rights to be accepted in the UK. (Sports Business Group, 2001: 42)

It is generally agreed that the USA is coming to maturity with regard to naming rights; existing deals have yet to conclude. Therefore, brand managers are looking to Europe for future sponsorship development. Within the European market it is recognised that Germany has the biggest sponsorship market. With that in mind, event providers should be aware of the sea change for corporate sponsorship shifting its focus to the European and the global market. With the assistance of major sporting events which rotate around the globe such as the Cricket World Cup, the UEFA European Football Championship, the Rugby World Cup and many more, awareness of international brands and the tangible benefits that sponsorship can bring is building internationally.

CASE STUDY   LONDON MARATHON

According to Arts and Business (2011) the UK sponsorship market was valued in the order of £934 million in 2007. Outside of the UK, the North American market has the largest spend in sponsorship $16.8 billion, as reported by IEG in the UK sponsorship landscape publication (2011). It is universally known within academia and the event sector that sport sponsorship consistently receives the highest spend in sponsorship year on year globally. In the UK, sport sponsorship accounts for 51 per cent of all sponsorship spend (UK Sponsorship landscape, 2011).

The London Marathon is a major sporting event, dating back to 1981. An estimated 20,000 people signed up for the race that year; 7,747 were accepted and there were 6,255 finishers. In its first year it was televised by the BBC, consequently 90,000 applications arrived in 1982, and the race was limited to 18,059 runners. The race has continually grown each year in terms of numbers and popularity, to become one of London's signature events. With that growth the BBC has continued with a live broadcast each year. Currently the event is televised in 150 countries. 'A total of 746,635 runners have completed the London Marathon since it started while a record 35,694 people finished in 2007' (Virgin London Marathon, 2010: 10 [online]).

The title sponsor for the first three years was Gillette. The initial sponsorship deal amounted to £75,000, which continued for another 2 years. Impressed with the results and media acclaim, Gillette increased their sponsorship to £100,000 in 1982. In the same year a major strategic decision by the International Amateur Athletics Federation decided that athletes should be paid. Therefore, all elite athletes who take part in similar events all over the world expect to be paid, and this has continued to the present day. This decision marked a major change in the professional approach surrounding the London Marathon. From a corporate point of view it raised the event to a higher commercial sponsorship value. In 1984–8, Mars, the confectionery company, paid £150,000, then £217,000 and then £350,000 in 1986. This growth in sponsorship allocation went on unabated, so that by 1989–92, 6 corporate companies were bidding to become title sponsor for the event; ADT eventually won the contract. This recognition and media attention did not go unnoticed by the International Association of Athletics Federations (IAAF). They co-opted the event within the World Marathon Cup in 1991, the third year of the IAAF competition. (Previously, the event had been held every four years, but after Japan the event was scheduled biannually.) At the end of the sponsorship deal with ADT in 1992, the London Marathon was firmly recognised

(Continued)

(Continued)

as one of the world's leading marathons. In 1993–5, NutraSweet was able to capitalise on the success of the event thus far but also pushing it to new levels of excellence. The race saw an increase in entry figures and a change to the route, with the new finish line at the Mall, with Buckingham Palace as the backdrop.

The longest sponsorship period in the history of the London Marathon was 1996–2009, with Flora, with 2010–14 seeing a new chapter in the commercial history of the London Marathon. Virgin Money financial services put down £17 million in sponsorship and has taken up the mantle as the new title sponsor. Virgin Money has put together a strategic plan for runners to raise £250 million by 2014 for charitable organisations; this will be linked via the Virgin Money official website. Money raised will go direct to the designated charities as more and more runners sign up to the Virgin system. As with so many of the previous sponsors Virgin has also taken the naming rights. As title sponsor Virgin will also be in competition with other commercial sponsors/suppliers of the London Marathon. They include adidas, London Pride, Holiday Inn, Lucozade, Realbuzz.com, Renault, Times, TNT, Nestlé Pure Life, and a number of media broadcasters such as BBC Radio 5live and

Figure 9.1   London Marathon winner 2011

BBC Sport. The obvious commercial relationship for some of the current sponsors is very clear. Nestlé Pure Life and Lucozade provide refreshments at designated water stations throughout the route. As the event is also seen as a destination event within a tourism context, runners, spectators and sport aficionados will seek out appropriate affordable accommodation in London, which ultimately draws upon the Holiday Inn association.

The London Marathon has also seen a significant growth in participants raising money for charities. The organisation was incorporated with charity status in the early years; runners raised £46.5 million in 2007, and this made it the largest single fundraising event in the world. In 2010, it was estimated that over £500 million would have been raised for charitable causes from 1981–2010. In 2010 the London Marathon listed 27 official charities linked directly to the event.

The Trust has pledged £6 million to help several Olympic facilities after the 2012 Games. (Virgin London Marathon, 2010: 12)

It is quite easy to see why Gillette became the title sponsor in the early years of the marathon, as the target audience at that stage, including the athletes, reflected a high percentage of male participants. Over the years marathons and half marathons have proliferated in the UK, with an increasing amount of female participants. The change in demographics and increase in gender split could also be one of the reasons for the increase in charitable donations. To increase the commercial attractiveness of this event, political and social pressure for UK population to get healthy has seen a significant rise in the number of road races up and down the country. As with the London Marathon, there are a number of similar events that receive significant amounts of commercial sponsorship and media representation from the BBC and other TV broadcasters. This ultimately increases the commercial value for any sponsorship deal.

CASE STUDY   DPERCUSSION SPONSORSHIP PROPOSAL

In 1996 Manchester was targeted by the Provisional IRA. The terrorist bomb attack was not the first on the British mainland, but inflicted substantial structural damage to retail units in the city centre. The result of the terrorist attack was to infuse Manchester with the will to rebuild the areas worst affected. On the back of that redevelopment, the people of Manchester came together a year later through a live music event in Castlefield outdoor arena. In 2007, the event celebrated its tenth anniversary, and is now known as Dpercussion. The event is managed and produced by a local event company Ear to the Ground. Currently the event went through an internal process of restructuring and seeking financial assistance through sponsorship and government-assisted grants. In previous years the event in the main was supported financially by Ear to the Ground. As the event has developed and established itself within the city as a free live music event celebrating

(Continued)

(Continued)

diverse music cultures from all areas of Manchester and beyond, it has therefore marked itself within the Manchester calendar of events as the free one-day summer live music festival. A number of companies over the years attempted to associate their product or brand with the event, but not enough to secure its long-term strategic security.

Ear to The Ground developed a sponsorship package, inviting potential sponsors to consider associating themselves to the long-term sustainability of this event. Within this proposal they adopted many of the aspects drawn from the marketing mix.

The document set out to inform potential sponsors of the history of the event and the potential audience figure for 2007.

Specific information about the music content was also included, giving a flavour of the range of musical production. A catalogue of bands listed who previously had made their debut at Dpercussion. Apart from the music the document also gave a description of the diverse forms of entertainment associated with the event.

As with every sponsorship proposal, it included the audience demographics, a vital part of the decision-making process for any potential sponsor. This looks at age range, along with areas of interest, spending potential and lifestyle, etc.

The attendance figure for each year was also given, with reference to a sustained incremental rise. The method behind this approach was to demonstrate the continual success of the event in reaching the target audience in Manchester and beyond.

As part of the visual layout of the document, and where the event has a historical heritage, it is a good idea to include some visual imagery to enhance the proposal. New media processes can also communicate the message beyond the usual marketing/advertising channels. Within the Dpercussion document, the organisation adopted some of the established methods of marketing, juxtaposed with new media techniques.

Areas where new media was integrated include giving the event a Myspace.com home page with a facility to join and become friends of Dpercussion.

With the information from this particular site the event company was able to build a profile of their audience. The event also has a dedicated website with a facility to upload personal information. This audited information is owned by the event provider under the Data Protection Act and is crucial to building a profile of the audience and advertising campaign if required. It also allows the event organiser to communicate through emails directly to the target audience. Customer relationship marketing (CRM) has become an integral element within the tool kit for event organisers who produce and manage their own events.

Exclusivity deals through sponsorship and ambush marketing

The European Capital of Culture was launched on 13 June 1985. Over the years, many cities within the European Union have been given the privilege of holding the title. Liverpool was awarded the title in 2008, following a successful bid to the European Parliament. The previous time a British city had hosted this event was Glasgow in 1990.

This particular event does require a certain amount of finance, which is generally raised through commercial sponsorship, local government funding, central government and associated agencies established to donate financial assistance. Therefore, the organising committee in Liverpool put together four categories within their sponsorship package, signifying the level of sponsorship and the benefits attributed to each. The first category is Official Partner; this category is limited to 12 companies, and with this a sponsor will receive exclusivity rights across all communication channels including digital and print media. The Liverpool Culture Company responsible for the sponsorship agreements had to ensure that no form of ambush marketing interrupted the sponsor's agreement at any of the events planned. Ambush marketing is a way of usurping the advertising or marketing of another product or service without the authorisation or permission of the negotiated client. In essence, ambush marketing obtains free marketing/advertising rights. The value of a sponsorship deal is sometimes balanced on how well an organisation can ensure that exclusivity is consistent throughout. All major events are susceptible to ambush marketing, given their duration and scope, and the audience attendance at various locations. It may become difficult to manage consistently; adidas achieved ambush marketing at the opening ceremony of the Commonwealth Games at the City of Manchester Stadium. David Beckham, ex-Manchester United footballer, presented the Commonwealth torch to the Queen in the main arena wearing a specially-made adidas tracksuit. Adidas was not listed in any format or arrangement within any of the sponsorship categories for the 2002 Manchester Commonwealth Games.

The second category of sponsorship is Official Supporter; at this level an organisation was given the opportunity to enjoy full involvement in the Capital of Culture programme of events. In the first and second categories, hospitality involvement came with the sponsorship deal. It must be noted that hospitality has become a major element to the event experience. For some events it is one of the highlights of the occasion. Hospitality could involve simply supplying beer at an event, or providing a full three-course banquet as part of the celebration. Where hospitality has a role to play within the event experience, consideration should be given and opportunities explored for commercial sponsorship. Sponsorship at the level which has been discussed in this chapter carries with it an immense knowledge of contractual negotiation to ensure that both parties are fully represented and achieve their desired outcomes. To present and manage a sponsorship deal, lawyers are continually used to draft, negotiate and conclude the process.

Summary

The main focus of this chapter was to illustrate different types of events and assess the sponsorship arrangements, drawing on similarities in the sponsorship proposals and how sponsorship can be obtained.

The chapter highlighted major iconic events such as the Olympic Games, and charted the development of advertising, marketing and sponsorship deals. The chapter also made it explicitly clear that sponsorship acquisition and management has become a sophisticated and complex animal. This was indicated by presenting case studies around some high-profile events such as the Manchester Commonwealth Games, Liverpool European City of Culture, and a North West regional event titled Dpercussion. The cultural, sporting and music events were selected on the basis of their distinct difference, but they also illustrated similarities in many areas.

One particular similarity was evident in how sponsorship deals are given various categories and associated benefits that meet each category. The chapter also touched upon the emerging trends in sponsorship and in particular on naming rights.

An economic viewpoint was highlighted demonstrating the potential for growth within the UK and European market. This was not just connected to sporting and entertainment facilities but included some of the major outdoor live music events within the UK. In closing, the chapter stressed the importance of research by an individual or organisation before approaching a potential sponsor.

■ Discussion questions

Question 1

Outline and discuss the various categories of sponsorship available within a sponsorship document and explain the need for differentiation in each category.

Question 2

Naming rights is an area within sponsorship that is a recent development within the UK market. Explain some of the cost benefits to an organisation when considering naming a live music facility.

Question 3

Explain some of the global impacts that can have a negative effect on corporate sponsorship for major sporting events.

Question 4

What can be argued as the single contributing factor for sport sponsorship financial allocation over and above any other form of event sponsorship?

Question 5

Put forward a commercial response as to why road races within the UK have become an attractive commercial vehicle.

CASE STUDY 1   MANAGING A SPORTS EVENT SPONSORSHIP FOR A NATIONAL COMPANY

The situation

One of New Zealand's largest and oldest life insurance companies had undertaken research which showed it lacked visibility in their largest potential market – Auckland. Having recently undergone a name change, there was a clear need to supplement the usual means of communication through advertising, direct mail and media activity, with sponsorship of a major sporting or cultural event. The new chief executive asked the Crabtree Associates Ltd, a public relations consultancy, to assist in obtaining sponsorship rights to New Zealand's biggest fun run, Round The Bays, and if successful, to manage the promotion and public relations programme for the company.

The programme

Crabtree Associates wrote the proposal to the organising committee which secured this sought-after sponsorship ahead of two multinational companies. By this time, the event itself was only five months away – half the normal time frame usually available to organise a programme for an event of such magnitude. The race organisers had also decided to add a new element to the event – a competitive section, which had also to be explained to the public.

The consultants recommended a launch function at which the new logo would be unveiled and, to attract media attention, preceded by a novelty race down the main city shopping thoroughfare. The race consisted of teams of four athletes from various groups and organisations, pulling harness racing sulkies which were 'driven' by the five mayors of the major cities in the region, plus two media personalities and the chief executive of the sponsoring company. This occurred two months before race day proper.

In the lead-up to the event regular weekly news releases were organised, covering aspects of the organisation, personalities involved, new elements which needed explanation and general information. Six radio stations were involved in promoting the event. In the seven days before the race, regular 'phone-outs' were organised with three stations to increase the flow of information.

Crabtree Associates recommended and organised: the building of a 'lighthouse', the company's symbol, which was towed to promotional sites by trailer for display purposes; a huge

(Continued)

(Continued)

banner for draping across the frontage of the company's Auckland office block to promote runner registration; banners to be hung on lighting poles and on other high density traffic routes around the city – promoting registration and the date of the event; special T shirts to be printed; a video of the launch event to be shown to staff at other cities and towns to enthuse them about the event; crisis management when a story broke in the media that barbed wire may be used to 'control' athletes at the start; coordinated placing of signs at the finish and presentation sites.

On the day of the event, two consultants assisted with media liaison, cooperated with organisers, minor sponsors and VIPs, and directed still and video photographers. After the event, the coordinated release of results and photographs to media outside Auckland was organised.

The results

A survey conducted by the client company showed that awareness of the company in its target market had risen by 50 per cent, while awareness of the company as the sponsor of the race stood at 15 per cent. Given the long history of association of previous sponsors – this was regarded as most satisfactory. Staff in the Auckland region expressed their pleasure at being involved in a community event.

Most importantly, registrations increased by over 12,000 on the previous year and the nominated charity received a cheque for $180,000, being the proceeds from registrations – the highest amount ever in the Round The Bays' 20 year history.

Source: Crabtree Associates Ltd (n.d.) [online]

CASE STUDY 2   SPECIAL EVENT PLANNERS IDENTIFY SPONSORSHIP CATEGORIES FOR FUNDRAISING EVENTS

Although organising such an event may sound like 'fun' to some, there's a tremendous amount of work that goes into planning a community fundraising event. And, keeping an eye on the bottom line, event planners must stay focused on creating value for event sponsors, which underwrites a significant portion of event costs and funds raised.

Sponsors also play a critical role in the ongoing success and expansion of community walks, explains Liz Klug, director of special events for the Y-ME National Breast Cancer Organization. Y-ME established its first walk in 1991 and has expanded the event to 15 cities for 2008.

'I think that there are many reasons why sponsors get involved,' Klug explains. 'Special event planners need to recognise those hot buttons: some participate to gain employee engagement, some are there to brand build, some want to extend sampling opportunities, some want their executives in front of an audience, and some want an activity where they can get in front of the media.'

Sponsors are also interested in the demographic of who will participate in the event, and determining the best method of getting their message in front of those folks. Y-ME and other organisations hosting a community event also know the important role of media visibility, pricing, and use of event logo rights.

Sponsor fees usually cover the operating budget of the event, 25–30 per cent.

Sponsorship categories

Y-ME has established three categories for national sponsorships for the Walk to Empower program, which includes a full range of visibility on all marketing, advertising, promotional and event levels (excluding booth sponsorship level). They include:

- national presenting sponsor ($250,000, maximum of 3);
- national official sponsor ($100,000);
- multi-market booth sponsor ($1,750 to $4,000 per site).

Most event planners limit the number of top category sponsors. As a point of reference, national presenting sponsors of the Y-ME walks include McDonald's, sanofi-aventis and Walgreens. And national official sponsors include Bumble Bee, Grant Thornton, Pfizer Oncology and United Airlines.

Y-ME has established five categories for local sponsorships. Packages start as low as $2,000 and go as high as $65,000 (for local sponsorship) depending upon the market. They include:

- local presenting sponsor;
- local official;
- local co-sponsor;
- local supporting;
- local booth.

One of the most desired benefits that all sponsors hope to secure with their sponsorship is category exclusivity, and community event organisers such as Y-ME certainly understand that request. However, it is usually tied to the higher levels of sponsorship, and that's also the case with the Y-ME Walk to Empower events. Event sponsorship at the Y-ME walks breaks down as follows:

Common benefits included in sponsorships

- Logo inclusion on event marketing materials.
- Right to use event logos.
- Logo inclusion on the cause's event website.
- Recognition at all event meetings and ceremonies.
- Dedicated team area for walk day program.

Value-added benefits for higher sponsorship levels

- Logo visibility on walk-t-shirts.
- Banner place at walk site.

(Continued)

(Continued)

- Right to exclusive sponsorship of a related program activity.
- Speaking opportunities for company representative at ceremonies.

Exclusive benefits for top level sponsors

- Category exclusivity at their respective level.
- Right to exclusive sponsorship of a related program activity.
- Speaking opportunities for company representative at ceremonies.

Source: Hard (n.d.) [online]

Further reading

Incentives and Meetings International (I&MI) – the worldwide network for professional buyers and planners of international meetings, incentive travel programmes, congresses and corporate events: www.i-mi.com/Marketreview

Crabtree Associates Ltd (n.d.) 'Managing a sports event sponsorship for a national company', CAL Public Relations [online]. Available at: www.calpr.co.nz/case_study_sports.html [accessed 7 January 2012].

Hard, R. (n.d.) 'Special event planners identify sponsorship categories for fundraising events' [online]. Available at: www.eventplanning.about.com/od/eventplanningbasics/a/event-sponsors.htm [accessed 10 January 2012].

Lee, M.-S., Sandler, D.M. and Shani, D. (1997) 'Attitudinal constructs towards sponsorship: scale development using three global sporting events', *International Marketing Review*, 14(3): 159–69.

Virgin London Marathon (2010) Media Guide [online]. Available at: http://static.london-marathon.co.uk/downloads/pdf/Media_Guide.pdf [accessed 7 January 2012].

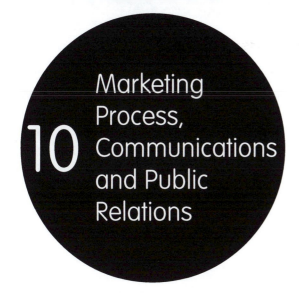

Marketing Process, Communications and Public Relations

In this chapter you will cover:

- the history and theory of marketing;
- application of the marketing concept to events;
- events marketing research and planning;
- the five stages of marketing research;
- estimating attendance and evaluation;
- consumer behaviour at events;
- the consumer decision-making process;
- the events consumer and segmentation;
- the events marketing mix;
- marketing communications;
- relationship marketing for events;
- the move to online marketing;
- experiential marketing;
- summary;
- discussion questions;
- case studies;
- further reading.

The aim of this chapter is to apply marketing process models to the events industry from conception to evaluation, to examine marketing research, segmentation, targeting and positioning of specific events as examples, and to highlight the application of marketing research. The focus will be upon positioning an event favourably in the mind of its target market in order to ensure long-term success.

The chapter will begin with a brief look at the history and theory of marketing followed by a discussion of marketing concepts and marketing research in relation to events. The chapter will then examine the behaviour of consumers and how they can be segmented. A detailed discussion will then follow on the marketing mix and its constituents: product, price, place and promotion, as applied to events. Finally, how events could be positioned within the marketplace to compete successfully and how relationship marketing could be applied to achieve repeat visitors and loyalty will be discussed.

History and theory of marketing

The *marketing era* could be said to have begun in the early 1950s (see Figure 10.1 below), when the public appetite for new goods and services appeared insatiable. In Western markets consumption rose substantially as prices fell. This was also the period when independent commercial television was launched and this became the marketer's most powerful mass market communication medium. The influence of marketing was such that consumer spending doubled during this time (Egan, 2011).

Research in marketing grew in the 1960s and it was during this decade that Borden (1964) introduced the twelve elements of the marketing programme

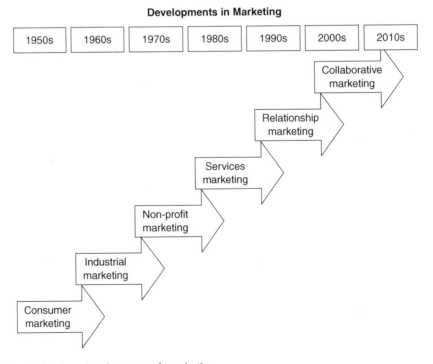

Developments in Marketing

| 1950s | 1960s | 1970s | 1980s | 1990s | 2000s | 2010s |

Collaborative marketing

Relationship marketing

Services marketing

Non-profit marketing

Industrial marketing

Consumer marketing

Figure 10.1   The development of marketing

(see Figure 10.2), which were later simplified further by McCarthy (1978) to what became known as the *4Ps* of marketing or the *marketing mix* (see Figure 10.2).

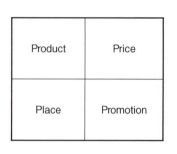

Product planning	Personal selling	Display
Pricing	Advertising	Servicing
Branding	Promotions	Physical handling
Channels of distribution	Packaging	Fact finding and analysis

Product	Price
Place	Promotion

Figure 10.2   Borden's and McCarthy's models compared

Application of the marketing concept to events

Marketing is one of the concepts in management which is difficult to define. If you ask people within a business what they understand about marketing and the role of the marketing department, you could be expected to get a variety of answers including:

- Marketing is about advertising.
- The people who work in marketing put brochures together.
- It is the company's sales activities.

There have been numerous definitions of marketing and no one definition is correct. They are simply opinions of how people view marketing. Below are just a few of the definitions which have been used.

> Marketing is the social and managerial process by which individuals and groups obtain what they need and want through creating and exchanging products and value with others.
>
> (Kotler and Armstrong, 2012: 10)
>
> Marketing is the achievement of corporate goals through meeting and exceeding customer needs better than competition.
>
> (Jobber, 2010: 918)

The above definitions do seem to be different. However, what is needed is an explanation which will apply to every company in every situation. In the UK, the definition given by the Chartered Institute of Marketing is widely accepted:

> Marketing is the management process responsible for identifying, anticipating and satisfying customer requirements profitably.
>
> (Chartered Institute of Marketing, 2011)

This definition is an elegant description of what marketing means. Of the many definitions that are available it is the most to the point. It emphasises the wide scope of marketing, ranging from the initial identification of customers' needs by means of research, right through to eventual, profitable satisfaction of those needs.

Academic research on marketing in events management has been slow to get off the mark, as Shannon noted in his article when discussing, in particular, sports marketing:

> The primary focus of most of the sport marketing publications, to date, appears to be in the marketing communications (advertising/promotion) and consumer behaviour areas of marketing. There appears to be less research in the pricing, product, and distribution/place areas of the marketing mix. These areas provide rich research potential for future studies in sport marketing. (1999: 517)

Taking into consideration the broad definitions of marketing, events marketing can be defined as:

> Event marketing is a management process to achieve the objectives of an organisation through identifying and meeting the needs of the customers who attend an event.

In order to satisfy the customer an event organisation must identify what business it is in and the purpose it is serving to satisfy the customer requirements.

The following list shows the number of marketing activities that an event manager should undertake to produce a successful event or festival:

- Analyse the target market to establish appropriate event components, or products.
- Establish what other competitive events could satisfy similar needs, in order to ensure their event has a unique selling proposition.
- Predict how many people will attend the event.
- Predict at what time people will come to the event.
- Estimate what price they will be willing to pay to attend the event.
- Decide on the type and quantity of promotional activities needed to inform and attract the target market to the event.

- Decide how the tickets to the event can reach the target market.
- Establish the degree of success for marketing events.

All the above activities are important in the organisation of a successful event. In order to achieve these marketing principles, the business will carry out a series of marketing functions such as:

- managing change;
- co-ordinating marketing planning control;
- managing the effects of competition;
- ensuring the survival of the business.

The success of any business depends on its ability to satisfy the customer. This statement suggests that the main purpose of the marketing function should also be the purpose of other functions within the organisation. The enterprise stands to win or lose by its ability to attain such a goal. To enable organisations to satisfy their customers effectively there are a number of questions which need to be asked.

- Who is our customer and what exactly are his or her needs?
- Who is responsible for satisfying the customer?
- What do we need to 'know' before we can commence the task of planning the process of satisfying customers, now and in the future?
- To what extent do our customers expect us to be creative and innovative in whatever we do?

Events marketing research and planning

Marketing research has a specific function which is to aid effective planning and decision making in markets. It plays an important part in designing and implementation of an effective strategy. There are three areas of activity involved in successful marketing management of events (see Figure 10.3).

Analysis

This is a crucial area of marketing. Its aim is to find out about the market in which the company operates or which the company is planning to enter. Through systematic market research, present and future needs can be identified, analysed and evaluated. To gain a comprehensive view of the market behaviour and opportunities both qualitative and quantitative assessments should be taken.

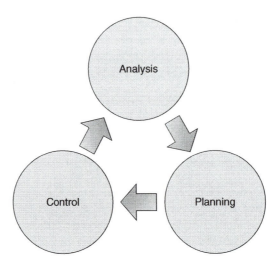

Figure 10.3   The process of designing and implementation of marketing management of events strategy

Planning

Planning is critical in professional marketing. It follows logically from the analytical approach. From the data derived from the marketing research process, management should be in a position to select markets suitable for exploitation. Products and services designed to satisfy the identified needs of specific markets should then be developed.

Control

Control is the third area of successful marketing. It is important for the productivity of the business or any type of organisation. Standards of performance need to be set and closely monitored. Marketing management should recognise that success in markets depends substantially on total commitment to management control throughout the business and an awareness of the need for specialists in marketing, design, finance, purchasing, personnel etc., to work creatively together to achieve the objectives of the organisation to which they belong.

The five stages of marketing research

There are five sequential stages of the marketing research programme as discussed below.

Stage 1: Brief research

This initial stage is where clients and researchers can identify a clear indication of the marketing problems. Some areas the company or event manager may discuss are: the industry background and the nature of products made by the company; the proposed topic of market investigation; and the extent of market research activities.

This stage is critical because it will determine the type of research and the research activities to be undertaken. At this stage the marketing problem must be clearly defined to enable the survey to be carried out effectively.

Stage 2: Research proposal

Information collected from stage one will be studied by researchers who will then submit a detailed proposal to clients for approval. The proposal should be carefully checked before moving on to the next stage.

The proposal is likely to contain the following information:

- A clear statement of the marketing problems to be investigated.
- A definition of the product or service to be investigated.
- A definition of the survey population to be sampled.
- The major areas of measurement.
- The methodology.
- The degree of accuracy of survey findings.
- Any costs involved in the survey.
- Any conditions applying to research survey.
- The experience of the researchers.

Stage 3: Data collection

Data can be collected using a number of different methods. The two main areas of data collection are primary and secondary. Primary data refers to data collected at first hand, such as observations, surveys or questionnaires. Secondary data refers to information which already exists. Secondary research is also known as desk research. This information can be obtained internally or externally. The acquisition of secondary data depends on four factors:

- availability;
- relevance;
- accuracy;
- cost.

Each factor must be carefully assessed to ensure that relevant, valid and cost effective information is obtained in specific enquiries.

Stage 4: Data analysis and evaluation

This is one of the final stages of the survey. It involves editing of survey forms, coding of answers and tabulation.

Stage 5: Preparation and presentation of the report

After the first four stages have been completed, the information has to be communicated in an attractive manner. This will usually take the form of a survey report.

Estimating attendance and evaluation

Generating accurate estimates of attendance is an important aspect of event evaluation (see Figure 10.4). It is quite simple for ticketed events or restricted number events, but complications can arise when the events are open or semi-open.

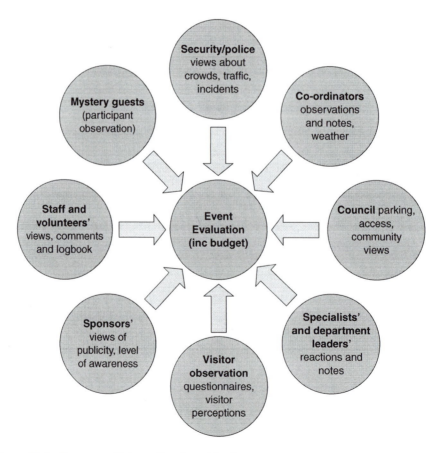

Figure 10.4   Sources of information for evaluation
Source: Adapted from Shone and Parry (2010: 246)

Consumer behaviour at events

The marketing concept is just as important to the event industry as it is to any other service industry. This is because the service in events is often intangible, separable, variable and perishable.

Why is the service intangible?

Unlike buying a product, the customer cannot pick, touch or try an event before the ticket is purchased, so the customer therefore has to make a decision based on expectations that a need or desire will be met.

Customer expectations may often come from the following sources:

- Recommendations from family and friends.
- Word of mouth.
- Promotional or advertising campaigns from the marketing organiser. For example through posters, television advertisements, leaflets, etc.
- The brand image of the event.

Before the event, expectations have a great impact on the levels of satisfaction and future purchase behaviour. If customers have high expectations of the event, then once they have attended the event, if it has not met their expectations then future business may be lost. On the other hand, if an event exceeds customer expectations then event managers would expect to see an increase in the sale of tickets in the future.

Why is the service inseparable?

The service the customer receives is inseparable from the consumption of the service. This is due to the fact that production and consumption of the service are inseparable, unlike purchasing a product from the shops and consuming it elsewhere.

Why is the service perishable?

If on the day of the event or festival the weather is not as expected – for example, if the event has been organised outdoors and it is wet and windy – the attendance level would be affected, but unsold tickets may not be sold at a later date when the weather improves.

Why is the service variable?

The event service is variable because people have different perceptions of the same event. This is because when markets are tightly segmented into a group of people with a common interest, members of the group may have differing perceptions of the benefits they have received from the event experience. Also, the event service is based on many variables which hamper continuity – artists, staff, environmental conditions, etc.

Consumer decision-making process

The following acronym helps to explain the customer decision-making process:

PIECE

- Problem recognition
- Information search
- Evaluation of alternatives
- Choice of purchase
- Evaluation of post-purchase experience

To influence customers to arrive at a decision about attending an event, marketers need to understand the needs, motives and expectations of their potential customers. Many event organisers do not carry out thorough customer-orientated research as either they believe in their own ability to know what their customers want, or they lack the resources to do it.

The start of the marketing process is to identify which of the customer needs will be satisfied if they attend the event. Many choices are available to customers to satisfy their needs or wants. Events must compete with other forms of leisure and events. There may be barriers which may not allow the customer to take part in the events, for example:

- personal reasons – time, social influences, money;
- event-related reasons – location, accessibility and cost.

Events are designed to satisfy all levels of needs, although not necessarily at the same time. People come to events with a variety of motives and expectations but there is no guarantee they will all be met.

The events consumer and segmentation

The majority of events do not appeal to all consumers, therefore when the event organiser is carrying out marketing planning for an event or festival, an understanding of the behaviour of the visitors must be included. This can be done by identifying market segments.

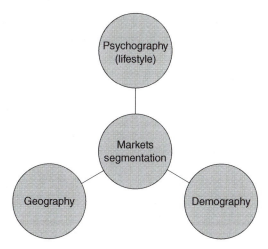

Figure 10.5   Market segmentation routes

Geographic segmentation

This is to do with where people who are visiting the event reside. For example, the organisers of a community festival will most likely decide that the local residents should be the starting point of their segmentation activity. However, the event or festival may be of interest to other people outside the residential area, and so the marketing network could be increased to include day visitors from outside the area, domestic tourists both local and national, school excursions and international inbound tourists. The chosen geographic segmentation depends on the experience provided by a festival or event.

Demographic segmentation

Demographic segmentation is about the measurable characteristics of people including:

- age;
- gender;
- occupation;
- education;
- income;
- cultural economic group;
- socio-economic group.

Men and women have different needs, which some event organisers may arrange to cater for in order to satisfy them. The age of the consumers can also affect the way they look at life, their attitudes, values and interests. When events are organised they may often be targeted at more than one generation, there-fore creating a desire for people to attend events as families and spend quality time together.

The particular stage that consumers are at in their life cycle will often determine the type of event or festival they will attend. For example, 'empty nesters' in socio-economic groups AB will tend to visit cultural events featuring quality food and drink, whereas consumers with families would be more interested in attending events which cater for both adults and children.

Psychographic segmentation

This is another method which event organisers find useful when planning event segmentation. This is based on the consumers' lifestyle and their values.

Psychographic segmentation has many limitations for the marketer. One of the main limitations being that it is very difficult to measure lifestyle segments quantitatively. This method can, however, be useful for marketers when trying to identify the characteristics of the target market.

The events marketing mix

The marketing mix is the term used for the four marketing variables the com-pany can control when organising events. The marketing mix consists of the 4 Ps: product, price, place and promotion.

When marketers are deciding on a marketing plan for the event, they can control any of the 4 Ps to enable them to make the event a success. This can only be done when they have carried out some market research and analysed the results to find out who their potential customers are.

Product

Products are usually considered to be tangible. That is to say, consumers can see the product, look at its appearance, touch the product and even try it. However, with events or festivals the product is not tangible. Consumers are not able to do any of these things and have to make a decision whether to attend an event or festival simply by the way the product is marketed.

Often when choosing an event, consumers tend to look at brand names. This helps them because they feel more confident visiting events they know will provide them with the product which will satisfy their needs. As with any other product, events also have different stages. This is known as the product lifecycle. The stages are as follows:

- introduction;
- growth;
- maturity;
- decline;
- stagnation;
- rejuvenation.

For example, an event or festival which is popular today may not continue to have the same benefits in the future, unless the event is changed or organised in a different way in order to keep pace with the expectations of the consumers. By making a change to satisfy consumer needs, the event may be rejuvenated.

Another method marketers could use to attract people to events is to launch a new product into the market which would be of interest to them. In order to bring the new event to the public attention there would need to be a variety of advertising campaigns to attract the public to attend the event. Once this is done the organisers must try their best to satisfy the needs of their customers, in order to achieve an image which will attract consumers to attend the event in the future and even promote it by making recommendations to family and friends who may have similar interests.

Price

Events organisers need to set prices for their products including admission to the event, merchandise, vendor rentals, and sponsorship fees. Even events that are normally free enforce a price on customers in terms of travel costs, lost opportunities and time.

In business terms, price is a simple expression of the monetary value of the product, service or asset. Price is a very important tool for management and key to the marketing mix of the company to gain competitive advantage. A pricing policy needs to be in harmony with the organisation's strategic goals and compatible with the market. Economists argue that price is an exchange strategy between goods or services that pay for the company's expenditure. It is important for events and festival companies to apply a pricing strategy which is achievable and accepted both by the market and by competitors. Another theory of price, stated by economists and marketers, is that the market price reflects the interaction between two different concepts. On one hand the price is determined by demand considerations based on marginal utility; on the other hand, price is determined by supply considerations based on marginal cost.

In general, pricing can be seen as the use of simple methods to calculate and allocate prices to certain goods or services; in reality it is not simple for companies to manage price. Therefore, it is vital for events managers to understand and effectively use pricing strategies in order to set the price for events, by managing the price in line with industry.

Place

Place normally refers to the physical location where the event is held, which could be a building, set of venues or space. Within the marketing mix, place also considers the atmosphere and how this may be created through lighting, set and design.

Place could also mean the distribution of event products or how they may be sold to the customers.

Promotional mix

The marketing communication mix is sometimes referred to as the 'promotional mix' within the event industry and consists of advertising, promotion, personal selling and public relations. Marketing communication is an important part of the marketing mix and affects all the other parts of the mix – product, price and place. Therefore, the task of marketing communications is to present the event in the most appropriate manner.

As it can be seen above, the role of marketing communications in events management is very important. The following sections will explore marketing communications in more details.

Marketing communications

The purpose of marketing communications is to provide information to a target audience in a way that encourages a positive response. Integrated marketing communications emphasises the benefits of harnessing synergy across different media types to establish brand equity of products and services in achieving that response. Marketing communications is defined by Fill as:

> a management process through which an organisation engages with its various audiences. Through an understanding of an audience's proffered communication environments, organisations seek to develop and present messages for its identified stakeholder groups, before evaluating and acting upon any responses. By conveying messages that are of significant value, audiences are encouraged to offer attitudinal, emotional and behavioural responses. (2009: 16)

This definition has three main themes: engagement; audiences for marketing communications; and response. Taking into consideration these three themes, marketing communications relating to events can be defined as:

> the management process of engagement between an event and its audience and how the audience responds to the marketing communications.

But the key question is: how does marketing communications work? There are several conceptual models that are presented in the marketing communication literature but the model put forward below in Figure 10.6 perhaps best describes this process. It has eight elements:

- Sender: the party sending the message to another party.
- Encoding: putting thought into symbolic forms.
- Message: communication channels message is sent through.
- Noise: unplanned static or distortion during the process of communication.
- Decoding: the process through which receivers place meaning on the sender's transmitted symbols.
- Receiver: the party receiving the message (audience).
- Response: set of reactions following exposure/reception of message.
- Feedback: part of the response transmitted back to the sender.

In this model the communication is a two-way process, as response and feedback mechanisms are built in and the sender or source may alter the message and media as necessary.

Marketing communications consists of various functions: advertising, sales promotion, direct mailing, direct marketing, personal selling, public relations, E-Marketing and viral marketing. Marketing communications works best when these different functions are integrated to achieve the overall marketing goals and thus the corporate goals. In the following sections

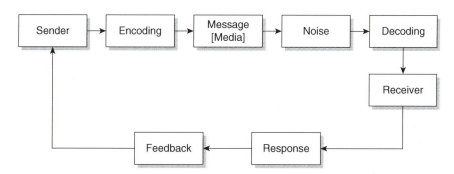

Figure 10.6   Elements in the communications process

each function of marketing communications is introduced and commented on in relation to events.

Advertising

Advertising is defined by the American Marketing Association as:

> Any paid form of non-personal presentation and promotion of ideas, goods or services by an identifiable sponsor.
>
> (www.marketingpower.com)

The purpose of advertising in events is to move the audience along a continuum stretching from complete unawareness of the event to taking action to come to the event.

Advertising communicates information to a large number of recipients, paid for by a sponsor. It has three main aims:

1 To impart information.
2 To develop attitudes.
3 To induce action beneficial to the advertiser.

For example, an advertisement for a motor exhibition is paid for by the exhibition organisers to achieve a greater number of visitors to the exhibition; a rock group will pay to advertise the concert to sell more box office tickets. It must be remembered that advertising is only one element of the communications mix, but it does perform certain parts of the communicating task faster and with greater economy and volume than other means.

How large a part advertising plays depends on the nature of the event and the number of times it is repeated. It contributes the greatest part when:

1 the event has features which are not obvious to the customer, i.e. the buyer's awareness of the event is low;
2 opportunities for differentiating a particular event are stronger than other similar events;
3 event industry sales are rising rather than remaining stable or declining;
4 a new product or new service idea is being introduced at an event.

Planning an advertising campaign

There are six distinct stages in planning an advertising campaign:

Identify the target audience

The target audience will be determined by the segmentation process, which will define the group that the event is trying to target. Creativity in the ads could be used to highlight mood, atmosphere and environment for brand usage, usually relying on non-verbal communication such as background setting for an advertisement (indoor/outdoor, relaxed or tense environment, type of music, use of colour schemes, appearance of models etc.).

Specify the promotional message

The intended function of the campaign will determine the promotional message that needs to be specified. This function could be:

1   to change perceptions;

2   to stimulate the desire;

3   to produce conviction;

4   to direct action;

5   to provide reassurance;

6   to pass on information.

Each function can suggest an appropriate form for, and content, of the message.

Selecting the media

The media selected provides access to a certain type of audience. The type of media includes: national newspapers, regional newspapers, magazines and periodicals, posters and transport advertising, cinema, internet and radio.

The media selected will be the one that is able to contact an optimum number of potential customers for an event at the lowest price. The choice of medium will depend on who the advertiser wishes to reach with the advertising message.

There are advantages and disadvantages with each of the various media types. Television is watched by viewers from all social groupings and is an ideal medium for advertising an event targeting mass consumers. Certain media may reach audiences with special characteristics: e.g. the cinema is visited mainly by young people; many magazines and local newspapers are read mainly by women; and there are trade magazines for certain industries. Events often use flyers and posters which can be mass produced at low cost and widely circulated locally. The size of the circulation for a particular audience is also an important factor in deciding which medium to use.

Another important consideration is the cost of advertising. This consists of:

1 the cost of producing the advertisements;
2 the cost of the exposure in the media.

The cost of exposure is often far higher than the cost of producing the advert.

Scheduling the media

An advertisement needs to be repeated several times because many of the target audience will miss it the first time it appears. It has also been found that a large target audience is reached by advertising in several newspapers instead of just one, and again, in several media instead of just one.

Setting the promotional budget

A budget needs to be set which will meet the objectives for the chosen media to convey the required message. The promotional budget is often linked to sales using:

- a percentage of last period of sales;
- a percentage of the target sales;
- a percentage of the target profit.

Evaluating promotional effectiveness

The problem with evaluating the effectiveness of an advertising campaign is that it hardly takes place in a vacuum. Other factors in the marketplace, such as competing events, changing attitudes and price changes, can all affect the advertising effect.

Sales promotion

Sales promotions are largely aimed at consumers, but also aimed at the 'trade', e.g. exhibition organisers, wedding planners, festival organisers, travel industry etc. Sales promotion is a more cost effective way to communicate with the target markets than conventional media advertising.

One important characteristic of sales promotion is its short-term nature. Rarely does a sales promotion last for more than six months, and the majority last for much shorter periods.

In general, sales promotion seeks to add value to the decision to purchase or attend, and to communicate a sense of enthusiasm. Two of the most common types of sales promotion are direct marketing and exhibitions.

Direct marketing

Direct marketing creates and develops a direct relationship with the event organisers and their consumers on an individual basis. It is a form of direct supply, embracing both the variety of alternative media channels (like advertising) and a choice of distribution channels (like mail order). Direct marketing methods include:

1 **Direct mail** This is the use of the postal service to distribute promotional material directly to a particular person, household or firm.

   The usage and acceptance of direct mail is increasing rapidly, and with the increasing sophistication of computerisation, advertisers can now segment and target their markets with greater flexibility, selectivity and personal contact.

   Direct mail can be used to sell a wide range of products or services, and its uses are also varied.

2 **Direct advertising** This is perhaps one of the oldest methods of reaching the consumer, with printed matter being sent directly to the prospect by the advertiser, often by mail, but sometimes through the letter box as a personal delivery, handing out to passers-by or left under the screen wiper of a car.

3 **Mail order** Mail order advertising aims to persuade recipients to purchase tickets for an event by post, with delivery of the tickets being made through the mail or other carrier or through a local agent. Thus, it is a special form of direct mail, seeking to complete the sale entirely by mail and being a complete plan in itself. Mail order is a type of direct mail, but not all direct mail is mail order.

4 **Direct response advertising** This is a strategy of using specially designed advertisements, usually in magazines or newspapers, to invoke a direct response, such as the coupon-response press ad, which the reader uses to order.

Exhibitions

Exhibitions are another form of below-the-line promotional activity. As with many other below-the-line methods they are growing in use and popularity. Exhibit marketing is a rich and flexible promotional practice that spawns new applications and has the power to adapt to changing situations. A recent example of new exhibit marketing is called the 'pop-up store'. This is a temporary retail set-up that may last a few months and is often used for seasonal products and services. The pop-up store is an unusual and novel idea which generates considerable publicity and promotional value. They can be found in major US cities, malls and airports and include both mainstream retailers and firms with new products to introduce (Pitta, et al., 2006).

Exhibitions come in three basic forms:

1 those aimed at the consumer;

2 those aimed solely at the trade;

3 those aimed at both.

Most exhibitions start off as trade exhibitions and then after the first week or so when all of the 'trade' business has been conducted they are usually opened up to the public. The public usually pays an entry fee that brings in revenue for the exhibition organiser and helps to pay for the costs of actually staging the exhibition. The general public may have an actual interest in the products and services being exhibited, for example clothes shows, motor shows and home exhibitions. Sometimes the products and services are of little direct interest to the general public. That is, they are highly unlikely to buy any of the products on show, but nevertheless attendance at the exhibition can be a 'good day out' (e.g. an agricultural show or an air show) and the public is prepared to pay for this privilege.

Personal selling

The sales force is an important part of the communication mix. It engages in 'personal' selling, as compared with the 'non-personal' selling of advertising and sales promotion activities.

The task of selling involves the following:

- Communicating the advantages of the event to the customers.

- Securing a sale of the event.

- Prospecting for additional customers. This involves perhaps visiting prospective customers several times and then making a sales proposition.

- Gathering information about what customers want from an event.

An important decision is to decide the possible size of the sales force but this can be increased or decreased depending on the size of the event. However, management need to have an effective, supportive, informative and persuasive communication with the sales force in order to achieve a successful operation.

Public relations

Traditionally, advertising may have been the main communication function in organisations because of budget size. But recently, it is not too uncommon to find large budgets for public relations (PR).

The Chartered Institute of Public Relations defines public relations as:

[t]he deliberate, planned and sustained effort to establish and maintain mutual understanding between an organisation and its public. (www.cipr.co.uk)

Public relations and publicity are used interchangeably sometimes. There is, however, a distinction between public relations and publicity. Publicity may be any form of information from an outside source used by the new media. It is largely out of the hands of the organisation as the source of the news item will have little control over how and when the story will be interpreted. While public relations may be concerned with publicity, not all publicity derives from public relations. The responsibility of public relations is to create and influence publicity in such a way that it has a positive impact on the event.

Public relations require that organisations relate to the public in some manner. In events, for instance, the public could be the media, event organisers, customers, financial investors, employees and potential employees, opinion formers and the local community. However, the type of audience will depend on the nature of the event but it is critical that the key audience for a particular event is identified.

Functions of public relations

PR carries out a range of different functions and Figure 10.7 identifies a number of these.

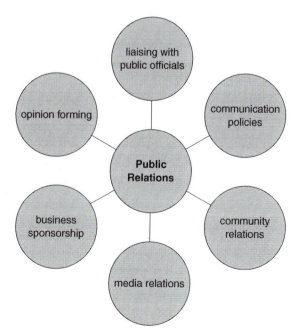

Figure 10.7   Functions of public relations

In some instances events will need to be created to provide an opportunity for 'hospitality' which can be extended to clients and customers of the organisations. At other times PR will take the form of participation in conferences and exhibitions, the themes of which are relevant to the functions of the company.

Relationship marketing for events

According to Grönroos:

> Relationship marketing is to identify and establish, maintain and enhance and, when necessary, terminate relationships with customers (and other parties) so that the objectives regarding economic and other variables of all parties are met. This is achieved through a mutual exchange and fulfilment of promises. (2007: 29)

Basically, the idea of relationship marketing is that event organisers attempt to develop relationships with visitors so that they will repeat their visit and promote the event to their friends and families. This will result in reduced marketing costs in targeting new customers.

In a general sense, relationships require at least two parties, who are in contact with each other. For example, the basic relationship of marketing is that between an event organiser and visitor. Nevertheless, within an event there will be several other players involved and a relationship may need to be developed between the participants in a network.

The move to online marketing

There appear to be at least three different sources of marketing changes. Firstly, the internet is altering our culture and the ways in which customers react to marketing stimuli. Secondly, the internet is changing the way businesses operate and as a result the speed and style of marketing is changing. Thirdly, this new way of communicating has given rise to e-marketing or internet marketing.

E-marketing

E-marketing can be defined as the use of the internet and related digital technologies to achieve the marketing objectives and support the modern marketing concept (Chaffey et al., 2008). These technologies include internet media and other digital media such as cable and satellite, together with the hardware and software which enables its operation and use.

Because of e-marketing the nature of the ways in which partners interact has also altered (O'Toole, 2003). McWilliams (2000) stresses that information technology is challenging the power balance in many relationships. For example, the creation of online communities has challenged firms to respond to strong, more vocal, united consumer groups.

Additionally, interactive television (t-commerce) and m-commerce facilitated through the new WAP mobile phone technology are yet more examples of remote interfaces through which customers will be able to interact with their suppliers.

Viral marketing

Viral marketing refers to marketing techniques that use previous social networks to produce increases in brand awareness, through self-replicating viral processes. This can be through word of mouth or online. The internet is very effective in reaching a large number of people rapidly.

Viral marketing on the internet can make use of blogs, chat rooms and websites designed to promote a new event. The purpose of viral marketing is to create media coverage using viral stories that are greater than the budget of advertising for an event.

Viral marketing is increasingly becoming popular for the following reasons:

- it is relatively easy to carry out a marketing campaign using viral marketing;
- effective targeting;
- low cost;
- the high and rapid response rate.

The main strength of viral marketing is its ability to target a large number of interested people at a low cost.

Viral advertising assumes that people will share interesting and entertaining content. This can be achieved through interactive games, images, funny video clips and text.

Through the use of the internet and e-mail advertising, organisations can have a greater impact in acquiring and retaining a large customer base compared to other marketing tools. Unlike spam mail, viral marketing encourages potential consumers of an event to tell a friend through positive word-of-mouth recommendation.

Experiential marketing

Events are in reality experiential, interactive, targeted and relational, and as such these characteristics are highly appropriate and desirable given the modern marketing environment. These features are consistent with other communication forms, notably within the wider, and expanding field of experiential marketing (Schmitt, 1999).

The term experiential marketing refers to actual customer experiences with the brand/product/service that drive sales and increase brand image and awareness. It's the difference between telling people about features of a product or service and letting them experience the benefits for themselves. When done right, it is the most powerful tool to win brand loyalty. Experiential marketing is defined by Lanier and Hampton as:

> [t]he strategy of creating and staging offerings for the purpose of facilitating memorable customer experiences. (2009: 10)

With the right kind of experiential marketing strategy, event organisations should be able to demand a higher premium for their offerings. However, without the real understanding of what experiential marketing entails, the rush to achieve a presence among experience providers has led many organisations to design and implement experiential marketing without proper preparation. Regrettably, with poor planning as to what needs to be achieved through experiential marketing as part of their overall marketing strategy, these event organisations often have ended up dissatisfying rather than delighting event goers.

Therefore, through experiential marketing, the idea is that experiences will positively influence the perception of brand both during and after the consumption phase of the event. Lanier and Hampton further add that brand experiences must offer 'added value' and fit the 'sign system' and audience profile/expectations of the event concerned (2009: 13). 'Adding value' means that the brand must do more than simply offer a spectacle.

Summary

At the heart of marketing is a focus on meeting the needs and wants of the customer. This chapter has demonstrated that marketing is more than selling and advertising, a misconception held by many within the event and festival industry. The main marketing principles include: anticipating marketing needs and opportunities to stage events; satisfying event visitors' expectations; generating income and/or profit from the event, maximising the benefits to the event organisation; and managing change and competition. Furthermore, marketing involves co-ordinating activities such as marketing research, planning new product development, pricing, advertising, personal selling and developing relationships in order to satisfy event visitor needs and at the same time meeting the objectives of the event organisation.

In order to achieve these marketing principles, the event organisation will carry out a series of marketing functions including: co-ordinating planning and control; implementing the marketing mix (the right event in the right place with the right promotion at the right price); and ensuring the survival of the business.

In this chapter the various functions of the marketing communications mix such as advertising, sales promotion, direct mailing, direct marketing, personal selling, public relations, e-marketing and viral marketing have been discussed. When deciding how to properly use the marketing communications mix to meet the marketing objectives, it is important to consider the relative strengths and weaknesses of each component of the mix. It should also be noted that marketing communications is most effective when each of the functions are integrated to achieve the overall aims and objectives of marketing and thus the long-term goals of the organisation. In addition, as an event manager, you should be knowledgeable about the different marketing communications functions so that you can communicate effectively the objectives of the event to the people responsible for the different functions.

Furthermore, the total budget (generally defined in the marketing and/or business plan) needs to be defined first, and a decision needs to be made as to the best way to leverage the different elements of the mix to maximise the return on event organisation investment. The various parts of the mix should be balanced to not only create an integrated approach to event marketing communications but also to ensure that enough resources are in place for each component to be successful.

■ Discussion questions

Question 1

Do you think that the customer is always right? Discuss.

Question 2

What sort of internal data might be useful when carrying out a marketing research project for a particular event?

Question 3

In groups or individually, try to list some of the purposes of good after-sales service for an event. Some are fairly obvious, others may need a little thought.

Question 4

Provide at least two event scenarios of your choice where you think integrated marketing communication has been deployed well.

Question 5

Discuss the relevance of PR for events.

Question 6

How can the internet be used effectively to market an event?

CASE STUDY 1   AERO HOT CHOCOLATE EXPERIENTIAL CAMPAIGN

Nestlé wanted to move into the hot chocolate category with Aero Hot Chocolate. iD, an experiential marketing agency in the UK, was selected to run a nationwide sampling campaign in 2007 to launch the product into the marketplace.

In 2008, once the product was established on the shelves, Nestlé approached iD again to run a bigger, more 'experiential' campaign.

The challenge was to 'develop an integrated through the line marketing campaign that builds on the success of 2007. The activity must champion our key differentiator and key brand attribute; bubbles,' instructed Aero Brand Manager, Vicky Hall. According to Vicky Hall, they really do make a difference to the taste of the product and help reinforce consumer perceptions of Aero Hot Chocolate.

The iD answer

To up the ante after the 2007 campaign, iD built a huge Aero Bubble dome to house an unforgettable bubble-inspired experience. The dome was taken on the road to the UK's key Asda and Tesco supermarkets during a six-week campaign. Using iD trained brand ambassadors, consumers were lured into the bubble dome with dry sample giveaways, an interactive prize-giving floor and lashings and lashings of Aero Hot Chocolate!

The dome acted as a consumer chill-out zone, giving families a place to relax, away from the stresses of the weekly shop.

Figure 10.8   Aero hot chocolate promotion

The result

This was one of the most successful campaigns in iD's history. During and post campaign the sales figures were increased by 3,000 per cent. Importantly, this figure didn't immediately drop once the campaign moved on either – consumers continued to buy the product at all of their locations.

This shows that the campaign opened consumers' eyes but the product won their taste buds – an example of how a great product makes a great campaign.

Aero Hot Chocolate is now the category leading Hot Chocolate product in the UK, kicking Cadbury off the top spot in just its second year in the game. Thanks in no small part to Nestlé's commitment to good, integrated experiential event marketing.

Source: http://www.utalkmarketing.com

CASE STUDY 2   LINCOLNTON-LINCOLN COUNTY CHAMBER OF COMMERCE MEMBERS ARE BETTER INFORMED THAN EVER

Located 29 miles northwest of Charlotte, North Carolina, Lincoln County is home to 76,000 residents and the businesses, associations, and organisations that serve them. The Lincolnton-Lincoln

(Continued)

(Continued)

County Chamber of Commerce works with its 700 members to enhance the quality of life and foster economic health by hosting numerous events and programs, including a 'Shop Local' campaign. Email marketing and event marketing by Constant Contact, a web-based event company, contributes to the chamber's success by keeping everyone well informed.

Challenge: making the most of Constant Contact

Lisa Wallace can recall what it was like to communicate with the membership of the Lincolnton-Lincoln County Chamber before 2007, when the business organisation joined Constant Contact. For Lisa's first four years at the chamber, where she serves as office manager, announcements for every event and a bimonthly newsletter were printed and mailed to members. 'It was very time consuming,' she remembers. 'You'd compose the newsletter, send it to the printer, and wait to get it back, and then go through the standard mailing process. By using Constant Contact, we're able to give much more immediate news and information.' Today, the chamber strives to use email and event marketing to the fullest potential – and plans to try using social media as a further means of promoting the chamber and its members.

Solution: learning and working with email and event marketing

The chamber first heard about Constant Contact through a member's recommendation. Then, a visit to a neighbouring chamber of commerce that uses email marketing revealed the ease and professionalism of member communications. 'It was something that I immediately wanted because I'm the one who does our newsletter,' Lisa recalls, adding, 'The board of directors was sold on it just like I was.' That was three years ago. Since then, the chamber has added event marketing.

Members receive *The Buzz*, the chamber's email newsletter, twice a month, with articles, member spotlights, announcements, recaps and photos of past events, and a calendar of all upcoming events. Event marketing is used to promote all chamber programs, seminars, and functions, plus more than 40 'grand openings' held at member locations throughout the year. Because each opening gets a dedicated email invitation and event homepage with detailed information, Lisa loves that she can set up several events at once and schedule distribution to the membership in advance.

Email and event marketing allow members to link directly to registration pages, eliminating the need to phone or email the chamber to reserve a spot. 'The best feature is members can automatically register, pay, and add it to their calendars,' Lisa says. 'They can do it sitting at home in their pajamas if they're checking email at home. It has helped our registrations come in more quickly.'

Lisa continually explores email and event marketing functionality and relies on Constant Contact's regional development director, online chats, and customer service to maximize her use of the programs. 'Any time I've needed help or had a question, people have been very responsive, very knowledgeable,' she reports. 'You can tell they enjoy what they do – they have that smile in their voice.'

Results: ready now for social media

In the seven years that Lisa has worked for the Lincolnton-Lincoln chamber, the membership has grown from 425 to 700 and the email list is nearing 1,000. Whereas printed communications were sent primarily to a single contact at a member business, email communications can be targeted to additional members within a company.

'Our information is now getting into the hands of the people who really need it,' Lisa says, noting that this helps increase registrations without additional cost. The email list is managed on a monthly basis, which results in a less than 1.7 per cent bounced email rate per mailing. In addition, the open rate averages 28 per cent, which Lisa attributes in part to great subject lines. 'People are very busy today and I think you have to capture them right off the bat with the subject line,' she explains.

Delighted with the professional look of their communication, the positive feedback from members, and the ease and efficiency of working with email and event marketing, the Lincolnton-Lincoln County Chamber is now exploring the use of social media to further promote its activities and its members.

'Right now we're talking about beginning to use Facebook,' Lisa says. Materials produced using email and event marketing can be automatically linked to various social media, such as Facebook, Twitter, and LinkedIn simply by checking a box as the email or event is created. 'Some of our board members do this for their businesses and they see it as another way to promote our chamber.'

Source: http://www.constantcontact.com/event-marketing/customer-examples/lincolnton-lincoln-county-chamber-of-commerce.jsp

Further reading

Brown, S. (2009) '"Please hold, your call is important to us": Some thoughts on unspeakable customer experiences', in A. Lindgreen, J. Vanhamme and M.B. Beverland (eds), *Memorable Customer Experiences: A Research Anthology*. Farnham: Gower Publishing, pp. 253–66.

Carter, P. (2009) *The Complete Special Events Handbook*. London: Directory of Social Change.

Chaffey, D., Mayer, R., Johnston, K. and Ellis-Chadwick, F. (2008) *Internet Marketing – Strategy, Implementation and Practice*. Harlow: Prentice Hall.

Egan, J. (2011) *Relationship Marketing: Exploring Relational Strategies in Marketing*, 4th edn. Harlow: Financial Times Press/Prentice Hall.

Fill, C. (2009) *Marketing Communications: Interactivity, Communities and Content*, 5th edn. Harlow: Pearson Education.

Grönroos, C. (2007) *Service Management and Marketing*, 3rd edn. Chichester: John Wiley and Sons.

Jobber, D. (2010) *Principles of Marketing*, 6th edn. Maidenhead: McGraw Hill.

Kitchen, P.J. and Schultz, D.E. (2000) 'A response to "Theoretical concept or management fashion"', *Journal of Advertising Research*, 40(5): 17–21.

Kotler, P. and Armstrong, G. (2012) *Principles of Marketing*, 14th edn. Harlow: Pearson.

Lanier, C.D. and Hampton, R.D. (2009) 'Experiential Marketing: Understanding the Logic of Memorable Customer Experiences', in A. Lindgreen, J. Vanhamme, and M.B. Beverland (eds), *Memorable Customer Experiences: A Research Anthology*. Farnham: Gower Publishing, pp. 9–23.

Morgan, M. (1996) *Marketing for Leisure and Tourism*. London: Prentice Hall.

O'Toole, T. (2003) 'E-Relationships: emergence and the small firm', *Market Intelligence and Planning*, 21(2): 115–22.

Pitta, D.A., Franzak, F.J. and Flower, D. (2006) 'A strategic approach to building online customer loyalty: integrating customer profitability tiers', *Journal of Consumer Marketing*, 23(7): 421–9.

Schmitt, B.H. (1999) *Experiential Marketing*. New York: The Free Press.

Shone, A. and Parry, B. (2010) *Successful Event Management: A Practical Handbook*, 3rd edn. Andover: Cengage Learning.

Uysal, M., Gahan, L. and Martin, B. (1993) 'An examination of event motivations', *Festival Management and Event Tourism*, 1: 5–10.

www.marketingpower.com

www.cipr.co.uk

www.utalkmarketing.com

Yehsin, T. (1999) *Integrated Marketing Communications*. Oxford: Butterworth Heinemann.

New Multimedia Technology for Events Organisers

In this chapter you will cover:

- **proliferation of new media within the event experience;**
- **smart phone marketing and communication;**
- **definition of terms;**
- **consumer interaction;**
- **privacy and permission marketing;**
- **early adopters within the sector;**
- **current trends;**
- **summary;**
- **discussion questions;**
- **case studies;**
- **further reading.**

The aim of this chapter is to investigate the technological development of m-commerce; charting its growth over the past 15 years, thus establishing a relationship with the consumer as a viable marketing avenue for consumer interaction leading to brand penetration. The general term m-commerce will be consistently referred to throughout this chapter as defined by Balasubramanian, Peterson and Jarvenpaa (2002). This term denotes the type of hand-held communication device known as a mobile phone or smart phone.

This chapter will set out and chart the short history of new media and its relationship with the event industry. The chapter will take into consideration events that are considered as early adopters of this technology, and it will also look at the current audience experience. The basis of this chapter is to explore the ways in which smart phone-embedded technology, associated with other media devices, can drive content to a consumer market via a live event. Two case studies will also assist in highlighting the typology of events that have embraced new media as a tool to enhance audience experience and help to drive brand performance in a competitive environment.

Proliferation of new media within the event experience

New media as a stand-alone term has many different connotations; its use and potential proliferation is only tempered by the technological capacity of the infrastructure that enables it, coupled with the hardware and software available and the potential knowledge and understanding of the end user. There are a number of factors that will ultimately impact on user experience, such as legislation, permission, privacy and financial outlay. While the term new media has not been disputed and is now part of the global marketing framework, there are many speculative and empirical hypotheses surrounding the technologies and their current applications. This push and pull application will only have full functionality with third generation mobile devices. It is this 3G technology that has transformed the method of interaction for marketers to communicate and actively engage with consumers. With extensive literature available on m-commerce, this chapter will also illuminate current research theory and demystify the relationship between consumer and mobile technological advancements.

The first mobile phone call in the UK was made on 1 January 1985 on the Vodafone network. In the early 1990s, applications embedded into mobile phones were two-dimensional and appealed to a distinct consumer group who saw ring tones, games, SMS interaction, and payment models as attractive features. Mobile operators invested a considerable amount of time and money in software development and handset advancement throughout the mid to late 1990s, which saw a sharp increase in consumer purchasing of mobile phones. Jaap Haartsen and Sven Mattisson developed the Bluetooth application while working for Ericsson in 1994. This software function is a feature in all second and third generation mobile smart phones. This technology is also included in headsets and earpieces, digital cameras and computers.

In 1997, the UK had four mobile operators: Orange, Vodafone, Cellnet and One 2 One. They all had licences for second generation mobiles. Wireless application protocol (WAP) was brought to the market 1999–2000 by Unwired Planet, a combination of the leading telecommunication companies. This is a technological advancement that allows a mobile user to operate in the same virtual environment as a wireless laptop user, uploading and transferring data, and it became a very attractive option to the consumer and especially the business user. The beginning of the new millennium saw a rapid expansion in the sale of mobile devices and a new generation of phones – also known as smart phones – with applications to enhance the consumer's way of life. On 27 April 2000 the British government concluded the sale of the third generation mobile phone licence for £22 billion. This watershed moment was the start of a technological mobile revolution within the UK market; the mobile handset now had a viable technological potential to compete with computers. Apart from becoming a viable communication interface, smart phones are also marketed and exploited by the user as a must-have consumer item. Along with the UK, Europe and the international market were also transforming the communication protocol with the third generation communication licence.

The smart phone revolution in the UK is moving rapidly into a new era, which will position the UK in line with most of Europe and the USA. The 4G mobile licence will go for auction before 2013.

> Ofcom has today announced plans for the largest ever single auction of additional spectrum for mobile services in the UK, equivalent to three quarters of the mobile spectrum in use today and 80 per cent more than the 3G auction which took place in 2000. Ofcom (2011)

This much-needed capacity will ensure the further increase of advertising spend to smart phones, which has currently overtaken printed media. The increased data service will be comparable to the bandwidth on today's laptops. The new spectrum on offer will be auctioned to the four mobile operators in the UK.

The recent advances in software development, commonly known as 'apps' or applications, were pioneered by BlackBerry with the 'phone as a computer'. This was then revolutionised and fully exploited by the Apple iPhone, which now has 90 per cent of the apps market share. Although it had a relatively late introduction into the consumer market, the iPhone has become for many the consumer product of choice. In 2009, Apple launched the App Store, only available to iPhone customers, with a choice of over 250,000 downloadable apps available.

This technology allows a user, or multiple users, to connect through wireless application, mobile internet, to a satellite and draw down updates of a specific nature. It must also be stated that each mobile operator (or mobile platform) has apps designed specifically for their devices. With the software known as app it is now possible to send that format as a multimedia file via Bluetooth function to a mobile phone.

Smart phone marketing and communication

Bluetooth and SMS technologies make it possible to send messages to individual mobile phones through which consumers can be called for action. This might be to respond to a survey, to use a forward link to online information, to receive coupons or other multimedia files, or to be directed to an m-shop through which a mobile transaction (payment) can be made. Through Bluetooth marketing it is possible to create a strong, personalised conversation (targeted according to time, place and need for information or communication). Other advantages are the visual transfer of messages and opportunities for strong interactivity. Other direct marketing characteristics that can be related to Bluetooth marketing include: a forced confrontation level; a limited information exchange; a limited online processing of messages after reactions; and low costs per customer.

To counteract that low cost and high impact there is also the risk of higher irritation levels which could be similar to cold calling. Current research and case studies have demonstrated that different demographics have significantly different responses to smart phone-embedded applications.

When Bluetooth marketing is applied, you need to consider a multi-channel approach, and the mobile campaign needs to be supported by an online website or offline follow-ups (preferably in the direct physical environment).

With mobile applications you can facilitate a platform related to an event offering information, and also let visitors communicate and interact with each other in order to create value and relevance to the context of that event. This not only leads to a more valued consumer experience but also to stronger brand, consumer loyalty and retention.

Consumers are attracted to mobile apps because it is clear who the provider is (an event organiser), what's in it for them (relevance, context, social interaction), that other visitors use it too (consumers tend to show and share it with friends and thus be part of a community), and whether it contains invitations to contribute to get something. Event driven marketing can bring strong results, especially when consumers' own actions invite more interaction. Research from the German-based Brand Science Institute (BSI) showed that mobile users show and share their new apps with friends and families. Each app reaches 14 new persons in this way, on average. Also these applications lead to stronger brand recognition than applications and widgets in social networks.

Definition of terms

Mobile applications require an active action to opt in (that is, to download it from an App Store), and the user can grant access to be localised and receive updates. Thus marketing and communication becomes a consumer-directed process.

Danish researchers Sundbo and Hagedorn-Rasmussen (Sundbo and Darmer, 2008) define three stages in the development of new experience productions and innovative systems: the *backstage* (where the focus is on all e-business and e-commerce processes); the *stage* (where the created experience is being offered and communicated from the perspective of the producer); and the *frontstage* where the consumer is going through an experience with others but also actively influencing the participation in and creation of that experience. In terms of the use of digital media for events, we focus on events websites and social media services that are used by the festival organiser. The frontstage in this context relates to the consumer interaction with the created festival, but also to expressing feelings and experiences to and with others. Frontstage is all about socialising, sharing and communication that can be enabled with the use of mobile and social media.

In today's communication market, information is integrated for many users via a mobile device. The level of impact of this integration for users will be discussed as we go through this chapter. One of the most popular functions associated with mobile phones in the second millennium is sending SMS. A modern third generation phone has the capability and functionality to not only communicate through the device itself but also to allow the user to acquire knowledge, experience entertainment and earn a living.

To acquire knowledge, entertain and earn is made possible by mobile applications. The advantages of mobile devices are immediacy, simplicity, and context. When those are combined with usefulness, we begin to see a different type of software application which has transformed the way consumers use mobile phones.

The theoretical framework around this subject highlights a number of promising areas for discussion, including: user interaction across age, gender and social class boundaries; technology and compatibility across mobile operators for push and pull applications; privacy and permission marketing; and behavioural boundaries. All of these will become key areas within a partially unregulated marketing environment.

Consumer interaction

One of the intrinsic problems encountered with m-commerce is the instability of the provider to maintain an unbroken connection to any application. This breakdown in service has the potential to seriously hinder sponsorship and brand penetration to the collective consumer group, thus creating an intangible void, loss of trust with technology and also loss of the marketing message. To circumvent this potential inhibitor a number of platforms are incorporating a location sensitive GPS system (Balasubramanian, Peterson and Jarvenpaa, 2008). Next to that the third generation smart phones are equipped with camera, compass and access to broadband mobile internet (3G networks). These attributes make it possible to serve out personalised information and multimedia applications based on the location of the consumer.

Mobile usage within the UK among a target audience has presented some interesting figures on consumer acceptance of mobile functionality. The taking and sending of photos were the two most popular non-core mobile services among UK users in 2008, according to data supplied by telecoms.com in collaboration with research specialist TNS. Data also show that 65 per cent of UK mobile users have taken photographs with their handsets, and 44 per cent have then sent files to other users. TNS results come from a large sample range of 15,000 customers aged 12 and above during 2008 (Hibberd, 2009 [online]).

It also shows a high percentage usage within the 12–18 age range of all services apart from internet browsing. The oldest group, 55 years old and above, shows the lowest usage of all demographics. Of the ten services listed, Bluetooth ranked third with 36 per cent penetration in 2008. Taking pictures was top with 66 per cent penetration.

According to Comscore (2011 [online]), the holders of information from many of the major mobile operators, Nokia represents 34 per cent of mobile media users, almost double the market share of its nearest rival Samsung, which has 18 per cent. Sony Ericsson has 14 per cent of the market share of mobile media users.

Not much difference was seen between male and female users, with a marginal increase for females in taking photos and sending images. Male users were more inclined to use Bluetooth, play games and listen to music. Of all the manufactured devices, Nokia scored as the handset of choice, with the iPhone making an appearance in third place. Research has consistently shown that targeting a young audience is far more productive in transmitting the marketing message. When that message is service rather than introducing a physical product it has a greater level of success (Dickinger, Scharl and Murphy, 2004). Through a push and pull activity marketers can tempt consumers to purchase, and where that information is personalised upon delivery it gives the user a level of legitimacy.

Privacy and permission marketing

Privacy with this industry is racing ahead of the legislators; consumer concerns regarding infiltration without consent could hinder marketing initiatives. As explained by Myles, Friday and Davies (2003), GPS positioning devices can enable an operator to recognise a user by this service embedded in smart phones. Within the European Union mobile providers and developers of mobile applications have to confirm to set privacy laws within EU nations (national law) and within EU law itself.

Early adopters within the sector

In 2010, V-festival launched their first app, only for Nokia users; 2011–12 will see the app roll out to iPhone, Android, Blackberry and Nokia. As with the Lowland Festival in the Netherlands, V-festival also introduced a friend finding functionality using the Facebook powered friend finder tool.

Glastonbury Festival launched their first free app in 2010, which also had an augmented reality feature: by scanning the phone at the stage, the customer can receive specific data on performers linked to the stage in question. This app was designed and promoted in association with the Orange network and available for iPhone and Android users. Early consumer online comments show that the Glastonbury Festival app received more favourable reports from its users in 2011.

Current trends

It could be argued that event organisers within the UK are late adopters in comparison with our European partners. However, within the UK, V-festival and Glastonbury Festival are early adopters and currently setting the bench-mark standard for the 7.7 million domestic and overseas people who attend UK festivals. According to a report titled 'Destination: Music', UK Music (the umbrella organisation for the UK's commercial music industry) attributes a cumulative spend of £1.4 billion to these music tourists (UK Music, 2011 [online]).

2011–12 has seen a small surge in UK festivals lining up to release their first downloadable app. Reading and Leeds Festival (owned by Festival Republic) launched their first free app in 2011 with availability for iPhone users.

Orange developed the Glastonbury app in 2010, and in the same year the Isle of Wight festival app appeared, supported by Vodafone UK and available on the Android market. The two apps share similar characteristics and functionality.

Current trends show that mobile marketing is currently taking off – even though mobile advertising is still in its infancy, it is expected to grow to $5.7 billion in the next five years (Comscore, 2011 [online]). The early success from this increase in advertising will be with organisations that grasp this social revolution through the hand-held device and develop software that allows groups and communities to actively share, notify and engage in global com-munication. As improvements in the devices themselves continue, this will also play a major factor in advertising growth. According to Comscore data (2011 [online]), as compared with European countries within the study – France, Germany, Italy, Spain – the UK population has a higher degree of usage regarding phone functionality, with taking pictures (66 per cent) as the number one function used on a mobile phone. Just using the phone for talking declined to 18 per cent in terms of the overall usage for UK mobile users. When looking at the development of apps within the market the most popular are gaming apps, with 53 per cent of app users in the EU playing games – which equates to 20 million users in 2009.

The case study below discusses the active use of the mobile phone as a marketing tool.

CASE STUDY   LOWLANDS OUTDOOR MUSIC FESTIVAL, NETHERLANDS

The Lowlands Festival is a three-day, progressive outdoor festival that focuses on alternative music, but offers much more than just that, with a complete programme of stand-up comedy, film, visual arts, literature and (street) theatre. For three days in August, a city rises in the middle of Holland: a township with 55,000 inhabitants, several hundred performances, many bars and global restaurants, a market, hippie hangouts, campsites with showers, radio broadcasts, a daily newspaper, and a unique currency. It's all there, divided over three areas and eight stages. Lowlands is one of the largest festivals in Holland. In 2009 and 2010 tickets were sold even before the final artist line-up was announced.

Over the years MOJO Concerts has developed a multi-channel marketing strategy with a strong focus on the use of new media (website, online community, mobile application for iPhone users and recently a mobile website). The goal of MOJO Concerts is to create the Lowlands Experience. The use of new media supports the creation and sharing of the festival vibe by mainly focusing on providing updated festival information. Another reason for developing mobile applications with cutting edge features is that MOJO Concerts wants to show its innovation capacity in the festival industry. MOJO develops these applications based on a sponsor and partnership program.

Lowlands Mobile Guide

First developed in 2007, this mobile application combines three types of WAP application. Firstly, it provides context text-based information (festival program, news and artist information), whereby users can create their own festival program by selecting artist performances on a favourite list. An RSS news feed also offers information on changes in the program. Updates are available every time the application is restarted; the costs are dependent on the mobile provider. The images in Figure 11.1 are taken from the smart phone apps, and give an indication of the type of information displayed and the level of detail for the consumer.

There are a number of features within the app that allow festival goers to access information about the festival with a degree of immediacy. Information such as scheduling for bands is available and the app has the ability to inform users if changes arise.

Secondly, it is a community-based application that enables users to interact through chat and instant messaging (in self-enabled channels). Thirdly, it is a service-based

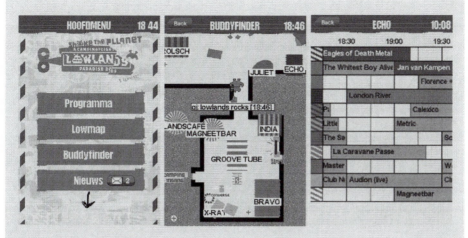

Figure 11.1   Examples from the Lowlands Festival smart phone apps

application based on GPS location that offers an interactive festival map where visitors can find their friends and send SMS messages. Users have the opportunity to stimulate friends to download the guide as well by sending an SMS message; they can also make arrangements to meet each other via a private Buddy Finder channel.

Apart from facilitating a platform for social interaction between visitors, the application also offers some 'goodies' from the sponsors. Converse was distributing rain ponchos or sun milk to festival users who could show them the mobile guide at the Converse Compound.

Radio 3FM offered a link to their mobile website (mobiel.3fm.nl) through which visitors could listen to the radio channel, also offering updated festival news. With the Buddy Finder users can create a channel by giving it a tag and a nickname. Users with the same tag are shown on the festival map, pinpointing their exact location, and their nickname and messages are displayed in a scroll bar. Within the channel they can exchange messages based on instant text messaging (SMS).

Although consumer interaction and brand penetration are their general marketing goals, MOJO Concerts has no hard marketing goals described for the mobile application. The festival organiser is aware of all the possibilities to use consumer data for marketing purposes. At this moment that is not the main target of the Mobile Guide. The main goal is to provide visitors with festival and artist information, to offer a platform for consumers to interact with the festival and each other. By showing its innovativeness MOJO is strengthening the brands of Lowlands and MOJO with festival visitors. The Lowlands Mobile Guide is developed with different partners and is financed through a branded sponsorship with Converse and Radio 3FM. The overall marketing strategy of MOJO for Lowlands is that commercial outings are minimised during the festival. Banners, posters and other promotion tools are not allowed, on site or digitally. MOJO doesn't intend to be a marketing platform for all their partners. The consequence is that sponsors are not allowed to send SMS messages to mobile users. Next to that MOJO is operating very carefully towards SMS marketing, having only sent one text message

(Continued)

(Continued)

to previous mobile guide users to announce a new updated version just before the festival started. Sponsors were given the opportunity to send messages in the festival news feed, but didn't use that communication channel last year.

In 2009 the Lowlands Mobile Guide was downloaded 15,530 times on 377 different mobile phones. The top five mobile phones were iPhone (37 per cent), Nokia 6300 (3 per cent), Nokia E71 (2 per cent), Nokia N95 8Gb (2 per cent) and Nokia N95 (2 per cent).

The mobile application was distributed across different channels, of which the SMS installations were most popular. In practice it turned out that the SMS download channel experienced quite some installation failures. Due to technical difficulties (both on provider and receiver sides) the number of 'uninstalled' applications went up to one quarter of all requested downloads. Other popular channels were the online application stores (both for iPhone and Android smart phones).

For Lowlands 2010 the organisation intended to build an iPhone native application only, because of the functional opportunities that an iPhone offers, the large share of this smart phone use amongst the audience and the technical stability of the platform itself. The intention was to make more use of the option to publish festival updates (based on a continuous RSS feed). The updates were to consist of festival news, the festival vibe, and programme changes combined with news from the *Daily Paradise* (a daily printed newspaper for the visitors). In order to monitor consumer experiences the messages in the Buddy Finder channel were saved and accessible, but only monitored to feel the existing vibe at the festival. It acted as a good thermometer, nothing more. For consumer evaluations during the festival MOJO organised a 'breakfast meeting' with a number of consumers at the festival itself. It was more important to get response on the ongoing festival and on any quick improvements that could be made. During all festival stages MOJO monitored online communities (like FokForum or PartyFlock) to get an insight into consumer's remarks about the festival. MOJO found that festival visitors were more open on third party platforms than on their Lowlands Community site. MOJO's policy was to monitor the content of the exchanged messages, and to intervene only when facts are wrongly communicated. For Marketing Manager Bente Bollmann, it was nice to see Lowlands visitors using the Mobile Guide to find artist information on a totally different pop festival.

Festival visitors were not 'spammed' by marketing outings in the Buddy Finder channels or through direct marketing actions. The Buddy Finder tools were used and experienced as a nice gadget. But the functionality can be improved. MOJO is confronted with technical issues and difficulties with GPS localisation (especially for the indoor facilities) and the speed of processing the sent messages. Overall, this functionality needs time to be working with it. Consumers need to localise themselves and then send a message. For the new iPhone application, MOJO is considering offering and/or integrating functionality from location-based applications like Foursquare or Gowella. In those applications the user localising him or herself with the use of GPS, then user-generated content like text messages, photos and videos can be combined with a more specific localisation. Another option is to work more closely together with the iPhone applications of

Hyves (a Dutch social network community like Facebook), as long as MOJO can find the right balance in using mobile functionality and commercial use or marketing purposes.

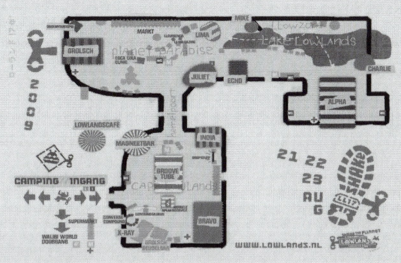

Figure 11.2   Lowland festival site map for smart phone users

Permission and privacy

MOJO has experienced no difficulties with festival users in terms of permission and privacy. Each festival visitor makes a private decision whether or not to download the Lowlands Mobile Guide. By downloading and installing it from the App Store or through an SMS service delivery, the consumer gives permission to the mobile provider and the festival organiser. As a festival organisation MOJO has access to particular consumer data (name, phone number, number of updates and so on) but does not use this data for marketing purposes. Phone numbers are not used for event-driven SMS or Bluetooth campaigns.

Privacy is protected by law (national mobile providers and 'anti-spam' policy) and the organisers' policy, that is, not sending commercial messages to the users and not using consumer data for hard marketing purposes. In our opinion, MOJO is focusing more on a pull marketing strategy, or consumer-demanded approach, which means that the visitor can download updates (that can include sponsor messages) if and whenever he or she needs updated information. With that permission guaranteed, the regulated and edited news feed from the festival organisation respects consumer privacy as well. The future is bright. MOJO envisions a wide range of opportunities for smart phones, native applications and offering improved functionality to consumers when making good combinations. The overall goal is that the identity and image of the festival should stay the same. That is why developers of future leisure-related applications should have an open option to design and protect these applications for commercial usage by sponsors or partners. On the other hand these applications bring new challenges and options for promoting and publishing leisure or tourism-related information services to consumers.

Summary

Technological advances have brought us to the point where there is no longer a need for a computer to undertake personal or financial transactions, as all this can be done with a 3G mobile device (Gunasekaran and Ngai, 2005). Extensive research from an international perspective has shown that mobile technology has developed significantly within the last ten years. With that development comes a number of challenges for the user in understanding the technology and its capabilities. Mobile operators have attempted to introduce the service levels to consumers via a number of innovative marketing campaigns. However, research has shown that a larger number of users only use a limited number of applications embedded within their phone. Taking pictures and sending a text are the most highly used applications and activities.

What is interesting, and requires further research and development, is the age differential for integrating with consumers. At the younger age range, 18–24, users become prolific users of smart phones and have less resistance to any intrusive marketing messages. This sliding scale of acceptance drops off as the consumer is older in years. This could have potential challenges for some events with an older audience profile. The level of privacy becomes an important issue for this target market and care must be taken to have pre-announcements before content is pushed to their smart phones.

The technology at present is robust and can deliver all types of media files to an intended audience. This will become more stable when the fourth generation licence is released to the UK market. However, timing for content delivery to mobile phones must be taken into consideration, and care must also be taken where alcohol has a feature within the event.

The rapid development of different functions in mobile applications (such as mobile payment or integrating AR-sensitive movies with on-screen action depending on your location) reveals that much will be possible for organisers and consumers in the near future. The question arises as to how these new media tools can be integrated into consumer orientated strategies by the leisure and entertainment industry.

As a marketing medium, third generation smart phones have broken some of the traditional rules of communicating to a target audience. With that has come legislation to protect the user from the intrusive marketers. From a sponsorship/brand positioning perspective, this technology has many long-term advantages for brand recognition and positioning. Used in conjunction with user activity levels, the degree of acceptance can increase exponentially.

On the other hand, new uses of the mobile phone, such as NFC coding for keys and mobile payment, will increase the number of touch points and hence the opportunities to advertise on mobile channels. Mobile advertisers will have to think of new ways to reach users, as services become more direct and more personal. The bottom line is: ads will only get through to the user if they are able to add the right value at the right time. With that knowledge event organisers and marketers have to consider the user of a mobile device as a global citizen who can strengthen brand positioning but also communicate immediate response in a consumer-led environment.

■ Discussion questions

Question 1

Name the four major phone operators who were part of the UK Government auction for the third generation mobile licence in 2000.

Question 2

Describe in detail the technical application of Augmented Reality as a feature within the Glastonbury festival app.

Question 3

Smart phones have become a common feature for consumers within the UK market, and it is widely known from data gathered that some phone functions have a higher usage rather than the phone itself. List the top five functions used by UK consumers.

Question 4

As recently as 2010, two UK outdoor music festivals launched festival apps. Discuss some of the developmental stages of those apps from initial release to the current date.

Question 5

With the impending release of the 4G licence to the UK market, discuss the potential benefits it will bring for consumers and event organisers.

Question 6

Research has shown that privacy and permission marketing within the smart phone revolution has become a topic of discussion on a global scale. Discuss the merits of considering this aspect when delivering content to consumers via their mobile phones at an event.

CASE STUDY 1   VAN GOGH AUGMENTED REALITY NETHERLANDS

Layar is a mobile platform for discovering information about the world around you. Using Augmented Reality technology, Layar displays digital information called 'layers' into your smart phone's field of vision.

A web browser can be seen as a window into the virtual world. Instead of seeing web pages inside that browser window, you see the environment around you; except with an added layer of data on top of it. Layar's augmented reality operates within that context. Augmented reality (AR) is a term for a live direct or indirect view of a physical real-world environment whose elements are augmented by virtual computer-generated imagery. It is also related to a more general concept called mediated reality in which a view of reality is modified. Consumers can install Layar on their mobile phone; this adds an information layer to the camera imaging with which information about locations or objects can be sought. Layar is currently only available on the iPhone 3GS and Android phones with GPS and compass.

Walking through the Dutch village of Nuenen, Vincent van Gogh fans can be introduced to the life and work of this world famous artist. With a mobile phone in hand, visitors to Nuenen are able to view Vincent van Gogh's life by watching detailed information, photos, audio and video files which are related to real buildings and places linked to the great artist. Routes to the points of interest are shown on a Google Map, and directions as to how to get there are given too. Customers can step into the route at any point, it is not necessary to walk a planned route. All this is done by building a Van Gogh browser (layer) in the mobile AR-application Layar. The Van Gogh layer is developed by Vrijetijdshuis Brabant, Ordina and 'Schatten van Brabant', the cultural program of the state of Noord-Brabant. With the Van Gogh layer they try to unlock important places in the life of the great artist for a new generation. Digital natives have the future, but now also have access to the past. The layer shows nine points of interest (on (GPS) locations) indicating where Van Gogh lived in Nuenen and created his world famous paintings (i.e. Aardappeleters). Many buildings and décors from 1885 still exist in Nuenen. This layer is one example of what will be developed in the near future.

This innovative demo is not related to specific marketing goals and the story in itself is not complete. More interesting is the question of what the leisure and tourism sector can gain with these new opportunities. For the leisure industry, mobile applications and services create new opportunities in product development and entrepreneurship. The challenge is to develop consumer-oriented services that create added value for their leisure experiences. Another layer already developed is offering the agenda of 'Uit in Brabant', which provides an event calendar of leisure activities of all the cities and places in Noord-Brabant. All of these are of course shown and displayed in terms of those 'nearest to you' based on GPS location and the direction of the Layar sensor. The information offered is related to events per day in a five-kilometre range and links are provided to find detailed information. Layar is built on a two-layer model. The first layer is geographically based on a point of interest and gives summarised information (title, short description, image and link). In the second layer a mobile website can be presented that offers more information or adds multimedia files. Layar is developed for the Android platform, based on an open source software development program.

At the moment Layar is most suited for use in the Netherlands; one reason for this is the availability of and access to broadband (mobile) internet and the increasing market share of 3G smart phones. The current telecommunications network offers the capacity needed and supports GPS location services. This example shows that it is possible to create and deliver rich stories based on local content related to a specific location. Text, photo, video and audio files can be used to create a multimedia package. However, not all multimedia formats are supported (think of the difficulties in presenting Flash files on an iPhone), but it is likely that these problems will be challenged in the near future. From the marketing and communication perspective, mobile applications like Layar can function as an extra channel to deliver information services to customers. For customers, more interest is created if an extra layer of additional content is offered (like Wikitude or multimedia presentations), or if the application is combined with other mobile services or tools like SMS or Bluetooth marketing.

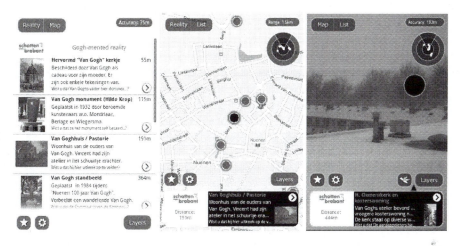

Figure 11.3   Examples from the Van Gogh browser in Layar

Permission and privacy

In the Layar example it is the customer who gives permission within the application to show a certain layer of information. Customers can download Layar as an application package and install it. Within Layar you can then 'scan' the surrounding area through the camera and select a certain information layer from the library list. Customers can adjust the settings via which related information is provided.

By installing the application customers must agree to the privacy conditions of Layar. Personal information and mobile numbers of users are available to Layar (as owner of the application) and mobile providers. Both parties have to comply with national and European privacy and spam laws. Personal user details are not shared by Layar with content developers. Developers only receive statistics on the number of downloads, updates and layer requests and the number of users. It is possible for developers to add self-created statistics (like Google Analytics). When it becomes possible to add interactive elements in the second layer, such as contact forms or collecting mobile numbers for SMS alerts, then developers could obtain that information.

CASE STUDY 2   MANCHESTER PRIDE

Manchester Pride is Manchester's annual lesbian, gay, bisexual and transgender (LGBT) festival which is traditionally held over the August bank holiday weekend. The aim of Manchester Pride, themed 'Best of British' is to celebrate LGBT lives and to work towards greater mutual support and co-operation. Manchester Pride attracts participants and spectators from across the UK and around the world.

Manchester Pride has traditionally always been a fundraiser for local HIV and LGBT communities. During recent years and ever increasing in numbers, North West Ambulance Service NHS Trust have participated at Pride through attendance in the Parade during the August Bank holiday and having an Expo stand providing information on the service and gauging user experience. The pride festival can trace its heritage back to 1990 when the first event was just a jumble sale to raise money for HIV and Aids. The location hasn't changed but the event management team has seen many individuals come and go. The organisation moved from a local team to a City Council collaboration linked to Marketing Manchester and it is now part of the City Tourism destination strategy. The gay village, as the location where the event is held each year is famously known in Manchester, was unfenced in 1998 but a wristband was required to get into the bars and clubs. In 1999, Mardi Gras was run from an office in Manchester town hall, the gay village was completely fenced off, and £10 entry tickets were introduced.

Under a new corporate name (GayFest), the festival reverted back to being free to enter in 2000 and 2001. In August 2002 the event went back to being called Mardi Gras, but although still free, was cancelled completely with just a few weeks to go. This was due to a dispute between the police and organisers regarding alcohol drinking restrictions on the public highway and crowd safety. In 2003 the event went ahead and was titled Europride; in the same year, Marketing Manchester was collaborating with organisers. Over the years, Manchester's August Bank Holiday gay event has been known as the Carnival of Fun, Mardi Gras, GayFest, Manchester Europride and most recently Manchester Pride.

In 2003, Operation Fundraiser deducted its own running costs (£59,520) from the ticket and collection bucket money it had gathered (£388,946). It handed over £200,000 to Manchester Europride (Marketing Manchester) to cover its running costs and the remainder (£129,426) went to good causes. In 2005 over £115,000 was raised for charity.

Key 103 Manchester radio station and Pride Parade broke all previous records that year, featuring over 78 floats in a huge procession that went through Manchester City Centre, watched by an estimated 50,000 people. The Big Weekend saw another boost in attendance, with ticket sales before and during the Big Weekend up 50 per cent on the previous year. The first ever PrideGames saw teams from across the world participate in a variety of sports and athletic disciplines, promoting equality and diversity in sport.

Source: www.g7uk.com/manchester-pride-investigation.shtml

Further reading

Balasubramanian, S., Peterson, R.A. and Jarvenpaa, S.L. (2002) 'Exploring the implications of m-commerce for markets and marketing' *Journal of the Academy of Marketing Science*, 30(4): 348–61.

Bauer, H.H. and Barnes, S.J. (2005) 'Driving consumer acceptance of mobile marketing: a theoretical framework and empirical study', *Journal of Electronic Commerce Research*, 6(3): 181–92.

Camping flight to Lowlands Paradise (2012) [online]. Available at: www.lowlands.nl [accessed 1 April 2012].

Comscore (2011) 'Mobile' [online]. Available at: www.comscore.com/Industry_Solutions/Mobile [accessed 1 April 2012].

Layar (2012) 'Get more out of AR with Layar Vision' [online]. Available at: www.layar.com [accessed 1 April 2012].

MOJO Concerts (2012) 'MOJO concerts' [online]. Available at: www.mojo.nl [accessed 1 April 2012].

Myles, G., Friday, A. and Davies, N. (2003) 'Preserving privacy in environments with location-based applications', *Pervasive Computing*, January–March: 56–64.

Ngai, E.W.T. and Gunasekaran, A. (2007) 'A review for mobile commerce research and applications' *Decision Support Systems*, 43: 3–15.

Ofcom (2011) 'Ofcom prepares for 4G mobile auction' [online]. Available at: http://media.ofcom.org.uk/2011/03/22/ofcom-prepares-for-4g-mobile-auction/ [accessed 1 April 2012].

Scharl, A., Dickinger, A. and Murphy, J. (2005) 'Diffusion and success factors of mobile marketing', *Electronic Commerce Research and Applications*, 4: 159–73.

TNS (2008) 'TNS launches world's largest syndicated study of mobile markets' [online]. Available at: www.tnsglobal.com/news/news-CBEFA9AEB07 F4B16960BC6326F31573E.aspx [accessed 1 April 2012].

Vrijetijdshuis Brabant (2012) Vrijetijdshuis [online]. Available at: www.vrijetijdshuisbrabant.nl [accessed 1 April 2012].

Section D

Preparation and Operation

12 Events Assessing, Planning and Monitoring

In this chapter you will cover:

- events planning and monitoring concepts;
- key stages within the planning process;
- planning for festivals;
- planning for conferences;
- planning for events;
- case study: In the City – the UK's International Music Convention and Live Music Festival;
- summary;
- discussion questions;
- case studies;
- further reading.

The purpose of this chapter is to explain and discuss the assessing, planning and monitoring of festivals and events. The chapter will present an integrated model for the successful planning of events, based on the author's approach to planning as a generic subject area. In order to understand the planning of an event we will identify the fundamental elements of the planning process and work through them in a logical order. We will incorporate business planning alongside these main elements in order to develop an integrated approach.

(It is worth noting here that the chapter will focus on event planning and not organisational planning, which is concerned with strategic process and positioning of the overall organisation and all of its business operation.)

This in-depth integrated analysis will be illustrated with practical examples, presenting different types of events that have a regional, national and international perspective. These case studies will illustrate academic and industrial perspectives on each topic area. This process will be a prelude to the presentation of a successful event plan, constructed around seven key stages – this is a model first suggested by Watt (2001: 6), which allows the event planner to integrate business and event planning approaches. We will develop this according to our own research and thinking, into a more logical structure of seven stages (see Figure 12.1). The chapter will refer to legislation, regulation and guidelines, where they have universal application, and we will also draw upon the relevant industry working documents.

Events planning and monitoring concepts

Once an organisation has decided or been asked to plan and deliver an event, it must first consider the reason for the proposed event, therefore establishing its aims and objectives. Watt has highlighted the need for a feasibility study, in which research into the external and internal environment is conducted. Watt (2001: 6) sets out seven stages within the planning process: idea and proposal; feasibility study; aims and objectives; implementation requirements; implementation plan; monitoring and evaluation; and future practice.

In Watt's model, the feasibility study, then, is followed by an investigation into the aims and objectives of the event, which will necessitate looking at customer demands and the client's plan. Watt (2001: 6) has taken a customer-led and strategic approach to setting aims and objectives, and this is evident in stages 2 and 3 of his model. The next stage of the process is to look at implementation requirements, which covers marketing, budget, resources and availability. Although these areas will have been covered in stages 2 and 3, this stage also looks at the economic effect of these on the business, event and the wider environment. The implementation plan stage develops the logistical relationships and partnerships associated with the event. This part of the plan is integrated in stages 3 and 4. Watt's final two stages involve monitoring and evaluation and future practice.

The planning process, mechanism or system that an organisation employs to realise an event is, in part, embedded in past experience, so before we deconstruct and reinvent suitable integrated planning mechanisms let's have a look at an integrated reinterpretation.

Key stages within the planning process

Figure 12.1 shows the seven stage model which we have developed out of Watt's basic ideas. In our model, stage 1 of the planning process begins with an assessment of the aims and objectives presented by the business, client or key stakeholders. With clear aims and objectives in place, the organisation can set specific benchmarks and build a process for developing an event. This stage

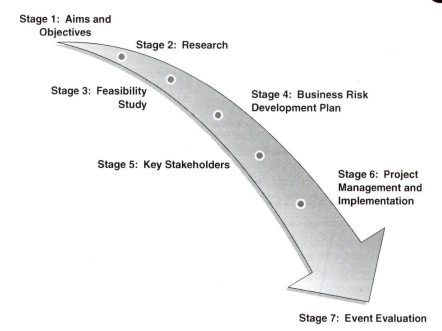

Figure 12.1   Seven stages of the event planning process

is also vital if the event is to be evaluated meaningfully at the end of the process; since the overall success and outcomes can only be determined if it is clear what the event was intended to achieve.

Stage 2, the research phase, involves accumulating data on all the key areas that support the event, business and existing sector. Armed with that information, stage 3, the feasibility study, will have a definable focus. The feasibility study should examine and conclude whether the event is viable within the economic climate or business constraints, taking into account internal and external relationships and partnership arrangements. Stage 4, the business risk development plan, will measure all financial risks to and other possible impacts on the business from the event. It should also investigate the likelihood of both positive and negative effects on the external environment.

Stage 5 identifies the key stakeholders and will ascertain in what way and at what level they affect the planning process or event. They may, for example, be linked to the event by sponsorship, partnership arrangements, financial investment or they may be participating directly. Once their level of commitment has been determined, the role of the stakeholders can be integrated within the planning process. At this stage, event planners also need to select the appropriate personnel to head the process and to ensure the integration of its elements.   .

Stage 6 is the detailed operational, project management and implementation period. The key concern here is how best to manage the event within the constraints that exist around it, in order to meet its key objectives. Event evaluation, stage 7, is vital if the organisation is to learn, develop and build upon the failures and successes of the event. The evaluation of an event from a business perspective must draw from the aims and objectives, the feasibility study and the key stakeholders. (Customer evaluation would be undertaken at stage 6.)

Planning for festivals

We can define a 'festival' as an event that celebrates culture, art or music over a number of hours, days or weeks. Festivals require all emergency services that need access to the event to be represented within the planning process. Apart from the emergency services, a number of agencies should also play a significant role within this process. These may include the Borough Council, Local Authority or London Authority and associated departments (Scotland has a different legal precedence and process).

Festivals, by definition, are a collection of events, which may be held in outdoor spaces, indoor venues or a combination of both. They are therefore bound by legislation and regulations. These legislative and regulatory frameworks will be presented as a guiding thread as we outline the planning process. The business administration, such as financial marketing, advertising and promotion, can also have a limiting impact on the process if it is not fully integrated within the process.

We will start by considering the planning of a festival. Most outdoor festivals are held on civic-controlled park land, national heritage grounds or private land. A suitable site or sites should have been identified and researched before embarking on the licence application.

In selecting the site, the organisation will need to determine whether it is likely that a licence can be obtained, and whether the location is appropriate for the audience, facilities, and external infrastructure. The selection and design of a site by the event manager must take into consideration all of these components if the event is to be successful. As part of this process, the event team should assess the services and utilities available on the proposed site. This assessment should consider, for example, whether the external lighting on site will be adequate for safety and security, and whether the type of roadway is accessible to emergency vehicles, customers and contractors and is likely to remain so for the duration of the event. This particular aspect must be assessed in all weather conditions and should take account of predicted attendance levels throughout the event.

As part of their assessment, the event team should identify external power conduits to be used by contractors and the event production team. Direct feeds can be connected where external power outlets are operational. An on-site communication network can be established using the landline supply service if a connection is accessible through underground network cabling. This can also be a contingency in the event of a power failure during the event, since communication can be re-established. Such eventualities should be covered by the emergency procedure plan, which is drawn up by the event team in association with other agencies.

Within the planning process, the movement of people within the site boundary must be clearly defined. To maintain control and safety, it is vital to identify the areas where contractors can obtain access, both prior to, during and after the event. Those attending the festival must be allocated sufficient space for movement at any given time throughout the event, taking into consideration the health and safety issues arising at different times of the day and night and from all possible weather conditions. In planning the site layout, overspill areas for customers should be identified, and where these may impact on the safety of customers, it must be indicated within the emergency plan.

Early consultation with the relevant authorities is vital. The accessibility of the site to emergency vehicles will determine whether the licence agreement is granted and renewed. The event team should therefore consult the local emergency services (fire, police and ambulance) on the choice of site and its layout before applying for a licence.

Where hazards in and around the site have been identified, sufficient measures should be put in place to reduce the risk of harm or injury to contractors, emergency agencies, customers and other personnel working on site. As the planning process develops, so too must the risk assessment document, if the event planners are to ensure that such hazards can be assessed and managed according to health and safety regulations. However, hazards arising from the *construction* of the site need to be assessed before a full licence agreement will be granted for the event. An initial assessment of anticipated hazards must be presented before a full licence is granted. It is also necessary for the event organiser to produce a written document outlining the site rules and regulations. Contractors must be given a copy of this before commencing any work on site.

As part of the licence agreement, and especially where the event site is located within a populated area and/or is likely to have an adverse effect on the local environment, the planning process must consider the potential impact of the event. Under the licence agreement and in accordance with the 2003 Licensing Act, the local community must be informed via a local newspaper and information posted in and around the local environment for a stated duration, prior to the provisional licence being granted. It is therefore prudent to consult the local community before applying for a licence to gauge the degree of support and anticipate any likely opposition that could be presented at the licence hearing.

Investing in consultation with the local community can produce a number of cost benefits for event planners. Such consultation can help to establish a long-term licence agreement with the local authority, which means that the event can be held on a regular basis. Marketing, sponsorship and financial budgeting can thus be planned strategically over time. Securing the support of the local community should also shorten and simplify the application process, thereby reducing the cost of legal representation.

A significant number of outdoor festivals are sponsored by commercial organisations, including V-festival and Carling Festival Leeds. The allocation of sponsorship monies and deals requires long-term planning; however, this type of arrangement guarantees sustainability and longevity.

Before a licence is granted, the event planning team will be required to prepare and present a number of documents, in line with industry guidance, legislation and regulations. For example, when constructing outdoor events, demountable structures will generally be required and the *Temporary Demountable Structures Guidance* will apply. Published by the Institution of Structural Engineers, this guidance provides a benchmark for procuring, erecting, maintaining and dismantling temporary structures.

The local authority planning and building control department will give guidance and make safety checks on the structure(s) during construction and/or on completion. The fire safety officer from the local fire department operates under the Fire Precaution Act 1971 and Guide to Fire Precaution in Existing Places of Entertainment and Like Premises. The Fire Service will issue the event with a fire safety certificate to cover temporary demountable structure(s), where the event requires the structure to be accessed by the general public, contractors or event personnel.

Further documentation will also be required by the local authority. This includes a risk assessment under the Health and Safety at Work Act 1974, which should be presented with the licence. The licence application and the fire safety certificate states that a risk assessment must be undertaken, and an emergency evacuation plan should also be written and presented alongside the fire safety certificate.

In preparing for their planning meetings with the local authority, emergency services and contractors, the event team must acquire and develop an appropriate plan of the site and surrounding areas. This site plan will be an essential tool in designing the site layout and facilities. It is also a requirement of the application process. The plan also gives the event manager/licensee a clear visual sense of the event and hence enables their strategic control of it.

The scheduling of performers and performances is a key task for all event planners. This must reflect the type of venue, the audience, the theme of the event, the intended impact and the profile of the performer/performance. These factors should be documented alongside the proposed schedule for the event and presented within the licence application.

Once the event team has undertaken adequate consultation with outside agencies, the local community and emergency services, and has obtained a provisional licence for a site under the 2003 Licensing Act, they should consult the *Purple Guide*. This is an industry document endorsed by the Health and Safety Executive and used by many local authorities, emergency services, contractors and associated organisations. The *Purple Guide* also has an international reputation as the definitive guide for outdoor festivals and similar events.

The *Purple Guide* provides detailed guidance for on-site services, management and operation, both prior to and during the event. It also describes the regulations that may impact on various aspects of the event, making particular reference to health and safety guidelines. The document gives direction on suitable site design and the layout of amenities and basic services. It directs event planners to the other guidance documents, legislation and regulations that they need in order to manage an outdoor festival.

Planning for conferences

A conference has a number of distinct differences within the planning process, as compared to festivals and other events. Although the first, preparatory, stage should be present in all event planning processes, the development of festivals is strongly influenced by the type of licence required. The structuring of a conference, on the other hand, will be greatly influenced by the building or location in which it will be held. The planning of other events may be constrained to varying degrees by licence, location and building factors.

Although there will be similarities to the processes used in festival planning, there are also specific issues to be considered when planning for a conference. Such an event clearly focuses on the key speaker(s) and delegates. A conference may also be described as a 'destination event', since the location is an integral element which can shape the entire planning process.

A conference has many similar characteristics to other events and this section will outline the common characteristics within the planning process. The conference organiser should firstly undertake research and conduct a feasibility study. This process, as highlighted in the previous section, will examine the nature of the business and its ability to hold this particular type of event. An organisation should always undertake this aspect of the planning process before starting to plan all new or existing events. Alongside the feasibility study, a business risk development plan should highlight potential adverse effects for the overall business and assess the level of risk for each.

There are a number of specific factors which must be taken into account when planning a conference. A conference must cater for an agreed number of delegates; it should be housed at a location that is easily accessible to the intended guests; and the event may include an overnight stay tied into the proceedings or offered as an option to delegates. Sufficient research should be carried out and the feasibility study should explore cost, availability and quality. Many conference facilities have developed an all-in-one package for conference organisers. These typically include venue and equipment, hotel, hospitality, labour and external entertainment. Where such a package is offered, it remains the responsibility of the organiser to research every element independently to assess operational levels of service quality.

The financial business risks of the conference are directly associated with the number of delegates, and cost of attending must be factored into the equation to cover all costs to the organisation developing and delivering the event. The overall cost of all external facilities that will contain the event for the given period must be included.

A cost benefit analysis should be conducted, especially where there is a high financial risk to the organisation of failing to attract sufficient delegates. This analysis should incorporate all costs associated with the event, including the cost of services provided in-house by the organisation and those purchased from external contractors. Where external operators are required, there may be additional costs due to transportation, seasonal cost variations or fluctuations in currency, and these must also be fully investigated, if relevant. Only after these areas have been priced accurately can the charge for delegate places be set. This must, however, also reflect acceptable price levels for this type of conference. The overall cost of the conference cannot be met by the total projected income from delegates' fees.

Many conferences have business-to-business relationships attached to the theme. Therefore most conferences are paid in full by the company or companies that host them, since they act as a promotional exercise for their business. However, some conferences require publicity to encourage participation. In The City international music conference, which is held annually in Manchester, England, attracts approximately 2,000 international delegates. In 2005, the cost to each delegate was £575 + VAT. For an event of this scale, the planning process must ensure continual marketing, including the production and distribution of promotional information from the previous event. Marketing can influence the number of delegates who attend this type of conference and the marketing strategy should identify and use effective communication platforms to transmit information across international boundaries. Since the conference has a yearly timetable of delivery, researching and targeting both existing and new customers will be a key and continuous part of the strategy.

Commercially-driven conferences, apart from relying on delegates who pay to attend, can also get financial assistance with overall costs from sponsors. This is the case for the international music conference mentioned above. In this instance, key stakeholders must play a significant role within the planning process in determining the aims and objectives. This will be more apparent where key stakeholders contribute to the event directly, for example, by supplying free or reduced cost venues and equipment. If a conference is a not-for-profit event, economic assistance may sometimes be allocated from local authorities if the event meets the basic criteria for the area. Where financial assistance is factored into the event planning process, event planners must ensure that the event's aims and objectives are linked to the criteria for assistance and must demonstrate this within their evaluation of the event.

As highlighted previously, delegate registration does not always include accommodation and hospitality; if it does not, then this cost must be borne by the delegates. In developing an overall package, deals should be negotiated with hotels to allocate a block booking for the number of delegates at a reduced cost if possible.

As in the case of festivals, conferences have legislative requirements which can determine the scope of the event. A building in which a conference is to be held must have a licence; though it is the responsibility of the venue operator, rather than the organiser to apply for this. The venue operator and the organiser are, however, jointly liable for fire safety, risk assessment, insurance, and health and safety. The venue or location must always meet the operational requirements of each Act of Parliament. All regulations, be they European or UK, including the health and safety regulations and the British standard on fire retardant materials, must be cross-checked with the insurance risk assessor, venue risk assessment and fire risk assessment. All the documentation pertaining to risk and health and safety must be easily accessible to all organisations and individuals concerned.

If the event is to be successful, the business must allocate adequate resources to the planning process. For example, where the feasibility study and business risk development plan identify tasks such as financial accounting and marketing as significant, the organisation should provide appropriate human and financial resources to support these areas.

The Association for Conference Organisers produces guidance on the planning and delivery of conferences and can direct event planners to other sources of support. The British Association of Conference Destinations plays a major role in the area of venues and locations for conference organisers.

Planning for events

All seven stages must carry equal weight when developing and planning the process. Where issues are presented that can affect the business or event, appropriate measures must be instigated to reduce the risk of failure or of a negative impact on the business. Where other organisations, contractors or the emergency services play a major role in the licence application, it is a good idea to involve a representative from each organisation within the planning process.

If a significant level of entertainment and hospitality is included within the event or is required by customers it is necessary to ensure that the facilities can sustain these demands and that the location is accessible for the duration of the event. Again, where sponsors are crucial to the overall event, they should be identified and involved at an early stage in the planning process and their aims and objectives for their sponsorship of the event should be established.

Once the seven key stages have been explored and developed the conference is entitled to function as an event. Each step along the process requires continual correlation with the stages, and the process should be monitored throughout.

CASE STUDY   IN THE CITY: THE UK'S INTERNATIONAL MUSIC CONVENTION AND LIVE MUSIC FESTIVAL

This case study will describe an event that has to take a dual approach to planning, in that it is both a conference and a music festival. In addition to the 2,000 international delegates who attend this industry conference on an annual basis, an area within the event is also open to members of the public who wish to attend the unsigned live music acts. The case study will demonstrate how stages within the planning process become an integral integrated business approach.

The 2005 In The City music event (ITC) was supported and sponsored by The North West Development Agency, Radio 1, Lastminute.com, Manchester City Council, Manchester City Music Network, and England Northwest. As part of the event, the city hosted 500 bands in fifty venues over five days. It is estimated that over 100,000 people attended the live music event.

The conference is primarily for industry professionals, who attend various workshops, interviews and discussions presented by specialist panels. These meetings and discussions are scheduled within a one-day programme at the main venue, which for 2005 was The Midland Hotel in the city centre. Due to the number of people attending this event, a selection of hotels within the city offered reduced rates to registered delegates.

In The City could be described as a 'destination event' for Manchester. Manchester City Council, in association with Marketing Manchester and the Tourist Board of Greater Manchester, uses events as a way of furthering the city's key objective to be seen as a culturally diverse and creative environment. The target for this particular objective is to raise Manchester's profile from a regional and national to an international destination location.

In The City music convention is an annual event that was initially launched in Manchester and has subsequently travelled to Liverpool, Dublin, New York and Glasgow. In recent years, it has been held in Manchester City Centre and is usually scheduled for late September.

An event of this magnitude requires a significant amount of planning, logistical operation and control, given the number of artists and venues. The event is a commercially-driven venture and is sustained by vital sponsorship. Therefore, the key stakeholders are not just circulating around the sponsors; the 2,000 registered delegates will dictate the style and content of the convention, along with the level of service quality and venues that will support this event.

Integration of the planning process

It is essential for the In the City event to have a distinct commercial aim and objectives at the heart of its planning process (**stage 1**). The event's aims and objectives are shown in Figure 12.2.

To bring together industry professionals from all over the globe and create business to business opportunities

To promote new and unsigned artists to the music industry and a wider audience

To share knowledge for the advancement and sustainability of a fast changing global music industry

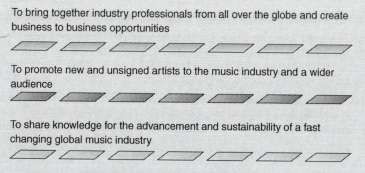

Figure 12.2   In The City festival's aims and objectives

Some of the aspects of the event that require a significant amount of research include: venues, hotels, potential or previous sponsors, travel arrangements, **panellists/speakers**, and interesting and relevant topics for sessions, e.g. new technology for the industry (**stage 2**).

At **stage 3**, the feasibility study should assess all the information accumulated at the research stage. It will look at hotel cost and availability, venue cost, scheduling and contra sponsorship deals, informative and current/explorative areas for workshops, interviews and discussions.

The business risk development plan (**stage 4**) will assess the business, event and the wider environment. The majority of data presented will be financial. The business must determine the overall cost of the event and assess market trends in relation to pricing for delegates. It is vital to identify the break-even point in order to set the correct pricing structure. Where there is a projected shortfall in income the remainder must be acquired by sponsorship/contra deals. The business must also assess the likely financial impact and human resource implications of the event's planning process on it (**stage 5**). For example, human resources may be required for web development, press and public relations and regional, national and international promotional advertising. The event by its design and facilities needed to support this venture, external factors may have a negative impact on the event. Scheduling of the event must take into consideration other events that may reduce hotel availability and participation from the wider audience at selected venues.

Stage 6, project management and implementation, then becomes the litmus test; the success of this stage will depend on how well the first five stages have been carried out. A great deal of logistical and operational management is required throughout the entire event. Therefore, appointed individuals who are fully briefed should deliver the event schedule, with room for flexibility where sudden changes are deemed necessary.

(Continued)

(Continued)

Stage 7 is the evaluation of the event. Quantitative and qualitative feedback can be collected from ITC delegates at the point of contact. Business evaluation will also be necessary due to organisational changes, which may include human resource issues or the acquisition of new business opportunities. This can be carried out with information obtained at stage 4.

This case study has presented the seven key stages of the planning process as they apply to the ITC event. It has shown that planning must be an integral part of any business when undertaking a new or existing venture. It has also set out clear and distinct stages that need both to be understood and realised by the organisation planning the event. A strategic view and effective leadership of the planning process is therefore vital, and all constituent parts and their impact on the process should be monitored continually.

Summary

This chapter has demonstrated that planning for an event is a logical, systematic, and yet fluid process. Developing a generic planning process that integrates not just the event, but the business and sector that supports it, should enable the event planner to gain a clearer understanding of the event, the business and the impact of each on the other.

We have also seen how the research and feasibility study is connected to outcome and success. Where a business undertakes a new type of event, the business risk development plan can ascertain the level of financial impact on the business in sustaining the process and delivery of the event. The process has shown the stakeholders' contribution and their relationship to the outcomes highlighted in the aims and objectives.

The chapter has also made reference to recent events that have a national and international profile in order to illustrate the issues pertaining to planning and to give a greater understanding of the organisation supporting the planning process and event. We have also explored this from a financial perspective and looked at the expertise and resources required to sustain delivery. Planning can be a long and arduous task even with all factors taken into consideration.

The chapter has demonstrated the seven key stages within the planning process. This seven-stage model can provide a starting point for the planning of festivals, conferences and events. It has been shown that each stage is integral and must be fully integrated with the day-to-day operational business of the organisation. If you are developing a type of event that falls outside of those discussed here, the seven stage model can be used as a template.

■ Discussion questions

Question 1

Within the event planning process, why should event management clearly identify goals in relation to critical success factors and measures?

Question 2

Within the planning process, outline why is it necessary to undertake a feasibility study.

Question 3

Outline some of the positive cost benefits (to an organisation) that can be derived from community consultation when planning an event.

Question 4

Within the planning process the event manager should look at a method for analysing the event. Explain in detail the Delphi method of evaluation and why this method is an appropriate tool to obtain an understanding of the event from the customer's point of view.

Question 5

Within the planning process a number of stakeholders can determine to a greater or lesser extent the outcome of an event. To ensure that stakeholder relationship remains positive, what mechanism can an event manager put in place to bring about a stable working environment?

Question 6

As part of the planning process event evaluation can take on two data gathering techniques. Outline how a mixed method approach can be of value when assessing data.

CASE STUDY 1   MANCHESTER HISTORIES FESTIVAL 2009

In 2009, a selection of public and private institutions came together to celebrate the illustrious history of Manchester. The event was scheduled for March 2009 at the iconic Town Hall building.

The two-day festival orchestrated and planned to occupy several rooms and halls within the Town Hall. Day one (Friday 20 March) had a specific remit to target local school children within Manchester, with the main festival activities taking place all day on Saturday 21 March.

The event had the support of Manchester Metropolitan University, the University of Manchester and Manchester City Council. Furthermore, The Welcome Trust was one of the major financial sponsors for this event. The event also sought further sponsors, who would eventually become part of the evaluation process.

The event was the first of its kind within the city, open to the general public, with a long-term strategy to become an annual or biannual festival. The festival was designed around a number of activities which gave a particular flavour of Manchester history to each target group, including:

1   Lectures (students, general audience)
2   Thematic display
3   Displays and exhibits (general audience, family)
4   Performance of drama and music (general audience and children)
5   Archive film and tape recordings (general audience plus 40)
6   Ask your question' sessions (general audience)
7   Historical walks (general audience and family)

All the activities that made up the festival from a customer experience were included within the evaluation strategy. Prior to the event it was crucial to identify how and where respondents could be approached to make certain data could be collected alongside all the activities taking place on Saturday 21 March.

Target audience

The audience profile for this event is multi-faceted and covers various different demographic groups. A comparable distribution of participants between students, general audience and families and school children make up a large part of the audience profile. In a bid to capture all target groups a clear distinction between these was developed in line with the activities throughout the day. Where there were a large number of participants interacting with a particular performance or general exhibits, contact details were sought prior to entering or engaging with an activity. This selection process took into account age, gender and ethnicity. This type of arrangement allowed the team to contact potential responders at a later date without disrupting their overall enjoyment of the festival.

In a bid to support the evaluation strategy, the official website had a page for consumer data collection with a view to becoming part of the evaluation. This was an explicit undertaking through the design of the site prior to, during and post event.

Evaluation strategy

Event evaluation was a significant requirement within the event planning and delivery process. It has a remit to present techniques, ascertain and correlate quantitative and/or qualitative data.

The evaluation paradigm employed a number of methods to acquire the relevant data, with the activities delivered throughout Saturday forming the major part of the evaluation. The Friday evaluation was covered by another team within the organisation who had sufficient knowledge and understanding of the target audience coupled with the activities.

It must be emphasised that the evaluation was not designed around collecting data for an economic impact or environmental study. It was delivered around perception, attitude shift and an understanding of particular artistic and historical interpretation born out of Manchester's industrial, commercial and artistic history.

Due to the nature of the particular evaluation and the complexity of the event activities, the design required a pre-test and post-test evaluation strategy.

A longitudinal evaluation strategy was adopted to give a complete view from a pre-, during and post-event analysis. Interacting with the customers pre- and post-event also helped to ensure that a significant volume of data could be collated without directly interfering with the respondents' events experience and thereby avoiding the research becoming obtrusive.

The Delphi method was widely used to establish hypotheses about how scenarios/outcomes were likely to develop with intended or eventual outcomes.

In designing the research methodology for the study, it was recognised that the Histories Festival as a particular 'event' with a confined duration, as opposed to a 'season' of opera or ballet, would be an excellent vehicle for employing the long-established Delphi method of evaluation. The Delphi method originated as a post-war movement with the rationale behind the method being to address and overcome the disadvantages of traditional forms of 'consultation by committee', particularly those related to group dynamics. Delphi is primarily used to facilitate the formation of group judgement. It developed in response to problems associated with conventional group opinion assessment techniques, such as focus groups, which can create problems of response bias due to the dominance of powerful opinion-leaders.

To alleviate strong-minded respondents from dominating the content in a focus group scenario, the study adopted an individual approach to key figureheads within the event. Each individual was given the opportunity to express their opinion through a structured questionnaire without fear of contaminating the views of others. The Delphi method was conducted in two rounds pre- and post-event. As stated earlier, the evaluation process took a longitudinal approach to capture data to gauge the level of interest, understanding and long term impact associated with activities connected to the event. It was seen as appropriate, if not essential, to contact respondents at least three months after the event to determine a differential or divergence between early perception and residual impact. The final element of data collection when analysed should feed directly into the future conceptual framework with recommendations for hosting the event again.

As for the major stakeholders, the evaluation strategy looked at a range of attitudinal aspects associated with the brand in order to ascertain whether, and to what degree, the sponsorship of the event could induce attitudinal change in audiences' perception of a brand.

Where the sponsor had key objectives these needed to be measured and the process had to identify and deliver in accordance with the criteria.

An ethical and confidentiality agreement was a crucial part of the strategy for respondents. This was vital to encourage objectivity and participation in the process.

Where a large number of respondents were required as part of the evaluation, a quantitative approach was adopted. This approach was developed in line with the stated aim and objectives. It followed the format of a five-point Likert scale, for example, objective 2, where 1 = not at all, and 5 = extremely well.

The festival set out clear objectives that became a significant part of the event delivery. It also had a requirement to measure the extent to which each objective could be observed, categorised and analysed.

Objectives

1 Bridging the gap plus removing barriers across generations and institutions.

2 Inspire pride in Manchester.

3 Be a celebration.

4 Present Manchester's past, present and future.

5 Highlight the different communities throughout an historical timeframe and how each has changed over time.

6 A mechanism to introduce and bring together communities and institutions.

In the main, the evaluation team consisted of undergraduates from the Events Management course. Overall operational responsibility for each individual to acquire data rested with the Histories Festival organising team and Project Officer.

Through the evaluation process a number of salient issues were presented, therefore, an unbiased and balanced interpretation of information was essential in concluding the final report.

The major stakeholders identified in the event all had individual objectives to achieve through involvement with the Manchester Histories Festival. Any evaluation process therefore needed to encompass these objectives and utilise these as a starting point for developing an applicable evaluation strategy. Prior research has established that longitudinal tests relying on data collected pre-, during and post-event, provide a powerful instrument for assessing behavioural/attitudinal changes in groups of respondents. Due to the quantitative nature of the data collated it facilitates and eases the statistical analysis and comparisons between the individuals and groups identified for this evaluation. KPI's identified in the evaluation process were then fed into future planning and development of the event by providing a crucial benchmark against which to perform. Moreover, decisive opportunities were identified for potential sponsors seeking to associate themselves with this unique festival.

Source: www.manchesterhistoriesfestival.org.uk/

CASE STUDY 2 URBAN MUSIC AWARDS

The Urban Music Awards is the premiere R&B, hip-hop, soul and dance music awards ceremony in the world. The Urban Music awards ceremony had its ninth appearance in 2011, as an annual event which takes place in the USA, France, the Caribbean, and Japan with plans to expand to Asia, Dubai and Africa. The Urban Music Awards was born out of the need to build a worldwide awards ceremony to recognise the achievement of urban-based artists, producers, club nights, DJs, radio stations, record labels and artists that are or were previously unrecognised within their country of origin and are a product of the current dance/R&B, hip-hop, neo soul, jazz, and dance music scene. The event is supported by and in association with British Music Week. British Music Week (BMW) pays homage to the legacy of the UK music industry and is a long-term strategy to promote and safeguard the future of British music.

As one of the premiere entertainment industry events in the United Kingdom, the Urban Music Awards is set to establish itself worldwide and will be the event that the business's top movers and shakers cannot afford to miss.

The Urban Music Awards is the only UK award ceremony to represent 100 per cent British-based urban and underground artists, DJs, musicians, labels, and club nights that make up the vibrant underground music scene here in Britain and others who are currently emerging on the urban music scene.

(Continued)

(Continued)

BMW utilize London's most popular music halls and clubs to promote the best British talent. Conferences, seminars and workshops held in venues such as Wembley, Equinox, Hammersmith Palais, 10 Rooms, Rouge, Mean Fiddler, and The Music Rooms will open their doors to the industry and fans for four full days of star entertainment. As a multi-site event with an international profile, this requires a significant amount of planning and logistical operation.

The BMW event has grown considerably from its early introduction to the market in 2001, and had its last showcase event in 2009. British Music Week and the Urban Music Awards combined their resources during that period to promote and highlight urban talent.

The UMA has been the showcase for BMW since its creation; its mission is to give recognition to the best of underground dance and urban music and by broadcasting it across the world to enable global appreciation. It aims to reach a diverse worldwide target audience of males and females aged 18–45.

Historically the event had an exclusive 500-person, invitation only, guest list that included mixture of celebrities, TV stars, sports and entertainment personalities, artists, A&R representatives, artists' managers, filmmakers, internet companies, DJ's, booking agents, concert touring companies, distributors, record label presidents, media executives, press, producers, and songwriters, etc.

The 2004 Awards were sponsored by Samsung mobile; other sponsors included Tynant & Alize. Media coverage in 2004 was by ITV, Channel 4, 20 other independent television stations, 53 local radio stations and 42 magazines. In 2005, the event included the launch of the World Online Music Awards, with and national coverage by BBC1, newspapers and magazines.

With the digital revolution fully integrated within the consumer market it only took a matter of time before events would realign their objectives to follow consumer trends. The World Online Music Awards is the first of its kind to acknowledge, celebrate and reflect the online revolution, promoting the most popular talent online, independent labels and artists.

Source: www.urbanmusicawards.net/2011/07/urban-music-awards-2011

Further reading

Gursoy, D., Kim, K. and Uysal, M. (2004) 'Perceived impacts of festivals and special events by organizers: an extension and validation', *Tourism Management* 25: 171–81.

Greater London Authority (2004) 'Notting Hill Carnival: a strategic review'. Available at: www.london.gov.uk

In The City: the UK's International Music Convention and Live Music Festival. Available at: www.manchesterwide.com/2009/08/10/in-the-city-music-convention-and-live-music-festival-manchester-18th-to-20th-october-2009/

Manchester Histories Festival 2009. Available at: www.manchesterhistories festival.org.uk/

Urban Music Awards: www.urbanmusicawards.net/2011/07/urban-music-awards-2011

Watt, D.C. (2001) *Event Management in Leisure and Tourism*. Harlow: Pearson Education.

Event Logistics –
13 an integrated
approach

In this chapter you will cover:

- event logistics;
- external and internal factors affecting event logistics;
- on-site event logistics;
- transportation logistics for events;
- logistical challenges for the future;
- case study: Green Festival Denmark;
- summary;
- discussion questions;
- case studies;
- further reading.

This chapter introduces the term logistics, and gives a definition of it based on current academic and industry thinking. Using examples and case studies, it explores the relationship between logistics and the event management experience. By using logistics as a business model, we will also be able to demonstrate how it is directly associated with customer satisfaction and the inclusion, and an integral part of business operations. The chapter will draw upon events across the industry spectrum to create an understanding of the effective application of logistics to achieve efficiency and stabilise cost. Logistics looks at the movement of resources to areas/places where they are required. It is the effective forward and reverse flow and storage of goods and services to meet customer satisfaction. The chapter will explain these terms, and offer a complete approach to achieving a logistical management framework.

Event logistics

Logistics has a direct historical heritage from a military perspective, which dates back to the Roman Empire. However, this term still has usage and relevance within a modern-day military framework, with the movement of resources and people over large distances and geographical areas. Over time there has been a refinement of the process and adaptation of it within the business world. The process has now influenced the teaching and physical application of event operations management. The notion of logistics, may conjure up an image of mega-freight in super tankers travelling to international ports on the far side of the globe. Logistics has come to mean many things but essentially it always comes down to one single quote which defines the process.

> The basic task of a logistics system is to deliver the appropriate supplies, in good condition, in the quantities required, and at the places and time they are needed. (United Nations, 1993: 9 [online])

Event logistics can be considered from a number of areas within the event planning process. The event planning process can include logistical aspects brought in at different stages in the research, development, implementation or delivery of an event. With this in mind a logistical framework is entwined within the event planning process. An organisation should develop logistical requirements for the movement of products, plant/machinery or people to a particular destination/location. This may also require the same identified items to be stored (inventory) or returned to their original place of departure.

In the process of developing a logistical plan it is paramount to bear in mind a number of variables that may have a direct impact on the logistical process. This point will be explained in more detail throughout the chapter. It is impossible to protect the logistical plan from all potential problems or issues born out of unforeseen or completely random circumstances. However, it is possible to manage the logistical plan if sufficient care and attention to detail is implemented consistently throughout, with a review process that allows for continual updating of the plan.

Most organisations will appoint a logistics manager to develop a system, to maintain control of that system, to track progress and to amend any problems that may arise. The logistics manager must implement a process to obtain information from each relevant department/operational area to allow the development of the plan. Areas such as financial management, marketing and human resources will become a necessary requirement in the management and delivery of the plan.

The logistical plan should never be considered as an independent operational process to the entire event planning process. The interconnected relationship between all areas will determine in a large part the success of the logistical plan.

Within the event management setting it has become essential to implement logistics as a management requirement. This is certainly the case when working on mega-events, such as the Olympic Games, or hallmark events, such as the Commonwealth Games. The lessons learned and skills acquired from these events have been well documented within the event management forum.

When developing a logistical plan for an event within an organisation, it is essential to differentiate between procurement, purchasing and outsourcing within a supply chain management setting. All these aspects are essential elements within the event management process and will have a direct relationship on the success/failure of the plan. Let's have a look in more detail at each of these three aspects.

Procurement

When an organisation sets out to procure, this process involves obtaining goods or services from one location and moving them to another for the purpose of use at the event. The financial transaction around this process may also include hire purchase or lease agreements. It is essential to remember that this particular activity will be replicated a number of times for different goods or services. In the process, this particular activity will develop into what is commonly known as the 'supply chain'. Where an organisation has a number of companies supplying goods or services to an event over a given period of time, and where each company is connected, this creates a supply chain.

The procurement process has no definite time span; for an event it can be implemented a year or two years in advance. With that in mind, long-term planning is a requirement; it is prudent to negotiate terms well in advance. It is therefore necessary from a financial point of view to establish a method of payment in line with inflation, once the pricing has been agreed between the event management financial controller and the outsourced company. It will become a joint operation to ensure that the goods or services arrive at the event in good time, and also that proper storage is arranged if necessary at the location, so that the goods are ready for their intended use. As indicated earlier, procurement has become a fundamental business requirement for event companies. Therefore it is important to implement systems that ensure the logistical process does not implode on itself because of disconnected levels of internal business communication. The logistics manager must secure from the accounts manager/financial controller the required sum of money to action a process of procurement and payment terms. Service agreements, warranties and insurance, etc. will remain in the domain of the operational manager and within the logistics manager's area of control. Documentation, as mentioned above, if not supplied prior to finalising the procurement deal, may hinder the logistics process. Other departments within the business should also engage with the logistics process. Human resources may be required at various stages within the process of procurement, delivery and use.

Where agency staff are required for setting up a particular product the event company must ensure that the correct levels of staffing have been sourced/requested, and that competent staff are in place to carry out the intended task over a particular staffing period in line with employment and Health and Safety laws. As the event sector continues to grow, staffing has and will become a bone of contention for many event providers. This is more so when sourcing staff from employment agencies. The availability of trained/ competent staff and in particular at peak season will impact on the event if not considered at a very early stage. Where staff are required to work over a period of more than one day, adequate accommodation should be booked in advance and payment terms with accommodation agreed prior to arrival. This type of forward logistics planning allows the event manager to deliver the event as planned. The human resource issue will have a major impact on any event if not requested and sourced if required prior to the roll out of the logistical plan.

Purchasing

Purchasing within logistics has two main areas of concern: items for consumption; and resaleable items. The purchasing of goods on behalf of the event relates to the amount of people who may attend the event. This can be calculated by looking at the number of pre-ticket sales, the capacity of the venue, and previous knowledge of similar events. If potential customers are purchasing tickets on arrival, the logistics manager will consult with the marketing team and investigate the strategy for customer awareness. The latter is a less accurate method to calculate purchasing; however, if this is the only method available, a sale or return arrangement for non-perishable goods could be part of the purchasing deal. The operations manager, in association with the logistics manager, could also look at suppliers within the supply chain who are able to work on quick delivery according to fluctuating demand (also known as just-in-time delivery). Demand-based management meets customer needs by changing the staffing requirement throughout various stages of the day and different periods of the event.

The final game for the Cricket World Cup 2007 saw an increase in ticket sales, and a corresponding increase in customers' consumption of perishable goods. It is evidently clear that an increase in staffing procurement is essential to meet customer satisfaction in this case. The ratio of staff and the number of potential customers for the sale of goods at key demand moments will give a greater return on sales to the organiser and thus customer satisfaction.

Outsourcing

Outsourcing at a logistics level has developed in areas where a deficiency exists within the business/organisation, or where it is cheaper or more efficient to use outside agencies. The International Cricket Council for the West Indies nominated GL Events as their official supplier for temporary structures and all plant and machinery that needed to be erected, decorated and maintained for the period of the event. GL Events is a UK-based company with an international profile in many areas of event management. With specialist knowledge developed over time in delivering corporate hospitality environments through the use of temporary structures, the company has a key market position which helped them to secure a working relationship with the ICC West Indies Cricket World Cup 2007. As part of delivering the event the ICC had to enact a number of outsourced requirements to meet the project deadline. Each organisation therefore needed a logistical framework to arrange in line with the event planning process.

External and internal factors affecting event logistics

In some areas of the event management field, and in particular outdoor music festivals, logistical issues are based around seasonality factors, competitive pricing for suppliers, high demand across the transportation network, and the need to increase marketing strategies to bring about customer awareness including temporary staff, both qualified and non-qualified.

In the events business, long-term partnership relationships are necessary in order to meet seasonal demand, and so this becomes a strategic function of the event planning process. Contractors are sourced at least a year in advance, or deals can be negotiated on a rolling contractual basis. This allows the main contractor to implement a supply chain if necessary to meet the client's needs. These logistical supply chains are found at many large-scale outdoor events, particularly where one company is over-stretched in the supply of goods or services in high season. The movement of goods and services via the transportation network also becomes an essential logistical issue. Where goods may have been used prior to the arrival at the intended site, contractors may be required to undertake an inventory of goods at a designated location before sending them out again. It is important to take a full and complete inventory at the original place of departure. A key representative must be present on behalf of the company to assess the goods before transferring to another event provider. Time allocated for drivers on the road, maintenance of vehicles to meet industry regulations, and alternative travel routes to ease traffic congestion all become part of the logistics criteria.

Within a highly competitive industry some suppliers operate a fluctuating price strategy in line with demand and seasonality differences. This price is also related to the fixed cost of the business along with replenishing old stock and ongoing maintenance/repairs. Music festivals, by design, function within a high-demand seasonal window. Therefore, higher costs for goods and services become the mainstay of the business relationship. In this type of environment it may be necessary to develop supply partnership arrangements. In the long term this could stabilise cost and achieve continuity throughout.

On-site event logistics

This section will look at the specific elements that make up event logistics. It will assess the interconnected relationships of each management area for the delivery of a safe and successful outdoor event. Event logistics should be explained as on-the-ground activities in meeting event and customer expectations. In logistical terms, an outdoor facility only differs from a permanent structure on the grounds that movement of people, machinery and products are restricted by little else other than weather, space and access. All legal, health and safety requirements must apply in both settings. Restrictions and permitted actions associated with the licence agreement should be followed for both settings.

Communication, emergency planning, fire safety management, crowd management, on-site transportation management, waste management, venue site design, medical facilities/welfare, barriers and fencing are all categories which need to be applied to an outdoor event.

Transportation planning

On the selection of a suitable site for an outdoor event, there are many logistical issues to take into consideration. Site access for all emergency vehicles must be the first priority. If the site is within a residential area consideration should be given to the local community, so that the event does not disrupt local traffic. If necessary, the event provider should apply for a road closure order to roads that are immediately adjacent to the site, with access allowed only for local residents and event traffic. This method needs to be applied and enforced for the pre-set up, event delivery and de-rig.

The event provider should also look at car parking for customers and staff. Where the event organiser can negotiate deals with public transport suppliers bringing customers to the event, this should be considered in order to reduce carbon emissions, and to reduce car transportation ultimately leading to fewer vehicles on site. National and local bus, rail and coach companies are the preferred option. Car parking on site should be outsourced, if affordable, to an on-site traffic management company. They will have an obligation to liaise with the police, the Highways Agency and the local authority in developing a traffic management system for customers and staff.

Emergency planning

When developing an emergency evacuation plan, the primary importance is the safety of the customers attending the event. The plan should be constructed taking into account all possible scenarios that could have a negative impact on customers. Therefore, adequate evacuation routes must be clearly marked, with stewards/security positioned at those exit points at all times during the event. Those routes must also be kept clear at all times. The emergency evacuation plan will be closely allied with the fire safety management plan, and all site layouts must have fire accessibility around and on the overall site. Remember also that an emergency plan must look at the vehicle access to the site for all emergency vehicles. An evacuation zone should be located so that customers and staff have a safe place to relocate.

First aid, welfare and medical provision should have a strategic location on site available on a 24-hour basis. Access to these facilities must take into account emergency vehicle egress and ingress. Customers should also be able to access the facility without too much difficulty. Therefore, all on-the-ground security staff and stewards must have clear understanding of the exact location.

It is evidently clear that all three emergency services must be given full consideration when developing the logistical movement of people and traffic to and around the site. When applying for a temporary outdoor entertainment licence under the 2003 Licensing Act, the police service must take specific instructions from the event licensee as to the movement of police vehicles on site. The police must also follow vehicle curfews unless they are responding to an emergency situation. This also applies to fire and ambulance service.

Crowd management

Crowd management can be developed from a number of standpoints. Firstly, one should develop crowd management strategies in line with the intended capacity and location. Further development will be consistent with amenities and basic facilities, such as toilets and food concessions. Areas of entertainment which make up the major part of the event must be given serious consideration. Where there is a main stage on site, due diligence should be paid to the area immediately in front of the stage, where there should be a considerable viewing area with access for emergency staff and security. Beyond that there must be enough square footage of space for more than 60 per cent of the customers on site. However, this should take into account what other activities are also running concurrently with entertainment on the main stage. Therefore, scheduling of activities throughout the site must allow for the movement of large numbers of people from one location to another, without adding to bottlenecks or congestion points. The free flow of people throughout the site will be the test of the scheduled entertainment within the main arena. The location of basic amenities will assist in this process. During the close down of the main arena further announcements should be made by display screens if available, or via strategically-placed stewards/security staff who can give customers clear directions to the designated exit point.

On-site transportation

On-site transportation (as opposed to car parking) requires some special measures to remove potential harm to staff and customers. The first restriction should be an overall speed limit for all vehicles. Where the event runs over more than one day due consideration should be made for the movement of non-essential vehicles at night. If there is a high volume of customers at any given time throughout the event an announcement should be communicated to all personnel who have control over vehicles. A vehicle curfew should be announced and monitored for its duration. Where camping on site is part of the event entertainment, specific access should be given to emergency vehicles, with the demarcation of fire lanes throughout the campsite. Each campsite should be identified by large signposts for customers, staff and emergency operatives. Observation towers may also be useful within the campsite; they should have a strategic location to assist in the movement of campers and act as a vantage point for staff and emergency vehicles as they move around the location. To complement this process, fencing around the site and along walkways throughout the campsite will assist in the flow of customers. To ease the movement of traffic and customers throughout the site at night, floodlighting should be placed at all entry and exit points, near food concessions, observation towers and main walkways around the site. If an event has an arena and overnight camping, a clean sweep of the arena is required to remove all customers. At this point the waste management systems can come into operation. All waste vehicles should be allowed into the arena area for the collection of consumable rubbish, and of human waste from sanitation areas. This can only take place once the arena is closed or a section is closed from all customers. The event provider must ensure that all vehicles working at night use hazard warning lights when moving around and keep to the speed limit. All personnel working within that area must also remember to wear high visibility attire at all times.

In managing the movement of all vehicles and personnel associated with each management system around the site, it is best to use a map with grid referencing.

Clear communication channels should be in place and an appointed individual charged with the responsibility of delivering communication messages throughout the site. A site map with grid referencing should also be distributed to all emergency services and non-essential services prior to arriving on site.

To assist in the traffic management of vehicles coming to the event site, an accreditation system for all vehicles must be part of the overall management. Vehicles should display at all times a valid vehicle entry pass. Passes should denote areas of access and limited access. If the site is fortunate to have a number of ingress and egress points, these should be ear-marked for contractors arriving or leaving the site along with other event traffic. While the event is up and running, specific notification must be made to ensure that designated points of arrival are clearly signposted. Public transport, taxi collection and drop-off points must be kept clear at all times. The effect of the heavy volume of traffic approaching the event should be taken into account, with diversion routes set up on local roads if appropriate. Heavy vehicles have weight restrictions and therefore must be taken into consideration before procurement and acquisition of goods. In collaboration with the Highways Agency and local police, overhead motorway traffic information boards should warn other road users about the event in advance and while the event is under way. Monitoring of the major road network to the site and around the site is also the domain of the event provider, and this should be done in collaboration with the Highways Agency and police. If traffic accidents occur on the road network and have a significant impact on event traffic, the event provider must have measures in place for communicating information to customers.

Disability access

Disability access, the location of amenities and viewing platforms must also be given sufficient consideration at outdoor events. Where appropriate the location of viewing platforms must take into consideration access for emergency vehicles. Disabled toilets and car parking must also reflect accessibility at all times during the event. Designated staff and on-site vehicles may also be required for transporting disabled and vulnerable adults throughout the event.

Transportation logistics for events

If an organisation is delivering any type of goods there are a number of factors to consider. The first question to ask is, what is the nature of the product that needs distributing? Is it perishable, chemical, expensive, etc.? If your goods are of a chemical nature, there are strict requirements for packaging and labelling the goods, and for the training of drivers. Further advice can be obtained from the Department of Transport Dangerous Goods Branch.

There are some items within the logistical framework that may require the service of couriers, hauliers and freight forwarders. A courier service is normally used for small goods. Couriers specialise in speedy and secure delivery nationally and internationally, but will only deliver packages up to a certain weight.

Hauliers, on the other hand, will collect goods from your premises and deliver them to your chosen destination. This type of arrangement will be done by road and could prove to be expensive if your goods don't fill up the entire vehicle.

Freight forwarders specialise in 'consolidation'. They combine your goods with other consignments in a single container or vehicle, reducing the cost. Due to the nature of their business and international logistical operation, they generally offer related services, e.g. organising the paperwork for export. They can manage the entire transportation process, tracking goods, and providing warehousing and local distribution centres if necessary. For further advice, contact the British International Freight Association (BIFA), who can assist with many of the logistical requirements.

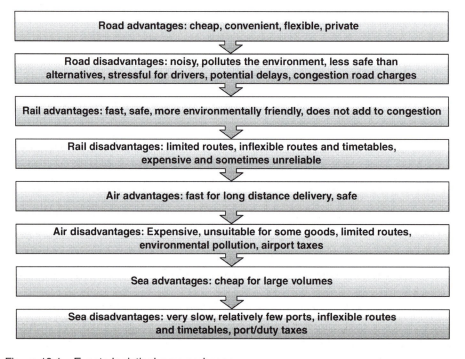

Figure 13.1   Events logistical pros and cons

With so many event companies working internationally, an understanding of the available services has become an important part of event logistics. With all these service providers there are ultimately pros and cons with each mode of transportation, depending on distance, destination, volume and type of goods. Figure 13.1 highlights the pros and cons associated with each service.

Before developing a logistical plan that may require the services of companies that specialise in this sector, sufficient forward planning is essential to develop a mix of services that best meet the requirements of the event profile. As with all event planning processes it is also essential to attach a credible contingency plan that looks at all potential variables including weather-related impacts.

Logistical challenges for the future

The automation of logistical services has been seen to improve operations and reduce costs to the business in most companies where the supply of goods is essential to the business operation. That is not to say that event providers should adopt an expensive automated service to achieve better cost benefits to the business and customers. However, there are aspects that can be highlighted and if appropriate could be deemed a successful addition to meet the challenges of the future.

Many companies today that have a large geographic area to cover set up local distribution centres to meet customer demand. Where appropriate, event providers should actively seek distribution centres or contractors in close proximity to the event. This helps to save travelling time, reduce cost and where perishable goods are required, local produce can be obtained.

Contractors who supply equipment to events can also look at labelling and security tagging of their goods prior to leaving their premises for use at an event, and for their safe return to their original location. A proper inventory is therefore essential at both locations if the company is to meet supply and demand effectively.

Although the fundamentals of supply chain management have not changed greatly over the years, in that it is still based around planning procurement and outsourcing, the scope and control around this aspect of logistics will continue to change and develop. As pointed out earlier, supply chains will continue to grow in length due to demand and at peak season.

An interesting feature of the future is the likely reduction in the use of HGVs, with a corresponding increase in the use of smaller goods vehicles (LGVs). Predictions on transportation congestion, and in particular urban delivery vehicles, throughout the UK indicate that this is a likely trend.

Other future trends in the industry might include:

- Consolidation on transportation, with the polarisation of different supply chain strategies.

- Better collaboration between event providers and suppliers; where goods and services follow a similar continuity, duality could assist the new challenges ahead of us.

- Procurement delivery to site, as is seen within the construction industry, where construction materials are cut and delivered to order. Translating this to the event industry is acceptable in some sectors such as exhibition design and build, and could help to reduce overall cost, human resources and time.

- The carbon footprint and possible carbon tax is a challenge – particularly in how to measure it and set the boundaries.

With the Far East becoming a major source for imported goods, traffic at ports will also become congested areas in the future. Cities outside of London have implemented, and are thinking of implementing, congestion charges for road users. In January 2012 the low emission zone was introduced in London, to reduce Pm10 particulates in the atmosphere, which are a direct result from vehicles that consume diesel. The case study below, Green Festival Denmark, provides the model which has been used by the Denmark festival organisers for managing traffic at festivals and events.

CASE STUDY   GREEN FESTIVAL DENMARK

Denmark is home to a number of well-established outdoor music festivals, one in particular is the Gron Koncert, which translates as the 'Green Festival'. This is the largest touring outdoor music festival in Northern Europe. It dates back to 1983, with an original concept that remains to this day, as a registered charity which raises money for muscular dystrophy.

Logistically this festival travels to eight cities in Denmark over a two-week period. For 2012 the festival ran from 19–29 July, concluding the tour in Copenhagen, the capital city of Denmark. Over the years this festival has migrated to a number of cities but remains true to the original concept. Audience figures at each location have fluctuated between 15,000–50,000 due to relocating to other outdoor sites. Vejle is a city on the east coast of the peninsula to the west of the country, with a population of 50,000. In 1986 the Green Festival toured to that city and visited again every year until 2002, with an estimated capacity of 15,000 customers each year. In 2003 the festival was cancelled in Vejle because of rain and never returned to that location. The year 2010 saw the highest number for audience figures over the eight locations, with 187,000 people attending. In 2011 the collective audience figure dropped to 135,000; the Green Festival attributed the fall in numbers to bad weather conditions that year. A survey from 2011 of 2,600 festival goers gave the festival a 96 per cent satisfaction rate.

The Green Festival travels to each location where performers play live from 1.30–9.30 pm. At the end of each day the festival goes through a complete de-rig and is transported to another location where it goes through a complete rebuild ready for the next day and new set of customers. The distance between Kolding and Randers, the first and second cities on the tour for 2012 is 111 km. The festival then travels from Randers to Arhus (36 km); from Arhus to Aalborg (101 km); from Aalborg to Esbjerg (198 km); from Esbjerg to Odense (122 km); from Odense to Naestved (89 km); and the final run from Naestved to Copenhagen is 70 kilometres. Between the 8 locations the festival crew, equipment, performers and contractors will cover approximately 727 km, which equates to 451 miles.

No other outdoor festival in Northern Europe can claim to have a logistical operation of this nature. This type of logistical arrangement requires substantial planning and contingencies to mitigate any potential road hazard that could inhibit the set schedule. The documenting and inventory of equipment becomes an essential element to maintain operational fluidity between the locations. Equipment stored in boxes will have identification marks or colour coding to ensure they are stored on the correct truck and taken to a specific location at the next site. Secondary equipment, if within the budget, will also be part of the plan along with preferred suppliers at each location if essential equipment is needed at short notice. This event must run similar to a small mechanistic army moving from one location to another ready to do battle upon arrival. Each site will have a small team of operatives who will manage the location before the contractors arrive to set up. As with most major festivals, planning for the Green Festival commences directly after the last performance in the tour date. In 1983 the volunteer force was 40; for 2012 the aim was to have 700 volunteers. The majority of volunteers will travel with the festival to each location, collecting more volunteers at other sites as it goes through the tour dates. All volunteers have their food, travel and accommodation taken care of to ensure they are ready to work each day. Accommodation for volunteers is not on the festival site but in local schools at each location.

Volunteers relocate stalls, fences, stages, light and sound equipment from one town to the next overnight. For that purpose the 700 volunteers use a car park for 50 articulated lorries (each of which weighs 15 tons), four fore-carriages of 5 tons each, 16 buses and several trucks and fork-lift trucks. Volunteers erect the stage and the tents, they sell food and drinks during the concerts, and finally they dismantle all the gear and transport it to the next town on the tour – all this in less than 24 hours. The crew takes down the stage starting at 9.30 pm, just after the music has stopped, and the last truck with equipment leaves the concert site at about 1.30 am.

The crew, which builds the stages in the next town/city, commences work at 4.30 am. They finish building six hours later. Cabling for all electricity on the outdoor site amounts to more than 13 km in length.

The title 'Green Festival' is not linked to its sustainable credentials, rather to its main commercial sponsors, Tuborg, who have sponsored the festival from its conception. Carlsberg, the owner of the alcohol brand Tuborg, has trademarked any event that promotes the word 'green' in association with an event of any discretion throughout Denmark. Therefore 'green' is only used as a commercial representation linked to the corporate colour of the brand.

(Continued)

(Continued)

Figure 13.2   The Green Festival, Denmark

Summary

This chapter has highlighted the significant use of logistics within the event management framework. It has shown how the process has been developed into a credible business model. Further development of the process has shown its flexibility in applying the process to on-site event logistics. This process and application has synergy with all types of events and the location. Logistics for event managers is not only a business requirement but has methodologies that translate to pre-event, during the event and close down. Logistics are now a paramount concern when applying for an entertainment licence under the 2003 Licensing Act, where licensees have a duty of care to ensure that customers leaving the event have appropriate access to transportation, without causing harm to themselves or others in the process.

A report was compiled in 2006 by the HSE Management Standards for Workplace Transport. In this document there are some alarming statistics which relate to transportation injuries and fatalities.

> On average, annually there are around 70 fatalities related to workplace transportation (in 2003/04, 57% were 'struck by a vehicle' and 7% were 'falls from vehicles').
> (HSE, 2006: 1)

These statistics exclude transportation by rail, public highway, and water transport.

This has given rise to a whole new conceptual model for managing outdoor events. In this chapter, we have looked at logistics from a wider perspective than just the standard recognisable setting of transportation logistics. The term logistics was presented alongside and partnered with a number of operational management processes, including supply chain management, demand management and inventory management. Case studies were presented to show the diverse application of logistics in the overall business of running an event company and event.

We have also seen that fire safety has close links with the emergency evacuation plan, and that all site layouts must have fire accessibility around and on the overall site. The chapter has shown that crowd management can be developed from a number of standpoints, but that crowd management strategies need to be developed in line with the intended capacity and location.

The scheduling of activities was discussed, and the provision of a site plan, which is needed to allow for the movement of a large number of people from one location to another. The location of basic amenities can assist in this process.

■ Discussion questions

Question 1

Demonstrate your understanding of the business relationship between event logistics and supply chain management. Outline your concept within an event management context.

Question 2

Outline two challenges that will face event organisers in the future when developing their logistical transportation plans.

Question 3

Demonstrate how seasonality issues within the outdoor event sector can have a negative impact on transportation logistics for event providers.

Question 4

Outline and discuss some of the logistical challenges inherent in the 2007 Cricket World Cup in the West Indies.

Question 5

When delivering the Cricket World Cup 2007 in a different location discuss some of the logistical, cultural human resource issues in acquiring technically competent personnel.

Question 6

Transportation as a logistical operation for spectators attending an event is an aspect that must be addressed by the event planning team. Discuss the type of transportation methods that can be introduced to reduce the impact of traffic on a host community.

CASE STUDY 1   HUMAN RESOURCES AT THE 2007 CRICKET WORLD CUP IN THE WEST INDIES

There are many logistical human resource issues in delivering an event of this type on time and to the requirements of the client, event organisers and consumers. This event was held over five islands throughout the West Indies. Apart from the overall management team with the core contingent from the five islands, resources for specialist skills in other areas were brought to the event. Security, media, and event management, alongside the large contingent of local crew and voluntary workers, were brought together in the pre-event stage to form a sound foundation for the event Training and adequate management of staff enabled the event to be completed and opened on time. This type of event resource would have been undertaken with the assistance of local knowledge by way of employment agencies and previous events held in those islands. This type of forward planning to meet the event schedule for erecting temporary structures primarily for hospitality use was carried out four months in advance.

As outlined earlier, the supply chain is the cornerstone of the logistics process, and in particular where long-term event planning with suppliers is necessary. Therefore, supply chain management, the control process to enable the supply chain to function without too much difficulty, must also be an integral part of logistics. In developing long-term business relationships with suppliers, the current industry trend looks towards supply partnerships. This particular thinking encourages suppliers to have a vested and shared interest with the client's strategic vision for a sustainable working relationship. Within a logistics framework this is an encouraging situation, where the long-term benefits to both parties emerge over time. Procurement deals with third party suppliers will smooth over internal and external factors affecting both organisations. The Confederation of British Industry and the Department of Trade and Industry are working closely to bring about Supply Partnership as a business philosophy across all industries, large or small.

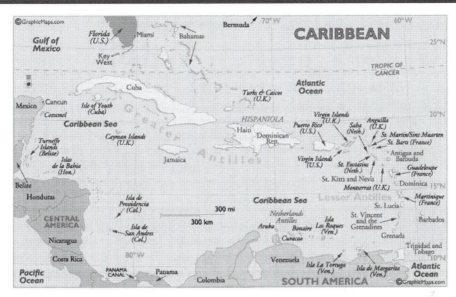

Figure 13.3 Map of the West Indies

It was estimated that in excess of US$ 100 million was invested in construction and infrastructure in Barbados in advance of the Cricket World Cup (CWC).

The country had an expectation of 20,000 visitors during the CWC, and as the event was held during the high season for tourism, the logistical challenge to accommodate all the visitors would ultimately test the Barbados government. Current room stock is estimated at 8,000 rooms, so to alleviate this situation the government of Barbados created a Bed and Breakfast/Home Accommodation Loan Fund. This fund was available to house owners who wished to develop their homes for bed and breakfast accommodation. Saint Lucia was also selected as one of the eight venues to host matches for the CWC 2007. (Initially Saint Lucia submitted a joint bid with Barbados, but eventually the country was able to make a bid on its own.) Within the bid, Saint Lucia made reference to their national stadium for cricket.

> The Beausejour Cricket Ground (BCG) is a modern fully serviced cricket stadium, constructed to international standards, with a seating capacity of 12,487 and completed in 2002 at a cost of US$16 million. It will be upgraded to 21,000 seats, 7,878 of which will be covered, for 2007. (The Saint Lucia Bid for Cricket World Cup West Indies – 2007 (2004): 4[online])

The report also alludes to initiatives to meet the international challenge. To dispel any anguish regarding Saint Lucia's ability to have enough staff available and trained to the international standard, the government implemented ahead of 2007 an extensive volunteer programme, including special training under a new government initiative.

Transportation within Saint Lucia was developed and documented in the Match Day Transportation Plan (MDTP). A Park and Ride system linked to five dedicated parking areas used 30- and 40-seat shuttle buses to move spectators from one ground to another. Parking at the official c ground was designated for VIPs, team vehicles emergency transportation and shuttle buses.

CASE STUDY 2   LAME HORSE NIGHT CLUB – RUSSIA

In December 2009, a fire at the Lame Horse night club in Russia killed 109 people. Officials from the Urals city of Perm, where the incident took place, investigated why so many people lost their lives. The incident in question has similar characteristics to the Station night club fire in 2003, at West Warwick, Rhode Island, in the USA, when 100 people died when pyrotechnics set off on the stage as part of the performance ignited flammable accoustic foam at the rear of the stage. It was stated that fire engulfed the club in 5 minutes 30 seconds.

Following the incident in Perm, mobile phone footage from the night was broadcast on Russian television, showing a large section of the audience dancing as sparks ignited the ceiling. As with the Station night club, pyrotechnics were set off inside the club hitting the ceiling which was covered in decorative twigs and plastic sheeting. Officials investigating the fire stated:

> "Russian authorities say the tinderkeg-dry wooden ceiling, the single narrow exit for a space capable of holding more than 400 people and the indoor use of fireworks, were all strictly against local fire codes and other laws that should have been enforced". (http://www.csmonitor.com/World/Global-News/2009/1207/russian-nightclub-fire-corruption-behind-lame-horse-tragedy)

Firefighters who were stationed directly opposite the club arrived on the scene in minutes.

The Lame Horse night club only had one exit point; the Station night club had more than one.

Rules and regulations inherited from the old Soviet Union were reported to have exacerbated the high death rate. Some 18,000 Russians die in fires every year, with safety rules often

Figure 13.4   The Lame Horse night club before the fire

Figure 13.5   Dancers at the Lame Horse night club before the fire

unenforced and safety precautions ignored. President Dmitri Medvedev ordered new fire alarms to be put into all care homes after the country's previous record disaster, when 67 died in a nursing home blaze in 2007.

Packed night clubs have previously turned into death traps. In 1981, 48 people died when a blaze broke out at the Stardust club in Dublin. The worst ever such disaster happened at the Cocoanut Grove night club, in Boston, in 1942, where 492 people lost their lives and hundreds more were injured.

History can reveal that a significant number of people have died at venues throughout the world due to ineffective monitoring, management, enforcement or regulatory require- ments to protect individuals attending places of entertainment. Event managers must therefore take very close account of the legal requirements when deciding to admit members of the public into venues. Management, legislative, design, psychological and enforcement issues should all be taken into consideration when investigating any incidents of this type.

How does one prevent an incident of this type from engulfing a venue again? There are a number of agencies that can assist and enforce legislative requirements from a UK perspec- tive. A cumulative approach to existing legislation and European directives will enable event managers to understand and apply the necessary requirements to minimise the potential fire risk at venues.

Further reading

The Saint Lucia Bid for Cricket World Cup West Indies – 2007 (2004) 'Media Guide' [online]. Available at: www.stlucia.gov.lc/docs/CWC2007BidExec Summary.pdf [accessed 11 March 2012].

United Nations (1993) 'Disaster management training programme' [online]. Available at: http://iaemeuropa.terapad.com/resources/8959/assets/documents/ UN%20DMTP%20-%20 Logistics.pdf [accessed 1 April 2012].

14 Event Production, Design and Lighting

In this chapter you will cover:

- identifying equipment in different venues;
- exhibitions and production;
- commercial music events and production;
- live public events;
- developing a business relationship with a production company;
- what the production company needs;
- final handover;
- associated agencies and organisations;
- lights and associated equipment in common usage in venues and events;
- Regulations, legislation and standard documents explained;
- production procedure for temporary structure erection;
- summary;
- discussion questions;
- case studies;
- further reading.

How do you identify and select the appropriate equipment for a particular event, in association with venue facilities and performers? This chapter will cover these areas in terms of legal requirements, contractual responsibilities, regulations, policies and procedures, aligning the discussion to industry standards and best practice. We will also look at how event producers select universal equipment when touring internationally. Technical procedures will also be redefined, to allow for changes in regulations. A practical approach to applying lighting at events and venues will be outlined by using current industry practice, underpinned by theoretical understanding. The chapter will also demonstrate the atmospheric and psychological approach to lighting at events to achieve customer satisfaction. Health and Safety regulations will be presented along with lighting equipment and technology which can help to achieve management and operational control.

Identifying equipment in different venues

The term 'production' is both a process and a business entity, within the very wide spectrum of organised events. In this chapter we will look at production as an outsourced requirement for developing aspects that are generally associated with the finer points of live performance/entertainment. Where static, mechanical or electrical equipment is being used, certified and trained individuals become a requirement. The chapter will provide a minimum working standard and develop a framework that allows event management companies the ability to engage in a business relationship that is mutually beneficial to both parties. The framework is aimed at organisers (who will know what they expect to receive), the production company (who will know what they expect to provide) and associated agencies that are also connected with the production process.

Production within the event industry has many specialist roles and responsibilities. The principal working practices are governed by the Health and Safety at Work Act 1974 and the Management of Health and Safety at Work Regulations 1999, with numerous UK and European regulations attached to this process. Event production and control as a business entity also covers many areas within the event experience and should take into consideration the different type of venues and how they are regulated.

Firstly, this chapter will outline the different types of events covered by production and identify some of the specific areas within events that are relevant to it. Through this process we will build a clear understanding of the integral role of production as a tool to enhance the quality of the event experience.

In today's global business environment 'production' can be located in many events. The corporate sector of event management has remained at the cutting edge of technological advancement through its use of ground-breaking multimedia equipment; especially where a corporate event has a speaker or performer demonstrating a product or a service to an invited audience over a given time span, multimedia is used to engage and focus the attention of the audience and enlarge the physical presence of the presentation. A large video wall, satellite links with live feedback or pre-programme information accompanied by laser, amplified sound and lights can be combined to achieve a memorable and powerful experience. Alternatively, single elements may be selected or further combinations, perhaps including static or mechanical equipment, may be specifically designed to generate a memorable and visual impact.

Exhibitions and production

The exhibition industry also has a far-reaching and global appeal with many internationally recognised venues throughout the UK, such as Earls Court London and Birmingham NEC. Exhibitors are constantly developing ways of competing within a closed environment, on a designated floor space to a trade or consumer audience. Where budgets are sufficient, exhibitors may employ professional production personnel to create an element of excitement and visual presence. This type of event experience can be linked in part to a marketing strategy or something new for the intended audience. Essentially, it may have heritage from the company's corporate colours displayed using lights and gobos (a metal stencil attached to a light fitting that enlarges and illuminates an image over a surface or distance). The exhibition environment may also employ moving images projected and displayed strategically on walls surrounding the designated area. Ambient amplified sound may also be used within a semi- or fully enclosed area of the exhibition stand. Exhibition stands are essentially constructed to carry a marketing message so production equipment will usually serve to expand on and amplify the company image. The installation of production equipment at exhibition venues must comply with regulations linked to health and safety in the first instance. As these are venues where all the structures are made of temporary material that could cause damage when exposed to extreme heat for a long period, all materials must be fire retardant and meet with the BSI standard along with the venue safety officer checks that may be carried out on all exhibitors prior to allowing customers into the space. The intensity of heat emitted from light fittings within an event production setting can render an environment unsafe if not checked.

Commercial music events and production

Music events, both in closed venues and outdoors, are amongst the biggest exponents of light, sound and stage equipment, since these are the core elements that create a powerful, dominating and hopefully memorable atmosphere. There are many possible combinations, generally determined by the budget, performers and creative production team. All of this must be closely monitored in line with fire regulations, health and safety and UK and European regulations. At music events, professional sound engineers have a duty to amplify sound in a way that both meets the artist's/band's requirements while giving the audience audible sound. They are also required to work within the license agreement on allocated hours for performance and decibel levels. Professional lighting engineers at large outdoor music events can sometimes be working with up to 30–50 individual lighting units arranged on a lighting rig above the stage. Some lighting rigs supported above the stage can be static or mechanically operated. It is the responsibility of the lighting engineer to pre-programme the rig and lights to work in tandem with the music and performance. Technology today allows lighting and sound engineers a greater degree of flexibility in achieving artist and customer satisfaction. Sound and lighting desks at live music performances can be operated manually or can be pre-programmed at source with an option to store the information on a CD, disk or memory stick, thereby enabling pre-programmed information to be transported electronically across international boundaries. Again, we can draw comparisons with many other areas of the events industry and begin to build our knowledge and understanding of the use of production, equipment and personnel. In setting up an environment which follows international protocols for live band performance, be that in a stadium, live music arena or outdoor field, the equipment's cost to purchase can run to hundreds of thousands of pounds. A professional sound desk can cost somewhere in the region of £200,000. Therefore adequate insurance liability for production equipment must meet with the market cost.

Live public events

Events that involve the use of lasers, fireworks, strobe lights and outdoor bonfires, are regular features within the UK calendar. When open to the public, these events have additional regulations and guidance for the safe control, use and management of fire. Fireworks must comply with The Fireworks (safety) Regulations 1997, which has now been updated by the Fireworks Safety (amendment) Regulations 2004, which has a principal responsibility for consumer protection. The British Standard 7114 (1989), although not law, is called up in the Fireworks Safety Regulations. Supplementary guidance is provided in The British Pyrotechnics' Association (BPA) and Explosive Industry Group (EIG) Fireworks Handbook 2000/01. The enforcement of fireworks law rests with the Health and Safety Executive (or their agents), the Department of Trade and Industry and local authority trading standards. Firework operators at public events must work with the local authority to establish the safe storage, safe fall-out area for projectiles and the amount of explosive intended for use at the event. Certification for personnel handling fireworks should be forwarded to the local authority by the event organiser or contracted agent setting up the firework display. Laser operators who are not fully conversant with their equipment should obtain guidance from the Entertainment Laser Association. Laser operators under the HSE have a duty of care to the public who are exposed to lasers, be they customers or operators. This is also the case for strobe lights, which can induce fits for people with epilepsy. Clear information must therefore be included in pre-event publicity and before entering venues/sites. Information should also be displayed throughout the venue and announced through the use of an amplified sound system if one is available. Such procedures enable the event manager to operate with due diligence under the Health and Safety Act and create a safe environment for employees and customers. With production equipment that has the potential to cause harm or injury to customers or employees, event managers have a responsibility to limit, reduce or remove risk of injury or harm. This can be done through information, public announcements or limiting exposure over a given time span.

So far this chapter has introduced events of different size, audience profile, location and content. What is constant and apparent is the use of production personnel and equipment.

Production equipment may include mechanically operated machinery designed for its purpose and assembled on-site; or an integration of special effects such as lasers, fireworks and strobe lights. Multi-media technology is used to enhance customer enjoyment by creating a memorable experience. This is also the case at large-scale music events where amplified sound and light become the driving force behind presenting and promoting a live stage performance.

To gain a greater understanding of the production process and the procedures that support the successful integration of these elements within the event management experience, we must first illustrate the working principles of a production house and personnel. A production company located within the event industry generally operates as a specific and specialist supplier of equipment and trained/qualified personnel. On the whole, event management companies outsource to production companies when required. The working relationship between the event management company and the production company will be critical to achieving a successful outcome.

Developing a business relationship with a production company

A reputable production company prides itself in the first instance on key personnel who are able to translate ideas into a working solution on time and within budget. It must also maintain high standards which must be demonstrated through inspections and the production of certification documents. These companies may be affiliated to a UK association recognised by the industry as acceptable.

They will also have trained and qualified personnel (if required) who are responsible for the maintenance and use of a particular type of equipment. Depending on the exact nature of the work undertaken by these companies, it may be necessary for them to show permits and certification before work can proceed. The production company, in agreement with the organiser, local authority and suppliers if required, will assess the type of activity and assign a particular type of equipment and personnel to complete a task.

It is the responsibility of an organiser to request, if not presented with, certification and permits for activities/equipment that are to be used both at the pre-build stage or during the event itself. It is necessary to obtain this information as the event insurance liability cover may be invalid if work is carried out without clear supervision, certification or permit if required. Insurance therefore becomes a significant issue for all production companies and event organisers should request a copy of the insurance cover from the production company before any work commences. Insurance liability cover for equipment and personnel will fluctuate from company to company. Mechanical machinery and flammable substances that are used either to generate power or to install and erect both off-the-shelf and specifically designed equipment should have a premium cover that is commensurate with the type of activity. Individuals who carry out a particular task on behalf of the production company, whether freelance or employed directly by it, may also require significant employee insurance liability cover and a permit to work if the activity or task has been assessed as potentially hazardous to health. This is sometimes the case for people who work at heights. If an event is held within a venue which has the structure to allow working at height, the venue manager should insist that persons wear a harness when working above head height. Again, if this procedure is not adhered to the venue insurance cover could be invalidated, along with the insurance cover held by the production company, including the venue licence, in some cities and venues in the UK.

Within the production company there are a number of operational procedures that require validation and support.

A health and safety policy/statement, risk assessment and method statement are fundamental operational procedures for production companies. If they are to fall in line with the Health and Safety at Work Act and the numerous UK and European regulations whilst also safeguarding their insurance liability, adherence to these procedures must become the common working practice.

What the production company needs

An order to commence work on site/venue can resemble a logistical and military operation. The production manager will draw up a checklist and site supervision order. It is the responsibility of the production manager to appoint roles and responsibilities for all personnel and any sub-contractors. The production manager will set up a method for communicating with all production personnel and appointed sub-contractors and will compile an emergency procedure plan if one is not already available. This document must be verbally announced and/or given to all personnel before they commence work. The emergency procedure should conform to the health and safety policy.

The production manager may be required to set up an office on site/venue if one is not already available. The office is where all documentation and agreements pertaining to the production set-up should be held. If any inspecting organisation, agent or authorities (fire officer, local authority operative, etc.) make an appearance on site/venue, information should be made available to them. If an inspection is carried out by any expert adviser, agencies or departments from the local authority, a copy of the documentation relating to the inspection should be held with the production manager on site. If erecting a temporary structure outdoors for a commercial or public event under licence, it is advisable for a fire officer to inspect the structure before allowing public admittance. A fire certificate will be presented to the production manager stating the fire regulations for that structure and its readiness for use. Some temporary structures may require a qualified structural engineer to inspect and sign off before allowing further work to commence within the structure.

It may also be a requirement to have a qualified professional to inspect an area or structure before allowing any personnel to carry out work. This is likely to be the case where a stage/platform or temporary tented structure has been erected. The risk transfer and liability will rest with the professional upon completing an inspection and signed documentation (to show that the site/venue is fit for purpose).

The production manager should also appoint a site supervisor if the type of event requires a considerable number of sub-contractors, personnel and equipment over a lengthy time period. This division of labour allows the site supervisor to deal with site deliveries, construction requirements and on-the-ground health and safety issues. This may include monitoring the working procedures of each contractor on site. Large-scale events like outdoor festivals catering for 40–80,000 people will require all of the above production personnel with the possible addition of an appointed health and safety officer. This type of arrangement is common at large-scale air displays (e.g. Farnborough Air Show) where a safety officer is appointed by the event organiser to monitor all contractors on site.

If the production site/venue requires mechanical handling equipment, there is a legal responsibility for each production manager to ensure that contractors provide adequate and proper training for the use of cranes and lifting appliances in accordance with the manufacturer's test certificate and the load test certificate. All this information should be made available for inspection on request.

Security at a production site must be considered a necessity, especially if working outdoors. It is the responsibility of the event organiser to appoint an accredited security firm to monitor security on site. Accredited security guards should wear distinctive markings or uniforms in line with the Private Security Industry Act 2001. Further guidance for the event industry can be obtained from the Security Industry Authority publication.

Final handover

A final checklist should be used by the production manager to bring any outstanding issues to the attention of the event organiser, inspecting officer or associated agencies. This part of the production process can act as an official handover once the checklist is completed and the organiser and authorities are satisfied. The official sign-off for the production can then take place and full responsibility for the event reverts back to the organiser.

Production managers have a great deal of documentation to process prior to and during an event. The Event Safety Guide for Pop Concerts and Similar Events (known as *The Purple Guide*) published by the HSE has been designed in part with this process in mind.

Associated agencies and organisations

So far in this chapter we have touched briefly on the relationship of production with associated agencies. There are a number of regulated agencies and organisations that have an integral part to play within the production process. We will now consider how legislation under governance and agencies sits within the production process and allows production managers expediency in delivering an exciting and memorable element to an event.

When developing a production process that has a direct relationship to an entertainment licence (under the 2003 Licensing Act) of some description, a production manager must take considered or specific instructions from that licensing authority. Where an event has a public audience, the onus will be placed on the organiser and production manager to demonstrate that elements of the event that have a risk attached have been investigated adequately and constructed to fit the intended use, without causing harm, injury or disturbance to the audience, workforce or resident community.

A number of stipulations regarding the use of equipment prior to and during the event may thus be inserted into the licence agreement. For example, a road closure order may be required where large vehicles are supporting the set-up process for the event, delivering equipment, and the event is located in a residential or business area that has a high throughput of traffic. Such an order can be obtained from the local police station in advance of the vehicles arriving. The licence agreement may also indicate that machinery that might disturb local residents can only be operated within agreed times. Where an event (be it indoors or out) has amplified music that might cause a disturbance to the local residents, a decibel level could be set in place by the local authority or venue. Checks are sometimes carried out by the licensing authority to ensure that the event does not break any of the conditions set. As an event manager, it is vital that any such conditions are brought to the attention of the production manager and sound engineer.

The testing of sound equipment will be allowed only within permitted hours as in the agreement. Any public entertainment licence obtained from a local authority will have a number of conditions set, which may either be statutory or specific to the location/venue and community. Breaching these conditions may risk the licence being revoked or a fine levied against the organiser. Once the local authority licensing department has granted a licence, the organiser must appoint a licensee approved by the local authority to take full responsibility for the licence.

In addition to the local authority, another key associated agency is the fire service, clearly having a principal responsibility for fire safety. They have the authority to have full access to the venue/site at all times. An appointed officer from the local fire service will be given the authority to check that any electrical equipment, material or environment temporary or otherwise meets with fire regulations. They will check that appropriate firefighting equipment is within the venue and in good working order, with clear signs in line with European law. They will also check if any flammable substances are being used at the event and that they are stored and managed as prescribed by regulation.

Lights and associated equipment in common usage in venues and events

Apart from the documentation and legislation accompanying the area of production we also have sound and light. These two particular aspects to the event experience have become a fundamental element in creating a memorable and lasting impact. This section will highlight the benefits of sound and light equipment, specification and implementation within the production process.

Alongside this it is essential to organise a set-up procedure for sound and lights. This will involve a full list of equipment and personnel, with a production schedule that demonstrates the full implementation process of all equipment to a designated location. This information is crucial as most production managers are working to a finite deadline. Within the product schedule it is also necessary to include rehearsal time for performers.

Sound

When working with amplified sound it is essential to assess the type of venue in relation to overall floor size, internal material finishes, audience capacity, venue proximity to other buildings or adjacent rooms, type of performance and the number of people performing. Apart from the areas mentioned above there may be other areas that could impact on the type of sound system that is required for use within a chosen venue. There may be a restriction on decibel level set by the local authority, particularly if the venue is located in a residential area. Other restrictions may cover aspects such as hours within the day or night that amplified music can be played or the type of performance allowed within any particular venue. To accompany this there is also the HSE Noise at Work Regulations 2005. This regulation does not apply to members of the general public who make an informed choice to enter noisy places, rather it applies to employees who work in a noisy environment.

Under this regulation, employers must undertake a risk assessment, provide hearing protection, look at ways to reduce noise level, limit the time spent in a noisy area, check that suppliers are aware of their duties and keep records of the decision process to help show that they have met their legal duties.

Within the production process it is essential to delegate to and communicate with a qualified sound engineer, where sound equipment will be brought into a venue to meet the performance and audience requirements. A sound engineer can determine the type of equipment to achieve the set outcomes. Amplified sound operates within a frequency range of high to low frequency. A qualified sound engineer can set the frequency range as required for the performance or venue. As sound propagation can be a very personal experience, it is essential to monitor sound levels throughout the venue and in particular when full audience capacity has been obtained. This can be done by the sound engineer or any member of the event team. The golden rule is, if you can't hear it there is a good possibility that your audience is having the same difficulty.

Therefore, when selecting a sound system it is essential to have a clear idea of the type of performance you are planning. In creating the right type of audible sound, various speaker systems and arrangement of those systems will go far in setting quality sound and atmosphere. The most common type of speaker arrangement is to house them in cabinets; this is designed for all types of sounds. This method is commonly used in home hifi systems. Each cabinet could have a three-band arrangement including low band, mid band and high band; this will be the frequency range emanating from the speaker cabinet. Or all three bands could be separated within individual speaker cabinets.

When operating within a closed environment such as a school hall or medium-sized music venue with a capacity of approximately 1,000, with the entertainment positioned at one end of the venue on a stage/platform, speakers should be placed where they can provide a good distribution of sound across the venue. If speakers are placed on a platform/stage or suspended from the ceiling, better distribution of sound will be achieved within the venue. Speakers suspended above head height, positioned to direct sound into the audience, are commonly applied to larger venues such as arenas, sport stadiums and outdoor live music festivals, where sound must travel over a greater

Figure 14.1   Millennium Square Leeds. Demonstration of sound and lighting equipment, high powered lasers

Figure 14.2   Virgin Festival 2002 main stage speakers

distance and maintain its frequency range along with clarity of sound. All this should be achieved by a competent sound engineer.

Delay speakers, as the name suggests, allow music to be heard at a greater distance from the stage with the same frequency range and clarity. As sound travels over a greater distance it can be interrupted and become unintelligible. Again these can be of use in larger venues such as arenas, sport stadiums, concert venues and outdoor live music festivals.

To achieve consistency with the music coming from the stage speakers, delay speakers are set with a minimum delay to coincide with the performance on stage. Any member of the audience standing in the locality of the delay speakers should hear an audible and clear sound. The average speed of sound is 340 metres per second. This depends on wind speed, humidity and air temperature. The equation for setting delay time is the distance in metres from the stage divided by 340 and multiplied by 1,000, which equals the time in milliseconds. From the information presented thus far it should become clear why a competent sound engineer is required when selecting and setting up sound systems. So far, we have only just touched upon some of the elements associated with sound systems. Apart from a sound engineer it is essential to have a qualified electrical engineer available at all times. This individual, apart from ensuring the power distribution is commensurate with venue supply, must also give their signature as part of the final handover process. Once the set-up/installation has been achieved to meet the legal standards of health and safety and fire risk assessment, handover to the event manager is the final stage.

For live music performances with individuals performing with musical instruments, it is essential to work with a sound engineer if the final outcome is to achieve quality sound. This individual will have control over what is called a 'sound desk', which allows music to be mixed and distributed appropriately through the speakers within the venue. The sound engineer (generally positioned some distance back, facing the stage) can also mix the music for the performers on the stage. This process enables the band to have an indication on the quality of sound produced, to check if they are playing in time with each other, or to hear only themselves or another member of the band if they wish. To achieve this, each performer on stage must have their own independent mix, via a microphone which in turn is linked back to the sound engineer at the sound desk/front of house desk.

To achieve sound quality that is commensurate with the status of the performers, sound equipment on stage mixes the sound that is produced by the performers (Figure 14.3). Once this process has been achieved it is distributed

Figure 14.3   Millennium Square Leeds, demonstration of sound equipment on stage
with effects rack

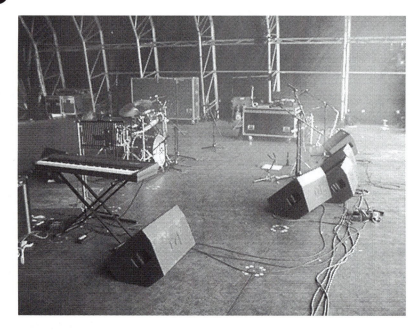

Figure 14.4   Millennium Square Leeds, demonstration of sound equipment. 5 wedge
monitor speakers for each performer

automatically to the front of house sound desk where it is then channelled to the speakers for the audience. The sound desk on stage is called a monitor desk. The monitor operator can mix the sound for all performers on stage. It can be channelled to each independent performer via a wedge monitor speaker (Figure 14.4) which is located in front of each performer.

Within the collection of sound equipment to achieve quality sound, a sound engineer must also work with power amplifiers, graphic equalisers and an arrangement of effect racks enabling him or her to stabilise and deliver quality and audible sound. The effects rack, along with the power amplifiers, has a similar heritage to a quality home hifi system. A stacked home entertainment system comes with an independent amplifier and graphic equaliser. However, the amount of equipment and cables required to set up a quality sound system at an event can fill up an entire truck. Therefore a crew should be made available to unload equipment at the designated location.

Lighting

As touched upon earlier, sound equipment can help to create a memorable experience. To enhance that experience sound engineers also work in partnership with lighting engineers. This joint partnership is also carried forward with the performers who communicate to a large extent the type of lighting arrangement that is required.

A lighting designer, just like a sound engineer, can undertake a number of courses in developing their skills. But on-the-job training is the true test of any lighting designer.

In today's environment the majority of lighting desks are pre-programmable. This allows the lighting designer to work from a lighting arrangement stored on a disk. It also allows the lighting engineer to have a degree of flexibility with each performance on stage. In association with that process there may be a requirement to interpret a lighting plot. A lighting plot will enable a lighting designer to have a clear idea on the amount of trusses needed, and the cabling required for patching into the dimmer rack.

There are common features that have been translated into the events and entertainment industry from the theatre sector. For example, chalk positions on stage will help follow spot operators to pinpoint performers effectively, and with the positioning of performers and stage equipment. Equipment brought in from the truck can also be colour coded according to its eventual location on stage, stage left and right or front of house.

Lighting arrangement on stage comes in two basic formats, fixed and moving lights. To accompany that there are also special effect lighting, such as strobe lights and lasers. Moving lights (Figure 14.5) can be controlled via the lighting desk as designed by the manufacturer. Fixed light can also be controlled by the lighting desk adjusting the intensity of the light, which is sometimes covered with a colour filter.

The distance to which each lamp can illuminate an object or area without losing intensity is governed by the inverse square law. If the distance between each light/lamp is doubled, the light intensity is reduced to one fourth the original. Even though you may achieve a greater spread of light over a surface, the optimal range from that light will diminish as the distance increases. Therefore it is necessary to know the optimal working range for each light fitting.

Lighting on stage can have an adverse effect on performers, as the intensity of light is far greater than what is used within the general home or working environment. The average bulb, or lamp as it is called within the trade, could be 1,000W. There is no particular legislation or regulation that determines how many light fittings can be positioned on stage, neither is there any regulation covering the amount of light emitted from each bulb.

Each performance determines the lighting arrangement. There are many different types of light fittings, and the most popular light fitting used across all types of performances, venues and events is the PAR can (parabolic aluminised reflector). They come in a range of sizes with the largest labelled as PAR 64 (the number indicates the diameter of the lamp in eighths of an inch).

Figure 14.5   Taking Liberties. Vodka fields outdoor event, Bramham Park, Leeds, 2001

Working as a lighting engineer requires a good degree of creativity in selection, arrangement and interpretation of the performance to the audience. When setting up a lighting arrangement, venues may have the facility to hang lights from a roof structure. This structure is generally called a lighting truss; it may be fixed to the ceiling or have the capability to be lowered to floor level. The lowering of the truss allows easy access for connecting the light fitting to the structure.

Production personnel attach chain supports to a triangular truss before lifting it above the stage. Prior to the truss being fully raised the PAR 64 in a bank of six with colour filters will be attached to the truss. Before lifting commences all lamp connections will be checked. The truss will be checked for tightness and safety. Once the truss has been lifted into position it must be checked that it is level otherwise undue stress on the structure can cause it to fail.

When it comes to connecting light fittings to a structure one should have a rigger who has their own insurance and permit to undertake a job of work.

An outdoor music event that runs into the late evening must look at installing independent general lighting at strategic areas throughout the site. Portable lighting units (as seen in the Figure 14.7) are powered independently by an internal generator.

Figure 14.6   Ear to the Ground outdoor live music event (Dpercussion) Castlefield
Arena, Manchester, 2006

As sound and lighting equipment have a tendency to consume a large
amount of power, it is essential when selecting a venue to ensure that independent power units are available to run sound and lighting equipment separately.
The amount of power for a lighting system depends upon the number of lamps
and their wattage. The power for a sound system is calculated by the amplifiers
driving the speakers. If too much power is drawn from a venue the result is a
blown fuse or blackout. To operate a sound and lighting system for a live music
concert in a stadium or arena type venue three-phase and single-phase independent power units are required.

Apart from having lights fixed to the stage via a lighting rig or trusses.
Some performers may request a spotlight, commonly known as a follow
spot, with an operator who ensures that the light follows the performer on
stage as and when the cues dictate. A follow spot is a very powerful light
unit and should only be operated by a trained individual. Part of the process
of lighting is the amount of cables needed. Cables that are used for lighting
at events should never be left tightly wound. The cables have the potential
to create an enormous amount of energy/heat and thus can burn the cable's
outer casing. Cables should never have restrictions on their route, be strung
up above fire exit doorways or run through a duct. The electrical connection
process should be made in this order: lamps, dimmer rack, power, with the

Figure 14.7   Ear to the Ground outdoor live music event (Dpercussion) Castlefield Arena, Manchester, 2006. Portable lighting units

lighting desk connected to the dimmer rack. The dimmer rack's main purpose is to vary the amount of electricity sent to a lamp, thus controlling the brightness. This process is no different to a common dimmer on a house light. Theoretically, a dimmer does not switch off, therefore keeping efficiency and heat low. To conclude, the operational process requires a level of communication between lighting personnel. The front of house lighting operator will need to communicate with operatives on the stage or riggers attached to the truss. An intercom system not only allows the team to set the lights as required, it also enables continuous communication throughout the performance.

Regulations, legislation and standard documents explained

As stated earlier in this chapter, the Health and Safety at Work Act 1974 is the overarching legislation, and therefore covers all areas of production within the UK. Many regulations come directly from Europe but not all are embedded into UK law. Compliance by employers and employees is sometimes questionable across various industries. It requires robust monitoring and evaluation from the Health and Safety Executive and its regional offices, trade unions and their representatives, to ensure that employers and employees understand and implement regulations throughout. With appropriate reporting of incidents to their regional office, the local authorities can work directly with the HSE and employees to raise working standards.

It was also mentioned that UK and European regulations have a major impact on production equipment and personnel. Let's have a closer look at these two specific areas. Prior to the European Parliament announcing new regulations for all new member states, it was the domain of the UK govern-ment to update the working practices by way of regulations. The Working at Height Regulations started life as a UK regulation; it consolidated European Council Directive 2001 and replaced all previous regulations. The Health and Safety Executive has reported that in 2003–4 there were 67 fatal accidents and 4,000 major injuries in the UK workplace. This particular regulation was brought about to prevent deaths and injuries caused each year from working at heights. The translation of this regulation is crucial within the event produc-tion field. Working at height can relate to anyone up a step ladder, suspended from a fixed roof truss, climbing a scaffold structure or operating an extend-able mechanical cherry picker – these are just some of the areas associated with this regulation. Within event production be it exhibitions, conferences or outdoor live music events there will generally be some aspect of working at height. As stated earlier some venues throughout England do not allow work-ing at height unless a permit has been applied for to the local authority, and the person also has adequate personal insurance including a recent risk assess-ment. If an individual is employed directly by an organisation or event produc-tion company, it becomes the responsibility of that company to ensure that all documentation is completed to support that particular task. The 2005 regula-tion sets out employers' responsibilities relating to the type of activities under-taken. The general responsibilities as stated in the Work at Height Regulations 2005 are:

> Avoid work at height where they can; use work equipment or other measures to prevent falls where they cannot avoid working at height; and where they cannot eliminate the risk of a fall, use work equipment or other measures to minimise the distance and consequences of a fall, should one occur. (Work at Height Regulations 2005, p. 3 [online])

It must also be noted that working at height remains a high risk activity, there-fore the area underneath where a person is working (known as a sterile area) must be designated a hazardous zone by the Health and Safety officer or appointed production manager.

As indicated earlier there are numerous regulations covering this area. The Health and Safety Executive website gives a full catalogue of regulations applicable to various types of industries and working conditions.

The 'Six Pack' regulations, introduced in 1993, are aimed primarily at management within the Health and Safety at Work Act 1974. Figure 14.8 outlines six regulations that need to be followed.

When working within the field of production it is essential that whoever has operational/health and safety responsibilities must understand and implement where necessary these regulations listed in Figure 14.8.

It is very common that regulations 1, 2, 4, 5 and 6 on the list will have a universal application on most sites/venues where production equipment and personnel are required to undertake a degree of physical work.

Occupational health has become a major and significant area of understanding for all industries, including the production industry. The Health and Safety Executive report from 2004, titled Thirty Years On, and looked forward to the development and future of the health and safety systems in Britain.

> One of the trends that has been increasingly evident in our work is the growing emphasis on occupational health matters. (Health and Safety Executive, 2004: 6 [online])

Occupational health assessors are becoming a common attachment to many industries and in particular the public sector, with companies assessing the

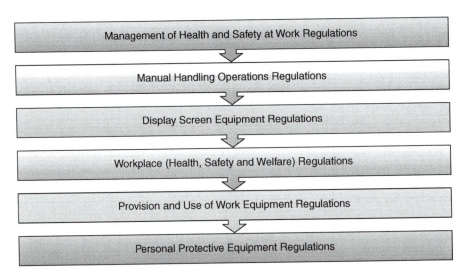

Figure 14.8   Health and Safety at Work Regulations

health of new or existing employees before allowing them to undertake a particular task. Such assessments must also become standard practice for production companies, as cases may be subject to industrial tribunals or legal proceedings if companies are found negligent or non-compliant to assessing the health risk associated with employees at work. Therefore, when developing a health and safety policy, occupational health assessments must take centre stage.

Production procedure for temporary structure erection

There are specific roles and responsibilities for an event manager in erecting and maintaining an indoor or outdoor stage.

When implementing a management procedure within the area of production related to a specific task, it is essential to outline the manpower required to carry out the task. This should include all technical, qualified and non-technical individuals. It is also a requirement to ascertain which regulations will relate to a particular working practice or situation.

Any working environment or situation has an overarching legal requirement, the Health and Safety at Work Act 1974. This act governs the working practice and situations common in all working environments under UK law. To accompany the 1974 regulationss there is the Management of Health and Safety Regulations 1999.

Establish which company you intend to hire your stage from, then ascertain if the stage will come with competent individuals who are qualified in the erection of the structure. If the stage will be erected with manpower under your control, it is essential that the structure when delivered should be accompanied with an outlined method statement.

For erecting an outdoor stage, you will require a technical/qualified team, including:

- a qualified site surveyor;

- a trained and licensed forklift operator;

- a competent foreman;

- a trained and competent workforce with appropriate working attire under health and safety regulations;

- a qualified and licensed structural engineer;

- a trained and licensed rigger with personal insurance indemnity.

Legal regulations applicable to this situation include:

- Health and Safety at Work Act 1974
- The Management of Health and Safety at Work Regulations 1999
- Lifting Plant and Equipment Regulations
- Manual Handling Operations Regulations 1992
- The Event Safety Guide, Health and Safety Executive 1999

When choosing an area on the site to erect an outdoor stage, you will need to check the following:

- Does the ground need draining?
- Does it have sufficient load-bearing capacity?
- Do you require a qualified survey to level the ground before erecting the stage?
- The stage should be erected within an area that does not infringe or does not cause danger to surrounding vegetation. Adequate access should be maintained at all times for emergency vehicles and a good distance from nearby buildings.

If your event is regulated by an occasional entertainment licence, the conditions within the licence will indicate the checks and procedures that your licensee must undertake to manage the event effectively.

Under the authority of a competent production manager/foreman the build sequence can commence. Mark out the area where the stage will be erected; if on grass you can do this with string and tent pegs. Place the base level so that it is levelled and squared. This can be undertaken with a qualified surveyor and competent workforce. If a method statement is available all directions relating to the structure should be followed to the letter. Any further inquiries should be directed to the supplier. Any recent test certificates should be requested and supplied with the structure; this information is required if requested by the fire officer or any member from the local authority. A 'no unauthorised access' area should be maintained around the build-up process.

Any machinery employed in the build process of the stage should be accompanied by a trained and licensed individual or competent person. All documentation related to that machinery and individual must also be filed at the site office.

If riggers are employed in the erection of the stage, a designated area below their working environment must be labelled as a 'no unauthorised access' area until work has been completed. The rigger undertaking their job of work must at all times wear a full body harness.

Any equipment that is attached to the structure must be within the load-bearing capacity of the structure and a secondary mechanism must be used to support that equipment in the event of failure. A D-shackle is the preferred safety device. This equipment is a steel cable with a calculated hanging and breaking strain.

Once all light, sound and scenery equipment has been hung from the structure, a structural engineer must undertake a full calculation of all equipment on the structure. These figures should have been presented prior to the build and checked on completion.

When the structural engineer is satisfied with the fully-erected stage and equipment attached, a signed certificate must be presented to the production manager and filed in the site office.

A fire officer will also undergo a final check, for correct fire extinguishers and evacuation procedures along with fire certificates for fire retardant materials.

Information should be available to all performers indicating fire procedures and emergency evacuation from the stage. Continual safety checks must be made throughout the duration of the event. All scenery draped or hung from the erected structure must be fire tested and fire retardant and carry a test certificate to authenticate it. All documentation associated with the temporary structure must be held at the site office.

Summary

In this chapter the production process has been identified from a particular point of view, and it has been illustrated with a number of relevant regulations and legislation appropriate to achieve successful outcomes within the area of sound and lighting. Not all regulations have been identified in this chapter, so it is important to research the HSE website to make sure you have a full and complete understanding of all regulations associated to this particular area. A great deal of the focus has hinged upon health and safety as the main driver for successful event producers. This chapter should have given you an insight into the very complicated area of work within an aspect of event management. It has shown how integral the working relationship of various skilled individuals is to achieving a quality production. This chapter was not written to enable an event manager to become a sound or lighting engineer or even a production manager. It was developed to enable a level of communication and understanding between two parties who are ultimately working towards the same end. Further reading and training is therefore suggested in order to develop your knowledge and understanding in this particular field. There is one highly recognised trade organisation within the UK that represents production personnel. The Production Service Association is a trade organisation with a website that gives help and guidance to people within the industry. It has a database of members and information on training courses along with recruitment plus general news within the sector.

The chapter has also given an insight into some of the aspects related to the job of the lighting and sound engineer, in particular where it would have an impact on regulations and legislation. A diluted approach was outlined demonstrating some of the equipment and processes required to achieve quality at live music at events.

■ Discussion questions

Question 1

Production managers working at events with special effects lighting have the potential to cause harm or injury. Describe the measures that should be taken to limit or remove risk to customers.

Question 2

Outline your understanding of the term 'rigger' and describe the documentation required by that individual before he/she can commence work.

Question 3

Outline your understanding of a lighting plot and discuss some of the key issues involved in supplying a lighting designer with a lighting plot.

Question 4

Outline your understanding of a 'method statement' and its relevance within the production process.

Question 5

Outline two methods available to the licensing authority if an organiser breaches the sound amplification level agreement stipulated in the licence condition.

Question 6

Within the 2003 Licensing Act there are statutory requirements attached to the licence, in that there are conditions on how to apply and control the licence within any given local authority. Describe why local authorities are able to make specific recommendations within the licence condition when referring to their local area.

CASE STUDY 1 OUTDOOR DANCE AND LIVE MUSIC FESTIVAL

This is a licensed site for 40,000 people, within a location on site that has full operational management of the event under licence. Event Control operates on a 24-hour rolling basis over night and day duties for Saturday and Sunday.

Duties include the management of all multi-agency operatives, licensing authority and environmental issues, with responsibility to the event licensing officer and safety officers. The licensee has full and complete responsibilities for all operational and licensing issues attached to this event. Safety officer main duties are health and safety and risk management issues reporting directly to event control and the licensee. Within the role of event manager one must respond and deal with many issues; most issues are operational or related to production equipment on site. Below are some of the general issues that may fall within the scope of an event manager within Event Control while carrying out their duty.

Operational incidents and actions taken:

1 Firework display not part of the licensing requirement and ignited on Saturday night. Complaints from the local inhabitants and reports given directly to the licensing authority. Final action: firework display cancelled for the duration of the event weekend.
2 Customer related death on site. Location within a dance arena within the licensed site. Emergency services in attendance, police, ambulance, security and licensing authority. Person pronounced dead on site by medical team. The location of death is now deemed a crime scene. Ordered by the safety officer to commence a show-stop in the designated area. All customers and artists to vacate temporary arena. Security and police to contain location from all non-essential personnel. Artist scheduled within arena given an option to relocate to another arena. Production schedule and timing adjusted to meet new demands across all existing arenas within the licensed site. Initial call for customer related incident came directly to event control from the production manager in the arena. The message was then passed on to the medical representative in event control including the location and potential situation at hand. Policies and procedures must be followed for all medical vehicle movements within the licensed site, and where a medical vehicle requires access through one of the main gates into the arena, security operatives must be informed prior to arrival to allow access.
3 As a response to the closure of one arena extra police personnel were drafted in to the licensed site as a precautionary method to manage crowd behaviour. This precautionary method was not required as no crowd disturbance was reported.

(Continued)

(Continued)

4　Within the licensed site fairground rides closed due to mechanical failure which left one customer trapped. Action taken: safety officer in consultation with fairground operatives and fire services to remove individual and make safe fairground structure. The injured individual was taken off site to a general hospital to be offered a comprehensive medical assessment. Fairground closed for the duration of the night awaiting assessment from the day safety officer issuing a new safety certificate to reopen fairground attractions.

5　Severe weather warning, 15 mm or rain within a 4-hour period, welfare given the responsibility of issuing space blankets to customers thereby protecting them from excessive heat loss.

6　Customer admitted to local hospital due to excessive intake of alcohol. Condition monitored over a 6-hour period before individual was deemed stable enough to be released.

7　Due to severe weather warning, main stage closed during the day. Stage deemed to be unsafe from a structural perspective. Artists and headline artists scheduled for main stage cancelled. Offered the option to perform in one of the temporary arena structures.

8　Related to capacity, numbers and production considerations, main stage closed for the duration of the event. Main stage cordoned off for all customers at a safe distance on safety officers' recommendation.

9　Shut down of all radio communication with all medical operatives on site. Action taken: licensee suggested that all medical operatives transferred to another free channel on existing radio frequencies.

10　Customer complaints through the customer complaint line of loud music. Licensing authority sent to check decibel levels in the local area. Decibel levels in excess of the licensing agreement. Information passed directly to all temporary arenas within the licensed site to adjust sound levels in accordance with the licensing agreement. Situation continually monitored and checked throughout the duration of the event.

11　Reports from campsite of excessive rainfall. Customers in need of facilities for drying clothes.

12　End of the event, tents in campsites checked to determine how many customers were still on site.

13　Communication to customers on site due to operational changes, via Bluetooth application on mobile phones. Security operatives also briefed at key locations throughout the site to disseminate operational changes. Information also posted on official website and communicated to external media representatives.

CASE STUDY 2　AMAECHI BASKETBALL TOURNAMENT

Media coverage and awareness

Manchester played host to the Haris Junior U18's International Tournament, in December 2009 at the Amaechi Basketball Centre. This type of spectator sport is unable to reach the international heights seen with the sport in the USA. On the whole, international sports receive more free coverage through television, radio and newspaper than any other part of the leisure sector. Evidently this helps to maintain awareness in the minds of the public and keep interest levels high, which subsequently could be capitalised upon to encourage attendance at sports events. However, a superficial scanning of both traditional and online versions of a variety of national and regional newspapers has revealed that as an individual sport, basketball struggles to achieve any prominent coverage and is often completely overshadowed by football, cricket, rugby and boxing. That is, the majority of the reviewed online media do not feature direct links to basketball on their homepages nor the sports section of the websites. For Amaechi Basketball Centre (ABC) and in particular the 'Manchester Magic' brand this 'glass ceiling' of media attention needs to be broken through within the Manchester area. To achieve this it is paramount to deliver an effective message designed to influence the target audience's perception of Manchester Magic. In addition, the club had to capitalise on building relationships with the media currently covering the sport, such as the Manchester Evening News.

The Olympic effect and match attendance

With London being awarded the Olympic Games 2012, subsequently there has been an increased focus on sports in general. Arguably the sports presenting Great Britain with realistic opportunities for winning medals will be at the centre of attention. These sports will not only benefit from increased governmental funding but moreover a rising consumer awareness and interest in live sports, which should be converted into wider match attendance and accordingly increased revenue for the clubs offering live events.

Although Team GB Basketball failed to qualify for the Beijing Olympics 2008, they did qualify for London 2012, so ABC and Manchester Magic should be able to build on the increased general interest in basketball.

Further reading

British Standards Institute (BSI) Introducing standards: raising standards worldwide. Available at: www.bis-global.com

Civil Aviation Authority (2003) Guide for the Operation of Lasers, Searchlights and Fireworks in United Kingdom Airspace. Available at: www.caa.co.uk

Event Industry News (2011) [online]. Available from: www.eventindustrynews.co.uk/2011/06/dbn-lights-parklife-festival.html [accessed 7th January 2012].

Health and Safety Executive (2002) Use of Contractors a Joint Responsibility. Liverpool: HSE.

Health and Safety Executive (2006) Consulting Employees on Health and Safety: A Guide to the Law. Liverpool: HSE.

Health and Safety Executive (2006) Health and Safety Law: What You Should Know. Liverpool: HSE.

Professional Lighting and Sound Association www.plasa.org

Section E

Events and Beyond

15 Sustainable Festivals and Events

In this chapter you will cover:

- sustainability framework;
- the global perspective;
- European and UK perspective;
- London 2012 sustainable challenge;
- sustainable development through the Olympic Games;
- case study: Park Life Festival 2011;
- summary;
- discussion questions;
- case studies;
- further reading.

This chapter examines and evaluates the subject of sustainability and aims to draw a clear link between the current global benchmark indicators from the United Nations and the European Union. With specific reference to the UK economic, environmental and social landscape, where those three pillars converge on sustainable issues they will be critically discussed. Where there is legislation, guidance documents and codes of practice to assist organisations in meeting the climate challenge, these will be introduced and explained as to their applicability within a given context. An industry specific case study with data collected during the period 2011 on a UK urban music festival will be introduced, to highlight the overarching principles and set out a method by which organisations can develop short- to long-term sustainable strategies.

Sustainability framework

Sustainability within a global context starts with one basic premise, CO_2 emissions. From the time of the first international climate conference in 1979, organised by the United Nations, CO_2 levels throughout the world were stated as significantly high, and the impending impact of those levels was said to present a significant negative imbalance on the world climate. The Intergovernmental Panel on Climate Change (IPCC) released their first document in 1990. The international community at this point made specific reference to the first report and developed policies to bring about change. International discussions amongst the global community commenced in 1990 and the first international agreement was signed by 154 states and the European Community in 1992.

The United Nations 2010 conference in Copenhagen brought together the international community to look at and discuss the conclusion of the Kyoto Protocol, which expires in 2013, and to set targets for the future. Climate change, when viewed from a European and UK perspective, has a far broader remit, due to the diverse social, environmental and economic disparities within each member state. Within the UK, climate change is generally included under the broad heading of 'sustainability'. Under this banner a number of government-appointed agencies have a specific remit to communicate strategies and set targets for all business sectors. The Environment Agency has a specific remit to develop a strategy for the disposal of commercial and non-commercial waste in the UK. Another government agency, the Department for Environment, Food and Rural Affairs, published a number of documents on the air quality in Britain. This agency has also published guidance documents for a number of business sectors including the event industry.

Clearly, the problems are complex and worldwide problems cannot be solved by a single planning solution and probably not by any single action. Moreover, there is a continuous discourse surrounding the dichotomy of economic and environmental principles, and the suggestion that one principle takes priority over another. Subsequently, social considerations are frequently given less attention. Within this book, and within this chapter, equal consideration is given to all three principles, including the implementation of social frameworks as fundamental to the concept of sustainable event management.

As a sector, the event industry is now facing many challenges to fall in line with the current wind of change. This has brought about many opportunities for some organisations, and costly operational changes for other businesses. In maintaining a competitive advantage, organisations must adapt to the impending global issues. There are some formidable barriers when attempts are made to translate the principles of sustainability into action in the context of events, such as lack of reliable information, individual and organisational inertia, employee perceptions and the failure to use planning and performance standards. In essence, events are fragmented – made up of many stages, many suppliers, many performance indicators and many clients. Therefore, any attempt at introducing a sustainable policy should be integral to all elements of the event, in the pre-, live and post-event stages and across the whole lifecycle of event management.

The nomenclature of events include mega, special, social, major, hall-mark and community events. Events are categorised according to their size, scope and scale. Moreover, events can be categorised according to their type or sector, such as conference and exhibitions, arts and entertainment, sports events, and charitable events. The Accepted Practices Exchange (APEX) *Industry Glossary* of terms (published by the Convention Industry Council) defines an event as:

> [a]n organised occasion such as a meeting, convention, exhibition, special event, gala dinner, etc. An event is often composed of several different yet related functions. (cited in Bowdin et al., 2006: 14)

Events are explicitly linked to fundamentals of the human race – social and cultural values, and the more basic ladders of social inclusion, a sense of belonging and a sense of identity. Dwyer et al. (2000) support the view that organising and managing a planned event involves many component parts and many stakeholders. Often the decisions to organise and host events are taken from different stakeholder viewpoints. Good economic rationale is a strong indicator, coupled with the social and cultural benefits to a destination, raising awareness of community/social issues, enhancing the exchange of ideas, net-working and business contacts. The social elements of the three pillars of sustainability are often neglected and often ambiguous. The scope of any framework should encompass those working, participating and attending the event and consider social inclusion as a key principle to widening participation and encouraging interest from all aspects of the surrounding community.

Significantly, the move towards the creation of a number of published frameworks for sustainable event management has provided not only a sense of professionalism in light of contemporary concerns, but highlighted best practice within the industry, advice and guidance, practical solutions, and an inward-looking sense of the importance of events in modern society.

The global perspective

Through the United Nations, the international community, has published a number of documents, including The Intergovernmental Panel on Climate Change 4th Assessment Report, in 2007. This outlines the global position in relation to environmental impact and in particular the four greenhouse gases: carbon dioxide, methane, nitrous oxide and sulphur hexafluoride. These four should be given due diligence when developing long-term policies for each state or member of the European community.

The European Parliament has also published and given clear guidance to the European community. In some aspects it has enacted specific regulations that require a uniform acceptance from all member states.

It is those gases that have become the main issue for many environmentalists and policy makers in determining the short- to long-term integration of change to ensure as a country the UK meets the international challenge of 'climate change'.

Even though this issue has been debated for over 20 years in the international arena, with clear guidance published to move this agenda forward, it is only over the past five years that the UK event industry has collectively and actively engaged with specific guidance and understanding to drive the sector forward.

In 2007, the British Standards Institute (BSI) published the BS 8901 specification for a sustainable event management system with guidance for use. This document was updated and re-published in 2009. In 2006, the Department for Environment, Food and Rural Affairs (Defra), a government agency, published Environmental Key Performance Indicators for UK businesses. To accompany that document in 2007 (Defra) published the booklet, *Sustainable Development Indicators in your Pocket*. Again, in the same year for the first time, the Department of Trade and Industry (DTI), another government agency, published *Meeting the Energy Challenge: a White Paper on Energy*. The UK government also introduced the UK Sustainable Development Strategy. This attempts to consolidate and present a way forward for business and the country as a whole. The very first international and highly-recognised standard came via the International Organisation for Standardisation, in 2004, the ISO 14001: 2004 and the ISO 14004: 2004. As a sector, we now have a considerable number of official documents from established, recognised agencies and organisations that can assist in the integration of environmental policies and standards. In 2008, the UK government brought into law the Climate Change Act, the first EU country to enact legislation of this type. This Act refers to a number of specific remits within the realm of sustainability and environmental impact. It presents a baseline figure for the reduction of carbon dioxide in the atmosphere by 80 per cent in line with 1990 estimates. This reduction is benchmarked and has direct correlation with the Kyoto Protocol published in 1997 by the United Nations, which referred to CO_2 emission and the need for reduction by the year 2012 in line with 1990 figures.

> The Parties included in Annex I shall, individually or jointly, ensure that their aggregate anthropogenic carbon dioxide equivalent emissions of the greenhouse gases listed in Annex A do not exceed their assigned amounts, calculated pursuant to their quantified emission limitation and reduction commitments inscribed in Annex B and in accordance with the provisions of this Article, with a view to reducing their overall emissions of such gases by at least 5 per cent below 1990 levels in the commitment period 2008 to 2012. (Kyoto Protocol, 1998: 3 [online])

European and UK perspective

It is clear how the Kyoto Protocol contributed in part to the introduction of the Climate Change Act, as the UK is a signed up member to the agreement. As a European member state a clear strategy is required that allows industry to enact appropriate policies with incentives to bring about a tangible reduction in CO_2 emission. In accordance with the Act, the European Parliament introduced the Carbon Accounting Regulations in 2009. This regulation is now part of UK law and allows each member state to trade carbon credits and set carbon budgetary levels. The levels set for each country have direct lineage from the Kyoto Protocol 1997. The 2009 regulation works in conjunction with the EU Emission Trading Directive from 2003.

Governance for this type of scheme in relation to trading and setting carbon budgets is controlled by the Environment Agency, a UK government organisation. The Environment Agency has set stringent rules in relation to the Kyoto agreement. Where carbon credits are surplus they will not be carried over but cancelled out. It has also been agreed by the Environment Agency that carbon credits generated outside the UK and used to meet the carbon budget must be cancelled out, and the method of double counting for credits will also be removed. It must also be noted that the UK carbon reduction commitment under this scheme is only 60 per cent of the UK carbon emissions. This scheme in the broadest terms has more relevance to the UK industrial sector and large energy emitters.

In order for small-to medium-sized businesses to contribute to this environmental initiative, and have a positive influence on the remaining 40 per cent, they must take control of their businesses from a unit level.

Local authorities in UK, and in other countries worldwide, are building Collaborative and integrated schemes, and planning to develop policies and guidance documents to bring about sustainable and long-term change. For example, Shoalhaven City Council (in New South Wales, Australia) is in the process of developing a sustainable events policy statement for the future (see Figure 15.1).

Shoalhaven City Council is planning a detailed policy to implement sustainable events strategies to ensure events held in Shoalhaven are organised and conducted in a sustainable manner. 'Sustainability' will be defined as using fewer natural resources, at the present, so that they are available for future generations. In practice, it means choosing suppliers or procedures, or products that have low impact on the planet and ensure the well-being of people and the environment.

Shoalhaven City Council wants all future events to be planned and implemented with the goal of reducing the impact of the event on the environment. The policy is being developed to achieve an outcome through encouraging events organisers to adopt the following strategies when planning future events.

There are a number of policies and legislation documents that can assist in the development of a clear and workable strategy. It is inconceivable that an organisation can enact wholesale change across a business operation in the first

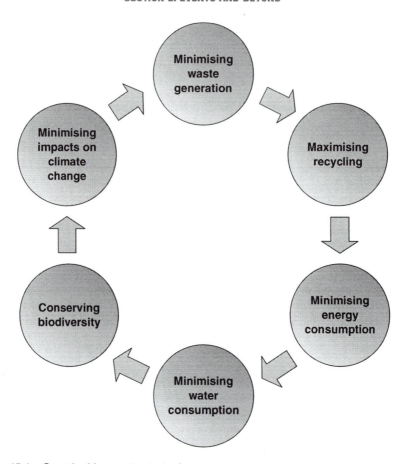

Figure 15.1   Sustainable events strategies

instance. This process of change should have a collective agreement within an organisation, which allows for sustained commitment, and which can then be communicated to suppliers, partners and business associates.

The implementation of the ISO environmental standard calls for a gradual approach to changing the business operation, with a continued assessment by the ISO on the potential business seeking ratification and continued certification under the terms of agreement. A business must clearly demonstrate. through developing policies and guidance for internal use, that employees have a full understanding of their specific remit when operating within the business unit and externally. Where a business has a need to engage with outside organisations to meet the delivery of their product or service, there is a requirement to implement change through dialogue and agreement. This aspect will become the cornerstone for a cohesive long-term environmental strategy.

The most high profile event in the UK that achieved ratification by the ISO was the London 2012 Olympic and Paralympic Games. The London Organising Committee Olympic Games (LOCOG) published a number of documents that outlined their requirement to meet the climate challenge, but also to educate the UK population and the international community.

'London 2012: Towards One Planet' makes specific reference to the fact that the Kyoto Protocol (published in 1997) set an expiry date of 2012 for the international agreements signed at Kyoto. Therefore, 2012 is a significant milestone for the future international debate on climate change and how international agreements signed at the Kyoto conference can move the agenda forward under a new agreement. The consolidation of the Kyoto agenda came about at the Copenhagen conference held in 2010. The Copenhagen Accord was signed by a number of countries, and also for the first time by China and developing nations. A legally binding agreement was not ratified by each country, however. What was agreed, was an aspirational goal of limiting global temperature increase to 2 degrees Celsius.

London 2012 sustainable challenge

As a mega event the Olympic Games has an impact over five major London boroughs Greenwich, Hackney, Newham, Tower Hamlets and Waltham Forest. In recognition of the likely effects of the Games on those boroughs, five sustainable objectives were put forward by London 2012.

Figure 15.2 highlights the foundation of London 2012's sustainable strategy. From the five objectives, inclusion in particular requires further investigation to draw a distinction with the social and political remits that need addressing by the UK government. Inclusion, according to London 2012, is:

> To host the most inclusive Games to date by promoting access, celebrating diversity and facilitating the physical, economic and social regeneration of the Lower Lea Valley and surrounding communities. (LOCOG, 2008: 6 [online])

It is generally noted that inhabitants of the five boroughs on which the London Olympic Games is centred are subject to higher levels of inequality. This theory is backed up by data from the Office for National Statistics (http://www.ons.gov.uk/ons/datasets-and-tables/index.html?pageSize=50&sortBy=none&sortDirection=none&newquery=hackney+crime&content-type=Reference+table&content-type=Dataset), which shows that there are significant differences between inner and outer London boroughs in the areas of crime, deprivation and health.

Inner London borough – Newham

1 Violence against persons: 7,003 incidents during the period April 2010 – March 2011.

2 Criminal damage including arson: 3,108 incidents during the period April 2010 – March 2011.

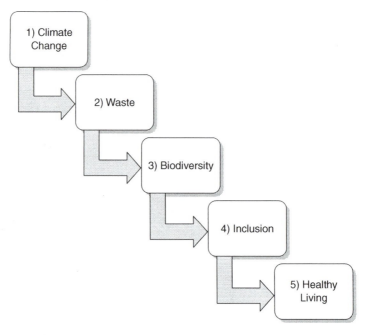

Figure 15.2   London 2012 sustainable strategy

3   Social services incidents: 1,299 during the period January 2006–December 2006.

4   Total number of county court judgements: 5,361, with a total value of £2,439.49.

5   Coronary heart disease cases for the period April 2007–March 2008: 3,950 admissions.

Inner London borough – Hackney

1   Violence against persons: 5,952 offences during the period April 2010–March 2011.

2   Criminal damage including arson: 2,205 incidents during the period April 2010–March 2011.

3   Social services incidents: 2,460 during the period January 2006–December 2006.

4   Total number of county court judgements: 4,256, with a total value £2,337.24.

5   Coronary heart disease cases for the period April 2007–March 2008: 2,369 admissions.

Inner London borough – Tower Hamlets

1   Violence against persons: 6,315 offences during the period April 2010–March 2011.

2   Criminal damage including arson: 2,803 incidents during the period April 2010–March 2011.

3 Social services incidents: 3,144 during the period January 2006–December 2006.

4 Total number of county court judgements: 3,155, with a total value £2,978.56.

5 Coronary heart disease cases for the period April 2007–March 2008: 787 admissions.

Inner London borough – Waltham Forest

1 Violence against persons: 5,456 offences during the period April 2010–March 2011.

2 Criminal damage including arson: 2,585 offences during the period April 2010–March 2011.

3 Social services incidents: 885 during the period January 2006–December 2006.

4 Total number of county court judgements: 3,860, with a total value £2,252.25.

5 Coronary heart disease cases for the period April 2007–March 2008: 3,206 admissions.

Inner London borough – Greenwich

1 Violence against persons: 5,435 offences during the period April 2010–March 2011.

2 Criminal damage including arson: 3,191 incidents during the period April 2010–March 2011.

3 Social services incidents: 1,482 during the period January 2006–December 2006.

4 Total number of county court judgements: 4,235, with a total value £2,191.55.

5 Coronary heart disease cases for the period April 2007–March 2008: 3,157 admissions.

When we compare these statistics with another London borough such as Camden, we see a comparable situation. Here, crimes of violence against persons accounted for 5,867 incidents during the period April 2010–March 2011. Criminal damage including arson registered at 2,269 incidents during the period, April 2010–March 2011. As for social service incidents, there were a total of 2,367 incidents during the period January 2006–December 2006. The total number of county court judgements was 2,469, with a total value of £3,473.53.

Outer London borough – Kingston-Upon-Thames

1 Violence against persons: 2,234 offences during the period April 2010–March 2011.

2 Criminal damage including arson: 1,327 incidents during the period April 2010–March 2011.

3 Social services incidents: 480 during the period January 2006–December 2006.

4 Total number of county court judgements: 1,529, with a total value of £2,865.32.

5 Coronary heart disease cases for the period April 2007–March 2008: 2,537 admissions.

Outer London borough – Barnet

1 Violence against persons: 4,438 offences during the period April 2010–March 2011.

2 Criminal damage including arson: 2,686 incidents during the period April 2010–March 2011.

3 Social services incidents: 1,314 during the period January 2006–Dec 2006.

4 Total number of county court judgements: 4,058, with a total value of £3,392.39.

5 Coronary heart disease cases for the period April 2007–March 2008: 3,491 admissions.

Outer London borough – Merton

1 Crime against persons: 2,874 offences during the period April 2010–March 2011.

2 Criminal damage including arson: 1,838 incidents during the period April 2010–March 2011.

3 Social services incidents: 621 during the period January 2006–December 2006.

4 Total number of county court judgements: 2,550, with a total value of £3,189.85.

5 Coronary heart disease cases for the period April 2007–March 2008: 2,441 admissions.

Outer London borough – Harrow

1 Crime against persons: 3,260 offences during the period April 2010–March 2011.

2 Criminal damage including arson: 1,577 incidents during the period April 2010–March 2011.

3 Social services incidents: 561 during the period January 2006–December 2006.

4 Total number of county court judgements: 2,771, with a value of £3,047.89.

5 Coronary heart disease cases for the period April 2007–March 2008: 3,433 admissions.

Outer London borough – Bromley

1 Crime against persons: 4,841 offences for the period April 2010–March 2011.

2 Criminal damage including arson: 2,808 incidents for the period April 2010–March 2011.

3 Social services incidents: 933 during the period January 2006–December 2006.

4 Total number of county court judgements: 3,073 with a value of £2,946.45.

5 Coronary heart disease cases for the period April 2007–March 2008: 5,265 admissions.

There are a total of 32 London boroughs, of which 12 are designated as inner London and 20 as outer London. There are significant differences between inner and outer London boroughs in terms of health, crime and social deprivation. Looking at one particular dataset across all boroughs leads to the conclusion that crime shows a wide and disproportionate impact in relation to particular locations. As for ill health, this is not completely predicated on where you lives but on how informed you may be on issues of healthy living. It is also important to bear in mind that clusters of ethnic groups in some inner London boroughs have a high propensity for coronary heart disease.

These statistics can also be linked with an independent study compiled by the Association of Public Health Observatories, which reported that the UK had the highest levels of obesity within the population of all our European partners. This particular issue needs to be tackled by our government, health professionals, food producers and retailers, and requires an immediate response. In 2009, the UK Government introduced a campaign titled Change4Life, a campaign that initially targeted children to become more active, although it has since increased its remit to include parents. The UK government can also take some lessons from our European partners. In 2003, Denmark was the first country in the world to outlaw food containing trans fats, a move which effectively bans partially hydrogenated oils (the limit is 2 per cent of fats and oils destined for human consumption). Switzerland followed Denmark's trans fat ban, and implemented its own in 2008. The National Institute for Health and Clinical Excellence (NICE) reported that trans fats contribute to 40,000 early deaths a year in the UK. Coincidentally, McDonalds and Coca Cola are global partners of the Olympic Games – by default a host nation must work with and promote those partners.

It is these and other issues that are on the political agenda which indicate why London 2012 has included healthy living and inclusion as two of the five objectives for the London Games.

Air quality

There is no direct reference to inclusion in the Kyoto Protocol and other United Nation documents linked to climate change., However, health associated with clean air has currency with the Clean Air Act and European regulations.

The Environment Act 1995 has a remit for all local authorities within the UK to assess and monitor their air quality. If the level of pollutants in the air rises above the limit set, the local authority will be designated an Air Quality Management Area and must draw up an action plan to remove the pollutants. There are seven pollutants identified in the Act, which local authorities must monitor; Manchester City, for example, was meeting the standards on six out of the seven pollutants in 2010. However, nitrogen dioxide (NO_2) is predicted to increase within the city, and is likely to be a problem for all major cities within the UK.

Alongside this legislation, the UK government and the European parliament have also drawn attention to the problem of PM10 particles, the main source of which is road transport, power generation and industry.

> Associated with respiratory problems, e.g. coughs, colds, shortness of breath and bronchitis, PM10 is made up of many substances, some of which may increase the risk of developing cancer.
>
> (Manchester City Council, 2006: 7 [online])

All of the five boroughs where the 2012 Games will impact (Hackney, Newham, Greenwich, Tower Hamlets and Waltham Forest) are currently under an Air Quality Management Area (AQMA) for nitrogen dioxide (NO) and particulates (PM10), and therefore an Air Quality Action Plan is in place.

The Hackney State of the Environment report, published in 2008, concludes that:

> Current levels of air pollution are still predicted to cause just over 1,000 premature deaths and a similar number of extra respiratory hospital admissions each year in London.
>
> (London Borough of Hackney, 2008, p. 14 [online])

London air quality is among the worst in the UK, according to the report. As in Manchester, Hackney has problems with the pollutants NO_2 and PM10, which have also become the concern for many metropolitan cities in the UK.

The UK Government is currently in breach of the 1999 Clean Air Act and European regulations. Since the regulations became legally binding in 2005, the UK has failed to meet these limits every year. The European Commission issued a final warning to the UK Government in 2009, with a potential fine of up to £360 million. To remedy this problem, on 3 January 2012, London introduced the Low Emission zone, which is in force 24 hours a day and 7 days a week. It targets vehicles of a particular size (from 4x4 cars to articulated trucks) that run on diesel fuel. If vehicles are found to be in breach of the Low Emission Standard, fines can be charged from £250–£1,000.

The introduction of the Low Emission Zone enables the London 2012 Olympic and Paralympic Games to meet one of the five objectives and measure with conclusive data a reduction in PM10 particles in areas of London identified by the European Commission which have been in breach of the regulations.

Sustainable development through the Olympic Games

In the short term, hosting the Olympic Games will increase consumer spending. In fact, experts estimate that the spending boost will reach £750 million during the Olympic Games period. During the Games there will be a lot of visitors who will spend in hotels, restaurants, shops, etc.

Secondly, the Games will raise the output of firms. This impact may attain £1.14 billion through the production of goods and services needed for the preparation and for the duration of the Olympic Games. The Olympic Games represent a real opportunity for national firms to raise their sales.

Thirdly, it will create employment. Indeed, this boost has happened during the preparation for the Games, with new employment created in the construction sector, in passenger land transport, business services and sports facilities. Besides this, many restaurants, hotels and shops will certainly hire additional staff to cope with the huge influx of people during the Games.

Fourthly, hosting the Olympic Games will lead to increased inward investments in the city and in the country as a whole. Some studies show that the city, and the UK, are attractive because of the preparation for the Games. Furthermore, London will have increased international exposure as the host city for the Olympic Games, so the city will receive additional investments for different projects. In the long term, hosting the Olympic Games will give to London and the UK a worldwide exposure and recognition, which will help to promote the city and the country to the world. For example, it is estimated that up to 2016, there will be 119 additional firms countrywide and 439 additional firms in London. Likewise, this exposure will have a second impact, increasing tourism in the long term.

Moreover, the Olympic Games will have a significant impact on GDP for the UK as a whole and for London. According to a study by Adam Blake, the UK GDP will increase by £1.9 billion during the period 2005–2016, and London GDP will increase by £5.9 billion.

The Olympic Games facilities, venues and infrastructures will contribute to the urban regeneration of London and especially the East end, including the Lower Lea Valley, a poor area of London.

CASE STUDY   PARK LIFE FESTIVAL, MANCHESTER 2011

In 2011, Ear To The Ground and the Warehouse Project jointly organised the Park Life Festival in Platt Fields, Manchester, for the second year.

This event was held on civic-controlled parkland designed in part to host outdoor events. Ear To The Ground event agency, located in Manchester city centre, was certified in 2010 with the ISO 14001 Environmental Standard. With that certification, Ear To the Ground must implement, review and develop environmental standards throughout all aspects of their business operation.

A methodology was designed in association with the event agency in the first instance to assess the Environmental Aspect and Impact Prompt List. Along with undertaking an environmental assessment of customers who attended the festival, this assessment measured customer attitude towards environmental issues and CO_2 emission as calculated from audience travel to the festival.

With a 20,000-customer capacity, Park Life Festival in 2011 had a number of environmental protocols aligned to the load in, event delivery and load out. A specific environmental policy was drafted to form the Environmental Aspect and Impact Prompt List for all traders, contractors and associated organisations. This document allowed traders and contractors to assess and monitor their overall impact on the environment. Prior to commencing work on site each trader/contractor was sent a copy of this document and asked to complete and return to the on-site event management team.

Assessment of environmental policy

Ear To The Ground supplied a list of 36 official contractors and associated organisations to take part in the environmental assessment study.

The first question put by the agency was: 'What was the initial response of the contractors to the Environmental Aspect and Impact Prompt List'. This question was first asked four weeks prior to the event, at which point it returned a negative response. This negative response was replicated when the question was asked for a second time, a day before event delivery to customers. The agency therefore developed an on-site approach to ascertain the level of engagement with the policy a day before the event commenced.

One of the organisations supporting the event was the police; however, their environmental impact was minimal due to the distance they covered to arrive at the site, and the fact that only one police car and few officers were involved in the pre-build stage. All wastes accumulated by that organisation were disposed of on site in the waste disposal bins located throughout the site. The police did not actively engage with any environmental policy and made no specific reference to the Environmental Aspect and Impact Prompt List.

One particular contractor went over and above the environmental policy – VSC Events Concessions ensured that all food traders followed their own environmental standard (rules and regulations).

Within the trader documentation, VSC Events highlighted waste management – reduce, reuse and recycle. To ensure a level of commitment to the rules and regulations a representative from VSC Events remained on site to monitor adherence to the standard. This also included the collection and disposal of cooking oil in a sustainable manner. This was also reflected in the type of waste material each trader could discard over the festival period. All water required by traders was taken from the on-site supply. Power for all traders was drawn from park generators.

Park Life Festival has the potential to become a major signature event for the student population of Manchester. With that knowledge, the festival can draw upon existing initiatives to bring about consumer acceptance and strengthen awareness within the immediate population.

Summary

The creation of a number of published frameworks for sustainable event management has provided not only a sense of professionalism in light of contemporary concerns, but highlighted best practice within the industry, advice and guidance, practical solutions, and an inward-looking sense of the importance of events in modern society.

It is clear that sustainability as a movement, political agenda or a stream of social consciousness, requires political support and strategic direction. Governments and in particular European member states should have a uniform approach to accepting Directives and EU Regulations into their legal statute. Where we have discrepancies among member states in pushing forward one or all of the issues there will be significant disparity between member states. This will present itself in the health of a nation, its economic strength to provide alternative energy supplies at an affordable cost to meet long-term demand, and increased taxation on goods and services to change consumer attitude and purchasing decisions. These are just a few of the major issues that now become milestones for small to medium size business.

By analysing Office for National Statistics data, we can conclude that social deprivation and crime is comparable across a large percentage of inner London boroughs. In contrast, the outer boroughs show a significant difference in the quality of life as compared with the inner boroughs. A significant number of inner London boroughs have levels of crime, deprivation and ill health which cause significant impact on inhabitants and can be debilitating for a sustainable community. We have also looked at the ways in which long-term sustainable effects of emissions policies can help to reduce the respiratory problems in young children, as indentified by NICE.

The chapter also looked at LOCOG's objectives for sustainability at the London 2012 Olympic and Paralympic Games. Each objective put forward by London 2012 must be evaluated to determine a marked reduction in the areas they have specified. This can be calculated, verified internally and independently on the objectives set. Biodiversity, waste and climate change cover a multitude of issues including energy, water resources management, infrastructure development, transport, local food production and carbon offsetting. Through their official website, LOCOG has released a number of documents which clearly show how they are moving forward with and meeting their objectives. However, healthy living and inclusion are two objectives which are particular to the UK and in need of long-term political intervention post 2012.

■ Discussion questions

Question 1

Discuss the social and health benefits to the community of London of the introduction of the Low Emission Zone in London in January 2012.

Question 2

In 2007 the British Standards Institute (BSI) introduced a sustainable guidance document for the event sector. Discuss the perceived difference between the ISO 14001 Environmental Standard and the BSI guidance for sustainable events.

Question 3

Within Britain there are a number of government agencies with a clear remit to develop strategies for business sectors to meet the climate challenge. Make reference to three of the agencies and outline their strategies to bring about long-term change.

Question 4

Within the case study data supplied, customers indicated that they were prepared to pay more for a festival ticket if the event demonstrated a shift toward an overt sustainable agenda. Discuss three aspects from a customer perspective that could be introduced to the festival to meet the climate change challenge.

Question 5

What strategic links, if any, does London 2012 have with the United Nations IPPC Fourth Assessment Report on climate change?

Question 6

The United Nations has organised a number of conferences on climate change. Discuss whether any of those conferences have been an instrument for international agreement and long-term policy change development for member states.

CASE STUDY 1   LOCH NESS MARATHON AND FESTIVAL OF RUNNING

Marketing review and impact assessment

In 2002, Caledonian Concepts staged the first Loch Ness Marathon with Baxters as its title sponsor. The event is now in its seventh year, and has been expanded to create a Festival of Running which includes: the Baxters River Ness 10k, the Healthier Working Lives 10k Corporate Challenge, and the Baxters River Ness 5k. The Festival currently continues to grow but relies on its sponsorship income for survival, and faces future challenges from a number of areas such as the current economic climate, and the growth of competitive events in the marketplace, coupled with a possible levelling out of participant numbers.

FEI was asked to look at the marketing of the event to help shape the next phase of its development and to explore how best it could secure its status and financial future. In addition, FEI was asked to manage the post-event questionnaire sent to in excess of 4,500 participants, to quantify economic impact and also to get feedback from participants to aid future developments in the event.

The marketing review was undertaken by FEI consultant Lucy McCrickard, a sports marketing, brand sponsorship and event management specialist with over 20 years' experience in major events. She managed Flora's sponsorship of the London Marathon for 13 years and continues her association with the event with Virgin. She is also commercial agent and manager for British Olympic Marathon runner Tracey Morris.

FEI's work included an assessment of the current position of the event, an examination of its future aspirations and identified how the distinctiveness of the event could best be safeguarded in a crowded market. We moved on to look at current and potential target audiences. We examined marketing and communication channels and looked at the current and potential partners for the event which would add value to the proposition. Charity has always played an important part in the Loch Ness Marathon and Lucy made suggestions as to how associations with charities could be best made to work in the event's long-term interests. We also looked at how best these developments might be financed and managed to maintain and protect the event. This work was encapsulated in a marketing review presented in August 2008.

Following the 2008 Marathon in October FEI also agreed the wording of the post-event online questionnaire with the client, managed its distribution and summarised the findings in an economic impact report delivered in November 2008.

Source: www.feiuk.com/Case_Study_03.asp

CASE STUDY 2   WINTER GARDENS PAVILION

Figure 15.3   The Winter Gardens Pavilion, Weston-super-Mare

As one of the largest conference centres in the Bristol region, the Winter Gardens on the seafront in Weston-super-Mare has always attracted customers because of its outstanding position, facilities and friendly service. However, in order to remain a competitive player within the hospitality market, it needed to continue to attract new customers and minimise costs and resource use.

In early 2005 the staff at the Winter Gardens decided that they wanted to go further in reducing the building's environmental impacts. Operated by North Somerset Council, the venue drew on the expertise within the authority and together became the first council service to pilot an Environmental Management System (EMS). The Winter Gardens catering partner, Parkwood Leisure, had already attained ISO 14001, so this seemed the natural next step.

From simple paper recycling, save-a-cup plastic cup recycling scheme and ensuring that computer monitors are not left on standby overnight, to installation of energy efficient equipment, everyone responded enthusiastically, and suggested ideas to help. One such idea led to plumbed-in water coolers being installed in office areas in place of bottled coolers, removing the need to transport the water – and saving money. The benefits of this have been recognised within the authority and it will soon be implemented throughout the rest of North Somerset Council.

One of the significant aspects that a venue like the Winter Gardens has is energy consumption. This has been dramatically reduced by upgrading the computerised building management system, giving greater control over consumption whilst improving the temperature control and comfort for customers. The Winter Gardens also purchases green electricity and the team behind ENVEC helped to install photovoltaic (PV) panels on the roof to help offset the carbon produced at the annual ENVEC event. The improvements programme, including attention to energy efficient lighting, is ongoing. Water consumption has also been reduced through initiatives such as the fitting of water saving devices to the toilets and urinals.

Another area that has been addressed in the EMS is the hosting of events and the various environmental impacts they create. Committing to meet the criteria of the **Greener Events** guide and promoting use of the guide to customers has helped to achieve one of the targets of the EMS by reducing impacts and raising awareness.

Figure 15.4   Looking across the harbour to the Winter Gardens Pavilion

New and existing customers of the Winter Gardens recognise the efforts to increase sustainability and have been keen to support the venue. A significant amount of new conference business has been won as a result of the **Greener Events** guide, demonstrating the growing awareness that event organisers have regarding sustainability issues. The experience at the Winter Gardens Pavilion has clearly demonstrated that an environmental ethos can have a commercial benefit and reinforces their long-term commitment for future improvements.

Further reading

London Borough of Hackney (2008) 'The Hackney State of the Environment Report' [online]. Available at: www.hackney.gov.uk/Assets/Documents/hackney_state_of_the_environment_report_2008.pdf [accessed 2 November 2011].

London Organising Committee for the Olympic Games (LOCOG) (2007) 'London 2012 Sustainable Plan November: Towards One Planet 2012' [online]. Available at: www.sel.org.uk/uploads/London-2012-Sustainability-Plan.pdf [accessed 2 November 2011].

London Organising Committee for the Olympic Games (LOCOG) (2008) 'London 2012: Towards One Planet, 2012 Sustainable Plan Update December' [online]. Available at: www.london2012.com/documents/locog-publications/sustainability-plan-december-08.pdf [accessed 2 November 2011].

Manchester City Council (2006) 'Greater Manchester Air Quality and Action Plan' [online]. Available at: www.greatairmanchester.org.uk/documents/LTP2%20AQ%20Strategy%20and%20Action%20Plan%202006.pdf [accessed 2 November 2011].

United Nations Framework Convention on Climate Change (1998) 'Kyoto Protocol' [online]. Available at: http://unfccc.int/resource/docs/convkp/kpeng.pdf [accessed 2 November 2011].

16 Long-Term Legacy and Impacts

In this chapter you will cover:

- impacts of events;
- long-term legacy of events;
- economic impacts of events;
- economic legacy of the Montreal Olympic Games;
- social and environmental impacts of events;
- summary;
- discussion questions;
- case studies;
- further reading.

The aim of this chapter is to critically review the development and implementation of long-term legacy and impacts of events on host destinations. The chapter will present compelling evidence on the economic and social impact linked to long-term legacy and impacts within the host location. The chapter will show that bidding for and hosting a mega event is not only predicated on a nation's ability to meet the international criteria, but that strategic alliances with international organisations are required, and the adoption of western political methods of governance can play a major factor in achieving the end game. The chapter will discuss the historical development of long-term legacy and impacts of events on a global platform with special attention to western democratic nations. A number of case studies will also be introduced to illustrate the broader issues from a positive and negative perspective.

Impacts of events

In the events industry impact studies are undertaken for a variety of purposes. Frequently they consider elements of cost-benefit analysis concerning the event, in comparison to income generation and visitor expenditure. Events give greater economic life to the host city and raise the profile by developing employment, increased tourism potential, additional trade and business development.

It could be argued that a catalytic effect ensues whereby following an increase in investment, additional monies are made available for local infra-structure and long-term promotional benefits are created. Further to this, other tangible benefits are improved tax revenues and increased property prices, with subsequent connections to the community.

However, event managers often put great emphasis on the financial impacts of events, and invariably become myopic concerning other possible impacts occurring during the event. It is important for the event manager to realise this potential situation and to identify and manage both positive and negative impacts resulting from the event.

Events provide the host city with great economic resources, which can leave a lasting legacy to the local community. In addition, local businesses rely on mega events and festivals to boost their income for the year; for many it may well be 'the icing on the cake'. Getz offers a definition of mega events:

> Mega events, by way of their size or significance are those that yield extraordinarily high levels of tourism, media coverage, prestige, or economic impact for the host community, venue or organisation. (2005, p. 18)

A wide range of events exists, and can involve cultural, environmental and social impacts. Each has its own popularity that helps to categorise the size and type. The Olympic Games is recognised as the world's largest sports mega event allowing substantial economic, social and political benefits for the host nation and local community.

Long-term legacy of events

> In order for the demands related to the Olympics to be satisfied, resources are required, and some of those resources may be diverted from other uses. To the extent that demands related to the Olympics absorb resources that would not otherwise have been utilised, such as labour resources, they will add to both employment and the total output of the economy. (Office of financial management research and information paper, 1997)

The term legacy has caused constant discussion (see Table 16.1).

Host cities for the Olympic Games

Up until 1968 the IOC awarded the Games to western democratic nations. From 1896–1964 the Olympic Games was held 17 times and over that period

Table 16.1   Types of legacy (International Olympic Committee, 2003)

Legacy	
Sporting	The introduction of a variety of sports within the area.
	Increased participation of women in the Olympic Games improves the percentage of females actively involved in sports activities in the host community.
	World class sporting facilities.
Political	Potential for improvement in education.
	Promote the Olympic Truce as a cultural aid.
	Introduction of various cultural considerations to the host community.
Economic	Difficult to measure due to constant variables.
	Long-term benefits for the community through regeneration projects.
Social	Builds upon national pride and traditions.
	Long-term recognition as a successful sporting nation.
	Used as an historical tool, educating the young community in its social past.

was subject to many economic and political intrusions. This chapter will show those intrusions at an international and national level and explore the ways in which they contributed to the social, economic and environmental impact of the Olympic Games for the host cities. The most obvious intrusions were the First and Second World Wars; during those periods the Olympic Games did not take place. However, at the end of each war countries that fell on the losing side were excluded from bidding for and participating in the Olympic Games for a short while.

In 1920 the games were awarded to Antwerp, Belgium; it was then given to Paris in 1924. In 1928 Amsterdam, Holland, was seen as a viable option due to its neutral status in the First World War. After the Second World War, London hosted the event in 1948. As the country was economically bankrupt after the war, it received approximately $4 billion in financial assistance from the American government under the Marshall Plan. Without this loan, Britain could never have maintained its balance of payment or world power at the centre of the Commonwealth. With that financial assistance, Britain was able to bid for and host the Olympic Games in 1948. In 1952 Helsinki was host to the Olympic Games, followed by Melbourne, Australia in 1956, then Rome in 1960. In 1964 Tokyo, Japan, was awarded the rights to host the Olympic Games. The city of Tokyo was devastated by bombing in the Second World War but also followed a western political style of governance. By 1956, Japan had joined the United Nations and from that point on was viewed as an economically strong and technological powerhouse of production.

In 1968 the IOC awarded the Olympic Games to Mexico. At that point in history Mexico was under authoritarian governance and with that came a number of political demonstrations by the young student population seeking political and civil freedom from oppression. On 2 October, ten days before the start of the Games, 44 student and civilian protestors were killed by government troops at a demonstration. It could be argued that this episode was one of the worst social impacts to a host nation because of the Olympic Games.

The long-term legacy of the London 2012 Games

Higgins (2008) identifies the five main areas in which the London 2012 Games needs to invest in order to develop its long-term legacy (see Figure 16.1).

Figure 16.1   Long-term legacy framework for the London 2012 Games

Costs of staging the Olympics, Beijing 2008

Table 16.2 identifies construction costs of hosting the 2008 Olympic Games and regenerating a city. Table 16.3 shows regeneration expenditure for Olympic and Non-Olympic related investments.

This improvement increases the standard of living for the city's residents and is therefore a positive impact for the host community.

Economic impacts of events

Historically, economic impact reports have been published as a prelude to the event and when the event concludes, particularly in the case of mega events. Academics and established independent organisations have consistently been

Table 16.2   Construction costs of the 2008 Beijing Olympic Games

Revenues	US$ million	%
Television rights	709	43.63%
TOP sponsorship	130	8.00%
Local sponsorship	130	8.00%
Licensing	50	3.08%
Official suppliers	20	1.23%
Olympic coins program	8	0.49%
Philately	12	0.74%
Lotteries	180	11.08%
Ticket sales	140	8.62%
Donations	20	1.23%
Disposal of assets	80	4.92%
Subsidies	100	6.15%
Others	46	2.83%
Expenditure	**US$ million**	**%**
Capital investment	190	11.69%
Sports facilities	102	6.28%
Olympic village	40	2.46%
MPC and IBC	45	2.77%
MV	3	0.18%
Operations	**1419**	**87.32%**
Sports events	275	16.92%
Olympic village	65	4.00%
MPC and IBC	360	22.15%
MV	10	0.62%
Ceremonies and programs	**100**	**6.15%**
Medical services	**30**	**1.85%**
Catering	**51**	**3.14%**
Transport	**70**	**4.31%**
Security	**50**	**3.08%**
Paralympic games	**82**	**5.05%**
Advertising and promotion	**60**	**3.69%**
Administration	**125**	**7.69%**
Pre-Olympic events and coordination	**40**	**2.46%**
Other	**101**	**6.22%**
Surplus	**16**	**0.98%**
Total	**1625**	**1625**

Source: BOCOG, www.beijing-2008.org

given the responsibility to produce reports, and have made available to the wider public, evidence that suggests mega events can bring a significant economic value to a host community, whether through tourism or major infrastructural

Table 16.3   Regeneration costs, Beijing 2008

Capital investments				Construction cost (US$ million)					
	2001	2002	2003	2004	2005	2006	2007	2008	Total
Planned non-Olympic expenditure									
Environment protection	1000	1000	1500	1500	1500	1300	827	0	8627
Roads and railways	547	592	636	636	636	313	313	0	3673
Airport	12	30	31	12	0	0	0	0	85
Olympic-related expenditure									
Sports venues	213			425	496	283	12	0	1429
Olympic village	111					159	135	38	442
Total	**1559**	**1622**	**2380**	**2573**	**2743**	**2055**	**1287**	**38**	**14257**

Source: BOCOG, www.beijing-2008.org

build programmes. In addition to this, economic studies have also been published by the host nations and official rights holders after each Olympic Games. The spending is reported as providing significant and worthwhile additions to the host locations. In most circumstances that infrastructure in the shape of homes, roads and commercial buildings are a welcomed addition to any city. However, the initial spend to acquire those assets to a large degree comes from the local and national taxpayers within the host nation.

In 2004 PricewaterhouseCoopers published a report that analysed the economic impact of the Olympic Games on host countries. It made a clear distinction between the overall financial costs for hosting the Games and those costs that can be met by revenue directly generated from the games. The report takes into consideration the size of the host nations, and measures economic effects at a local and national level, for example in the USA and in Greece. The report looks at pre-, during and post-Games impact. Broadcast revenue is also explored – this is the largest economic revenue driver from the Olympic Games, although the IOC will generally take a significant share of these revenues. In building an economic profile of the Games within a host city the report makes reference to what is known by economists as the 'multiplier effect'. This is an economic indicator applied to test and measure the economic performance via aggregated spend.

The report takes into consideration seven countries that hosted the Games from 1972–2000. Of the seven countries analysed within the economic report there was one anomaly that must be recognised: the Los Angeles Olympics, which was able to break the economic cycle of debt to the host nation. The local organising committee was able to secure all the financial outlay by way of sponsorship. No other country before 1984 or after has been able to finance and bring the event in with a surplus.

The economic performance within each country was measured over a period of 8–10 years to see if there was any significant impact on GDP, investment, private and public consumption and consumer expenditure. The report does not take into consideration, but draws to the reader's attention, global economic situations that could have an effect on growth and economic performance for some countries, such as with Greece with the Iraq war and increasing security budget. The report clearly shows that economic performance increases in the pre-Games impact stage for nearly all countries. However, in the Games impact and post-Games impact, economic performance related to GDP and the other indicators as mentioned earlier level out, and for some host cities economic performance drops off for a number of years.

The Australian Government reported, and the IOC concluded, that the Sydney Olympic Games in 2000 was an economic success. However, the PricewaterhouseCoopers report shows that GDP for the New South Wales economy dropped off and consumer expenditure and public consumption levelled out. In Sydney's bid for the 2000 Olympic Games, the budget was $AUS 3 billion (£1 billion), of which just $AUS 363.5 million would be borne by the public. In 2002 the Auditor-General of New South Wales undertook a further audit, confirming that Sydney Games had cost $AUS 6.6 billion and the public paid $AUS 1.7–2.4 billion. Such budget discrepancy can be seen with many bids, including that for London 2012, where the local organising committee decide to negate/exclude capital cost for facilities and infrastructure, which ultimately becomes the most costly aspect of the bid.

In 2005 the Department of Culture Media and Sport, in association with PricewaterhouseCoopers, published the Olympic Games Impact Study Final Report for London 2012 Olympic Games. The report draws a conclusion which detracts from the information contained in the 2004 economic profile of seven Olympic countries.

> It shows, for example, that there is an 84.4% chance that the Olympics will have a positive impact on UK GDP over the period 2005–2016: in London, the comparable probability is 95.3%. (PricewaterhouseCoopers/DCMS, 2005: 5 [online])

Before London won the rights to host the Olympic Games in 2005, the government undertook some extensive research and published a report: House of Commons Culture, Media and Sport Committee London Olympic Bid for 2012 (2002–3).

It detailed what the cost would be to host the Olympic Games in 2012. The report took into account factors such as infrastructure cost, inflation, land acquisition, uncertainties and assumptions of a ten-year project, with an investigation of the Athens, Sydney and Manchester Games. The final budget that was put forward was £4.674 million, with public subsidy set at £2,624 million by the Department of Culture Media and Sport (DCMS). Considering the fact the security budget alone for Athens 2004 was documented at 1.4 billion, and the Greek government required loans from the IMF to cover the cost of the Games, it is difficult to believe that the government with associated partners put forward such an underestimated cost to host the Games.

> The Secretary of State emphasised in oral evidence the risks involved in budgeting for the Games with reference to the experience of Sydney and Athens. She said that both had found their outturn to be double their estimated costs. We asked the DCMS what work had been undertaken to assess and avoid the failure of Sydney and Athens in predicting costs. (House of Commons Culture, Media and Sport Committee, 2002–3: 17)

The security cost for London 2012 was put at £600 million, as taken from the official website; current statements circulating on this issue now place the cost close to over £1 billion. Some media commentators draw the comparison with Athens 2004 security budget of 1.4 billion Euros. By 2007, the budget for the London Olympics had doubled in cost.

> The budget for the London 2012 Games, announced in March 2007 by the Minister for the Olympic and Paralympic Games and Co-Chair of the Olympic Board, was £9,325 million. (The Olympic Delivery Authority, 2011: 17 [online])

Taking into consideration the 2004 report, where Olympic cities did not show any significant movement in GDP post-event but in some cases economic performance dropped off, and assimilating this alongside other Olympic cities that were not included within the sample for the 2004 report, the evidence shows a very similar characteristic in terms of economic performance. It is therefore difficult to conclude that London 2012 has a high probability of achieving a significant economic profile.

When charting the economic impact of mega events on western nations we are confronted with a level of inconsistency regarding published data. This is compounded by a continued effort on the part of the IOC to demonstrate that hosting the Olympic Games is seen as a financial success and a status symbol for stable economies, emerging and developing nations.

The economic legacy of the Montreal Olympic Games

In 1996 a report was written and published by Michel Guay, titled, 'Legacy of the Olympic Games in Montreal – An Introduction'. In that report he categorically states that the Montreal Olympic Games did not have a deficit, in fact the Games brought about a surplus of over $223 million to the Government of

Quebec. Within the same report it makes reference to the tobacco tax that was earmarked to bring down the 'Olympic debt'.

> According to the Quebec Government original estimates in the budget for 76–77 (8), (when the new tobacco tax for the Olympic debt repayment was established), the repayment of the 'Olympic debt' was to be done by fiscal year 1981–82; and now, 15 years later than the planned date, there is still 'an Olympic debt'. Many thanks to our politician friends. (Guay, 1996 [online])

Here we have a clear indication of a divergent opinion on the same subject within one document. Many academic papers and independent reports allude to the mega debt that was levied on the population of Quebec for hosting the Olympic Games and in particular the payment attributed to the Olympic stadium. A $1.5 billion debt for the stadium was finally paid off in 2006. At current estimate it is reported that Montreal had the longest debt repayment for hosting the Olympic Games.

In the official report published by Montreal Olympic Games 1976, volume 1, it refers to the escalation of cost, which was initially set at $310 million to host the Games. The report attributes the cost escalation to a number of factors, including social and economic conditions within the country and globally. From 1973 over the following four years, Canada experienced an inflation rise of 40 per cent. The gap between the financial projection and reality has been attributed to technical difficulties, the under-estimation of material along with labour disputes on the Olympic site, and finally new construction techniques. The technical problems were considered to be one of the major factors as to why the Olympic stadium had a runaway cost. The French Architect Roger Tallibert, who designed the stadium, had not fully appreciated that building techniques were tested during the construction of the stadium on the Olympic sites. This ultimately presented many problems for the build process and caused many delays. Even after the initial build the stadium was blighted with many construction defects. In 1991 a 55-ton concrete beam fell from the structure; and in 1999 a 350m^2 section of the roof collapsed. Fortunately, no one was injured on either of these occasions.

Within western democratic nations and in particular in the UK, bidding for mega events is driven in the main by a policy known as 'urban regeneration' a product of urban neglect in many metropolitan cities. Coupled with that programme of redevelopment we also have social impact, a major addition included within bidding documents for mega events.

The policy of urban redevelopment comes directly from national government, but urban decline is also on the European agenda, as is evident in the European Commission Objective targets given to underperforming cities or regions. Objectives 1, 2 and 3 are status targets that give a social and economic profile to a city in the broadest terms. Liverpool was granted Objective 1 status by the

European Commission for nearly 20 years, as the city had recorded some of the worst economic and social impacts to communities within Europe.

It was not until 2008, when Liverpool was officially European City of Culture, that the city began to experience new investment opportunity and was removed from Objective 1 status.

This can also be seen with the location of the 2002 Commonwealth Games in Manchester, the 2012 Olympic Games in London and the 2014 Commonwealth Games scheduled to take place in Glasgow.

Manchester 2002 Commonwealth Games was located to the east of Manchester city centre, an area noted for its economic and social problems. Blighted by underinvestment in all areas, East Manchester required significant economic investment to turn around years of decline. Derelict land was earmarked for redevelopment with a sustainable long-term future. Manchester Commonwealth Games post-event analysis by a number of academics and independent organisations has presented significant success stories by way of new homes, jobs, improved transportation and road networks including sporting facilities which have sustained use from the local inhabitants. The London 2012 bid was located on contaminated and derelict land untouched since the Second World War. The event has a social, environmental and economic reach over five boroughs in London which rank as the worst performing in many social aspects in comparison with the outer boroughs. The 2014 Commonwealth Games in Glasgow is strategically located to the east end of the city. Again this area is ranked as one of the worst performing areas within the UK from a health perspective, and also manifests a range of other social problems linked to ill health. The European Commission also places it as one of the most deprived locations in Europe. It is no accident therefore that mega events have a strategic role to play when attempting to enhance the lives of the local inhabitants. The methodology applied across the three events gives a clear picture that mega events have the propensity to change the social and economic fabric of a city for the better.

Social and environmental impacts of events

Event organisers are now using historical and cultural themes to develop annual events in attracting visitors and creating cultural images in the host cities by holding festivals within community settings. Even so, many event organisers do not take into account the social and environmental impacts.

The impacts of events can greatly affect the quality of life of the local residents. It has been argued that strategies need to be adopted to take control of the social and environmental impacts of festivals and analysis is required when looking at the economic impact of each individual event. Event organisers may only take into consideration the economic implications and ignore the residents' perceptions, which provide an important non-economic dimension for gauging how events benefit or impinge on the host community (Hall, 1992).

Therefore, it is important for event managers to address the concerns of the local people and reduce the negative impact. Event managers should also deliberate on the perceptions of the local residents and show willingness to discuss the initial proposal of the festival with the local community. Many leading authors have suggested that it is important for event organisers to have a clear awareness and understanding of residents' concerns and attitudes. This, Delemere (2001) believes, will encourage a balance between social and economic development forces within the community. The view of the host community may also help to refine the analytical framework used by planners and policy makers in helping the industry to be sustainable in the long term (Jeong and Faulkner, 1996; Williams and Lawson, 2001).

Without the support of the local community the success of any event cannot be ensured so it is a matter of urgency and even commonsense to get the local community on board from the outset. Event organisers who do not take into account local feeling will only store up feelings of animosity and a sense by the local community that they do not belong, that it is no longer their event. This is only one of a number of potential problems with the measurement of event impacts, in that the costs and benefits are unevenly distributed, and may occur in the short or long term.

This is an extremely important point, which is likely to assert an influence upon the results of this study. Thus it is clearly important to establish both *how* and *who* are affected by the costs and the benefits.

Summary

The chapter suggests that the spending by visitors on local goods and services has a direct economic impact on local businesses and also passes the benefits more widely across the economy and the community.

The chapter has debated the validity of economic assessments and shown that there is disagreement regarding the most accurate method of assessing the performance of an event. Substantial attention, however, is still paid by governments and the events industry to the economic dimensions of impacts, as this is often regarded as a measure of the immediate success of the event and associated developments. The event organiser and local government only take into account the economic impacts and ignore the implications of social impacts of the events. As the events industry develops, it is the role of the event manager to catalogue and forecast possible impacts to stakeholders while creating plans to decrease all negative impacts.

Evidence clearly shows that social and economic impact within the mega event arena is a common issue that must be taken seriously by future governments when deciding to bid for international mega events. The long-term social scars for some inhabitants will remain long after the event is over. The fiscal debt which remains with the host inhabitants has created a great deal of resentment towards mega events in host communities. Official documents produced as a way of explaining the overall legacy and impact of mega events must follow consistent criteria and in particular when presenting financial data. Infrastructure cost must always be included when presenting a pre- and post-event impact report. Long-term financial projections should pay close attention to similar bids where the financial data gives an accurate account of fiscal spend.

Transparency and accountability should not be seen as a cursory comment tagged to a final report but used as a mechanism to address problems and set new standards for the future to nations who intend to bid.

 ■ Discussion questions ▬▬▬▬▬▬▬▬▬▬▬▬▬▬▬▬▬

Question 1

The social impact of mega events as seen with the Mexico Olympic Games can have a dramatic negative effect on the local inhabitants. Discuss the political relationship between the US and the Mexican government that led to the students' massacre in 1968.

Question 2

Economic impact reports from the host nation and appointed organisations have consistently shown that debt is a minor issue for the majority of countries who decide to host a mega event. Discuss the rationale as to why there is conflicting information published by credible and accredited bodies representing mega events.

Question 3

Urban regeneration is a political and government policy to redevelop areas within a region, city or town that has seen significant decline. Mega events have taken on this political agenda. From a UK perspective, put forward an argument as to why some bid documents have taken on urban redevelopment as a feature.

Question 4

The award of City of Culture 2008 had a significant impact on the city of Liverpool. Discuss some of the benefits that took Liverpool out of Objective 1 status as a result of hosting the event.

Question 5

Mega sporting venues have in some cities given a major boost to the economy by way of the events scheduled for those venues. Discuss the benefit of the Millennium Stadium to Cardiff.

Question 6

The Expo, when first introduced by Britain in 1851, had a major benefit to the nation's global status. Following on from that date the Expo was hosted in the main by three countries during a specific period in history. Name the three countries and discuss why the allocation of events remained with those three countries throughout a particular period.

CASE STUDY 1   SOCIAL AND CULTURAL IMPACTS OF THE EDINBURGH FESTIVALS

One of the most ground breaking areas of work is the analysis of the importance of the Festivals to cultural and social life in Scotland. The Edinburgh Festivals Impact Study asked local and visiting audiences, performers, teachers and media about 'the Festival effect' in a number of areas: such as, how well Festival events compare to competitor events nationally and internationally, how the Festivals inspire children and young people, how they encourage further visits to arts and culture, how they enhance the image and identity of Edinburgh and Scotland and how they foster a sense of community and well-being. This is the first time that such far reaching questions have been asked on this scale.

Some of the most striking findings in the study relate to the overwhelming impact the Festivals have on local pride and attractiveness as a visitor destination. There is very strong evidence of the Festivals' contribution to local, national and international profile. Eighty-two per cent of visitors stated that the Festivals were their sole or an important reason for their trip to Scotland. Similarly, 85 per cent of all respondents agreed that the image that the Festivals present of Edinburgh and Scotland is one of diversity and openness, showcasing a positive national identity.

At a citywide level, 93 per cent of tourists and visitors said the Festivals are part of what makes Edinburgh special as a city, and 82 per cent agreed that their experience at the Festivals makes them more likely to visit Edinburgh in the future. Local respondents also rated the Festivals extremely favourably, with 89 per cent agreeing that the Festivals increase their pride in their home city.

Furthermore, in the Summer period, the Festivals running concurrently is also seen as a major benefit, with 78 per cent of survey respondents agreeing that having the Festivals on at the same time adds to the overall appeal of the Festival City.

Many of the other key findings relate to the Festivals' role in widening access and participation. There were 32,055 attendances at dedicated workshops and educational events, 95 per cent of whom were children and young people. Ninety-three per cent of parents agreed that attending Festival events increased their child's imagination, rating Festivals events an average of 8.5 out of 10 when asked to score events on behalf of their families.

Impacts do not just extend to children, however, with 93 per cent of all audiences stating that the Festivals enabled them to see artists or events that they would not normally get to see; and over three-quarters of attendees (78.4 per cent) rate the quality of Edinburgh Festivals events as better as or much better than similar events elsewhere. Nearly two-thirds of Festival audiences said that their festival experience had made them more likely to take greater risks and attend less well-known performances.

Environmental impact

For some time the Festivals have been working hard to address climate change and resource depletion, introducing a number of initiatives to mitigate the effects of their offices and events such as minimising waste to landfill, monitoring and reducing energy use, printing on responsibly sourced paper and reducing paper usage overall. Many Festivals also present events, talks and films to promote understanding of environmental issues.

The study has helped support the environmental work the Festivals do, individually and collectively, in developing ways of benchmarking, monitoring and reducing the overall environmental impact of the Festivals for the very first time.

In the first attempt to record this impact, the study reveals that audience travel to events accounts for the majority of CO_2 emissions, and has been calculated as ~44,653 tonnes, equivalent to 1.34 kg of CO_2 per ticket sold. In terms of waste management, nearly half (48 per cent) of waste from Festival offices is recycled.

Given their temporary nature, assessing the operations and impact of many of the 'pop-up' Festival venues is a much more complex undertaking. To this end, however, the Festivals have been recently collaborating on a pilot 'Green Venue Initiative' which supports, facilitates and recognises those venues that are monitoring, measuring and reducing their environmental impact. The pilot year for this programme was 2010, and 27 per cent of Festival shows took place in a 'Green Venue'. It is anticipated that this figure will grow in the near future, enabling the full environmental footprint of Edinburgh's Festivals to be increasingly monitored and reduced.

Source: Edinburgh Festival www.festivalsedinburgh.com/sites/default/files/FestivalsImpact Release2011FINAL.pdf

CASE STUDY 2   IMPACTS OF SPORTS INFRASTRUCTURE INVESTMENT ON VISITOR NUMBERS TO CARDIFF

New sports venues that can attract major sporting events or host entire tournaments attract both UK and international visitors in large numbers. This article explores the effects of sport infrastructure investment on visitor numbers through the example of the sports venues available in Cardiff. It considers both existing venues and the sporting events they have hosted and future events or venues still in planning and their anticipated impact on the number of visits to the city.

In recent years, large towns and cities such as Manchester and Belfast in the UK have experienced significant growth in investment in sporting infrastructure. Either led by private finance, government development grants or both, funding has flowed into large infrastructure projects including stadiums, multipurpose sports venues, and supporting facilities.

The implications for visitor figures in locations that have received significant funding are clear. New sports venues that can attract major sporting events or host entire tournaments attract both UK and international visitors in large numbers. In addition, the cumulative effect of media coverage of major sporting events can help sustain a long-term visitor interest in a town or city.

The long-term tourist impact of this type of investment is very significant. The funding and development moulds a legacy that stretches well into the future, and completely changes public perceptions of the locations that are subject to the investment.

There can be few better examples of the boost to visitor numbers that this investment generates, than the city of Cardiff.

Tourism is an important component of the Welsh economy. In recent years, annual spending from overnight and day visits has been in excess of £2.6 billion, which is equivalent to approximately 7 per cent of Welsh GDP.

Investment in sporting facilities boosts national and international visitor numbers to a city, and generates a legacy that helps to sustain increased visitor numbers.

This has been recognised by many local development authorities, including Cardiff County Council who have outlined as a key part of their tourism growth strategy the importance of establishing Cardiff, 'as a leading short-break destination, in particular for sports and culture'.

The traditional perception of Cardiff

Over the years, the traditional perception of Cardiff was not that of a top-tier multi-sports venue, and was associated with little beyond its role as the traditional home of Welsh rugby.

This perception was not without basis. The most notable and largest capacity sports venue was the Cardiff Arms Park. Opened in 1962, by the mid-1990s it was an old and outdated stadium, lacking modern hospitality, parking or media facilities.

Up until the turn of the last century, the cities' other principal venues included the antiquated Ninian Park (opened 1910), Sophia Gardens Cricket Ground (opened late nineteenth Century), the Empire Pool (opened in 1958) and the Wales National Ice Rink (opened in the 1980s). Other additional sports facilities only included a small number of standard venues that themselves were often in need of significant investment and were incapable of hosting any kind of significant sporting events.

Although the city over the past century played host to numerous notable sporting moments, Cardiff lacked the capacity to host multi-sport higher-tier events that attract national or international attention.

Investment and transformation

Infrastructure investment is essential to the delivery of venues and venues are key to delivering events. Apart from the relatively small number of individuals who travel to specifically admire sporting venues, the vast majority of tourists generated by infrastructure come because they have tickets for major sporting events.

The organisers of events such as the Ryder Cup, the Ashes, FA Cup, etc. have to protect the reputation of those events. As such, they require a very high standard from the venues wishing to host those sporting occasions. Stadiums, pitches, hospitality, media and corporate facilities, parking, transport links, crowd control, etc. are all factored into the considerations, and the venues that are awarded the opportunity to host these events must be of a very high standard.

Sports infrastructure investment is essential to deliver these high-quality facilities and allow teams to bid for the big ticket sports events. Cardiff has been spectacularly successful in showing the link between investment, building, competition, awarding of events and the resulting tourist and economic benefits. Cardiff's sporting diary over the past 10 years has been impressive, including global sports events such as the Ashes (2009) and the Ryder Cup (2012).

Sports infrastructure development progress: built, building and planned

Wales Millennium Stadium

Around the mid-1990s a committee was set up to look at redeveloping the Wales National Stadium (old Arms Park) and linking the redevelopment to the regeneration of West Cardiff.

A review of the National Stadium at Cardiff Arms Park showed that it had long since been overtaken in terms of capacity; with Twickenham and Scotland having developed stadia with capacities of 75,000 and 67,000 respectively, and France about to build the Stade de France with a capacity of over 80,000.

As replacement for the Cardiff Arms Park, the Wales Millennium Stadium was opened in June 1999. At the time of its construction it was the largest stadium in the UK with a capacity of 74,500. The Stadium sits on the west bank of the river Taff, and a unique feature of the stadium is its proximity to the city centre. Fans leaving the stadium can literally stroll into the pub, bars and restaurants following the end of sports and entertainment events held in the stadium.

With the first retractable roof in the UK, the stadium is a multi-purpose venue. It has been awarded a UEFA 5-Star rating and has now hosted two Rugby World Cups, a Wales Grand Slam and six FA Cup Finals.

It had delivered a £725m financial boost for the economy of Wales, according to the findings of an independent survey carried out for the Welsh Rugby Union.

The economic impact survey reveals that more than nine million people have entered the stadium since it opened, helping it become the most visited attraction in Wales and one of the top ten in the UK.

Source: Tourism insight (2012) Sharing sector expertise, analysis and intelligence

Further reading

CIA (1968) 'Students stage major disorder in Mexico' [online]. Available at: www.gwu.edu/~nsarchiv/NSAEBB/NSAEBB10/mex03-01.htm [accessed 1 March 2012].

Edinburgh Festival available at: www.festivalsedinburgh.com/sites/default/files/FestivalsImpactRelease2011FINAL.pdf [accessed 1 March 2012].

Guay, M. (1976) 'Legacy of the Olympic Games in Montreal – An introduction' [online]. Available at: http://montrealolympics.com/mg_legacy.php [accessed 1 April 2012].

House of Commons Culture, Media and Sport Committee (2002–3) *A London Olympic Bid for 2012: Third report.* London: House of Commons.

Institution of Civil Engineers (2003) 'Impact of the Olympic Games as mega-events' [online]. Available at: http://epress.lib.uts.edu.au/dspace/bitstream/handle/2100/993/muen.157.3.209.49461.pdf?sequence= [accessed 13 March 2012].

Klyn-Hesselink, E., Stoter, J. and Van der Woerd, A. (2004) '1986 Commonwealth Games: the year of the boycott' [online]. Available at: http://sporthamilton.com/content/history/1986_Commonwealth_Games.pdf [accessed 1 March 2012].

Osawemen, M. (1987) 'Britain's relation with South Africa' [online]. Available at: www.niianet.org/documents/articles%20pdf/Britain%27s%20Relation%20with%20South%20Africa.pdf [accessed 15 March 2012].

PricewaterhouseCoopers/DCMS (2005) 'Olympic Games impact study final report' [online]. Available at: www.gamesmonitor.org.uk/files/PWC%20OlympicGamesImpactStudy.pdf [accessed 11 March 2012].

The Olympic Delivery Authority (2011) 'The ODA plan and budget' [online]. Available at: www.london2012.com/documents/oda-publications/oda-plan-2011.pdf [accessed 1 April 2012].

Tourism Insight (2012) 'Sharing sector expertise, analysis and intelligence' [online]. Available at: www.insights.org.uk/articleitem.aspx?title=Case%20Study:%20The%20Impact%20of%20Sports%20Infrastructure%20Investment%20on%20Visitor%20Numbers%20to%20Cardiff [accessed 23 January 2012].

17 The Future of the Events Industry

In this chapter you will cover:

- drivers for change in the global events industry;
- developments in technology;
- virtual events;
- the transferable personal skills of an event manager;
- sustainability in the event industry;
- summary;
- discussion questions;
- case studies;
- further reading.

The aim of this chapter is to discuss the future of the events industry. The chapter explains how sustainability, globalisation, innovation and technology will impact greatly on the industry. The global events industry has been growing rapidly in the west for the last decade. In particular, the experience and knowledge economy is in the ascendancy and therefore business events must be much more experience and knowledge oriented. Furthermore, the use of the internet, mobile technology and virtual applications will considerably affect the events industry. The internet will continue to shape conferences and seminars as delegates may no longer need to attend these events to gather information that is now available via the internet. With these future changes, the event professional will need to be adaptable, and have greater transferable skills.

Drivers for change in the global events industry

With the downturn in the economy, several organisations have cut their budgets and are reducing costs by getting rid of staff, cutting services and limiting business travel. Furthermore, due to climate change and the realisation that our natural resources are in short supply, many organisations are going green and investing in different ways to reduce their carbon footprint. These changes, coupled with cultural shifts, the search for original consumer experiences, the relationship between sports, economics and events, and developments in technology such as mobiles and virtual applications represent some of the challenges facing the events industry professional. In response, organisations have been looking for ways to cut costs and remain environmentally friendly, including looking at whether it is necessary to have face-to-face meetings.

Figure 17.1   Drivers for future changes in the global events industry

Shifting cultural class

Even today as consumers are becoming financially better off, they distinguish themselves by their use of cultural, experiential and social knowledge and individual identity. It is no longer about the wealth you have, but what you do with that wealth and who you know. The cultural capital of events is how communities and tourists talk about their experience of festivals and sporting occasions and their participation in them, hence the cultural consumption of festivals.

Search for original experiences

Event goers are continually searching for original and new experiences rather than the old traditional events. There is an increasing need to seek out experiences and products which are authentic and not contaminated.

Sporting events and the changing economy

Sport contributes considerably to the economy of most countries in terms of mega sporting events, print and digital media, health and well-being and amateur sports. Hosting mega sports events such as the FIFA Football World Cup is highly contested and prized, not least because of the potential positive impacts on the destination.

On the other hand, mega events have had negative impact on the economy of certain countries, such as Greece, where some have argued that the 2004 Olympic Games was a catalyst to the country's later economic problems. The 2004 Athens Olympics cost nearly twice as much as its initial budget. In 2010, more than half of Athens' Olympic sites were barely used or empty, although the Games did improve the transportation system with a new metro system, a new airport, and a tram and light railway network. However, given the looming fiscal deficits in many countries, arguments about the economic benefits of mega events will diminish.

Sporting events and politics

Sport has always been used by politicians as a means to influence political reform or as a way to bring about change in countries. For instance, during the cold war, some countries (predominantly Western) decided to boycott the Moscow Olympics, and during the apartheid era in South Africa several countries refused to play against them. More recently, there has been controversy as to whether the Formula One Grand Prix should have been held in Bahrain in 2012 when the regime there has treated very harshly protestors demanding political reforms motivated by the Arab Spring in the Middle East. Nevertheless, mega sporting events will continue to be influenced by politics and will also have influence on world politics.

Developments in technology

The internet and mobile technology

There are over three billion mobile phone subscribers globally. The mobile revolution has and will continue to transform the way that we communicate, get information, find our way around, buy things, and the way that event professionals do business.

There is a coming together of technology trends which is driving these changes. For instance, advances in phone hardware have led to mobile phones increasingly being used for far more than just making calls. Increasingly they are becoming mini-computers with functionalities such as advanced web browsing, geo-positioning, video, and contact management capabilities, to name a few. Smart phones will provide more powerful processing capabilities in smaller and more convenient packages.

In addition, advances in web technology have been the main delivery medium for software. Google and other major players are investing in web-based mobile tools, most of them at little or no cost to the user. The use of web technology has been greatly impacted by advances in high-speed broadband internet access through the wireless networks. Soon, everywhere you go, broadband internet, the carrier for the mobile web software tools mentioned above, will be available.

GPS (Geo-Positioning Technology) is already available in some phones but increasingly this will become a common cell-phone feature over the next few years. Finally, NFC (Near Field Communication) wireless technology (which is widely used in Japan with trials in the United States, Germany, Finland, Netherlands and a few other countries) will turn cell phones into secure credit or debit cards. A chip embedded in a phone will allow users to make a payment by using a touch-sensitive interface or by bringing the phone within a few centimetres of an NFC reader. Your credit card account or bank account is then charged accordingly.

These converging trends in mobile technology will affect how some events are organised and managed. For instance, several meetings-related applications, including mobile-based conference agenda, exhibition guide, and networking guides and web-based mobile phone guides, could help conference attendees to explore the conference agenda and enable the connection between exhibitors and other conference attendees. Mobile city guides and mapping programs will become increasingly helpful to convention goers in unfamiliar cities. The iPhone and its competitors, with robust web functionality, will make the many excellent location-based mapping websites (such as Ask City http://city.ask.com and Google Maps http://map.google.com) much more accessible.

Additionally, mobile products such as Google Mobile Maps (www.google.com/gmm) offer directions, real-time traffic, and satellite imagery. Geovector (www.geovector.com) is an example of a mobile-phone-based mapping tool allowing users in Japan to search for movies, restaurants, buy tickets, make restaurant reservations and more, and get step-by-step GPS-based guidance on how to get there. Advanced mobile-phone GPS capabilities are likely to be able to help attendees find hotels, reception locations, rooms in a convention centre and navigate efficiently while at events.

Furthermore, interactive audience response keypads are excellent tools that engage attendees and can provide very useful data. The challenge is that rental fees for these systems can be expensive costing up to US$10 per person per day. In the future, when a speaker or event organiser would like to use audience voting capabilities, attendees will be able to pull out their phones and use them as a voting keypad. Already, companies such as Log-On offer text message voting using mobile phones. In the future, using web-based survey products, this will become much easier with the ability to graph the results instantly on the screen. Additionally, companies such as VisionTree (www.visiontree.com) are providing advanced audience polling, surveys and continuing education tracking using any web-enabled mobile device.

There are many excellent web-based as well as proprietary hand-held business networking products which help people of like interests to find each other at events. The challenge is that the standard web-based tools are not very mobile and the hand-held tools can be too expensive for many groups. Better web-browsing functionality in phones will allow the benefits of both – high quality conference networking systems that are mobile and at lower cost.

This will likely be tied to a conference messaging system giving the meeting planner the ability to make broadcast announcements to all attendees or a subset (for example in the event of a major session change), and allow attendees to send messages to other conference goers.

The current system, where exhibitors are charged large sums by registration companies for barcode or magnetic bar code scanning equipment, will likely become outdated in the next few years. Using near field communication (NFC) enabled mobile phones, attendees will be able to easily exchange contact information. This can be between two phones or between a phone and an NFC-enabled badge and will be as simple as tapping the two devices together. Similar technology could be used for access verification (with an embedded ID photo), for electronic tickets, continuing education unit (CEU) tracking, tote bag distribution and more.

There are more than 1,500 technology products in 30 categories available as part of online registration processes designed to assist in the meeting planning process (www.corbinball.com/bookmarks). Many of these tools are web-based. With the increasing functionality of web-based mobile products, these tools will be increasingly accessible via mobile phones.

Online registration is just one example of many. A mobile-phone based registration solution could work as follows:

- Event attendee receives an email on a mobile-phone for an upcoming conference.
- The attendee clicks on the link to the registration page.
- Using the functionality of 'auto-fill', the registration form is completed and the authorisation for payment is carried out.
- By return the confirmation email contains a printable receipt and a confirmation bar-code (or NFC e-ticket).
- The attendee takes the bar-code or e-ticket received on the mobile phone to check-in on site.

These are just some of the ways that mobile phones are possibly going to change the events industry. The next generations of mobile phone will revolutionise meetings management and the business process in general in very significant ways.

While acknowledging that ever-changing technology makes it difficult to tell what might happen next, there will be certain parts of the events industry which are fundamental and will continue to require the need for meetings to take place face-to-face. For example, successful sales teams are built through zeal for a goal that comes from face-to-face meetings.

Microsoft has suggested that in the coming years, 50 per cent of US gross domestic product will be taken up by training and knowledge delivery. Progressive organisations will continue to bring people together to meet. Commentators have argued against the predictors of doom who claim that the meeting business is in a death spiral.

The constant reassessment and the desire for new innovative ideas is a key to staying ahead of the game. In order to achieve this, innovative organisations possess certain characteristics which are presented in Figure 17.2.

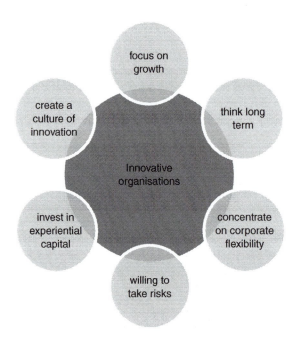

Figure 17.2   Characteristics of world class innovative organisations

Virtual events

Some organisations and businesses have begun to re-evaluate the necessity of face-to-face meetings and events and, in some cases, choose to hold them virtually. In 2010, over 70 per cent of event professionals felt that reduction in budgets would be their biggest challenge, and 38 per cent were planning to replace live meetings with virtual meetings or conference calls (Scofidio, 2009 [online]).

Consequently, organisations will increasingly use virtual worlds to hold meetings and special events. A study in 2009 found that 40 per cent of corporate brand marketers and 31 per cent of exhibition marketers hold virtual events; 71 per cent of respondents use virtual reality to accommodate geographically widespread workforces and customers, with webinars (81 per cent) being the most commonly used (Center for Exhibition Industry Research, 2009).

The virtual events market, consisting of many different products and services, is estimated to increase to around $18.6 billion from 2010 to 2015 (Market Research Media, 2010). Market Research Media (2010) identified a range of services included within the virtual conference and trade show market, which are shown in Figure 17.3.

The scope of virtual reality applications found within the event industry ranges from entertainment, to visualisations, to architecture/design, to education and training.

Virtual reality applications are becoming increasingly more relevant in these times of change; however, most event professionals do not have a clear understanding of what they are and how they may be employed to address business needs.

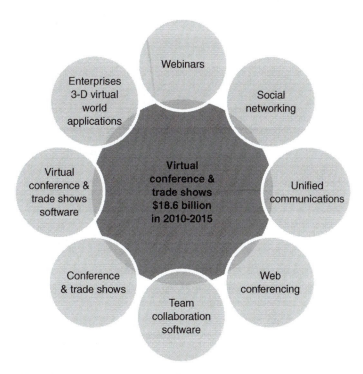

Figure 17.3   Virtual and conference trade shows spending

Source: Market Research Media (2010)

Virtual events can have benefits for both exhibitors and attendees. For exhibitors, virtual events can create new and lucrative opportunities for the organisation, increasing content delivery options, driving more robust networking, and extending sponsorship options while exceeding customer expectations.

Furthermore, virtual events can give event organisers the ability to increase revenue and cut costs, to extend the brand, to broaden the brand community, to track attendees, and to permit rapid response. The benefits for attendees include decreased costs and time associated with travel, which may lead to increased education and training participation.

In the face of changing technology and the quest for new products what is needed is continuous education and training for event managers who will need to adapt transferable personal skills to keep up to date with the developments in the industry.

The transferable personal skills of an event manager

Events are an exceptionally powerful medium of communication. People may not remember exactly what was said or heard, exactly what was done or seen, but they do remember how the event made them feel. This is true whether you are witnessing a major sporting achievement, a musical performance or keynote speaker, or whether you are attending an exciting exhibition, a well-orchestrated new product launch or your own perfect wedding.

If excellent event experiences are to be produced and the 'experiential marketing' of events is thus to be successful, then highly skilled event professionals are required. Such professionals share a set of common skills, whether they are organising concerts or conferences, meetings or matches, fashion shows or film festivals.

So what are the transferable personal skills of event managers? Having examined numerous job advertisements, descriptions and person specifications for event management posts, the following skills are invariably featured:

- organisational and logistical skills;
- time management skills – running to a schedule;
- leadership skills – a team player/team leader;
- motivational skills – self-motivated and able to motivate others;
- people skills – with a wide range of people at different levels;
- marketing skills – media, sales;
- public relations skills – generating interest, copywriting, contacts;
- communication skills – to colleagues, clients and authorities;
- presentation skills – in several forms and media;
- research skills – gathering and interpreting information;

- commercial awareness – finance, budgets and break even points;
- a positive and adaptable attitude – the 'make it happen';
- problem solving skills and can do attitude;
- innovation and creativity – generating the 'wow' factor.

Many of these skills, especially when combined together, are those expected at graduate level and this explains the increasing number of universities and higher education institutions around the world now offering events management programmes at both undergraduate and postgraduate level.

There are also professional development initiatives within the industry. These often bring together diverse aspects of the industry, for example, the Events Sector Industry Training Organisation (ESITO). ESITO is officially accredited by City & Guilds in the UK as the assessment centre for the Events National Vocational Qualifications (NVQs). Events NVQs are available to virtually everyone in the events industry, particularly those involved in organising events, working at event venues, exhibiting and supplying goods and services for events.

ESITO is supported by 12 leading organisations. They are:

ACE – Association for Conferences and Events

ABPCO – Association of British Professional Conference Organisers

AEO – Association of Exhibition Organisers

BECA – British Exhibition Contractors Association

EVA – Exhibition Venues Association

ITMA – Incentive Travel and Meetings Association

MIA – Meeting Industry Association

MPI (UK) – Meeting Professionals International

MUTA – Made Up Textiles Association

NEA – National Exhibitors Association

NOEA – National Outdoor Events Association

TESA – The Event Services Association

ESITO is involved in projects seeking to identify the common skills, knowledge and understanding required by international events organisers and managers. They are undertaking this research in the Czech Republic, Germany, Portugal and the UK.

The Association of Conferences and Events (ACE), which was the original founder of ESITO, began the first Careers Fair aimed purely at the conference and events industry in 2003.

Sustainability in the events industry

Within the events sector the pace of change is different, with a varying focus in each different country at the present. This is understandable, as the events sector is still developing as a recognised sector, and as a result it is difficult for education and customer service to be standardised in the same way across the globe.

Some parts of the events industry still do not really understand the term sustainability and while some countries show fantastic examples of fair trade, social welfare and heritage considerations these initiatives are not communicated under the label 'sustainability'. An example of the mindset change which may be required in the future, is the customer service attitude so integral to the event industry. For example, an event attendee last in line at a buffet lunch picking up the last roll and seeing food portions for one person would not think, 'this event has been well planned with the consideration of food waste'. Instead, the current industry attitude towards customer service would be, 'there is not enough food at this event – I do not feel well looked after'. Practitioners have suggested a change in customer service thinking could take place with the arrival of the next generation in the workplace (Pelham, 2011).

In Brazil, the existence of two large global events (the FIFA World Cup and the Olympic and Paralympic Games) was seen to be forcing the industry to change. The fact that the eyes of the world are on these events and that such large-scale events offer significant business opportunities for the host country means that both the 'carrot and stick' approaches to change are evident. In other words, there are business opportunities and external customer pressures which will influence the implementation of sustainability and change the host country event industry business model.

It is argued by some commentators in the industry that economics is one of the main barriers to the acceptance and widespread implementation of sustainability throughout the event industry. This is due to two reasons: firstly, the perception that becoming sustainable is costly; and secondly, there is a need to factor in the actual cost related to people taking the time and acquiring the knowledge needed. This barrier can be overcome by raising the profile and changing the perception of the event professional. Showing leadership in the field of sustainability, using the international best practice tools created by the industry for the industry (e.g. ISO 20121 and GRI Event Organiser Sector Supplement) is an opportunity for people to notice and recognise the strategic importance of the event practitioner role.

A study carried out by Pelham of events practitioners makes the following recommendations for sustainability in the events industry:

- Industry practitioners should not wait for there to be a definite demand for sustainability before changing their product/service offer. To do this would risk their brand and their client's brand with the event attendees potentially damaging both beyond repair.

- Governments and corporate clients are likely to lead the way in requesting sustainable events to align with their reputation and economic goals.

- Industry practitioners should research to see if their client currently reports on sustainability, as the growing number of corporate reporting on sustainability will result in an increased need for the consideration of sustainability in events.

- Large events, which create international public attention and widespread business opportunities (e.g. the Olympic Games) are likely to focus increasingly on sustainability and this will significantly drive the demand.

- Despite the existence of internationally recognised frameworks for the implementation of and reporting on sustainability (e.g. ISO 20121 and GRI Event Organiser Sector Supplement), the practitioners felt it likely that regulation on sustainability would hit the event industry in the near future to change the business model more quickly and to a more significant extent.

- Transparency was highlighted as an area where the industry will need to make changes to the current business models. For example, declaring commissions.

- The next generation of the event industry were recognised as passionate about sustainability and likely to bring a level of enthusiasm and even expertise. (Pelham, 2011: 6)

Summary

Reduced budgets combined with increased demands resulting from globalisation, environmental sustainability concerns and developments in IT have forced events practitioners to be innovative in meeting business needs. However, many have argued the events industry has been slow to adapt to its changing environment, including the adoption of IT solutions.

In the future the implementation of internet-based solutions will result in cost savings by presenting the opportunity of increased attendance at events due to lower costs, by expanding the reach to event goers. One such development that will continue to have an impact on the event industry will be the creation of virtual applications.

Several forward-thinking companies have adopted virtual reality applications that meet business needs while also addressing social concerns. Virtual meetings and virtual special events are environmentally friendly, less expensive, and provide alternatives to face-to-face meetings. They are innovative and viable methods to effectively and efficiently meet organisational needs. Virtual worlds represent a growing space for collaborative play, learning, work and e-commerce.

Strong competitive forces require the constant reassessment of competencies, and event practitioners must be accustomed to industry needs and wants if they are to be viable players in such a competitive environment. The awareness of such IT applications and the provision of such services may be a point of differentiation for organisations; it is only a matter of time before a business or organisational presence in a virtual world is as commonplace as a website is now for a business.

■ Discussion questions

Question 1

Discuss the future drivers of change in the events industry.

Question 2

Analyse the changes in the global economy and politics that will impact on the sports events industry.

Question 3

Explain how the developments in mobile technology will affect the events industry.

Question 4

Evaluate the various virtual applications which will force the events industry to change.

Question 5

In what ways will the event professional need to adapt to the changes in the event industry?

Question 6

Discuss the changing nature of the environment and its influence on the event industry.

CASE STUDY 1 BRIGHT FUTURE LIES AHEAD FOR EVENT, CONFERENCE INDUSTRY

Tourism officials and travel agents from across the Taiwan Strait recently pointed out that the number of visitors from Taiwan and mainland China could reach 10 million by 2014, thanks to the soaring number of mainland Chinese tourists visiting the island.

The participants in the 15th annual Cross-Strait Tourism Exchange Conference in Haikou City in China's southern Hainan province further highlighted Taiwan's potential in becoming the next 'MICE hub' in the Asia-Pacific region.

The local Meetings, Incentives, Conventions and Exhibitions (MICE) industry has seen strong growth in recent years as the government spares no efforts to promote the sector through the 'Meet Taiwan' program. Today, the island not only has state-of-the-art convention and exhibition venues, but has also nurtured a strong base of talents in the industry.

But, as many nations and regions also boast quality software and hardware for convention and exhibition purposes, what can help make Taiwan stand out? Many seasoned globe-trotting MICE experts will tell you that the answer is Taiwan's unique cultural and natural landscape as well as, of course, stronger MICE incentives.

One of Taiwan's strong points is its top-notch domestic industries. Taiwan's bicycle, automobile components, information technologies (IT) and tool industries are all global leaders in their own fields, making exhibitions in these areas automatically big events internationally. For instance, The Taipei Cycle Show, Computex and Taipei AMPA/AutoTronics, to cite just a few, are all world-acclaimed trade shows constantly in expansion.

In addition to first-tier MICE software and hardware, as well as talented local teams to execute MICE-related affairs, Taiwan's unique culture, its friendly people, its picturesque scenery and its local delicacies also attract many international organizations – especially from mainland China – to hold MICE tours and other important events in Taiwan.

As a host, the island allows guests to easily combine work with pleasure with its integrated, modern and advanced transportation infrastructure. The convenience of Taipei's Mass Rapid Transit and High Speed Rail (HSR) makes it possible to sightsee, shop, taste gourmet food and take care of business all in the same day.

The successful holding of major international events – the 2009 World Games, the Deaflympics, 2010 Taipei International Flora Exposition and more recently the 2011 International Design Alliance Congress – demonstrates Taiwan's ability to host world-class MICE events.

Meanwhile, Taiwan has won the bid to host the 2017 Summer Universiade, once again attesting its excellence in creativity and education. Launched in the Italian city of Turin in 1959, the Universiade is a biennial sports event for university athletes from more than 130 countries.

According to a survey conducted in 2010 by the Bureau of Foreign Trade, under the Ministry of Economic Affairs, to find out the level of brand-awareness for the MICE industry, about 58 per cent of survey participants who held conferences and exhibitions in Taiwan knew about the Meet Taiwan program. As high as 82 per cent of participants said they would consider holding future events in Taiwan, showing the positive results from Meet Taiwan's marketing efforts.

Ninety-two per cent of those surveyed expressed satisfaction with their experiences in Taiwan. Convenient transportation, safety, cultural characteristics, cuisine and quality of service were some of the things that survey participants were most satisfied with.

(Continued)

(Continued)

Today, Taiwan's rich experience in organising international exhibitions, high service quality, diverse culture, quality professionals and transportation should be the focuses of the government's future marketing plans – in mainland China and across Asia.

Meet Taiwan's website (www.meettaiwan.com), which acts as an important promotional platform for Taiwan's MICE industry, should also be improved by further integrating resources from the Tourism Bureau and the Government Information Office into a one-stop site for MICE search, travel, entertainment, procedures and benefits.

It may be hard for some people to locate the Republic of China on the world map, but Taiwan is definitely the place to meet for exhibitions, conferences, meetings and incentive events.

Source: www.chinapost.com.tw [accessed 26 April 2012]

CASE STUDY 2   FORMULA 1 TEAMS CRITICISE MEDIA FOR 'POLITICISING' BAHRAIN GRAND PRIX

Formula 1 team bosses have hit out at the way the sport was turned into a political battleground over the Bahrain Grand Prix, on the back of the media storm that erupted around the event.

With the Sakhir race becoming headline news, and various politicians stepping in to call for it to be cancelled, several team bosses say they are unhappy about the way the situation was portrayed outside the paddock.

Lotus team principal Eric Boullier told AUTOSPORT: 'I should not say it, but the media did not do for me what they should have done.

There are various issues, which are up to the country to fix. But there are issues in every country, even in England, France and other European countries, and the over-dramatisation was definitely wrong.

F1 is a sport and should be seen as a sport. We also know that it is very important for Bahrain to have this event, it is their biggest event of the year, and F1 should not be used as a political tool.'

When asked if the negative coverage could be a turn-off for potential sponsors, Boullier said: 'It is their choice, but politics is never good to mix with sport.

We have enough inside our paddock. We don't need to bring what is going on outside in, and that is what the media did. The media brought the external politics inside the paddock and that is not good.'

Red Bull team principal Christian Horner said his outfit did not spend much time worrying about how the event was being reported. But he feels that F1 should not have been forced into the political arena.

'It is difficult because you see an awful lot of enthusiasm for Formula 1 in towns and areas of the country,' he said. 'It is not right for Formula 1 to be dragged into a political debate. And of course it is deemed to be political if you race and it is deemed to be political if you don't.

So our focus has been on coming here to do a job and getting it done and I am delighted to say that we have.'

Force India deputy team principal Bob Fernley, who had to withdraw his team from practice session two because of safety concerns from his staff about travelling at night, said that there were positives that came out of the weekend.

'I am probably quite surprised by it all, because I believe irrespective of the criticism and some of the issues we have had, it puts Bernie [Ecclestone] and Jean [Todt] in a very visionary position,' he told AUTOSPORT. 'They have delivered F1.'

'For the Bahraini authorities – they have laid themselves bare to the world's media. If that is not transparency, what is?

'There have been issues, and all sorts of things that we could improve on for next year from an F1 point of view, but F1 should not be about looking back with regret. It should be quite proud of what it has done because the solution now for the politicians in Bahrain is there'.

'They now need to get into a dialogue away from F1 – and the fact that F1 was brave enough to go there, and the leadership was strong enough to do it, good for them.'

Source: www.autosport.com/news/report.php/id/99121

Further reading

Center for Exhibition Industry Research (2009) *Digital + Exhibiting Marketing Insights*. Chicago: Center for Exhibition Industry Research. Market Research Media (2010) 'Premium market analysis' [online]. Available at:www.marketresearchmedia.com/2010/02/07/virtual-conference/[accessed 1 April 2012].

Pelham, F. (2011) 'Will sustainability change the business model of the event industry?', *Worldwide Hospitality and Tourism Themes*, 3(3): 187–92.

Scofidio, B. (2009) '2010: Looking ahead', *Association Meetings Magazine* [online]. Available at: http://meetingsnet.com/corporatemeetingsincentives/news/1123-recession-meetings-impact/index.html [accessed 22 April 2012].

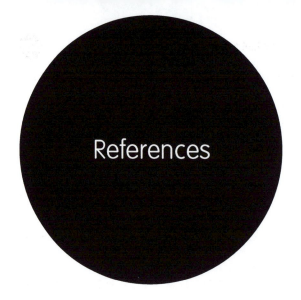

References

Books

Allen, J., O'Toole, W., McDonnell, I. and Harris, R. (2000) *Festival and Special Event Management*, 2nd edn. Milton Keynes: John Wiley & Sons.

Allen, J., O'Toole, W., McDonnell, I. and Harris, R. (2002) *Festival and Special Event Management*, 3rd edn. Milton Keynes: John Wiley & Sons.

Association of Accounting Technicians (1990) *AAT Study Text: Cost Accounting and Budgeting Paper 10*. London: BPP Publishing.

Berridge, G. (2006) *Event Design and Experience*. Oxford: Butterworth Heinemann.

Blyton, P. and Turnbull, P. (1992) *Reassessing Human Resource Management*. London: Sage.

Boella, M. and Goss-Turner, S. (2005) *Human Resource Management in the Hospitality Industry*, 8th edn. Oxford: Elsevier Butterworth Heinemann.

Bolton, B., Thompson, J. (2003) *The Entrepreneur in Focus*. London: Thomson.

Bowdin, G., Allen, J., O'Toole, W., Harris, R. and McDonnell, I. (2011) *Events Management*, 4th edn. Oxford: Butterworth Heinemann.

Brassington, F. and Pettit, S. (2000) *Principles of Marketing*. London: Prentice Hall.

Brayshaw, R., Samuels, J. and Wilkes, M. (1999) *Financial Management and Decision Making*. London: International Thomson Business Press.

Brearley, R. and Myers, S. (1999) *Principles of Corporate Finance*, 6th edn. Maidenhead: McGraw-Hill.

Brown, S. (2009) '"Please hold, your call is important to us": some thoughts on unspeakable customer experiences', in A. Lindgreen, J. Vanhamme and M.B. Beverland (2009), *Memorable Customer Experiences: A Research Anthology*. Farnham: Gower Publishing, pp. 253–66.

Brown, S., Blackmon, K., Cousins, P. and Maylor, H. (2001) *Operations Management: Policy, Practice and Performance Improvement*. Oxford: Butterworth Heinemann.

Burke, R. (2006) *Project Management: Planning and Control Techniques*. China: Everbest.

Butler, R., Davies, L., Pike, R. and Shaap, J. (1993) *Strategic Investment Decisions*. London: Routledge.

Carrell, M.R., Elbert, N.F. and Hatfield, R.D. (2000) *Human Resource Management: Global Strategies for Managing a Diverse and Global Workforce*, 6th edn. Dallas, TX: The Dryden Press.

Carter, P. (2009) *The Complete Special Events Handbook*. London: Directory of Social Change.

Center for Exhibition Industry Research (2009) *Digital + Exhibiting Marketing Insights 2009*. Chicago: Center for Exhibition Industry Research.

Chaffey, D., Mayer, R., Johnston, K. and Ellis-Chadwick, F. (2008) *Internet Marketing – Strategy, Implementation and Practice*. Harlow: Prentice Hall.

Davidsson, P. (2003) 'The domain of entrepreneurship research: some suggestions', in J. Katz and D. Shepherd (eds), *Cognitive Approaches to Entrepreneurship*, Vol. 6. Cambridge, MA: Elsevier Science, pp. 315–72.

Dessler, G. (2000) *Human ResourcesManagement*, 8th edn. London: Prentice Hall International.

Drury, C. (2004) *Management and Cost Accounting*, 6th edn. London: Thomson Learning.

Dyson, J.R. (2007) *Accounting for Non-Accounting Students*, 5th edn. London: Pitman.

Egan, J. (2011) *Relationship Marketing: Exploring Relational Strategies in Marketing*, 4th edn. Harlow: Financial Times Press/Prentice Hall.

English Heritage (2000) *Tourism Facts 2001*. Swindon: English Heritage.

Fill, C. (2009*) Marketing Communications: Interactivity, Communities and Content*, 5th edn. Harlow: Pearson Education.

Fowler, F.J. (2002) *Survey Research Methods*. London: Sage.

Freedman, H.A. and Feldman, K. (1998) *The Business of Special Events: Fundraising Strategies for Changing Times*. Chelsea, MI: BookCrafters.

Getz, D. (1991) *Festivals, Special Events Tourism*. New York: Van Nostrand Reinhold.

Getz, D. (1997) *Event Management and Event Tourism*. New York: Cognizant Communications Corporation.

Getz, D. (2005) *Event Management and Event Tourism*, 2nd edn. New York: Cognizant Communications Corporation.

Glasson, J., Godfrey, K., Goodey, B., Van Der Berg, J. and Absalam, H. (1995) *Towards Visitor Impact Management: Visitor Impacts, Carrying Capacity and Management Responses in Europe's Historic Towns and Cities*. Aldershot: Avebury.

Glautier, M. and Underdown, B. (2001) *Accounting Theory and Practice*, 7th edn. Harlow: Financial Times Press/Prentice Hall.

Goldblatt, J. (2002) *Special Events Best Practices in Modern Event Management*, 3rd edn. New York: International Thompson Publishing Company.

Goss, D. (1994) *Principles of Human Resource Management*. London: Routledge.

Grönroos, C. (2007) *Service Management and Marketing*, 3rd edn. Chichester: John Wiley & Sons.

Hall, C. (1992) *Hallmark Tourist Events: Impacts, Management and Planning*. Chichester: John Wiley & Sons.

Hall, C. (1994) *Tourism and Politics: Policy, Power and Place*. Chichester: John Wiley & Sons.

Hall, C.M. (1997) *Hallmark Tourist Events: Impacts, Management and Planning*. London: Belhaven.

Health and Safety Executive (2002) *Use of Contractors a Joint Responsibility*. Liverpool: HSE.

Health and Safety Executive (2006) *Consulting Employees on Health and Safety: A Guide to the Law*. Liverpool: HSE.

Health and Safety Executive (2006) *Health and Safety Law: What You Should Know*. Liverpool: HSE.

House of Commons Culture, Media and Sport Committee (2002–3) *A London Olympic Bid for 2012: Third report*. London: House of Commons.

Idowu, S. (2000) *Capital Investment Appraisal: Part1*. London: Association of Chartered Certified Accountants.

IMA Study Systems (2006) *Management Accounting Fundamentals*. Oxford: Elsevier Butterworth Heinemann.

Jobber, D. (2010) *Principles of Marketing*, 6th edn. Maidenhead: McGraw Hill.

Johnston, R. and Clark, G. (2008) *Service Operations Management*. London: Prentice Hall.

Kandola, R. and Fullerton, J. (1998) *Diversity in Action*: *Managing the Mosaic*. London: Chartered Institute of Personnel and Development.

Key Leisure Markets (2001) *Tourism in the UK*. London: MarketScape Ltd.

Key Note (2004) *Market Report 2004: Corporate Hospitality*, 4th edn. Key Note Limited.

Kotler, P. and Armstrong, G. (2012) *Principles of Marketing*, 14th edn. Harlow: Pearson.

Kotas, R. (1999) *Management Accounting for Hospitality and Tourism*, 3rd edn. London: International Thomson Business Press.

Kurdle, A. and Sandler, M. (1995) *Public Relations for Hospitality Managers: Communicating for Greater Profits*. New York: Wiley.

Lanier, C.D. and Hampton, R.D. (2009) 'Experiential marketing: Understanding the logic of memorable customer experiences', in A. Lindgreen, J. Vanhamme, and M.B. Beverland (eds), *Memorable Customer Experiences. A Research Anthology*. Farnham: Gower Publishing Limited, pp. 9–23.

Leslie, D. (2001) 'Urban regeneration and Glasgow's galleries with particular reference to the Burrell Collection', in G. Richards (ed.), *Cultural Attractions and European Tourism*. Oxford: CABI Publishing.

Lock, D. (2001) *The Essentials of Project Management*, 2nd edn. Farnham: Gower Publishing Limited.

Luecke, R. (2004) *Managing Projects – Large and Small*. Boston, MA: Harvard Business Press.

Lumby, S. and Jones, C. (2000) *Investment Appraisal and Financing Decisions*, 6th edn. London: Chapman & Hall.

Mabey, C., Salaman, G. and Storey, J. (1998) *Human Resource Management: A Strategic Introduction*. Malden, MA: Blackwell Publishers.

McCarthy, E.J. (1978), *Basic Marketing: A Managerial Approach*, 6th edition. Homewood, IL: Richard, D. Irwin.

McDonnell, I., Allen, J. and O'Toole, W. (1999) *Festival and Special Event Management*. Brisbane: John Wiley & Sons Australia.

McKoen, S. (1997) *Successful Fundraising and Sponsorship in a Week*. London: Hodder Arnold.

McKendrick, E. (2007) *Contract Law*, 7th edn. Basingstoke: Palgrave Macmillan.

Mercer, D. (1996) *Marketing*, 2nd edn. Oxford: Blackwell Business.

Meredith, J.R. and Mantel, S.J. (2009) *Project Management: A Managerial Approach*, 7th edn. Chichester: John Wiley & Sons.

Morgan, M. (1996) *Marketing for Leisure and Tourism*. London: Prentice Hall.

Mulligan, J. and Raj, R. (2008) 'Destination marketing', in C. Vignali, T. Vranesevic, and D. Vrontis (2008) *Strategic Marketing And Retail Thought*. Zagreb: Accent.

Mullin, R. (1976) *The Fund Raising Handbook*. Oxford: A.R. Mowbray & Co. Limited.

Mullins, L.J. (2007) *Management and Organisational Behaviour*, 8th edn. London: Financial Times/Pitman Publishing.

Murphy, J. (2007) *Street on Torts*, 12th edn. Oxford: Oxford University Press.

National Society of Fund Raising Executives (1996) *The NSFRE Fund-raising Dictionary*. New York: John Wiley.

North West Development Agency (2004) *Commonwealth Games Benefits Study: Final Report*. Warrington: NWDA.

Pembrokeshire Association of Voluntary Services (2005) *Developing a Fundraising Strategy*. Haverfordwest: PAVS, August, pp. 1–2.

Pike, R. and Neale, B. (2006) *Corporate Finance and Investment: Decisions and Strategy*, 5th edn. Harlow: Pearson Education.

Raj, R. and Morpeth, N.D. (2007) *Religious Tourism and Pilgrimage Management: An International Perspective*. Oxford: CABI Publishing.

Tribe, J. (1999) *The Economics of Leisure and Tourism*, 2nd edn. Oxford, Butterworth-Heinemann.

Richards, G. (ed.) (2001) *Cultural Attractions and European Tourism*. Oxford: CABI Publishing.

Richards, P. (2007) *Law of Contract*, 8th edn. Harlow: Longman.

Schmitt, B.H. (1999) *Experiential Marketing*. New York: The Free Press.

Shone, A. and Parry, B. (2001) *Successful Event Management: A Practical Handbook*, Thomson, London.

Shone, A. and Parry, B. (2010) *Successful Event Management: A Practical Handbook*. 3rd edn. Andover: Cengage Learning.

Silvers, J. (2008) *Risk Management for Meetings and Events*. Oxford: Butterworth Heinemann.

Stone, R. (2002) *Human Resource Management*, 4th edn. Brisbane: John Wiley & Sons, Australia.

Sundbo, J. and Hagedorn-Ramussen, P. (2008) 'The backstaging of experience production', in Sundbo, J. and Darmer, P. (eds), *Creating Experiences in the Experience Economy*. Cheltenham: Edward Elgar.

Tarlow, P. (2002) *Event Risk Management and Safety*. New York: Wiley.

Tribe, J. (1999) *The Economics of Leisure and Tourism*, 2nd edn. Oxford: Butterworth Heinemann.

Tomlinson, J. (1992) *Cultural Imperialism: A Critical Introduction*. Baltimore, MD: The Johns Hopkins University Press.

Turner, S. (2007) *Unlocking Contract Law* (Unlocking the Law), 2nd edn. London: Hodder Arnold.

Watt, D.C. (2001) *Event Management in Leisure and Tourism*. Harlow: Pearson Education.

Webster, I., Leib, J. and Button, J. (2007) *The Concise Guide to Licensing*. Leicester: Matador.

Weetman, P. (1999) *Financial and Management Accounting: An Introduction*, 2nd edn. Harlow: Financial Times Press/Prentice Hall.

Wickham, P. (2006) *Strategic Entrepreneurship*. Harlow: Financial Times/Prentice Hall.

Wood, F. (2005) *Business Accounting 1*, 8th edn. London: Pitman.

Yehsin, T. (1999) *Integrated Marketing Communications*. Oxford: Butterworth Heinemann.

Yeoman, I., Robertson, M., Ali-Knight, J., Drummond, S. and McMahon-Beattie, U. (2004) *Festival and Events Management: An International Arts and Culture Perspective*. Oxford: Butterworth Heinemann.

Yeoman, I. et al. (2004) *Festival and Events Management*. Oxford: Butterworth Heinemann.

Journals

Alkaraan, F. and Northcott, D. (2006) 'Strategic capital investment decision-making: a role for emergent analysis tool?', *The British Accounting Review*, 38(2): 149–73.

Balasubramanian, S., Peterson, R.A. and Jarvenpaa, S.L. (2002) 'Exploring the implications of m-commerce for markets and marketing', *Journal of the Academy of Marketing Science*, 30(4): 348–61.

Bauer, H.H. and Barnes, S.J. (2005) 'Driving consumer acceptance of mobile marketing: theoretical framework and empirical study', *Journal of Electronic Commerce Research*, 6(3): 181–92.

Borden, N.H. (1964) 'The concept of the marketing mix', *Journal of Advertising Research*, 4: 2–7

Dickinger, A., Scharl, A. and Murphy, J. (2004) 'An-Investigation-and-Conceptual-Model-of-SMS-Marketing'. Proceedings of the 37th Hawaii International Conference on System Sciences.

Dwyer, L., Mellor, R., Mistillis, N. and Mules, T. (2000) 'A framework for assessing "tangible" and "intangible" impacts of events and conventions', *Event Management*, 6: 175–89.

Erickson, G.S. and Kushner, R.J. (1999) 'Public event networks: an application of marketing theory to sporting events', *European Journal of Marketing*, 33 (3/4): 348–64.

Foote, D.A. (2004) 'Temporary workers and managing the problem of unscheduled turnover', *Management Decisions*, 42: 863–74.

Gursoy, D., Kim, K. and Uysal, M. (2004) 'Perceived impacts of festivals and special events by organizers: an extension and validation', *Tourism Management*, 25: pp. 171–81.

Hanlon, C. and Jago, L. (2004) 'The challenge of retaining personnel in major sport event organizations', *Event Management*, 9(1–2): 39–49.

Journal of the British Accounting Review.

Kitchen, P.J. and Schultz, D.E. (2000) 'A response to "Theoretical concept or management fashion"', *Journal of Advertising Research*, 40(5): 17–21.

Kobia, M. and Sikalieh, D. (2010) 'Towards a search for the meaning of entrepreneurship', *Journal of European Industrial Training*, 34(2): 110–27.

Krulis-Randa, J. (1990) 'Strategic human resource management in Europe after 1992', *International Journal of Human Resource Management*, 1(2): 131–9.

Lee, M.-S., Sandler, D.M. and Shani, D. (1997) 'Attitudinal constructs towards sponsorship: scale development using three global sporting events', *International Marketing Review*, 14(3): 159–69.

Maslow, A. H. (1943) 'A theory of human motivation', *Psychological Review*, 50(4): 370–396.

McWilliams, G. (2000) 'Building stronger brands through online communities', *Sloan Management Review*, 41(3): 43–54.

Mohr, K., Backman, K., Gahan, L. and Backman, S. (1993) 'An investigation of festival motivations and event satisfaction by visitor type', *Festival Management and Event Tourism*, 1: 89–97.

Myles, G., Friday, A. and Davies, N. (2003). 'Preserving privacy in environments with location-based applications', *Pervasive Computing*, January–March: 56–64.

Nanto, D.K. (2009) 'The Global Financial Crisis: Analysis and Policy Implications'. CRS Report for Congress. Congressional Research Service.

Ngai, E.W.T. and Gunasekaran, A. (2007) 'A review for mobile commerce research and applications', *Decision Support Systems*, 43: 3–15.

Office of financial management research and information paper (1997)Economic impact of Sydney Olympic Games. NSW Treasury page. 5 Web address: http://www.treasury.nsw. gov.au/__data/assets/pdf_file/0020/6644/TRP97-10_The_Economic_Impact_of_the_ Sydney_Olympic_Games.pdf

O'Toole, T. (2003) 'E-Relationships: emergence and the small firm', *Market Intelligence and Planning*, 21(2): 115–22.

Papatheodorou, A., Rosselló, J. and Xiao, H. (2010) 'Global economic crisis and tourism: Consequences and perspectives', *Journal of Travel Research*, 49: 39–45.

Pelham, F. (2011) 'Will sustainability change the business model of the event industry?', *Worldwide Hospitality and Tourism Themes*, 3(3): 187–92.

Pitta, D.A., Franzak, F.J. and Flower, D. (2006) 'A strategic approach to building online customer loyalty: integrating customer profitability tiers', *Journal of Consumer Marketing*, 23(7): 421–9.

Raj, R. (2004) 'The impact of cultural festivals on tourism', *Journal of Tourism Today*, 4: 66–77.

Rashid, T. (2006) 'Relationship marketing and entrepreneurship: South Asian Business in the UK', *International Journal of Entrepreneurship and Small Business*, 3(3/4): 417–26.

Scharl, A., Dickinger, A. and Murphy, J. (2005) 'Diffusion and success factors of mobile marketing', *Electronic Commerce Research and Applications*, 4: 159–73.

Shannon, J.R. (1999) 'Sports marketing: an examination of academic marketing publication', *Journal of Services Marketing*, Vol. 13(6): 517–35.

Stiernstrand, J. (1996) 'The Nordic model: a theoretical model for economic impact analysis of event tourism', *Festival Management and Event Tourism*, 3: 165–74.

Uysal, M., Gahan, L. and Martin, B. (1993) 'An examination of event motivations', *Festival Management and Event Tourism*, 1: 5–10.

Websites

Andranovich, G., Burbank, M.J. and Heying, C.H. (2001) 'Olympic cities: lessons learned from mega event politics' [online]. California State University, Los Angeles, available at: www. blackwellpublishing.com/images/Journal_ Samples/JUAF0735-2166~23~2~079/079.pdf [accessed 29 March 2011].

www.accountancyage.com/accountancyage/features/2141181/ [accessed 22 December 2011].

Ask City, http://city.ask.com [accessed 7 April 2012].

Auto Sport, www.autosport.com/news/report.php/id/99121 [accessed 26 April 2012].

www.barmitzvahs.org/ [accessed 09 April 2011].

www.bradfordmela.org.uk/bradford_mela_2011/site_plan_2011

British Standards Institute (BSI) 'Introducing standards: raising standards worldwide'. Available at: www.bis-global.com

British Tourist Authority (2010) 'The British Conference Market Trends Survey 2010' [online]. Available from The Business Tourism Partnership at: www.businesstourism-partnership.com/research [accessed 11 March 2012].

British Visits and Events Partnership (2007) 'Moving business visits and events up the agenda' [online]. Available at: www.businesstourismpartnership.com/pubs/BVE_Leaflet_low_pages.pdf [accessed 19th September 2011]. www.britishmotorshow.co.uk/[accessed 12 April 2011].

Bradford Mela, www.bradfordmela.org.uk [accessed 20 June 2012].

Bradford Telegraph and Argus (2009) 'Thousands celebrate mela's 21st birthday' [online]. Available at: www.thetelegraphandargus.co.uk/news/campaigns/campaigns_brilliant/campaigns_brilliant_news/4437692.VIDEO__Thousands_celebrate_Mela_s_21st_anniversary/?ref=rss http://brianmcgovern. com [accessed 14 April 2011].

Camping flight to Lowlands Paradise (2012) [online]. Available at: www.lowlands.nl [accessed 1 April 2012].

Canadian coalition of community-based employability training (CCBET) (2004) Leadership: Fundraising and resource development. Available at: www.savie.qc.ca/ Ccocde/An/ AccueilPublique.asp [accessed 12 April 2011].

CAROL website for European, UK and Asian financial reports, www.carol.co.uk [accessed 22 December 2011].

Civil Aviation Authority (2003) 'Guide for the operation of lasers, searchlights and fireworks in United Kingdom airspace' [online]. Available at: www.caa.co.uk

Chartered Institute of Personnel and Development (2011), 'Reflections on the 2005 Training and Development Survey', CIPD, London [online]. Available at: www.cipd.co.uk/guides [accessed 3 October 2011].

Chartered Institute of Public Relations www.cipr.co.uk [accessed 10 March 2012].

Chartered Institute of Marketing at www.cim.co.uk [accessed 21 December 2012].

China Post, www.chinapost.com.tw [accessed 26 April 2012].

CIA (1968) 'Students stage major disorder in Mexico' [online]. Available at: www.gwu.edu/~nsarchiv/NSAEBB/NSAEBB10/mex03-01.htm [accessed 1 March 2012].

Comscore (2011) 'Mobile' [online]. Available at: www.comscore.com/Industry_Solutions/Mobile [accessed 1st April 2012].

Corbinball, www.corbinball.com/bookmarks [accessed 4 April 2012].

Crabtree Associates Ltd (n.d.) 'Managing a sports event sponsorship for a national company', CAL Public Relations [online]. Available at: www.calpr.co.nz/case_study_sports.html [accessed 7th January 2012].

Department for Culture Media and Sport, www.culture.gov.uk/ [accessed 28 April 2011].

Edinburgh International Festival (2002) www.eif.co.uk [accessed 3 January 2012]. Edinburgh Festival also available at: www.festivalsedinburgh.com/sites/default/files/FestivalsImpactRelease2011FINAL.pdf [accessed 1 March 2012].

www.environment.nsw.gov.au/resources/warr/cs_koreanfoodfair2001.pdf

Eventia (2010) 'Britain for events' [online]. Available at: www.eventia.org.uk [accessed 19 June 2012].

Event Industry News (2011) [online]. Available at: www.eventindustrynews.co.uk/2011/06/dbn-lights-parklife-festival.html [accessed 7 January 2012].

Flora London Marathon (2006) www.london-marathon.co.uk [accessed 3 January, 2012]. http://entrepreneurs.about.com/od/entrepreneursinaction/a/Women-Owned-Businesses-Are-Proliferating.htm (2011) [accessed 10 April 2012].

The Football Association Premier League, www.premierleague.com [accessed 30 November 2007]. http://www.gamesmonitor.org.uk/files/PWC%20OlympicGamesImpactStudy.pdf

Geovector, www.geovector.com [accessed 6 April 2012].

GCB (2009) German Convention Bureau, Frankfurt, www.gcb.de/pdf/Meeting_und_ EventBarometer_Studie.pdf

Google Mobile Maps, www.google.com/gmm [accessed 6 April 2012].

Google Maps, http://map.google.com [accessed 6 April 2012].

Government Olympic Executive (2011) 'London 2012 Olympic and Paralympic Games Annual Report 2011' [online]. Available at: www.culture.gov.uk/images/publications/ DCMS_GOE_annual_report

Greater London Authority (2004) 'Notting Hill Carnival: a strategic review'. Available at: www.london.gov.uk [accessed 3 April, 2011].

Guardian, www.guardian.co.uk/commentisfree/2011/aug/07/are-pop-festivals-over-debate?INTCMP=SRCH [accessed 9 September 2011].

Guay, M. (1976) 'Legacy of the Olympic Games in Montreal – an introduction' [online]. Available at: http://montrealolympics.com/mg_legacy.php [accessed 1 April 2012].

Hard, R. (n.d.) 'Special event planners identify sponsorship categories for fundraising events' [online]. Available at: www.eventplanning.about.com/od/eventplanningbasics/a/ event-sponsors.htm [accessed 10 January 2012].

Health and Safety Executive (2004). www.hse.gov.uk/aboutus/reports/ 30years.pdf [accessed 30 April 2011].

Hibberd, M. (2009) 'UK mobile usage patterns' [online]. Available at: www.telecoms. com/10782/uk-usage-patterns-regular-service/

ICOMOS (1999) 'International cultural tourism charter' [online]. Available at: www. icomos.org/tourism/charter.html/ [accessed 22 December 2011].

www.inspiresme.co.uk [accessed 12 April 2012].

www.ipr.org.uk [accessed 9 March 2012].

Incentives and Meetings International (I&MI) – the worldwide network for professional buyers and planners of international meetings, incentive travel programmes, congresses and corporate events: www.i-mi.com/ Market review

In The City: the UK's International Music Convention and Live Music Festival: www. manchesterwide.com/2009/08/10/in-the-city-music-convention-and-live-music-festival-manchester-18th-to-20th-october-2009/

Institution of Civil Engineers (2003) 'Impact of the Olympic Games as mega-events' [online]. Available at: http://epress.lib.uts.edu.au/dspace/bitstream/handle/2100/993/ muen.157.3.209.49461.pdf?sequence= [accessed 13 March 2012].

www.investorsinpeople.co.uk/Documents/CaseStudies/edinburgh international conf bw.pdf

Kauffman Foundation (2012) Youth entrepreneurship survey, www.kauffman.org/youngen-trepreneurs [accessed 10 April 2012].

Key Note (2010) 'Leisure outside the home market review 2010' [online]. Available at: www.keynote.co.uk/market-intelligence/view/product/10374/leisure-outside-the-home?utm_source=kn.reports.browse

Keillor, G. (1995) [online]. Available at: www.nasaa-arts.org/Research/Best-Practices/State-Spotlight/Minnesota's-Scenic-Byways-Partnership.php [accessed 20 June 2012].

Klyn-Hesselink, E., Stoter, J. and Van der Woerd, A. (2004) '1986 Commonwealth Games: the year of the boycott' [online]. Available at: http://sporthamilton.com/content/ history/1986_Commonwealth_Games.pdf [accessed 1 March 2012] .

Layar (2012) 'Get More out of AR with Layar Vision' [online]. Available at: www.layar.com [accessed 1 April 2012].

Liverpool's Matthew Street Festival (Liverpool Culture Company). Available at: www. liverpool.gov.uk [accessed: 13 November 2011].

London Borough of Hackney (2008) 'The Hackney State of the Environment report' [online]. Available at: www.hackney.gov.uk/Assets/Documents/hackney_state_of_the_environment_report_2008.pdf [accessed 2 November 2011].

London Borough of Lambeth (2005) www.lambeth.gov.uk/NR/rdonlyres/ 7B786033-45F8-4ECE-A13C-E597A5F3F9DB/0/CPA2005 scorecard 151205. pdf [accessed 3 January 2007].

London Organising Committee for the Olympic Games (LOCOG) (2007) 'London 2012 Sustainable Plan November: Towards One Planet 2012' [online]. Available at: www.sel.org.uk/uploads/London-2012-Sustainability-Plan.pdf [accessed 2 November 2011].

London Organising Committee for the Olympic Games (LOCOG) (2008) 'London 2012: Towards One Planet, 2012 Sustainable Plan Update December' [online]. Available at: http://www.london2012.com/documents/locog-publications/sustainability-plan-december-08.pdf [accessed 2 November 2011].

London Organising Committee for the Olympic Games (LOCOG) (2012) 'London 2012 sustainability guidelines – corporate and public events', third edition [online]. Available at www.london2012.com/documents/locog-publications/ london-2012-sustainability-events-guidelines.pdf [accessed 15 July 2012].

Manchester City Council (2006) 'Greater Manchester Air Quality and Action Plan' [online]. Available at: www.greatairmanchester.org.uk/documents/LTP2%20AQ%20Strategy%20and%20Action%20Plan%202006.pdf [accessed 2 November 2011].

Manchester Histories Festival (2009). Available at: www.manchesterhistories festival.org.uk/

Marketing Power, www.marketingpower.com [accessed 12 March 2012]

Market Research Media (2010) 'Premium market analysis' [online]. Available at: www.marketresearchmedia.com/2010/02/07/virtual-conference/ [accessed 1 April 2012].

Michigan Business School (2004) 'Fundraising' (FACUM) [online]. Available at: www.aactmad.org/ppts/fac_UM_fundraising_slides.ppt#31 [accessed 11 March 2007].

Mintel (2004) 'Music concerts and festivals', Mintel Report, August 2004. Available at: www.academic.mintel.com [accessed 23 April 2011].

MOJO Concerts (2012) 'MOJO Concerts' [online]. Available at: www.mojo.nl [accessed 1 April 2012].

My Next Race's marathon (2011) www.mynextrace.com/2011/09/london-marathon-announces-impressive-charity-fund-raising-figures/http://www.nice.org.uk/newsroom/pressreleases/PressReleaseCVDPrevention.jsp

Ofcom (2011) 'Ofcom prepares for 4G mobile auction' [online]. Available at: http://media.ofcom.org.uk/2011/03/22/ofcom-prepares-for-4g-mobile-auction/ [accessed 1 April 2012].

Osawemen, M. (1987) 'Britain's relation with South Africa' [online]. Available at: http://www.niianet.org/documents/articles%20pdf/Britain%27s%20Relation%20with%20South%20Africa.pdf [accessed 15 March 2012].

The Olympic Delivery Authority (2011) 'The ODA plan and budget' [online]. Available at: http://www.london2012.com/documents/oda-publications/oda-plan-2011.pdf [accessed 1 April 2012].

Performing Rights Society for Music (2010) 'Adding up the UK music industry' [online]. Available at: www.prsformusic.com [accessed 19 June 2012].

Philanthropy UK (2011) 'Charitable sector overview' [online]. Available at: www.philanthropyuk.org/publications/guide-giving/how-give/charitable-sector-overview [accessed 9 September 2011].

PricewaterhouseCoopers/DCMS (2005) 'Olympic Games impact study final report' [online]. Available at: www.gamesmonitor.org.uk/files/PWC%20OlympicGamesImpactStudy.pdf [accessed 11 March 2012].

Production Services Association www.psa.org.uk [accessed 13 April 2011].

Professional Lighting and Sound Association, www.plasa.org

RainbowTrust (2005) www.rainbowtrust.org.uk/subpage.cfm [accessed 22 December 2011].

Scofidio, B. (2009) '2010: Looking ahead', *Association Meetings Magazine* [online]. Available at: http://meetingsnet.com/corporatemeetings incentives/news/1123-recession-meetings-impact/index.html [accessed 22 April 2012].

SEEDA (2009) 'Temporary structures for outdoor events: A market opportunity?' [online]. Available at: www.seeda.co.uk/_publications/332-FEI_outdoor StructuresReport.pdf www.soundadvice.info/amplifiedlivemusic/casestudies. htm

Sport Business Group (2001) 'How to develop effective naming rights strategies' [online]. Available at: www.sportbusiness.com/ [accessed 23 March 2011].

Sport England (2006) www.sportengland.org/index/news and media/common wealth-games2006.htm [accessed 24 December 2011].

The Saudi Arabia Information Resource, the Saudi Ministry of Culture and Information website and official News Agency of Saudi Arabia: www.saudinf.com

US Department of Labor, Bureau of Labor Statistics (2011) www.bls.gov/ooh/Business-and-Financial/Human-resources-specialists.htm#tab-1 [accessed 6 October 2012].

The Saint Lucia Bid for Cricket World Cup West Indies – 2007 (2004) 'Media guide' [online]. Available at: http://www.stlucia.gov.lc/docs/CWC2007 BidExecSummary.pdf [accessed 11 March 2012].

TNS (2008) 'TNS launches world's largest syndicated study of mobile markets' [online]. Available at: www.tnsglobal.com/news/news-CBEFA9AEB07F4B 16960BC6326F31573E. aspx [accessed 1 April 2012].

Tourism Insight (2012) 'Sharing sector expertise, analysis and intelligence' [online]. Available at: www.insights.org.uk/articleitem.aspx?title=Case%20Study:%20The%20 Impact%20of%20Sports%20Infrastructure%20Investment%20on%20Visitor%20 Numbers%20to%20Cardiff [accessed 23 January 2012].

T in the Park, www.tinthepark.com [accessed 23 November 2011].

White Book (2006) 'White book directory' (online database) www.whitebook.co.uk/about/default.aspx [accessed 12 December 2006].

Work at Height Regulations 2005 [online]. Available at: www.legislation.gov.uk/uksi/2005/735/contents/made

UK Events Market Trends Survey (UKEMTS) (2011) www.meetingsreview.com/news/view/64560

UK Music (2011) 'Music tourists contribute at least £864m a year to the UK economy' [online]. Available at: www.ukmusic.org/news/post/147-music-tourists-contribute-at-least-864m-a-year-to-the-uk-economy

Ultra Marketing, www.utalkmarketing.com [accessed 8 March 2012].

UNEP (2002) [online]. Available at: www.uneptie.org/pc/tourism [accessed 19 November 2011].

United Nations Framework Convention on Climate Change (1998) 'Kyoto Protocol' [online]. Available at: http://unfccc.int/resource/docs/convkp/kpeng.pdf [accessed 2 November 2011].

United Nations (1993) 'Disaster management training programme' [online]. Available at: http://iaemeuropa.terapad.com/resources/8959/assets/documents/UN%20DMTP%20-%20Logistics.pdf [accessed 1 April 2012].

UNWTO www.unwto.org

Urban Music Awards www.urbanmusicawards.net/2011/07/urban-music-awards-2011

US Department of Labor, Bureau of Labor Statistics, www.bls.gov/home [accessed 3 March, 2006].

VisionTree, www.visiontree.com [accessed 5 April 2012].

Virgin London Marathon (2010) 'Media guide' [online]. Available at: http://static.london-marathon.co.uk/downloads/pdf/Media_Guide.pdf [accessed 7 January 2012].

Vrijetijdshuis Brabant (2012) Vrijetijdshuis [online]. Available at: www.vrijetijdshuisbrabant. nl [accessed 1 April 2012].

X-leisure (2010) 'Making the case for leisure' [online]. Available at: www. x-leisure.co.uk/case/download.pdf

Yorkshire Evening Post (2002) Available at: www.thisisleeds.co.uk/ [accessed 24 December 2011].

Index

Page numbers in *italics* refer to figures and tables.

73550253R00223